Border Crossings

Border Crossings

An Introduction to
East German Prose

THOMAS C. FOX

Ann Arbor

THE UNIVERSITY OF MICHIGAN PRESS

Copyright © by the University of Michigan 1993
All rights reserved
Published in the United States of America by
The University of Michigan Press
Manufactured in the United States of America

1996   1995   1994   1993   4   3   2   1

Library of Congress Cataloging-in-Publication Data

Fox, Thomas C.
    Border crossings : an introduction to East German prose / Thomas
C. Fox.
        p.   cm.
    Includes bibliographical references and index.
    ISBN 0-472-09514-5 (alk. paper). — ISBN 0-472-06514-9 (pbk. :
alk. paper)
    1. German literature—Germany (East)—History and criticism.
    2. German literature—20th century—History and criticism.
    I. Title.
    PT3723.F68   1993
    838′.914099431—dc20   93-12125
                                                          CIP

A CIP catalogue record for this book is available from the British Library.

For Margaret and in remembrance of Charles

Preface

The 1989 revolution in the German Democratic Republic (GDR) concluded an era of peril and privilege for East German authors. In a society that had censored literature, that is, taken it seriously, writers had functioned *nolens volens* as public figures, and literature had served as an outlet for energies and ideas that Western societies channeled into politics, philosophy, journalism, or history. Before 1989, GDR authors could be intimidated, bought, muzzled, imprisoned, or expatriated. They were not, as in Stalin's Soviet Union, murdered. Hence many of them remained in their country as long as possible, convinced their presence mattered. Indeed, the doyen of GDR social scientists Jürgen Kuczynski often prophesied that to understand his country posterity would peruse not its scholarship but its literature. His prescient observation serves this study as starting point.

In the absence of an official political opposition, East German literature possessed the privilege to oppose and to provoke. Although censored, it maintained more autonomy than the closely controlled press, which served as a mouthpiece for Party propaganda. The relative independence of literature resulted in part from the very exigencies of literary form and language, with the resulting gaps and ambiguities; East Germans became expert at writing and reading between the lines.

Aesthetic dangers exist when artists must double as journalists. Nonetheless, for many years Eastern Europe, along with Latin America, produced one of the world's most vibrant literatures. The American reading public knows the works of the Polish exile and Nobel Prize laureate Czeslaw Milosz, the novels of the Hungarian György Konrád and of the Czech exile Milan Kundera, and the poetry of another Nobel Prize winner, Jaroslav Seifert. Many Americans, however, find it difficult to name even a single East German writer. My book seeks in part to address that lacuna.

To reach as wide an English-speaking audience as possible, and also in the hope that my audience will want to read the works I discuss, I have generally limited myself to novels, novellas, and stories available in English. I envision an interdisciplinary readership of scholars, teachers, and students of German Studies or Soviet and East European Studies. To that end I have attempted to avoid jargon, to minimize notes, and to provide plot summaries. Although I am not writing primarily for GDR specialists, I hope this study will serve them, since it presents one of the first attempts to write literary history after the demise of the GDR and hence contributes to the ongoing debate regarding the complicity and culpability of East German writers. I address a number of works (e.g., "The Time Together," *The Road to Oobliadooh, The Seventh Well, Approximation,* and *November*) that have received relatively little attention from scholars of GDR literature, and my examination of Stefan Heym constitutes one of the most comprehensive to date. In addition, I present a preliminary attempt to trace the reception of GDR prose in the United States and to compare that reception with East and West German reactions.

The title "Border Crossings" possesses a number of referents. It signifies most obviously the former German-German border and the fact that East German conditions for the production and reception of literature differed drastically from those in the West. It also signifies that East German cultural products provided a bridge over the Wall, as Günter Grass always insisted. In another sense, my title refers to the limits (e.g., on expression) transgressed by GDR writers. Finally, it acknowledges the linguistic border between German and English; it signals the process of cultural transfer from East Germany to America.

Although I generally restrict my discussion to literature available in English translation, my study nonetheless includes many of the most important GDR works in prose. Of course gaps remain. Numerous novels by Willi Bredel, Karl Heinz Jakobs, Hermann Kant, Erich Neutsch, Dieter Noll, Brigitte Reimann, and others are important within GDR literary history, but their often parochial orientation would have little appeal to U.S. readers, and they have not been translated. Important works from the 1980s—works by Volker Braun, Günter de Bruyn, Brigitte Burmeister, Fritz Rudolf Fries, Christoph Hein, Helga Königsdorf, or Irmtraud Morgner—are not (yet) available in translation. The GDR produced a number of very fine women writers—in addition to those above, one thinks of Helga Schubert, Helga Schütz, and Christine Wolter—but not enough have yet been translated.[1]

My research modifies David Bathrick's assertion that "seen from the broadest perspective of literary life in this country as defined by what books appear on bestseller lists, what works and authors are reviewed and discussed in the leading literary periodicals (such as the *New York Review of Books*, *New York Times Book Review*, etc.), what writers have had significant creative influence on American writers, there is practically no reception of GDR literature in the United States" (1–2). GDR works were not best-sellers and did not influence U.S. writers, but at least since the 1970s, East German literature was discussed with some frequency in leading U.S. review periodicals.

In the cold war atmosphere of the 1950s, GDR literature in fact had no reception in this country. Such authors as Bertolt Brecht, Anna Seghers, or Arnold Zweig, who had established a U.S. audience before 1945, were viewed as German writers who happened to live in East Germany. In the 1960s, mainstream U.S. presses published (and mainstream literary periodicals reviewed) experimental novels by Uwe Johnson and Fritz Rudolf Fries; *Bridges and Bars*, a book of stories by Rolf Schneider; and Wolf Biermann's *The Wire Harp*, a collection of poetry.[2] Articles in the *Nation* and the *New York Times* discussed literature by Johannes Bobrowski, Volker Braun, Peter Hacks, Hermann Kant, Günter Kunert, Erich Neutsch, Erwin Strittmatter, Christa Wolf, and others. The *Nation* also reviewed Christa Wolf's *Divided Heaven* in more detail.[3]

In the 1970s and 1980s, GDR literature made inroads with mainstream U.S. publishers and reviewers. During this time the U.S. public could read translations of works by Jurek Becker, Christoph Hein, Reiner Kunze, Ulrich Plenzdorf, Hans Joachim Schädlich, Christa

Wolf, and others. Publishers also reintroduced Stefan Heym, who had established a U.S. audience in the 1940s and 1950s. Michael Hamburger edited a volume of East German poetry in translation. Twayne and Ungar published volumes of GDR short stories.

It is unlikely, however, that these books or their reviews radically changed U.S. perceptions of Germans in general or of East Germans in particular, since most books published by mainstream U.S. publishers dealt with World War II or were highly critical of the GDR. U.S. reviewers generally de-emphasized the Marxist commitments of, say, Wolf or Heym. The more representative anthologies of prose edited by Peter and Evelyn Firchow (Twayne) and Roger C. Norton (Ungar) were reviewed only in *Publishers Weekly, Choice,* and the scholarly *Modern Language Journal.* The great majority of works by the East German Seven Seas Press, which printed critical but affirmative GDR literature in English translation, were ignored (British translations of GDR literature were also not reviewed until the 1980s). GDR feminist authors, many of whom believed that the East German state constituted a prerequisite for their feminism, were not translated in proportion to the impact they had in their country.

U.S. publishing and reception of GDR literature occurred within a literary marketplace characterized by discontinuity, a marketplace in which little contemporary German-language literature was (or is) translated into English (Rectanus 14). Furthermore, the most significant literary transfers from the GDR to the United States generally filtered through West Germany, where publishers first began to pay serious attention to East German writers in the 1970s. Most GDR literature published by mainstream U.S. publishers had been previously licensed to a publisher in the Federal Republic and had established an impressive sales record there. Indeed, some critical literature had only been published in the Federal Republic and hence constituted West German literature, at least according to copyright. To offset partially those ideological and economic filters, I have included in my discussion books published by Seven Seas Press.

As David Bathrick points out, translation and cultural transfer invariably entail a process of decontextualization and then recontextualization within a new and potentially revealing cultural grid. The receiving culture "misreads" the work in translation; if the misreading is productive, it may bring to the surface textual elements unnoticed in the original context (4). To an extent this describes the U.S.

reception of Christa Wolf, discussed in chapter 5. In general the decontextualization of GDR literature is less apparent than that of such best-sellers as Patrick Süskind's *Perfume*—Mark Rectanus believes that decontextualization by a popular audience is one prerequisite for an international best-seller (18)—if only because U.S. readers need a framework in which to understand a dissident work. One does perceive a greater decontextualization in the literature of the 1980s, but as I argue in chapter 7, this results from qualities inherent to the literature itself.

While not denying that Americans read (or misread) in a different fashion than East or West Germans, I have attempted to situate these texts in their sociohistorical context. For better or worse, many GDR texts lose luster, lose their specific meaning and brisance, when separated from that context. In most readings I have been guided by Pierre Macherey's theory that literary texts, in putting ideology to work, often illuminate gaps in that ideology. Paradoxically, much of a text's potential meaning would then reside in its silences. One function of criticism is to make those silences speak, for, as Terry Eagleton notes, "an ideology exists because there are certain things which must not be spoken of" (90). Macherey's theory concerns the unconscious production of ideology; nonetheless, I find it fruitful, at least heuristically, when reading GDR texts that consciously manufacture, confront, and/or undermine the ideology of their society.

I began this manuscript in the mid-1980s and completed it in late 1990. During the subsequent editorial process I have attempted to incorporate as much new information as possible.

NOTES

1. Several works by Anna Seghers, for many years president of the GDR Writers' Association, are available in translation, though most predate the GDR. I discuss Seghers in chapter 1. Some stories by GDR women writers have been translated in Altbach et al. and in Elling and Mielke. There is a growing interest in translating works by GDR women writers. Sarah Kirsch's *The Panther Woman: Five Tales from the Cassette Recorder* has recently appeared, and Nancy Lukens and Dorothy Rosenberg are preparing an anthology of GDR women writers in English translation. Most of Christa Wolf's literary production is available in English translation; I discuss her work in chapters 1, 2, 3, and 5.

2. By mainstream publishers I mean the larger trade presses (e.g., Har-

court Brace Jovanovich) with national distribution. As the Gerber and Pouget bibliography demonstrates, a good deal of GDR literature has been translated (they list 1,250 titles by one hundred and twenty-nine authors), but most of it in small journals and magazines with limited distribution.

3. See the *Nation* 17 April 1967, for a discussion of Hacks, Neutsch, Strittmatter, Wolf, and others. The review of *Divided Heaven* is in the *Nation* 13 Feb. 1967. The *New York Times Book Review* discussed *Divided Heaven* as well as the writers Manfred Bieler, Johannes Bobrowski, Volker Braun, Uwe Johnson, Günter Kunert, and Karl Mickel on 12 Sept. 1965.

Acknowledgments

A generous grant cosponsored by the American Council of Learned Societies and the Social Science Research Council enabled me to write much of this book. I received additional support from the German Academic Exchange Service and from the former *Liga für Völkerfreundschaft*.

Peter Demetz, Jeffrey L. Sammons, and Egon Schwarz read this manuscript at one stage and made many useful suggestions. Marilyn Sibley Fries brought the manuscript to the attention of the University of Michigan Press. I also thank Joyce Harrison and Christina L. Milton, my editors. Any remaining problems with the text are of course my responsibility.

I am greatly indebted to a number of people for their support during the last few years. In addition to those named above, I want to mention Stephen Brett, Anders Carlsson, Tom Davey, Mike and Joan Fox, Christine Hoffmann, Pascal Ifri, Paul Michael Lützeler, Charles Oriel, James F. Poag, Douglas Schöck, Manfred Stassen, and especially Susan Briziarelli. This book is for my parents, from whom I first learned about workers and farmers.

Colloquia Germanica for "*Sprachskepsis* or *Sprachkritik*? Reflections on GDR Prose," *Colloquia Germanica* 21 (1988): 2–11.

European Studies Journal for "The GDR after Biermann: Literary Dissent 1976–1986," *European Studies Journal* 4, no. 2 (1987): 38–59.

Germanic Review for "Oobliadooh or EIKENNGETTNOSETTIS-FEKSCHIN: Music, Language, and Opposition in GDR Literature," *Germanic Review* 61, no. 3 (1986): 109–16. Reprinted with permission of the Helen Dwight Reid Educational Foundation. Published by Heldref Publications, 1319 Eighteenth Street NW, Washington, D.C. 20077-6117. Copyright © 1986.

German Life and Letters for "A 'Jewish Question' in GDR Literature?" *German Life and Letters* 44, no. 1 (1990): 58–70.

German Quarterly for "Feminist Revisions: Christa Wolf's *Störfall*," *German Quarterly* 63, no. 3–4 (1990): 471–77.

German Studies Review for "Forms of Persuasion in Stephan Hermlin's *Abendlicht*," *German Studies Review* 13, no. 3 (1990).

Contents

Introduction

From Soviet Zone of Occupation to Workers' and Farmers' State (1945–49)

Officials of the German Democratic Republic formerly expressed ritual gratitude to the Soviet Union for liberating the Germans from fascism. But as East German writer Stephan Heym once remarked, in 1945 the Soviets were more concerned with defeating the Germans than with liberating them. When a group of German communists, led by Wilhelm Pieck and Walter Ulbricht, returned from Moscow to administer the Soviet Zone of Occupation, it confronted a formidable task.

Initial Soviet policies remained, at least on the surface, conciliatory, reminiscent of the *Volksfront* coalition of progressive forces in the 1930s. Ruling a hostile populace, one inculcated with fascist and anticommunist sentiment, the Soviets placed considerable value on reeducation, for which they turned not only to new teachers, whom they educated in intensive short courses, but to authors. The Soviet Zone of Occupation welcomed numerous well-known artists and intellectuals from exile: Johannes R. Becher, Theodor Plivier, Erich Weinert, and Friedrich Wolf from the Soviet Union; Anna Seghers, Bodo Uhse, and Alexander Abusch from Mexico; Bertolt Brecht, Ernst

Bloch, and Stephan Heym from the United States; Arnold Zweig from Palestine; and Stephan Hermlin from Switzerland.

On 9 June 1945 the Soviet Military Administration in Germany (SMAD) was established. Taking the West by surprise, the next day it permitted the creation of antifascist political parties. The first party to appear was the Communist party of Germany (KPD), which called not for socialism, especially on the Soviet model, but for the implementation of the revolutionary demands of 1848. The KPD platform supported a "democratic republic," with private enterprise and trade (McCauley 14). In 1945–46 SMAD initiated reforms in schools, judiciary bodies, and police forces, purging former Nazis and destroying old administrative structures. SMAD also effected land reform by breaking up large estates and those held by national socialists, redistributing smaller farms to individual peasants.

As relations worsened between the United States and the Soviet Union, both superpowers became increasingly concerned with integrating their occupation zones into their sphere of influence. In the Soviet Zone the KPD merged with the Social Democratic party of Germany (SPD) to form the Socialist Unity party (SED) in 1946; according to official explanations, the left wished to overcome the internecine struggles that had facilitated Hitler's rise. The principle of parity between former SPD and KPD members was undermined in the following years, with communists assuming more power; thousands of social democrats, as well as members of other parties, were imprisoned (Childs 22). Some political prisoners were deported to the Soviet Union for forced labor. Thousands of others died in former fascist concentration camps that the Soviets used for their own purposes between 1945 and 1950.[1]

In February 1946 the KPD proposed the nationalization of enterprises that belonged to "war and Nazi criminals." By 1948 the state owned most major enterprises, especially in heavy industry. State-run factories constituted only 3 percent of all factories, but they accounted for approximately 40 percent of gross production (McCauley 25).

In 1948 the Western powers introduced the deutsche mark into their zone. The Soviets then declared the ost mark the currency for their zone and for all of Berlin. The Western allies protested by introducing the deutsche mark as a second currency in West Berlin, whereupon the Soviets blockaded the Western sector of the city. The subsequent U.S.-sponsored airlift developed a sense of ideological cohesion among West Germans and West Berliners. It also allowed Americans to revise their image of the ugly German to one of the German as victim.

Although Germans on both sides continued to talk of reunification, two German states were founded in 1949: the Federal Republic, with its provisional capital in Bonn, and the German Democratic Republic, with its capital in East Berlin. Wilhelm Pieck served as the East German president and Otto Grotewohl as prime minister. The GDR could point to a democratic constitution and a multiparty system, but the SED, backed by the Soviets, maintained firm control. In 1950 Walter Ulbricht became general secretary of the SED and de facto head of state.

The 1950s

The fledgling state faced enormous difficulties. Its population proved mistrustful and rebellious, identifying the SED—correctly—as the "Russian" party. The GDR received no Marshall Plan assistance and little aid from the Soviet Union. SMAD had dismantled many German industries in the Soviet Zone, transporting them to the Soviet Union. Additionally, the Soviet Zone and subsequent GDR had to pay reparations to the Soviet Union. The country possessed few natural resources, and the former German provinces of East Prussia, Pomerania, and Silesia, areas rich in agriculture and/or natural resources, had been annexed by the Soviet Union or Poland. The GDR maintained only a small industrial base: 86 percent of German heavy industry lay in the British Zone (McCauley 25). Perhaps most ominous was the constant drain of skilled workers and professionals who left, among other reasons, for higher salaries in the West. Although the GDR patrolled its border with the Federal Republic, crossing from one Germany to the other continued to be a relatively uncomplicated affair. Furthermore Berlin, in the center of the GDR, remained under allied administration, and it functioned as an open city until the construction of the Berlin Wall in 1961. East Germans could purchase a light rail (S-Bahn) or subway ticket and, if they passed the fairly desultory controls, travel to West Berlin and another world. According to West German law, they were automatically West German citizens.

The GDR attempted to address its many problems by importing the Soviet model, including Stalinism. In the arts, for example, the government adopted the Soviet aesthetic dogma of socialist realism. Increasing SED control of the arts mirrored its rising influence in society at large: the "class struggle within" and the reorganization of the Party, state, economy, and society characterized the 1950s. The West German social scientist Peter Christian Ludz asserted that the SED leadership often utilized terror to achieve its goals; ideological and political in motivation, the terror tactics were directed at farmers, the middle classes, and the upper middle and upper classes (6). SED policy effectively vitiated the private sector. In November 1952 the government denied most self-employed persons and their families ration cards; the number of private factories declined by two thousand in 1953 alone. The government began to collectivize agriculture, and the number of large farms in private hands decreased by sixteen thousand, or one-third, in 1953 (McCauley 64).

Stalin died in March 1953. In June GDR workers, embittered by the disastrous economic situation, began a strike in East Berlin, an action that spread to other GDR cities. Protests against increased norms quickly escalated into demands for free elections, whereupon the Soviet Union, citing the danger of counterrevolution, restored order, and Ulbricht's standing, with its tanks. Anna Seghers presents a more or less official version of the uprising in her novel *Trust*, which I discuss in chapter 1, and I examine Stefan Heym's somewhat more differentiated version in chapter 6.

Ulbricht's SED found itself challenged again in 1956. During the Fourth GDR Writers' Congress in January, numerous writers representing a range of generations criticized, in Peter Demetz's formulation, "the oppressive ways in which Party authorities had made it difficult for even the loyal to be loyal" (*Fires* 113). Khrushchev's denunciation of Stalin in February 1956 strengthened the resolve of critical GDR writers. But labor unrest in Poland, the Anglo-Franco invasion of Egypt, and the armed uprising in Hungary once again reinforced Ulbricht's position, and the GDR contented itself with condemning Stalin's "cult of personality," even as Ulbricht constructed one of his own.

Between 1956 and 1958 Ulbricht successfully countered challenges from Party members who wanted real de-Stalinization and economic reforms. He also kept intellectuals reigned in. Wolfgang Harich, professor of Marxist philosophy and editor in chief of the *Deutsche Zeitschrift für Philosophie,* was arrested in 1957, and as of that year, the influential Marxist philosopher Ernst Bloch could no longer teach in Leipzig.

In 1959 the Party introduced the Bitterfeld Program, which encouraged workers to write and professional authors to work in factories. Peter Demetz is surely correct in viewing the program as a means of controlling the restive intelligentsia: "the Party again had doubts about its own intellectuals, and preferred to create an anti-intellectual counterforce of factory workers and peoples' correspondents to keep imagination on a close leash" (*Fires* 114). But I also agree with Wolfgang Emmerich that the Bitterfeld Program represented a genuine socialist initiative in the arts, one designed to render problematic the concept of "literature."[2] In the early 1960s, however, the Party let the campaign lapse.

With the exception of the Bitterfeld Program (inspired more by 1920s agitprop experiments or by Mao Tse-dung than by Soviet socialist realism), a restrictive, utilitarian interpretation of socialist realism did not allow for much distinguished achievement in GDR literature of the 1950s. John Flores has demonstrated that such poets as Peter Huchel, Bertolt Brecht, and Johannes Bobrowski proved perhaps most successful at avoiding the prescriptions of socialist realism and producing estimable literature. Writers of prose published numerous "novels of production" that dramatized resourceful workers overcoming all manner of obstacles in factories that now belonged to the people.[3]

Novels and stories emphasizing communist antifascist resistance have aged somewhat more gracefully. In chapter 1 I discuss two examples, Stephan Hermlin's "The Time Together" and Bruno Apitz's *Naked Among Wolves.* The texts reminded the world that some Germans, no matter how few, had resisted Hitler, and such literature normally ascribed to communists the leading role in that resistance.

As the two Germanys fought the cold war with cultural politics, the finest GDR novel from the 1950s, Uwe Johnson's *Speculations about Jakob,* could not be published there. Schooled on Western modernism, the book provided a radical break with both socialist realism and the Bitterfeld Program. Its West German publication in 1959 coincided with Johnson's departure for West Berlin. I discuss Johnson's novel in chapter 2.

The 1960s

During the 1950s the GDR experienced an annual population loss of approximately 0.5 percent—the highest in the world (Ludz 3). Severe industrial shortages in 1959–60, the forced collectivization of agriculture, and attempts by the Soviet Union to settle the Berlin question on Soviet terms only increased the flight West. In 1960 just under two hundred thousand East Germans left their country. In the early months of 1961 the monthly total rose toward fifty thousand (Krisch 14–15). On 13 August 1961 East German military and police units raised barbed wire around West Berlin, effectively sealing off that half of the city from GDR citizens. The East Germans soon replaced the barbed wire with tightly patrolled walls. GDR officials defended the barricades as they did the Soviet tanks in 1953, as a harsh but justifiable response to Western provocations. Christa Wolf presents some of those justifications in her *Divided Heaven*, published in the GDR during 1963 (see chapter 3).

Although the GDR secured its border and its labor supply, the economy stagnated for two years. With agriculture and industry nationalized (socialized industry contributed 85.5 percent of the gross national product in 1963), the SED launched its New Economic System of Planning and Management of the People's Economy (NES).

> The concepts of profit, cost, price, profit earning capacity, and economic cost-accounting were finally accepted as principles of industrial management in the GDR. Wages and bonuses were raised, and therefore the situation of the working population improved considerably. Even more important was the recognition—at first rather hesitant—of the performance principle. (Ludz 7)

The NES did not try to emulate the Yugoslav experiment, nor was it as radical as Czech experiments in 1968 or the Hungarian New Economic Mechanism, also introduced in 1968 (McCauley 110). Nonetheless, for its time it constituted one of the more daring economic reform experiments, in some respects anticipating Mikhail Gorbachev's *perestroika*.

In 1967 the SED replaced the NES with the ESS, or Economic System of Socialism. The Party intended the new designation to counteract the impression developing among some managers that economic and technological efficiency provided ends in themselves, regardless of socialism. Instead, as Wolfgang Emmerich points out, the Party wished to reassert its leading role (129). By asserting that the GDR had achieved a "socialist human community," the Party could argue against domestic and international critics that such terms as *profit* signified something qualitatively different in their state. Although the economic reforms and the scientific emphasis did not fulfill all the hopes of the SED, they helped the GDR achieve the position, according to some estimates, of eighth-ranked industrial state in the world.

Ulbricht accompanied his proto-*perestroika* with very little *glasnost*. His government encouraged criticism of U.S. involvement in Vietnam but arrested young people who protested GDR participation in the suppression of the Prague Spring. Intellectuals who had hoped that the Wall would provide their government with more security and them with more latitude found such hopes largely unfulfilled. However, Johannes Bobrowski published *Levin's Mill, Lithuanian Pianos*, and other finely wrought narratives (see chapter 1) that displayed considerable formal complexity. Bobrowski's texts demonstrate that despite the SED condemnation of modernism, GDR authorities were prepared to tolerate a modicum of literary experimentation, provided a work's content remained unobjectionable. Influenced by the Bitterfeld Program, Erwin Strittmatter's *Ole Bienkopp* (1963) and Christa Wolf's *Divided Heaven* (1963) present loyal criticism, as does Günter de Bruyn's 1968 novel, *Buridan's Ass*, all discussed in chapter 3. Featuring a librarian as protagonist, de Bruyn's novel reflects the influence of the NES, with its emphasis on planners and managers as opposed to workers.

During the 1960s the SED generally maintained the same hard line in cultural politics as in the 1950s. In 1962 authorities forced Peter Huchel to resign as editor in chief of the GDR journal *Sinn und Form*, which he had built into one of the most important forums for German-German literary communication. In 1963 Stephan Hermlin organized a poetry evening that introduced many of the GDR's talented young authors. According to the SED, Hermlin failed to channel appropriately the ensuing discussion, and as a result he lost his important posts with the GDR Academy of the Arts and with the GDR Writers' Association. In December 1965 the Eleventh Plenum of the

Central Committee attacked "anarchic" and "pornographic" tendencies in GDR literature. It blacklisted such critical writers as the poet and balladeer Wolf Biermann, the novelist Stefan Heym, and the playwright Heiner Müller. It is hardly surprising that a year later Fritz Rudolf Fries's *The Road to Oobliadooh*, a novel combining verbal brilliance, modernist techniques, political satire, and an ambivalent attitude toward the GDR, could only appear in West Germany (see chapter 2).

Christa Wolf set her novel *The Quest for Christa T.* in the GDR of the 1950s, but written during the 1960s, it comments indirectly on the NES and ESS as well, examining the alienation of the individual in an increasingly mechanized society. At the same time, the novel insists that only and precisely in socialism can such problems be surmounted. Formally and intellectually dense, Wolf's novel had a small but controversial printing in 1968; it was then suppressed until 1973 (see chapter 2). A second important novel appeared in 1969, Jurek Becker's *Jakob the Liar* describes life in a Polish-Jewish ghetto under Hitler (see chapter 1). Becker, a survivor of ghettos and concentration camps, fashions a subtle, melancholy piece that speaks the seemingly unspeakable.

The 1970s

By the early 1970s, Walter Ulbricht, who had displayed more longevity than any other Soviet bloc leader, had become an irritant at home and abroad. Ulbricht had forced the Sovietization of the GDR, but in the later 1960s he grew increasingly assertive vis-à-vis Moscow, and he irked the Soviets with his references to a separate GDR road to socialism. The one-sided East German industrial development also caused concern among the Soviets. Although in 1969 the GDR with seventeen million inhabitants had surpassed the 1936 industrial output of the German Reich with its sixty million citizens, consumer goods remained scarce, and similar shortages caused Polish citizens to riot in 1970. The SED terminated the Economic System of Socialism, of which Ulbricht was proud, in 1970. Under pressure, he reluctantly resigned as general secretary on 3 May 1971. Until his death in 1973, he held a number of increasingly ceremonial posts.

Erich Honecker succeeded Ulbricht. A longtime Party member, Honecker had come from the working class; he had also spent much of World War II in a Nazi prison. Honecker and his allies discarded Ulbricht's designation of the GDR as a "socialist human community," preferring to speak more realistically of "really existing socialism," of a "class society of a special type," in which the "birthmarks of the old society" remained, if to a decreasing extent (McCauley 153).

In the early 1970s Honecker fended off rivals; a number of achievements then helped him secure his position. GDR Olympic teams, which began to compete under their own flag in 1968, did exceedingly well at the 1972 games in West German Munich and Garmisch. The United Nations admitted both German states in 1973, and numerous countries recognized the GDR in that period—the United States in 1974. In 1975 the GDR signed the Helsinki Accord; subsequently, it emphasized clauses that sought to discourage interference in the affairs of other countries, while de-emphasizing clauses calling for human rights, including emigration. Economically, the GDR did well in the early 1970s, and the standard of living rose noticeably. Then the Arab-Israeli war, the oil crisis, and the rise in the price of other raw materials caused considerable difficulties for the resource-poor East Germans. Although the Soviet Union helped by supplying oil and other natural resources at below market cost, the GDR economy stagnated in the later 1970s.

After Honecker assumed power in 1971, he moved away from Ulbricht's pre-*perestoika* experiments, but with the economy functioning fairly well, he found it prudent to allow some proto-*glasnost*. In December 1971 he delivered an often quoted and analyzed speech, in which he declared that no taboos in the realm of art and literature should exist, providing artists proceeded from the firm standpoint of socialism. Thus the man who in 1965 had served the SED as mouthpiece for the denunciation of numerous GDR writers now ushered in the first real thaw in GDR cultural policies since the imposition of socialist realism. I discuss two important and emblematic works published during the thaw, Ulrich Plenzdorf's *The New Sorrows of Young W.* and Volker Braun's "Unfinished Story," in chapter 3. Christa Wolf's story "Self-Experiment" (see chapter 5) describes a sex-change operation and can stand as an example of the growing feminist literary movement in the GDR.[4]

Honecker's speech in no way abolished all taboos, since it remained the Party's prerogative to determine whether an artist in fact maintained a socialist standpoint. Nonetheless, the GDR witnessed a considerable outpouring of energy in literature and the arts. The relatively harmonious feeling between the more adventurous intellectuals and their state abruptly ruptured, however, when the SED expatriated the writer and singer Wolf Biermann in November 1976. Twelve leading GDR artists protested in a public letter, and over one hundred others ultimately joined them. The government responded with measures ranging from relatively mild rebukes to arrests, and the remainder of the decade proved an uneasy, often bitter time in the relationship between the writer and the state. In chapter 4 I discuss works from that time: Reiner Kunze's *The Wonderful Years*, Hans Joachim Schädlich's *Approximation*, Jurek Becker's *Sleepless Days*, and Rolf Schneider's *November*. None of these books appeared in the GDR.

Two important texts by leaders of the Biermann protest, Christa Wolf's *Patterns of Childhood* and Stephan Hermlin's *Evening Light*, did appear in the later 1970s (see chapter 1). Other writers, among them Kunze, Becker, and Schädlich, found it prudent to leave the GDR. Stefan Heym (see chapter 6), who had protested the Biermann expatriation as well as subsequent East German measures designed to restrict writers' expression, elected to remain in East Germany, though he was expelled in 1979 from the Writers' Association, blacklisted (not for the first time), and denounced indelicately by a well-known colleague in the Party newspaper *Neues Deutschland* (22 May 1979). In the 1970s, both before and after the watershed of 1976, GDR writers turned again and again in their work to the relationship between writers and society. Christa Wolf has acknowledged that her novella *No Place on Earth* (see chapter 5), which deals with two nineteenth–century German authors who commit suicide, was in part inspired by her despair regarding the GDR cultural situation in the later 1970s (Meyer-Gosau 89–90).

The 1980s

During the early 1980s the GDR economy grew on average 4.5 percent a year. As in the latter part of the previous decade, however, the later 1980s brought economic stagnation (Stinglwagner 129). East Germany had purchased a modicum of social peace by providing a rising standard of living, and GDR politicians had always used their country's various entitlement programs—free health care and education, subsidized food and housing, and full employment—as an argument for the superiority of their system. But the government paid dearly for such benefits (roughly one quarter of the budget in 1989), and in the 1980s numerous economists began to question whether the GDR could continue to afford them.

In international affairs, the collapse of détente could not leave the GDR unaffected, though even as superpower relations worsened, the East Germans strived to maintain, sotto voce, a German-German dialogue. Nonetheless, East Berlin supported the Soviet invasion of Afghanistan, and when NATO countries stationed Cruise and Pershing II nuclear missiles in West Germany, the Soviet Union responded by placing new SS-20 missiles in the GDR.

These latter events, combined with the expansion in the late 1970s of premilitary training in GDR schools—an action strongly opposed by the Lutheran church in Protestant East Germany—helped generate an underground, independent peace movement of some magnitude. Many East Germans, like their cousins in the West, feared that any European war, even a limited one, would be fought on German soil. Supported by the church, the independent peace movement called for disarmament, spoke of pacifism (traditionally scorned in the GDR), and attempted to expand the possibilities for conscientious objectors. Mindful of the subversive role played by the Catholic church in neighboring Poland, GDR officials exercised flexibility and some restraint when dealing with the independents. Some authors nonetheless insisted on crossing the borders of the permissible: Stefan Heym's novel *The Wandering Jew* (see chapter 6), which supports the independent peace movement, appeared in the Federal Republic in 1981 but was suppressed in the GDR until 1988; and when Christa Wolf's controversial *Cassandra* (1983) called for unilateral disarmament, her government censored it (see chapter 5).

In the 1980s a grass-roots concern with the environment grew increasingly vocal. The GDR economic miracle devastated the countryside, but the government kept statistics on environmental damage strictly secret, and public discussion of such issues remained for many years taboo. In 1980 Monika Maron could publish only in West Germany her novel *Flight of Ashes* (see chapter 7), an exposé of industrial pollution in the GDR city of Bitterfeld, which she decried as Europe's filthiest. By 1987, however, Christa Wolf could publish *Accident* in East Germany; in the story, she describes the anxiety and uncertainty that the Chernobyl catastrophe unleashed within her country (see chapter 5).

Many GDR writers enthusiastically supported the ascent of Gorbachev and his reforms. Formerly intellectuals had been commanded to acknowledge the leading role of the Soviet Union, but they now did so voluntarily, often to the embarrassment of the SED. Officially the East Germans supported *perestroika* and *glasnost* as necessary reforms—for the USSR. SED officials argued that their country possessed a well-functioning economy that might be derailed by reforms. Off the record they would add that East German citizens, living within broadcast range of West German television and radio, had always experienced at least passive *glasnost*.

The Tenth GDR Writers' Congress in November 1987 occasioned a test of wills. In front of SED officials, Jurij Koch delivered an impassioned attack on rapacious strip-mining in his province. Christoph Hein and Günter de Bruyn lambasted censorship and regretted the lack of a free press (in an ironic confirmation, the report in the Party paper shortened, defused, and falsified their remarks). In what numerous observers viewed as a response to the obstreperous spirit at the Writers' Congress, state security police raided the offices of the East Berlin Zion Church, searching rooms, seizing papers from the environmental library, confiscating copy machines, and arresting some members. The congregation responded with vigils and a protest march.

The mood of confrontation escalated in January 1988, during the annual parade commemorating Karl Liebknecht and Rosa Luxemburg, founding members of the German Communist party. Two unofficial groups—one demanding the right to emigrate, the other demanding increased civil rights within the country—attempted to join the march. The government arrested over one hundred demonstrators, and in the following days it detained numerous activists from the independent peace, environmental, and civil rights movements.

The arrests provoked strong protests in West Germany, where fifteen former GDR writers, among them Wolf Biermann, Reiner Kunze, and Hans Joachim Schädlich, published an open letter in support of the detainees. The extent of the protest in the GDR proved more surprising. In the name of ten younger GDR artists, Lutz Rathenow read a letter protesting the criminalization of literary, artistic, and political activities. Throughout the republic, various churches held services for discussion and prayer; up to three thousand people attended some meetings. Instead of destroying the GDR civil rights movement, the SED actions from November 1987 and January 1988 reinforced it (Spittmann).

GDR writers and, increasingly, literary scholars continued to press their government for concessions. Volker Braun's "Unfinished Story," long available only in a *Sinn und Form* issue not always attainable in GDR libraries, appeared in book form. A GDR publisher announced it would print Fritz Rudolf Fries's *The Road to Oobliadooh*, banned for over 20 years. The rehabilitation of Stefan Heym began: *The Wandering Jew* appeared in 1988, though his novel *Collin*, which deals with the Stalinist 1950s, remained on the government's index.

In 1989 the SED lost control of events. Hungary began to dismantle its barbed-wire border with Austria in May, and by the end of September over 25,000 GDR citizens fled by that route. An additional 13,000 sought asylum in West German embassies in Prague and Warsaw. They were taken in sealed trains through East Germany to West Germany. The passage of the trains through the GDR sparked a riot in Dresden, while in Leipzig and other cities street demonstrations demanding reforms commenced. The hemorrhage did not stop, and approximately 344,000 people left the GDR in 1989, as opposed to 40,000 in 1988 ("Chronik" 176).

On 7 October the beleaguered GDR government celebrated its fortieth anniversary, and the People's Police fought counterdemonstrators with some viciousness. Nonetheless, the ranks of those protesting in the street continued to grow, and on 18 October Erich Honecker resigned, supplanted by Egon Krenz. On 8 December Gregor Gysi replaced Krenz, and he presided over a caretaker government until free elections were held in March 1990. A center-right coalition allied with Helmut Kohl's West German Christian Democrats won decisively, making German unification only a matter of time.

Writers and artists played an important role in these developments. For many years the artistic opposition had functioned as the political opposition and had extended the borders of the permissible in the GDR. As events accelerated in the fall of 1989, artists often assumed leadership positions. In Leipzig, Kurt Masur, director of the Gewandhaus Orchestra, helped prevent bloodshed. Painter Bärbel Bohley cofounded New Forum, one of the largest opposition groups.

On 11 October, a week before Honecker's resignation, the Writers' Association called for "revolutionary reforms," and nine days later the Film and Television Association demanded an end to media censorship. On 24 October writers Christoph Hein, Stefan Heym, and Gisela Steineckert participated in a televised debate regarding political alternatives. Soon thereafter East Berlin writers organized a public discussion in which Stephan Hermlin, Stefan Heym, Christa Wolf, Heiner Müller, Volker Braun, and Christoph Hein participated. On 4 November various artists' associations organized the largest nonofficial GDR demonstration ever. In the heart of East Berlin, a half million people listened to speeches by Christoph Hein, Stefan Heym, Heiner Müller, and Christa Wolf. Five days later their government opened the Wall.

Writers and artists helped organize and focus the opposition, but after November 1989 they found themselves rather quickly in the margins. Volker Braun, Stefan Heym, and Christa Wolf, among others, signed a proclamation in late November calling for citizens to remain in the GDR and build a democratic socialism. But the majority of GDR citizens, having lived for forty years as the subjects of a social experiment gone grievously wrong, wanted no truck with new experiments. As they emphasized in March 1990, they did not want a writer-president, a Vaclav Havel. They wanted Helmut Kohl.

Vaclav Havel symbolized unbending resistance to a hated regime, and in the GDR, there was no Havel among the writers. Haunted by a guilty conscience concerning German atrocities in World War II, East German authors (as opposed to the Czechs and others) experienced difficulty distancing themselves from a state that defined itself as antifascist, since to do so would have entailed resisting the resisters. Many GDR intellectuals believed that capitalism had brought Hitler to power, and that it had generated all postwar "fascisms" in Korea, Algeria, Vietnam, Greece, or Chile. For those intellectuals the West provided no alternative.

Helga Königsdorf wrote in Die Zeit that she and other GDR authors had struggled to reform their state but had not questioned its legitimacy (8 June 1990). Unless they left their country, unless they published unauthorized books in the West or participated in the unofficial, largely self-contained art scene of East Berlin's Prenzlauer Berg,[5] East German writers were to some extent implicated in their system. They accepted prizes, salaries, pensions, and privileges (some could travel to the West). Those who criticized the system generally did so, to use Brecht's expression, in the language of slaves.

The sudden, unexpected collapse of the GDR and the publicity surrounding its numerous human rights violations have now exposed some authors to the charge of collaboration. It is not difficult to identify the worst opportunists, but even such respected authors as Christa Wolf have not remained unaffected. In 1990 Wolf published *What Remains*, written in 1979 and revised in October and November 1989. The story describes her fear and anger while being observed by the secret police; it also discusses her inability to break decisively with her government. The piece unleashed a far-reaching debate regarding the culpability of writers who had remained in the GDR. Did their critical works create an alternative public sphere, undermining the GDR while providing its citizens succor? They did, especially when one remembers Roger Woods's assertion that within an incorrigible system even would-be reformers functioned as de facto revolutionaries (19). But it is also true that by creating literary works that kept alive a utopian socialist hope GDR writers often suggested that East Germany provided the prerequisite for the realization of that hope. Thus they lent a bankrupt Party respectability. This study analyzes writing from an era in which heroism and sycophancy proved to be by no means mutually exclusive phenomena.

NOTES

1. After the collapse of the SED dictatorship, mass graves were discovered at several camps used by the Soviets from 1945 to 1950. When I visited the former Nazi concentration camp Sachsenhausen in 1990, a new exhibition documenting Soviet use of the camp estimated that between 13,000 and 20,000 political prisoners died there between 1945 and 1950. Eleven such camps existed in the Soviet Zone of Occupation.

2. Emmerich 87. All references to Emmerich are to the 1st ed. unless otherwise stated.

3. For a discussion of these novels, see Silbermann, *Literature*.

4. Other examples of GDR feminist literature from this time, examples available in English translation, include Sarah Kirsch's interviews with GDR women (*The Panther Woman*, 1973); Elfriede Brüning's "Heaven on Earth" (1974), which describes the suicide of an elderly woman who has been rendered marginal by East German society; Irmtraud Morgner's "The Rope," "Shoes," and "The Glad Tidings of Valeska," all self-contained stories from her experimental novel *Life and Adventures of Troubadour Beatriz* (1974); and

Christine Wolter's "I Have Remarried" (1976), which tells of a GDR woman who, after her divorce, begins to live with a woman.

5. In late 1991, Sascha Anderson, a poet and leading figure in the Prenzlauer Berg alternative culture, was accused by former dissidents Wolf Biermann and Jürgen Fuchs of having worked for the East German secret security police (Stasi) as an informant, charges that have since been verified. Such information has occasioned intensive debate regarding the political ramifications of an "unofficial" GDR avant-garde art that was often formally hermetic and thematically apolitical. Former GDR writer Lutz Rathenow has asserted that the Stasi in fact encouraged (or managed or even created) such art as a pressure valve.

1

Remembering the Past

> Like thousands of others of my generation, I came to Socialism
> not via the proletarian class struggle or starting from Marxist
> theory; I arrived at that different social order via Auschwitz. This
> is what distinguishes my generation from those before and after
> it, and it is this difference which determines our tasks in litera-
> ture.
> —Franz Fühmann, *Twenty-Two Days or Half of a Lifetime*

When East German schoolchildren made their required visits to the
former concentration camps of Buchenwald or Sachsenhausen, they
learned that an underground communist organization had liberated
Buchenwald in the final days of World War II. In Sachsenhausen they
visited the Museum of the Anti-Fascist Struggle of the European
People, which documented the leading role of communists in resisting
the Nazis and their allies. In Sachsenhausen the exhibitions occasionally ranged beyond 1945, for example to Greek or Chinese civil wars
in which, the observer learned, communists fought against Western
imperialists and their agents. Thus the museums suggested parallels
between national socialism and the Western capitalist democracies.

East German schoolchildren visiting the camps examined pictures
of "German monopoly capitalists"—Flick, Krupp, and Thyssen—labeled as the "commissioners"; immediately beneath the capitalists
hung pictures of Himmler and others who, according to the captions,
served as the commissioner's henchmen. Other exhibits emphasized

the economic use of the camps—Krupp had a branch at Auschwitz—
and the profitability of slave labor. Schoolchildren learned that Party
Chief Erich Honecker had resisted the Nazis and had spent time in a
fascist prison, while Austrian and West German leaders had not.
They learned that their state embodied the logical culmination of the
progressive forces of history, and that they constituted the "victors
of history."

The GDR utilized every opportunity to define itself as an antifascist state. It adopted the Soviet position, established at the Comintern
in 1935, that fascism represented the final, most brutal stage of capitalism. As opposed to the Federal Republic, which tends to hold a
small group of criminals responsible for fascist crimes, the GDR
viewed national socialism as systemic. This thesis assigned to the
capitalist Federal Republic the role of a restorative, protofascist state,
a haven for former Nazis and a breeding ground for future ones.
Proclaiming, and to some extent believing, the convenient fiction
that the Nazis were "over there," GDR officials could assert that they
had effected a clean break with the past. Among other things, this
allowed them to renounce any responsibility for Nazi genocide and
to refuse reparations to Jews.[1]

GDR writers reflected and transported the official view, but in time
they modified it as well. During the 1950s writers emphasized communist underground resistance, thus educating the Germans and,
not incidentally, serving the legitimation needs of the new state. In
the later 1950s and in the 1960s, writers pressed into service the
nineteenth-century form of the *Bildungsroman*, or novel of education,
to illustrate the transformation of a young fascist into a chastened
communist. In the 1970s, after a change of government, writers began to examine, as Christa Wolf noted in 1989, the fashion in which
the " 'victors of history' ceased to engage their real past as collabora-
tors, dupes or believers during the Nazi period." Their silence then
and later "made them unsuitable for resisting Stalinist structures and
patterns of thought, which for a long time were deemed a touchstone
of 'partisanship' and 'loyalty' " (qtd. in Jarausch 85).

These investigations were not always welcome in the GDR, where
such antifascist icons as Erich Honecker were also Stalinists. Discussion of the role of the KPD in the 1920s or 1930s—when it denounced
the SPD as social fascist, split the left, and facilitated Hitler's rise—
remained taboo. Public discussion of Soviet Terror in the 1930s (or in

subsequent years) was hardly possible, and writers and historians could not speak openly about the Hitler-Stalin pact of 1939. According to the terms of that pact, Stalin occupied parts of Poland, the three Baltic states, and began a war with Finland. He supplied the German war machine with natural resources and allowed the Germans to use a submarine base in Murmansk. Moscow ordered foreign communist parties to desist in their antifascist propaganda and, in the case of the French communists, to subvert the war effort against Germany. The Soviet Union also returned numerous émigrés, including those of Jewish origin, to Germany and its Gestapo.

Although specific examination of such themes remained nearly impossible, at least until the later 1980s, some GDR writers did begin to reexamine the Jewish question, modifying traditional Marxist analyses. Historian Martin Jay has asserted: "The more radical the Marxist, the less interested in the specificity of the Jewish question" (288). Another historian, Konrad Kwiet, once noted, "Antisemitism, the history of the German Jews and their persecution are not themes considered worthy of study for their own sake within the terms of reference of GDR historiography" (173). Beginning with the baptized Jew Karl Marx, Marxist thinkers have often subsumed anti-Semitism under the crisis of capitalism. Arguing that capitalists fomented anti-Semitism to distract the working classes, Marxists believed that the abolition of capitalism would bring the cessation of anti-Jewish sentiment.

Anti-Semitism persisted, however, in several East bloc states, where, as Ferenc Feher gloomily asserted in 1979, it was elevated in its pre-Auschwitz form to "official policy" (347). Just as an examination of Hitler's crimes led to thoughts of Stalin, investigations into the causes of fascist anti-Semitism led some East German writers to comparisons with East bloc practices. Such issues are properly the purview of writers concerned with remembering the past, but they constituted extremely sensitive subjects in the GDR. Due to interior and exterior censors, many East German attempts to write—and right—the past remained problematic, at least through the 1970s.

Antifascist Beginnings: A Portrait of Anna Seghers

Like Bertolt Brecht, Anna Seghers grew up in a comfortable bourgeois milieu, and like Brecht, she developed into one of the most influential socialist writers of this century. Anna Seghers (1900–83) was born as Netty Reiling in Mainz. Raised in a prosperous Jewish family, she studied art history and earned a Ph.D. with a dissertation on Rembrandt and Judaism. "Seghers" was the name of one of Rembrandt's contemporaries, and "Anna Seghers" was a heroine in an early story by Reiling, after which Reiling adopted the appellation as her nom de plume.

Seghers achieved literary recognition in 1928 with the publication of *The Revolt of the Fishermen*, which received the prestigious Kleist prize. That same year she joined the German Communist party. When Hitler seized power Seghers was arrested briefly. After her release, she fled with her husband and children to Paris. Her mother was later murdered in one of Hitler's camps.

Much of Seghers's writing from the 1930s—*On the Way to the American Embassy* (1930), *The Companions* (1932), *A Price on his Head* (1933), and *The Way through February* (1935)—demonstrates not only a clear commitment to the communist cause but her desire to employ such narrative innovations as montage or interior monologue in the service of that cause. Her work in prose parallels to an extent Brecht's own efforts to expand the formal possibilities of the theater. But the two authors (neither of whom spent World War II in Soviet exile) remained mavericks, especially after the Soviets imposed socialist realism on Party writers in 1934. In 1938 Seghers exchanged a number of letters with the influential Hungarian Marxist philosopher Georg Lukács (who was living in Moscow exile), in which she defended attempts to combine Marxist commitment with avant-garde writing. In opposition to Lukács's emphasis on German Classicism, she underscored the literary experiments of the German Romantics, which she traced to their sense of political disfranchisement.

When Hitler's army entered Paris in 1940, Seghers escaped to Marseilles and then to Mexico, where a number of German communists spent the war. In Mexico Seghers published her finest work: *The Seventh Cross* (1942), *Transit* (1944), and "The Excursion of the Dead Girls" (1946).

Published in Mexico and the United States in 1942, and filmed in the United States in 1944, *The Seventh Cross* describes the flight of seven prisoners from a German concentration camp in 1937. The Nazis place seven crosses in the camp, at which three recaptured prisoners must stand. Three more prisoners die or are murdered during their flight, and the crosses become their grave markers. The communist George Heisler, however, is able to avoid the fascists. Aided by countless "ordinary" Germans as well as by his Party, he ultimately escapes Germany on a Dutch barge, a symbol of international solidarity. The seventh cross remains empty.

The novel is at least in part an expression of the *Volksfront* strategy pursued by the communists in the 1930s, but Marcel Reich-Ranicki correctly points out that numerous people who assist George do so out of a sense of decency and humanity, not with regard to politics ("Seghers" 372). Heisler's passion, which does not end on the cross, symbolizes the mystical power unleashed by resistance to inhumanity. Ernst Wallau, a fellow escapee who later dies a martyr's death in the camp, admonishes George: "Remember what is at stake here, and that its being labeled George for a week is but incidental" (307).

The ramifications of George's escape spread rapidly through the Rhine/Main area. A German worker reflects: "An escaped prisoner, that is what counts. It always creates an upheaval. It raises a doubt as to their [the Nazi's] own omnipotence. It is a breach" (60). That doubt, that breach in what had until then appeared to be the seamless ideology of fascism, affects all who contribute to George's flight. But the most immediate beneficiaries may be the inmates of the camp, who watch as the former commander is dismissed and the seven crosses are dismantled: "All of us felt how ruthlessly and fearfully outward powers could strike to the very core of man, but at the same time we felt that at the very core there was something that was unassailable and inviolable" (338).

Seghers had also fled from the Nazis, traveling from Marseilles to Mexico via Martinique, Santo Domingo, and Ellis Island. In *Transit*, which Christiane Zehl Romero calls "probably Seghers' best, certainly her darkest, most probing book" ("*Seghersmaterial*" 74), the author describes the nightmarish world of Marseilles, where desperate refugees wander helplessly in a seemingly absurd, in any event impenetrable, bureaucratic maze. They struggle to acquire the documentation necessary to leave France: proof of citizenship, residence papers, exit permits, a paid ship passage, sufficient funds, character guarantees, and visas for transit and for the final destination.

The story is recounted in the first person by a nameless narrator to a nameless interlocutor in a Marseilles harbor bar (it is indicative of the story's elusiveness that we never learn the real name of the narrator). A nonpolitical German, the narrator had nonetheless struck a Nazi in a fit of rage and had consequently been imprisoned in a concentration camp. He had escaped to France and had ultimately reached Marseilles. In Marseilles the Mexican consul had confused him with an antifascist author named Weidel. Assuming Weidel's identity, the narrator had been able to secure the necessary transit papers. But shortly before his departure to Mexico, he had abruptly decided to remain in France, work on a farm, and resist Hitler.

Marcel Reich-Ranicki finds the conclusion unbelievable from a psychological point of view and suggests that it results from Seghers's acquiescence to Party discipline in Mexico ("Seghers" 376). His interpretation ignores important aspects of the novel, however. In *Transit*, as in all of Seghers's work, one finds a search for permanence, generally embodied by the concept of resistance. The title serves as a metaphor for betrayal, deception, and the transience of life itself. But throughout the novel the narrator longs for fixity: "Only what is permanent pleases me, only what is different from me" (264).

The narrator discovers several examples of permanence. Weidel's antifascist writing about the Spanish civil war survives the author's death (233). The crippled Spanish civil war veteran Heinz leaves traces in people (206), and he helps the narrator rediscover a sense of self (83–84), so that at the conclusion of the novel he can realize, in lines that echo *The Seventh Cross*, his own inviolability (304). Finally, Seghers continuously invokes the feeling of eternity emanating from Marseilles, its people, and the surrounding countryside (e.g., 302). Those impressions move the narrator to remain in France and to work with the resistance: "Even if I were to be shot I have the feeling they could not entirely efface me. . . . If we shed our blood on familiar soil, something of us keeps on growing there, just as it is with bushes and trees one tries to root up" (311). The narrator's decision to remain is entirely consonant with the metaphorical and psychological universe of the novel.

In Seghers's subsequent story, "The Excursion of the Dead Girls," a story Christa Wolf has characterized as one of the most beautiful in the German language ("Faith" 125), the narrator moves within a surrealistic, dreamlike narrative that blurs time and place. She leaves her Mexican exile and returns to a school outing she had experienced as a girl in Germany. The narrator recalls her classmates and at the same time merges those past memories with the biographies of these girls under fascism. The Nazi era brings death to them all, perpetrators and victims alike. The literary techniques employed by Seghers in this story demonstrate her interest in Romanticism but bear little resemblance to those of socialist realism.

That changed in her subsequent novel, *The Dead Stay Young*. Seghers wrote most of the book in exile, but after she returned to the Soviet Zone of Occupation in 1947, she revised it for two years, publishing it in 1949, the founding year of the GDR. Covering a vast panorama of German history from the end of World War I to the end of World War II, the book attempts to illustrate the reasons for Hitler's rise and fall.

The novel begins with the murder of the young communist revolutionary Erwin by three officers. The plot then traces the subsequent lives of the officers, all of whom become Nazi supporters. Although Erwin's son Hans knows nothing of his father, he also becomes a communist and, at the conclusion of the novel, is also executed on orders from one of the same men who had murdered his father. The murderer notices the resemblance—the dead stay young. The repetition of events demonstrates the brutal recurrence of repressive history, but the novel also indicates that the cycle can be broken, for like his father before him, Hans has left a woman pregnant, and the unborn child represents not least of all the GDR.

Following the standard communist interpretation, Seghers blames the rise of Hitler on the disunity of the left and on the machinations of German industrialists. A description of the left coalition in Saxony brings one of the few overt narrative comments: "This alliance between Communists and Socialists should have taught the whole Reich that such a friendship was possible" (91). (This is of course at the same time a gesture of support for the East German SED.) Councilor of Commerce Castrizius attends the 1932 Düsseldorf luncheon with Hitler and is impressed with the "solutions" the man has to offer (152–55). Later Hitler is described as a capitalist tool: "A couple of people gave the man his start, they say, hoping he would keep order in Germany. Because he, alone, knows how, with their help, to keep the rich rich and the poor poor" (287). At the conclusion of the war, however, the capitalists abandon Hitler and initiate contacts with

Britain and the United States. In *The Decision* and *Trust*, the sequels
to *The Dead Stay Young*, Castrizius and his circle have rebuilt their
wealth and reputation with Marshall Plan assistance, and these men
represent a threat to the vulnerable GDR.

Revised in the Soviet Zone of Occupation, *The Dead Stay Young*
describes the Soviet Union through Hans's eyes as a "land without
masters and slaves, where everyone could eat his fill" (395). Hans
glosses over the difficulties occasioned by the Hitler-Stalin pact: "So
far Hitler has never done anything that turned out well for us—Stalin
never anything that turned out bad for us. That's why we trust him,
even when we don't always understand at once what he means"
(373). After Hitler and Stalin partition Poland, we learn from Hans
that the Germans act like "beasts," whereas the Soviets open schools:
"I learned how a nation feels under Russian rule, how many schools
they have opened in Bessarabia and Russian Poland, and how, up to
now, those people were not allowed to learn how to read and write
and now they have learned" (376). Christa Wolf once indicated that
The Dead Stay Young was read more as a textbook than as a work of
art ("Faith" 126), and it was clearly to some extent written in that
spirit.

Perhaps the most intriguing figures in the novel are the women.
Returning to Germany in 1947, Seghers witnessed the work of the
Trümmerfrauen, who, in a postwar Germany bereft of men, cleared
the rubble and reclaimed building materials. Her novel demonstrates
the devastating effects of war on women of all classes. Although
Seghers's women are often relatively powerless, their very marginality allows them the "luxury" of an incipient conscience; Elizabeth
Lieven, an unsympathetic character, can at least be momentarily horrified by genocide that leaves her husband cold (422).

As the German army invades the Soviet Union, the soldiers find
themselves haunted by Soviet women who remind them of witches
and other fairy-tale creatures. After an aged woman predicts the
defeat of the German army, Hans "felt instinctively that there was a
bit of his mother in this old witch and, when he thought of home, a
bit of this old witch in his gentle, silent mother" (378). Hans's mother
Marie has Cassandra-like moments earlier in the novel. Later she
develops female solidarity amidst the bombs and ruins of Berlin.
Western critics have derided the striking final image of the novel, in

which Marie shares a bed with Hans's pregnant lover, the unborn child between them. Reich-Ranicki for example finds it not far removed from unintentional comedy ("Seghers" 380). But it can be read as an image of a female tradition, of female solidarity across generations. Later GDR feminist writers, especially Irmtraud Morgner and Christa Wolf, would emphasize and expand the potential for female resistance present in this and other works by Seghers.

The Dead Stay Young represents a work of transition; its two sequel novels, *The Decision* (1959) and *Trust* (1968), published while Seghers was president of the Writers' Association, maintain an unabashedly didactic tone. *The Decision* describes an attempt to rebuild the Kossin steel work in East Germany. Kossin had previously belonged to the Bentheims, now in West Germany, and they plot to reacquire their former property. The CIA works with former Gestapo agents, *Schutzstaffel* (SS), and war criminals, to lure away the leading Kossin managers. Though top management defects, the East Germans redouble their efforts and succeed.

The Decision advances some criticisms of the GDR, although Seghers's SED apologists invariably have recourse to the GDR self-definition as an antifascist state (many of Seghers's heroes fought for the republicans in the Spanish civil war and/or suffered in concentration camps) in order to seize the moral high ground. These antifascists must contend with U.S. "imperialism" and "fascism," and here the novel does not proceed in a very differentiated fashion, equating Hitler, Franco, the Americans in Korea, and the French in Indochina (325). There is no mention of Stalinist repression in the Soviet Zone or in the subsequent GDR; instead, Seghers emphasizes in a separate plot the corruption of Herbert Melzer, a writer formerly committed to the socialist cause who becomes a commercial success in the United States and falls comfortably into a pattern of censorship and self-censorship. The West German scholar Klaus Sauer asserted in 1978 that no evidence suggested Seghers practiced self-censorship herself (168), but a 1989 book by Seghers's publisher Walter Janka, in which he describes his show trial during the 1950s and Seghers's silence during his sentencing, has raised serious questions about her integrity.

Seghers attempted to deal with the Janka trial in her story "The Righteous Judge," which she wrote in 1957–58, but which could first appear in 1990. In the story a judge refuses to participate in a show trial. He is imprisoned, and he meets there the innocent victim who has been sentenced by a more malleable judge. In prison they are able to reaffirm their commitment to the communist ideal, despite its Stalinist perversion. Seghers scholar Ute Brandes notes that Seghers also had two conversations with Ulbricht concerning Janka, and that she interceded on behalf of writers who protested the trial. Seghers thus promoted her state publicly, as head of the Writers' Association or in such a novel as *The Decision*, while attempting to work behind the scenes—a process that, Brandes asserts, led to "acquiescence and political ineffectiveness in attempting to reform the Stalinist state" ("Real" 4). It remains unclear how precarious Seghers's own position in fact was; various East bloc show trials during the late 1940s and early 1950s had victimized communists of Jewish descent who had spent World War II in Western exile.

Seghers's novel *Trust* (1968) deals with the workers' uprising of June 1953. Klaus Sauer dismisses as less than a half-truth the accusation that Seghers blames the West for the uprising (163). But the novel contains a plenitude of Western agents and provocateurs (most of them former Nazis); the strike leaders go to West Berlin and return with instructions (314); and an SED man at one point asserts that, although the government had more or less acceded to the workers' demands, the strike occurred due to outside manipulation (329).

The most telling moments in *Trust* occur when Seghers challenges the taboo of Stalinism, for she moves beyond the usual GDR euphemism regarding Stalin's "cult of personality" and directs attention to his anti-Semitism, to show trials in Budapest and Prague, and to coerced confessions. At the end of the novel, Ulsperger, a communist who had spent World War II in Soviet exile, reluctantly reveals something about Stalin's purges of German communists:

> Yes, certainly, everything started well—then came a bad period. Although I was luckier than many others, because I already had real friends. Friends who never lost sight of me. Who had the courage to intercede on my behalf. It was like a miracle—I was set free. (*Das Vertrauen* 438; my trans.)

This revelation shocks Richard Hagen, the good Party man who had until then heard that Ulsperger had been treated well in the Soviet

Union; Ulsperger himself had never spoken of his imprisonment there. Reflecting on the man's silence, Hagen decides that his comrade's approach represented the correct one; to speak of such things would confuse people (438). He feels a tremendous respect for this man who has maintained his trust in the Party.

Seghers's careful mention of these matters hence does not invite further discussion. Indeed, the SED cannot have approved of a reference to earlier Stalinist show trials in Czechoslovakia at a time when the East German army joined the Soviets in suppressing the Prague Spring. Nine years later Christa Wolf even more discreetly returned to the subject of Stalinism in *Patterns of Childhood*, asking, "When will we start speaking of that, too?" (245).

Seghers's best writing in the GDR is located in her short prose from the 1960s and 1970s, in "Benito's Blue" or in the cycle of stories entitled "The Strength of the Weak." In these narratives Seghers demonstrates the unexpected reserves of strength available to ostensibly simple people who evince a quiet, matter-of-fact heroism, a word it would not occur to them to employ. Although the stories at times do not rise above socialist kitsch, in "The Reed" Seghers returns productively to her antifascist roots. In 1973 she published "Encounter on a Journey," in which Kafka, Gogol, and E. T. A. Hoffmann meet in a Prague coffee house and discuss literary technique. The story allows Seghers to defend anew several of the positions she had advanced over thirty-five years earlier in debate with Lukács.

Institutionalized as a socialist classic, Seghers functioned as a symbol for the marriage between power and the intelligentsia in the GDR: The 1987 Writers' Congress featured a large picture of her with Party Chairman Erich Honecker. Fritz Raddatz asserted in 1972 that Seghers's literary influence on other GDR writers had been negligible (*Traditionen* 232), but that was never true. Christiane Zehl Romero has for example demonstrated Seghers's importance for Christa Wolf ("Remembrance") and for playwrights Heiner Müller and Volker Braun ("*Seghersmaterial*"). If Brecht functioned for these writers as the father of GDR literature, Seghers assumed the place of mother. Seghers's antifascist writing reverberates for the authors in this chapter. Her impressive novel *The Seventh Cross* especially echoes in their works.

Heroic Resistance and Sudden Conversions:
Hermlin, Apitz, and Fühmann

Stephan Hermlin, "The Time Together" GDR 1949, GDR 1962
(Eng. trans.), GB 1962

Born in 1915, Stephan Hermlin grew up in a cultured, upper-middle class family, but he joined the communist youth organization in 1931. A tension between the aesthete and the activist henceforth structured his life and his art. Between 1933 and 1936 he worked for a Berlin printer and engaged in illegal antifascist activities. He emigrated in 1936. After the pogrom in November 1938, the Nazis arrested his father, a Jewish businessman, who then died in the Sachsenhausen concentration camp. Hermlin's brother joined the Royal Air Force and died fighting the Germans.

Hermlin's emigration took him to Egypt, Palestine, England, Spain, and France, where he fought in the resistance and was interned. He escaped to Switzerland in 1944. From 1945 to 1947 he worked for Radio Frankfurt in the American zone of occupied Germany, and in 1947 (after having lost his position due to his political views) he moved to the Soviet sector. During the 1940s Hermlin wrote poetry of considerable beauty, and in the 1940s and 1950s he also published a number of short stories.

Published in the founding year of the GDR, *City on a Hill* contains four World War II stories illustrating the need for solidarity and the consequences when it lapses. The most powerful story, and the most sophisticated from a literary point of view, is "The Time Together," which deals with the 1943 uprising in the Warsaw ghetto. After the war a German who in some ways resembles Hermlin comes to Warsaw for the first time and visits the ruins of the ghetto. There he reads (or remembers reading) a letter written by a Jewish fighter during the uprising.

In an analysis of "The Time Together," the West German scholar Christiane Schmelzkopf does not doubt the sincerity of Hermlin's intentions, but she finds his tone often questionable, at times even macabre and tasteless. Schmelzkopf believes that Hermlin, who was not a participant, has little right to write as he does. She objects in particular to his at times precious stylization of the victim's feelings; to his pathos, which, she asserts, often lapses into inadvertent kitsch;

and to his well-ordered, refined, and elegant sentences, which stand in too crass a contrast to the chaos he wishes to describe (30–33).

One can counter at least some of Schmelzkopf's objections with an analysis of the narrative techniques Hermlin employs in the story. At the conclusion, the narrator of the frame remarks, "It was still a matter of indifference to me whether what I had just experienced was really in the letter or not" (158). In a night of memory and mourning, the narrator of the frame infuses the events of the letter, which he had previously given a cursory reading, with his own subjectivity, until, as the East German scholar Silvia Schlenstedt notes, the narrator of the letter becomes an alter ego for the narrator of the frame (*Hermlin* 164). The latter narrator remarks, "His features were so near and must have been so like the face which I see every morning in the mirror" (95). Both narrators are thirty-four, and when the Polish narrator of the letter imagines himself in a small, northern, German town, we encounter the consciousness of the German narrator from the frame.

The two narrators in turn share traits with Hermlin, who was thirty-four when he first visited Warsaw. There is also some of Hermlin in Mlotek, the heroic communist Jew who leads the antifascist resistance: both have been in Palestine. Blending himself as author with the two narrators plus Mlotek, Hermlin presents an experiment in the creative process of remembering, making an attempt to empathize with the suffering of Warsaw's Jews.

Hermlin had earlier written a journalistic essay on the uprising, and he places "The Time Together" within a precise historical framework. The letter writer records dates and events of the uprising in his narrative, and Hermlin also integrates documentary material, such as the report of SS Scharführer Stroop, who was responsible for extinguishing the revolt (*Stroop Report*). Within that carefully constructed historical framework, Hermlin invents a tale that, in its ideology, corresponds to a communist understanding of the rules governing society and history.

Cleaving to the models presented by Anna Seghers and others, Hermlin's story emphasizes heroic resistance. The letter writer displays considerable impatience regarding the passivity of fellow Jews: "But of one thing I am sure, the face of *Bar Kochba* [who led a Jewish uprising against the Romans under Hadrian] must be hidden under the frozen features of Job" (102). Mlotek, the name of the Jewish communist who leads the Warsaw Jews, means "Hammer" in Polish; "Hammer" or "Hammer-like" is also the significance of the name Maccabee, the leader of the second-century B.C. battle for Jewish independence. As Christiane Schmelzkopf points out, Maccabee and Bar Kochba fought for *Jewish* independence and religious freedom, but in Hermlin's story they symbolize the struggle of Jews and non-Jews together for a better world (37). When the Warsaw Jews decide to revolt, they are helped by Jan and Stanislaus, two non-Jewish representatives of an outside organization that provides fighters, arms, and escape for women and children.

At the height of the revolt (which occurs during Passover), Mlotek and his fighters discover old men commemorating Seder: "This year still slaves, next year children of liberty. This year here, next year in Jerusalem" (137). Within the story, the second sentence functions metaphorically as a longing for freedom from oppression; the story explicitly rejects a literal interpretation, which would signify a Zionist alternative. Directly after the Seder, Mlotek reveals that he has indeed been to Palestine: "I should have been only too pleased to be convinced that people like us could stop anywhere without being bothered" (138). After becoming a communist, however, he finds himself harassed by British and Jewish police, who arrest and ultimately deport him. As Schmelzkopf notes, under capitalism a Jewish state can provide only illusory solutions; socialism would bring the cessation of anti-Semitism and would render such a state unnecessary (39).

Hermlin's vision of Jewish-Gentile solidarity was common among leftists at that time, especially among those in Western exile. Hans Mayer, who would work with Hermlin in Frankfurt before moving to the GDR to lecture in Leipzig, wrote that during his exile he encountered a concept of togetherness (*"Gemeinsamkeit,"* thus echoing the title of Hermlin's story, "Die Zeit der Gemeinsamkeit") that dismissed differences among comrades of Jewish and non-Jewish background as bourgeois prejudice and also as unworthy (259). Mayer describes his disillusionment after the war: "The anti-Semitism of Stalin and others could not simply be abolished by decree. To be sure, I realized this very late, after two world wars and during horrified observation of Stalin's anti-Semitic show trials in Moscow and Prague, Sofia and Budapest" (257; my trans.). When Hermlin published "The Time Together," the trials in Moscow and Prague waited in the near future, but those in Sofia and Budapest were occurring. In 1948, Stalin had initiated an anti-Zionist campaign, during which he purged Soviet Jews from the government and Party, banished them from universities, and closed Jewish institutions, newspapers, and presses; he also dissolved the Jewish Antifascist Committee, jailing and/or murdering its leaders.

Nonetheless, in Hermlin's story, the Soviet Union provides a great hope. Mlotek insists the Soviets are fighting for the Jews (110). The letter writer repeats several times that "there is something new in the world which has begun far away in the East" (101)—the German defeat at Stalingrad. The narrator hears an "echo of the cannonades of Stalingrad" in the picks and shovels the Jews use to dig their bunkers (106). Mlotek lectures on Lenin, and the narrator can imagine "Long live Poland!" in the same breath as "Long live the Soviet Union!" (147).

As with the vision of Jews and Gentiles united in a common struggle, the harmonious view of Polish-Soviet relations is idealized, hence problematic. It neatly divides the world into fascists and antifascists, with the Soviets leading the latter group. Yet Poles and the Polish Communist party fared particularly tragically under Stalin. According to one estimate, fifty thousand Poles living in the Soviet Union were executed at the time of the Bukharin trial (Spriano 47). In a secret protocol to the Hitler-Stalin pact of 1939, the Soviet Union and Germany divided Poland. Under Gorbachev the Soviet Union admitted responsibility for the massacre of thousands of Polish soldiers, most of them officers, in Katyn Forest. In Hermlin's story, the Jews regret that the Soviet army is still too far removed to aid their doomed uprising, but during the second Warsaw uprising in 1944, the Soviet army, camped across the Vistula, elected to watch the Germans tame the revolt and burn the city; then the Soviets liberated it. After the war the Soviets annexed large portions of previously Polish territory. Stephan Hermlin structures "The Time Together" with history, but much of his plot constitutes an ideological wish fulfillment.

Bruno Apitz, *Naked Among Wolves* GDR 1958, GDR 1960 (Eng. trans.), GB 1960

The small city of Weimar, in the south of the GDR, assumed in German history an importance usually reserved for capital metropolises. The home of Goethe and Schiller in the late eighteenth and early nineteenth centuries, Weimar became synonymous with German Classicism. Its name also characterized the first democratic republic in 1919. On the Etersberg, the hill overlooking the city, the Nazis built the Buchenwald concentration camp. The camp, erected in a beech forest (*Buchen Wald*), was not primarily an extermination camp in the manner of Auschwitz or Maidanek. Nonetheless, the fascists murdered an estimated fifty-six thousand there, including the chairman of the German Communist party, Ernst Thälmann.

Among the inmates was Bruno Apitz (1900–79). One of twelve children, Apitz grew up in working class poverty, had an apprenticeship as a diesinker, and joined the Communist party in 1927. Active in the antifascist resistance, he spent most of the Nazi period in jails or camps; he spent 1937 to 1945 in Buchenwald.

Set in Buchenwald, Apitz's *Naked Among Wolves* describes the last months of the war, as American units approach Weimar. With the front nearing, the Nazis panic. Some wish to destroy the camp and its inmates, while others believe that a demonstration of restraint, even at a late date, might win them mercy from the allies.

A Polish Jew, arriving from the evacuated Auschwitz camp, smuggles with him a three-year-old child, whom various inmates, including some communists, help hide. The communist leaders fear that such exploits endanger their underground organization, and they order the child out of the camp, even though the young boy will then most certainly die. The text thus creates a conflict between reason and emotion, between discipline and spontaneity, between means and ends. The inmates disobey the order and hide the child. Although some prisoners are tortured, they refuse to divulge information, and their comrades ultimately liberate the camp, overwhelming the remaining SS guards and uniting with U.S. advance units.

Apitz's novel proved a tremendous success in the East, becoming a best-seller with numerous printings. It was also filmed. The book attained the position of a classic within GDR literary history, not least because it supported East Germany's self-definition as an antifascist state and as the inheritor of the progressive, communist resistance.

By the early 1970s two million copies of the novel had reached twenty-eight countries in twenty-five languages, but West Germans of the 1950s and 1960s generally ignored it. That was in part due to artistic reasons: the characterizations are rather primitive; the language is often awkward; and the narrative style belongs to the nineteenth century. It may be, however, that the very "flaws" in the novel help account for its mass appeal, similar to another melodrama on a related subject, the television film *Holocaust*. Professional readers and literary critics often underestimate the ability of "bad" art to serve the good.

As Wolfgang Emmerich points out, the main obstacle to a West German reception was the cold war (91). Marcel Reich-Ranicki found Apitz's story not at all true to life (apparently he did not know Apitz based it on actual events), and in an extremely dubious interpretation, he attributed the novel's success in East Germany to the fact that communists disobey Party dictates in the name of a higher duty ("Apitz" 459–60). The conservative *Frankfurter Allgemeine Zeitung* was scandalized that a West German publisher printed the novel in 1963, and it was not until 1968 that the film could be seen in public theaters (Emmerich 91). One suspects that similar obstacles blocked the U.S. reception of Apitz's book, which was not reviewed by U.S. critics.

Matthias Brand, who attempts to find a middle ground between the celebration of the novel in the East and the tendency in the West to camouflage a political rejection with a discussion of aesthetic flaws, has some sensible objections to the book ("Stacheldrahtleben"). In Apitz's Manichaean universe, the good characters are almost all rather wooden heroes, with the result that the evil characters tend to be more interesting. Brand notes that for Apitz's heroes the camps and their evils remain externalized, something one does not find in other literature, documentary or not, about the camps. Brand also quotes Czeslaw Milosz's remarks on socialist-realist expectations for the concentration camp genre:

> How was one supposed to see a concentration camp? It is not hard to enumerate: 1) the prisoners should have banded together in secret organizations; 2) the leaders in these organizations should have been Communists; 3) all the Russian prisoners appearing on the pages of the book should have distinguished themselves by their moral strength and heroic behavior; 4) the prisoners should have been differentiated according to their political outlook. (Milosz, *Captive* 120)

Apitz's book satisfies all these requirements; it was written to measure. Not surprisingly, Apitz does not mention noncommunist resistance groups, though they existed; Brand also asserts that eyewitness reports of the liberation do not corroborate Apitz's glowing depiction.

Peter Demetz agrees that the novel follows the communist concentration camp genre established by Seghers and others; the "persecuted were seen in terms of class and party allegiances, and the genre itself was unwilling to perceive them as loyal or assimilated members of a religious or ethnic community" (*Fires* 26). Demetz notes that the Polish Jew who brings the Jewish child into the camp is only once referred to as Jewish, and that the prisoners prefer to speak of the child as Polish, not Jewish. When the Germans begin to evacuate the camp in the final days of the war, the disorganized Jews panic: "They shouted and wept and did not know what to do" (qtd. in *Fires* 27). In the plans of the communist committee to liberate the camp, the Jews do not figure at all. Demetz asserts that the novel "suggests a good deal about how Communists of the Weimar generation looked at their unorganized Jewish fellow prisoners" (*Fires* 26). Ruth Angress is more explicit and more severe: "The Jew as victim of the Holocaust is literally infantilized, and put into the shadow by the Comrades, as if Jews had been only incidental victims compared to the genuine, ideological enemy who preserved his integrity and knew how to fight back" (216).

These objections were, however, raised by scholars outside the GDR. Within that country, *Naked Among Wolves* assumed a central place in literary history. For GDR authors dealing with the past, Apitz's novel remained a presence to be confronted, a text within their texts.

Franz Fühmann, *The Car with the Yellow Star: Fourteen Days out of Two Decades* GDR 1962, GDR 1968 (Eng. trans.)

Born in 1922, Franz Fühmann grew up in Rokytnice, a town in northern Bohemia where many ethnic Germans longed to go "home to the Reich." Fühmann often commented on the influence his environment exercised over his early development. His father, the town apothecary, founded the local Nazi party, and young Fühmann participated in two Nazi youth organizations. In 1939 he enlisted voluntarily in the Wehrmacht and fought in Greece and in the Soviet Union. He also began publishing poems, some of which were printed in the weekly *Das Reich*, one of Goebbels's propaganda organs. Fühmann was, as he notes in an autobiographical statement appended to the English version of *The Car with the Yellow Star*, "a faithful soldier of Hitler."

In November 1982, twenty months before his death, Fühmann traveled to Munich to accept the Geschwister-Scholl-Prize, named after Hans and Sophie Scholl, the brother and sister who organized and led the White Rose resistance group in Munich during World War II. Unlike so many of his generation who claimed to have known nothing or to have merely followed orders, or who, like Kurt Waldheim, simply denied their past, Fühmann had relentlessly confronted his actions as a Nazi. For that reason this "faithful soldier of Hitler" could be offered such a prize. One of Fühmann's first works in prose, *The Car with the Yellow Star* shows us both sides of the author: the development of the fanatic, and the man who attempts to come to terms with his fascist past. It is far more convincing on the former count.

In keeping with orthodox Marxist thought, the novella advances primarily economic motives for anti-Semitism. The young protagonist, who has never seen a Jew, has heard that "they took money out of honest people's pockets by all manner of mean tricks and they were to blame for the depression which threatened to ruin my father's little druggist's business" (12). At the time Fühmann wrote, the GDR generally equated Jews with communists—Hitler had persecuted both, and both received special treatment in East Germany as victims of fascism. The novella attempts to demonstrate that fascists demonized communists as well as Jews for similar—economic—reasons.

Fühmann describes his early feelings toward communists with words comparable to those used in describing Jews: "[Communists] were criminals who refused to work and wanted to take everything away from honest people because they were so lazy; they plundered and murdered and stole" (28). After Hitler annexes the Sudetenland, many Germans come to work there, "for many jobs were now vacant where the Jews and Reds had worked before" (53).

The fanaticism of young Fujmann (as the narrator calls himself in this autobiographical novel) allows him to overlook obvious contradictions. When a state of emergency is declared in the Sudetenland, the Nazi youth group occupies the local school, convinced that an attack by "Czech-Jewish-Bolsheviks" is impending. They wait out the day in growing boredom, and they finally disperse sheepishly after three polite Czech policemen remind them that curfew approaches. "Next morning," the story continues, "we heard on the German radio of new and dastardly crimes perpetrated by the Czech-Jewish-Marxist mob" (41). The report describes a savage attack by Czech police on harmless schoolboys, who resist heroically and suffer fatalities. Fujmann admits, "We knew perfectly well that every word was a lie, but we listened with shining eyes and it did not occur to us to call it lies" (41). Later, when Hitler justifies the invasion of Poland with reports of Polish atrocities against Germans, the narrator writes with irony (though for his youthful persona the irony is entirely unconscious), "We knew all about atrocities against defenceless Germans, for we had experienced them ourselves" (57).

The young fanatic cannot free himself from all doubts, however, and the narrator traces a continued pattern of incipient questioning followed by rapid suppression. Already as a schoolchild in a monastery, for example, Fujmann finds himself thinking "a deadly sin, perhaps even unforgivable" (30): he hopes the communists will destroy the monastery. He confesses and must do penance for such thoughts. When he serves on the Russian front, the first successful Soviet counteroffensive causes him to recognize that the entire campaign is madness (81), but he can suppress these thoughts as well (88–89). After witnessing German atrocities (labor transports and hanged peasants), however, he begins to question his earlier conviction that Hitler had destroyed classes and had created a radically egalitarian society, a *Volksgemeinschaft:* "Does everything belong to the people, to Germany? Or are a few big industrialists putting everything into their own pockets as they did in the First World War?" (102). He also listens—and that is a mutinous act—to a Soviet propaganda broadcast that asks many of the same unsettling questions (102–4). After reading the Old Norse apocalyptic epic *Edda*, he has a vision of an army of hanged men invading Germany to take their revenge. Such thoughts shock him: "Loss of the war would mean Germany's downfall. How could such a thought have occurred to me, even the thought was a crime! I was desperately ashamed of having had such doubts" (118). The language and the psychology are similar to his schoolboy experiences in the monastery.

The Soviets take the narrator prisoner, and the remainder of the novella traces his reeducation in the Soviet Union. Whereas the story has examined the development of Fujmann the fascist in some detail, the transformation of Fujmann to a socialist is asserted, not described; telescoped, it remains unconvincing. Perhaps *Das Kapital* does not provide the stuff of drama:

> After the first lectures in political economy I felt the scales falling from my eyes, for here were the answers to all the questions which had always bothered me. Later on, when I had ploughed through the thick volumes of Marx' *Capital*, I could see right back through all the stages of my life, as clearly as I could see the desk in front of me. (166)

After Fujmann's Saul-like transformation, Fühmann the author presses his book into service for the East German state. Not surprisingly, GDR critics applauded the book, praising it, for example, as a "poetic documentation of the highest interest" (*Der Sonntag* 17 Feb. 1963; my trans.). Fühmann creates a dualism between East and West, excoriating the "bad news" from the Western zone of Germany, and celebrating the fact that, in the East, "the people had set up their own state" (167). When the protagonist returns to Germany, he visits a coryphaeus in West Berlin. This man, who is proud of his instant coffee, is a caricatured Westerner, but the protagonist too easily dismisses some important issues in the coryphaeus's library. He waxes indignant that the man possesses books by authors of protofascist sympathies, but the library contains books unavailable in the GDR: "And here was what he called freedom of the mind—Eliot, Camus, Pound and many others whom I did not know" (170). Later in his life, Fühmann admitted that upon returning to the GDR and discovering that his favorite poet Georg Trakl was proscribed by socialist realism, he felt he had been "struck by a whip" (qtd. in Demetz, *Fires* 127).

The narrator hails the merger of the Communist and Socialist parties into the Socialist Unity party (152), though history shows that it was a process of coercion. He attacks the anticommunist propaganda of the Western press but is relieved that at least the official SED paper tells the truth (172). He spotlights the optimism and hope that result from land reform, as the government divided larger estates and awarded parcels of land to individual farmers—"land of his own for the first time in his life" (174). By the time Fühmann wrote, however, the GDR had collectivized its farms, and its farmers were once again without land of their own.

On a more subtle level, the text maintains its dichotomies by setting up the East as an optimistic place and the West as a decadent, declining one. The coryphaeus speaks of "the loneliness of mankind, the despair, the mercilessness, the rejection" (172). But Fujmann has experienced solidarity, be it in the Soviet Union as he builds a road or in the GDR as miners sing in a train. In a 1968 Swiss edition of *The Car with the Yellow Star*, an edition greeted in the West with critical respect, Fühmann distanced himself from his final chapter, characterizing it as a break in style. He is in part correct, for the final scenes lack the irony and distance of the previous chapters. Nonetheless, the psychology remains the same and provides the book, against the will of the author, with a certain unsettling unity. As a prisoner in the Soviet Union, the narrator swears that "no power in the world is ever again going to make us take part in its plans" (150), but Fühmann's narrator moves rather quickly from fascism to socialism.

Jewish Victims in Bobrowski, Becker, and Wander

Johannes Bobrowski, *Levin's Mill* GDR 1964, GB 1970

Johannes Bobrowski was born and raised in Tilsit, a city on the Neman river. In 1917, when Bobrowski was born, Tilsit constituted part of Germany. (After 1945 the Soviets annexed the city and renamed it Sovetsk.) It was an area where many peoples and cultures—Poles, Germans, Lithuanians, Russians, Jews, and Gypsies—coexisted, often uneasily. Since the days of the Teutonic Knights (who founded Tilsit), the Germans maintained a sense of colonial purpose and manifest destiny in the East. In the nineteenth century, for example, Gustav Freytag's best-selling novel *Debit and Credit* depicted the exemplary, Horatio Alger-like path of a hardworking young German, whom Freytag contrasts with an unpleasant Jew and many lazy Poles. The racial, national, religious, and economic tensions between these groups turned genocidal with the arrival of Hitler's army. A foot soldier in that army, Bobrowski himself became part of German guilt in the area, and his entire opus, perhaps even more so than with Franz Fühmann, represents an act of penance. His theme, as he often repeated, became the Germans and the European East: "a long history of calamity and guilt, since the days of the Teutonic Order, which stand on my people's account. Not that it can ever be erased or atoned for, but it is worth hope and an honest attempt in German poetry" (qtd. in Flores 233).

After four years as a Soviet prisoner of war, Bobrowski returned to the Soviet Zone of Occupation and worked as a reader at publishing houses. He began publishing in 1954, helped by Peter Huchel. In 1962 Bobrowski received the West German Group 47 Prize, which helped him achieve international recognition. From 1962 until his untimely death in 1965, he commanded considerable national and international attention as a poet, and his four small volumes of poetry—two of which were published posthumously—remain some of the very finest written in the GDR.

Perhaps trying to realize the socialist-realist demand for popularity and comprehensibility, Bobrowski wrote several short stories in the 1960s (some of which have been translated in the volume *I Taste Bitterness*), and in the last two years of his life, he published two short novels. Bobrowski's prose makes demands on its readers, especially his novel *Lithuanian Pianos* and the masterful short story "Boehlendorff," which provided a demonstrable influence on later writers, such as Christa Wolf and Gerhard Wolf (Tate 184). Nonetheless, Bobrowski's prose remains generally more accessible than his poetry, and his first novel, *Levin's Mill*, received a widespread and positive critical response in both East and West Germany. The novel, which in its narrative techniques separates itself from the rather cumbersome and mechanical pieces of socialist-realist prose being published in the GDR at that time, remains too little known in the United States, where it was not reviewed.

The Russian Jew Leo Levin comes to Neumühl, a Polish village on a small tributary of the Drewitz, and builds a mill that takes business from Johann, the narrator's grandfather. The time is 1874, soon after the founding of Bismarck's German Reich, and the Polish village constitutes part of that Reich. Grandfather, a German and a Baptist who regards himself as a leading member of the village, feels threatened by Levin on a number of levels—economic, religious, and national—and he destroys a dam in the river, thus causing the wreck of Levin's mill. Levin sues, but Grandfather effectively bribes the

(German) legal system so that Levin's case is adjourned. Levin returns to his Russian home with the Gypsy Marie, but they have become outsiders there, and they continue to wander.

Grandfather's misdeeds extend beyond the wreckage of Levin's mill. In his attempt to bring "order" to the village, he buys the Baptist minister, driving that man's wife to alcoholism and suicide. He also burns down the abandoned house in which the Gypsies Marie and her father Habedank have been living. The Jews, Gypsies, and Poles fight back, however, turning Grandfather's victory over Levin into a Pyrrhic one. They make his life in the village unpleasant enough that he sells his property and moves to a city. Even there he finds himself confronted with the artist Philippi, who, when Grandfather demands to be left in peace, responds simply, "No."

The Germans in the novel, represented by Grandfather, are loud in their denunciations of the Poles; the Germans also mistrust Gypsies and hate Jews. Reading a popular family magazine, Grandfather is delighted to discover his own views confirmed there by the nineteenth-century writer Otto Glagau: "No longer may tolerance or miserable weakness prevent us Christians from taking preventative measures against the extravagances, excesses and effrontery of the Jewry" (123). Judith Ryan is certainly correct in reading *Levin's Mill*, set in Bismarck's Reich, as a comment on the Third Reich (130–31).

Grandfather Johann does not hesitate to inflame religious, jingoistic, or xenophobic sentiments for his ends, but his real motivations are economic. Class differences inform and structure the narrative. On the first page the narrator already informs us that the Germans were more prosperous than the Poles. The wandering flutist Johann Vladimir Geethe (the name combines that of Goethe with Lenin) tells us the Germans act as they do "because of money" (174). The narrator does not contradict this opinion, and we may take it as authoritative. In Bobrowski's novel, class interests cut across national and religious lines, hence indicating the preeminence of the economic argument. Gregor German is, despite his name, Polish, and also a rich farmer. Of him the narrator notes, "Gregor, we must admit, has had a little bit too much, lands and cattle" (190). Gregor asks the Gypsies and Poles who are celebrating on his farm to please go somewhere else. Like Grandfather Johann, Gregor German is interested in peace and order.

Order constitutes one of the leitmotifs used to characterize Grandfather, who keeps track of his bribes in an organized fashion by recording them in the back of his Bible. Grandfather attempts to control events, but he ultimately fails, for the Poles, Gypsies, and German outsiders conspire as Levin's allies to chip away at, and eventually subvert, Grandfather's imposed order. They do that with music, a form of protest and a mode of subversion. Grandfather's wife Christina generally suffers passively, but at one point she leads the village women in a church song aimed at Grandfather and his corrupt preacher, Feller (184). The Poles have songs that reverberate with a history of suffering, and they sing a ballad, written by another wanderer, Weiszmantel, commemorating the bloody Polish farmers' revolt of 1863 (176–77). The first words of the revolutionary ballad of the Polish revolt—"The time had come, this time I cried / My soul was sore oppressed" (176)—appear to echo Christina's favorite song, mentioned three times in the text: "Heart, my heart, when will you be free" (192). The Polish national anthem, "Poland is not lost yet," also functions as a song of resistance (190), and Weiszmantel's song of Moses (i.e., of Levin) publicly indicts Grandfather for destroying the mill (90–91).

These attempts to subvert the established order with music are expressed formally by the narrator's project, for he, too, wishes to undermine accepted structures. To this end he utilizes what might be called modernist techniques, but not, as in Uwe Johnson's *Speculations about Jakob*, to demonstrate the fundamental irreducibility and ultimate incomprehensibility of reality. For Bobrowski's narrator, there is a story that can be told and grasped. First, however, he must take apart our way of seeing the world. Thus the grandchild narrates, as he admits, in a circumlocutory fashion (42). Referring to Feller, Grandfather's paid preacher, he notes, "Of course, the world can be nicely arranged, in chapter and verse even, then everything fits together" (9). Yet it is precisely Feller's and Grandfather's order of the world that he wishes to undermine. Thus, although the narrator announces he will structure his story around thirty-four key sentences, he is not very concerned about counting them correctly (e.g., 58).

The narrator attempts to create his new order by educating his audience. Demonstrating the fashion in which the underprivileged overturn established structures, he provides exemplary scenes of what *might* have happened, of how history might have been—and can be—changed. But the narrator, writing some fifteen years after Hitler's downfall, is unsure of his audience. That explains his halting start: in the first two pages he must begin his story twice; he is afraid of misunderstandings (5); and the prospect plagues him that his efforts will be in vain, "just as futile as if I had dished it up then to my grandfather" (7). Thus, as Bernd Leistner astutely points out, Bobrowski's narrator has to create a community of reader-listeners (113–14, 122). One measure of the grandchild's success here, though Leistner does not name it, is the progression from "I," at the beginning of the story, to "we," from "my story" to "our story."

At one point Geethe plays a ballad that Weiszmantel narrates with "many Ta ta tas and La la las" (194). In a sense, that is the strategy of Bobrowski's narrator, who employs dialect, the Polish language, and vulgarities in an attempt to imitate an oral tradition—such as the ballad—of storytelling. This technique also signals, on a formal level, his sympathy with the Gypsies and Poles, the storytellers.

At the conclusion of the text, the grandchild brings together the themes of music, protest, and the responsibility of the artist:

> Come, let us sing.
> In Gollub the gypsies are playing.
> If we don't sing, others will.
>
> (230)

The last paragraph deals with the artist Philippi's harassment of Grandfather. The narrator has presented an act of solidarity with the Poles, Gypsies, and Jews. Like the Gypsies, he has "sung" against injustice; and like Phillipi, he has presented an example of the fashion in which writers should not leave the past, here represented in the grandfather figure, in peace.

Despite the exhortations to the reader at story's end, a sense of precariousness remains. Grandfather is ultimately driven from his village, but not before he has exiled Levin, turning him into a wandering Jew. Phillipi also writes some disturbing, Bobrowski-like lyrics near the end of the story: "I speak into the wind" (225). The sentence echoes the narrator's original doubts as to whether his story will be heard or understood. Similarly, a Jewish teacher in Russia sketches in the dust on the floor signs that no one will read: "In this world, he says, the laws wander around and stand in our rooms and have wide eyes and long ears and say: There shall be parting and no union" (210). Continuing in the language of prophecy, the teacher declares: "In the other world we shall see those who have parted, they'll be standing together, their arms around each other" (210). Bobrowski's narrator has tried to write signs that will be read. He has attempted to speak not to the wind, but to a community. His project has been to create the community and the solidarity for which the Jewish teacher longs—to transport the other-worldliness of Jewish messianism to political activism in the world.

Jurek Becker, *Jacob the Liar* GDR 1969, USA 1975

Like the Romanian Jew Paul Celan, who after suffering in a fascist camp wrote some of the most beautiful German poetry of this century, Jurek Becker maintains a highly ambivalent relationship with the language he controls so well. Born in Lodz, Poland, two years before the German invasion and the start of World War II, Becker spent his first years in Lodz's Jewish ghetto. Later he was transported to the concentration camp Sachsenhausen, near Berlin, where he survived until his liberation by the Soviet army in 1945. Becker remained in Berlin with his father, and at age nine he began to learn the language of those who had wished him dead.

The story of *Jacob the Liar*, Jurek Becker's first novel, unfolds during the last year of World War II, within the barbed-wire enclosure of the Jewish ghetto in a Polish city. While under arrest, former ice-cream and potato pancake vendor Jakob Heym accidentally overhears a radio report that the Soviets are fighting for Bezanika, a city perhaps five hundred kilometers away. By pure chance, the Germans release Jacob, the first Jew to return alive from the German police headquarters. That presents to him both a blessing and a conundrum, for no one will believe his glad tidings; or if they do believe him, they will think him a spy.

Hence Jacob invents a radio. He does it in an unpremeditated fashion, to prevent his friend Misha from a reckless act certain to result in death. He intends to clear the matter later, but he discovers that the hope he has unleashed has spread quickly through the ghetto. Trapped in his lie, Jacob must invent battles, generals, and strategies, all designed to bring the Red Army closer. Within the ghetto, the Jews begin once again to dream of a future, and the suicides cease.

Jacob's fiction cannot deter the ineluctable reality; the Germans continue to deport the ghetto's inhabitants, street by street. At the novel's conclusion, the remaining inhabitants, Jacob among them, crowd into boxcars that will take them to an extermination camp. En route Jacob meets the narrator and entrusts to him the story. The narrator survives; Jacob does not.

Jacob's fictional radio forces him to invent and tell stories. In a sense, as Rainer Nägele points out, Jacob's recounting of stories parallels the narrator's own project (212). To that end, the narrator employs the slang of spoken language, addressing readers (in the German text) with the informal pronoun "du," breaking distance and making us initiates. Like Bobrowski, from whom he learned, Becker repeats words or phrases in an almost formulaic fashion, adopting a narrative device from the oral epic. The Jewish narrator captures in German the rhythmic echoes of Yiddish and hence recalls a tradition of Yiddish storytelling that stretches from Scholem Aleichem to Isaac Bashevis Singer. If, as Jacob twice complains, he does not possess the talents of a Scholem Aleichem, the narrator does.

Felix Frankfurter, the father of Misha's lover Rosa, "likes nothing better than a story with a point to it" (40). The narrator follows that strategy, both in the larger structure of his text and within smaller narrative units, such as anecdotes or stories. He provides a paradigmatic example of his storytelling technique directly at the outset of the novel, when he relates the symbolic import of trees in his life:

> A few years later—I was about seventeen—I was lying with a girl for the first time in my life. Under a tree. This time it was a beech tree, a good fifteen meters high. The girl's name was Esther—no, I think, Moira. Anyway, it was a beech and a wild boar interrupted us. Maybe, there were even several—we didn't have time to turn around. And a few years later my wife Chana was shot to death under a tree. (4)

The style here, with its combination of humor, understatement, and abrupt abruptness, is characteristic for the novel. The movement from lovemaking to murder is shocking, and the narrator magnifies our horror by avoiding pathos; indeed, his very matter-of-factness appears almost scandalous. Yet it is precisely appropriate to his story of life in the ghetto, where death ruled in a sudden, arbitrary, and finally senseless fashion. Jacob's roommate Piwowa is shot by his supervisor in a shoe factory (22); Misha's roommate Fajngold disappears mysteriously, never to return (191); the inhabitants of entire blocks are deported according to a pattern unapparent to the ghetto populace (233). The narrator's matter-of-fact style represents an attempt to describe a "normal" situation in the ghetto, where one daily sees in the street bodies of Jews who have starved to death. Jacob's radio helps restore humanity to people trapped in an inhumane situation; Rosa and Misha, for example, begin to plan for a "normal" future (56–58).

If Jacob attempts to impose his story of the Russian advance between the reality of deportation to the extermination camps, the narrator attempts with his story to impose order on meaninglessness. If in his style he intends to approximate a sense of senselessness—the inexplicable suffering and death of a people—he also, finally, structures that meaninglessness. In so doing, he tells a story; despite his deference to his sources, to the "realistic" novel, he invents, sometimes freely. He provides a statement of intent early in his story:

> I'm telling the story, not [Jacob]. Jacob is dead. Besides, I'm not telling his story, but rather a story. . . .
> I say to myself it must have been approximately thus and so. Or I say to myself, it would be best if it had been thus and so, and then I tell it and act as if it fits. And it really does fit. (37)

Like the narrator in Christa Wolf's *The Quest for Christa T.* (1968), Becker's narrator underscores the fictionality of his undertaking.

We encounter that technique most clearly with the narrator's conclusion, or conclusions. Clearly dissatisfied with the drably "real" one he must relate, he invents an alternative one that satisfies his need for order and meaning. According to his alternative conclusion, Jacob is shot and killed while attempting to escape from the ghetto. Immediately thereafter the Russians liberate the ghetto, and the narrator hears in the Russian cannon a response to the machine gun that cuts off Jacob's life (254). He sees this expressly as vengeance for Jacob, thus giving his story a sense, an order, the point he misses in its "real" conclusion. The inhabitants Jacob fought to protect are saved, and both Jacob's life and death have meaning within a cosmic structure that brings revenge.

Of course, if the alternative ending had occurred, Jacob's story could not have been told, for he confides it to the narrator in the boxcar during the other conclusion, "the pale-cheeked and unpleasant one, the real and unimaginative ending whereby you are easily pushed to the silly question: What's the purpose of all that?" (256). The narrator gives this conclusion priority, for he realizes that if Jacob's story is to be told, he must tell it, that if sense is to be had, he must make it.

The novel shares many characteristics with the fairy tale, for the book is governed not by rules of necessity or even probability (37) but by the imagination and, in a sense, the miraculous. It is a miracle that Jacob returns alive from the police headquarters. It seems a miracle that the Soviets are near Bezanika, and that Jacob should have discovered it. Jacob's radio is a wonder and creates one, for it saves Misha's life and that of countless others. Later in the story, Jacob attempts to aid his depleted imagination by raiding a German outhouse and stealing the newspapers used as toilet paper. The toilet is for Germans only, and Jacob would be killed if discovered; unfortunately, a German soldier waits outside, and only a "miracle" can save Jacob (96). The miracle occurs: Jacob's friend Kowalski creates a diversion that frees Jacob in a "fairytale fashion" (95).

Lina, the eight-year-old orphan girl who lives with Jacob, has never seen a radio, but she suspects it talks in a "wonderful" fashion (145). After searching Jacob's apartment, she decides his petroleum lamp must be the miraculous radio—surely a reference to the tale of Aladdin's lamp. When Lina demands a demonstration of the radio, Jacob takes her into his cellar and, separated from her by a partition, narrates a fairy tale. The story tells of a young princess who languishes because she wishes to possess a cloud. The gardener brings her a piece of cotton as large as her pillow, and the lie, presented out of love, saves her life. Lina is not the princess, for she spies on Jacob during his radio presentation, becoming the only person in the ghetto who knows Jacob has no radio. The princess represents the Jewish people; the cloud, Jacob's stories.

At the conclusion of the novel, the fairy tale assumes added meaning. In the boxcars, the reality of which underscores the artificiality of Jacob's stories, Lina returns to the fairy tale, asking of what clouds really consist. The narrator then tells her of the "eternal circulation of water," of how clouds form from evaporated water; he tells her of steam from chimneys. Becker may be citing the German-Jewish Nobel Prize laureate Nelly Sachs, whose poem "O the Chimneys" utilizes chimneys as a conceit for the Holocaust (3); Paul Celan's famous poem "Death Fugue," also about Jewish death in the camps, contains the lines "then as smoke you will rise into air / then a grave you will have in the clouds" (53). The clouds, earlier representative of Jacob's stories, of life-bringing hope, become symbols of the extermination of the Jewish people.

Jacob's death—his absence—forces the narrator to recreate his presence in words; hence the presence of absence becomes a structural principle in the text (Nägele 212). Again, the radio functions as the central metaphor, for although it is a nonexistent entity, a fiction, it is also the most important "thing" in the ghetto. In fact it leads to the destruction of what is perhaps the only real radio in the ghetto. Felix Frankfurter, who has smuggled in a radio but is too afraid to listen to it, fears that news of Jacob's "radio" will lead to a house search by the Germans. He takes his wife into their cellar, shows her the radio, then destroys it. The scene adumbrates the later episode in Jacob's cellar, where Jacob "creates" a radio for Lina. Fiction replaces reality.

The narrator signals the presence of absence most clearly with the dead. In this he follows the tradition in which he writes: Scholem Aleichem's work seethes with ghosts and dybbukim. The presence of the dead also provides a technique of personifying the emotions of the ghetto inhabitants, who have, we realize, only *seemingly* accustomed themselves to the horrors about them. Jacob's two roommates, for example, are ghosts who maintain their reality for him. Misha's roommate, Fajngold, exerts a similar power, for after he vanishes mysteriously, his prolonged absence disturbs the lovers. Jacob's death forces the narrator to write, as does indeed the extermination of his entire ghetto.

Writing creates, however, a conundrum, for language balks at the Holocaust: the writer confronts an absence of language as well. The narrator hints at his problem in his description of Jacob leaving the police headquarters at the outset of the novel: "The latch is carefully depressed. Pity that there is no other word for 'carefully.' At best, 'very carefully' or 'infinitely carefully'—all just as far from what is meant" (15). The inability to express what we mean, a standard component of modern writing, reaches nightmarish proportions with the crimes of World War II. In Jacob's ghetto the inhabitants deal with their reality through primarily nonlinguistic means: gestures, looks, at most innuendo. The lawyer Schmidt, an outsider who does not feel himself a Jew, unwittingly breaks the unwritten rules of the ghetto when he asks whether Jews in a boxcar will be sent to a concentration camp: "Schmidt doesn't understand the game of allusions, that certain things are not mentioned and are nonetheless stated" (125). The rebuke, a statement of the code of communication that functions in the ghetto, contains at the same time an indirect statement of narrative technique. The narrator knows his limits, the limits of language, and as we have seen, he works with hints and understatements, with irony and textual "gaps" that invite our imaginative cooperation. Examples of his ironic understatement, often in a subordinate clause, include his description of the man who clears "the streets of rubbish and those who have starved to death" (161), or his description of the city of Pry, which "did not have its own ghetto because of its fortunate social structure" (244).

The narrator employs symbols and parables, such as the fairy tale of the princess; his own, private code is embodied, as we have seen, by trees. A natural phenomenon for a middle European, trees are forbidden in the ghetto—another example of absence that exemplifies the unnaturalness of the Nazi regime. Trees also function as a multivalent literary referent. Bruno Apitz's *Naked Among Wolves*, set in Buchenwald (Beech Forest), begins with a description of trees. As we have noted, the camp was located on the outskirts of Weimar, home of German Classicism. As if to underscore the polarities of German culture and German barbarism, the Nazis built Buchenwald on the site of the Goethe Oak, a commemorative tree they felled.

Trees can symbolize, then, the German culture to which Jews have contributed so handsomely, and from which, in Jacob's ghetto without trees, they are violently cut off. In the nineteenth century Annette von Droste-Hülshoff wrote "The Jew's Beech Tree," a dark novella of crime and Old Testament retribution; Eduard Mörike composed "The Lovely Beech," an often anthologized poem. In this century the Brecht poems "Bad Time for Poetry" and "To Those Born Later" feature trees as central metaphors: "What kind of times are they, when / A talk about trees is almost a crime?" (318). Becker's narrator would seem to have Brecht in mind when he begins his novel, "I can still hear them saying: A tree, what's so special about that?" Theodor Adorno once declared—polemically—that after Auschwitz, poetry was impossible. Jurek Becker is no poet, but he writes a poetic prose of great lucidity and sad beauty. His narrator presents a melancholy elegy to, and a continuation of, German culture, which after 1933 will never be the same.

German journalists reviewed Becker's novel with respect and very friendly words. In West Germany, Marcel Reich-Ranicki, the feuilletonist of Polish-Jewish origin who had lost many family members during World War II, reviewed the novel positively (*Entgegnung* 289–93). In East Germany's *Neues Deutschland* (14 May 1969), Werner Neubert also reviewed the book favorably, though he criticized Becker for neglecting class analysis and the role of the communist resistance. In an indirect reference to Anna Seghers and Bruno Apitz, Neubert explains the comfort he takes in works that show communist resistance; without such books, he asserts, a novel such as Becker's would allow sadness to gain the upper hand. In the United States, major newspapers and magazines unfortunately ignored the novel, perhaps because *Library Journal*, a bit like *Neues Deutschland*, wrote that it "does not end with the final hopeful note common to much of Holocaust literature, but rather leaves the reader with an overwhelming sense of futility" (15 Oct. 1975).

Fred Wander, *The Seventh Well* GDR 1971, GDR 1976 (Eng. trans.), USA 1976

Two years after Jurek Becker's *Jacob the Liar*, the GDR produced a second powerful work of fiction dealing with Jewish suffering in World War II. Compared with Becker's novel, Fred Wander's *The Seventh Well* evidences little plot. Instead, it offers a loosely connected series of anecdotes in which the narrator remembers his internment in various camps, as well as a forced death march between camps. He evokes the memories of other prisoners: Teichmann, a storyteller; Pechmann and Antonio, two musicians; and Pépé, a political prisoner. Like Becker, Wander refers to the shtetl and its tradition of Yiddish narrative. As in Becker's novel, storytelling may ultimately provide the only form of salvation available.

Fred Wander was born in Vienna in 1917, the son of a Jewish, communist businessman. After Hitler's annexation of Austria in 1938, Wander fled to France, where authorities interned him. Deported to Germany, he survived Auschwitz and Buchenwald. After the war, he worked as a journalist and photographer in Austria, then studied at the East German Johannes R. Becher Writers' Institute in 1955, moving to East Berlin in 1958. The West German scholar Georg Wieghaus believes Wander chose the GDR because it dealt in a more radical fashion with fascist criminals than did Austria or the Federal Republic (4). However, *The Seventh Well* displays no desire for vengeance. Instead, Wander wishes to remember the victims, and especially those qualities that allowed them to retain their humanity. One of those qualities was storytelling.

The narrator emphasizes his project from the outset, entitling his initial chapter "How to Tell a Story." He approaches the master storyteller Mendel (which means "Comforter") Teichmann, and asks to be initiated into his secrets. Later he overcomes the reluctance of an impatient revolutionary, Pépé, to whom praxis is all, and tells him a story until late in the night: "I was breathless, that wasn't me, it was Mendel Teichmann talking! What had Teichmann done with me?" (81).

The narrator notes that "for every blow, for every humiliation, and for the lewd jokes in the face of our death Mendel tried to find a formula, a redeeming word" (17). The narrator resurrects Teichmann's efforts, and he attempts with his redeeming words to rescue the dignity of at least a few victims from the facelessness of mechanical death: "I know the stories of the dead lying there on the front platform" (43). At the beginning of his story, he notes bitterly of his master, Teichmann: "Forgotten are his verses, his ashes lie strewn over Polish forests and fields" (19). At the end of the book, Teichmann and his verses are no longer forgotten: they live in the word.

The narrator hence accords the word near-magical qualities. It is life-inspiring, distracting the Jews from their bleak realities and, as with Becker, infusing them with hope. Words can suggest cities, with their Jewish quarters: "Meier Bernstein and Mendel Teichmann had taken turns telling stories, had reveled in words, had conjured up the aroma that pervades the narrow alleys on *yom tov*" (51). Language structures history: "In the word he lived his life through again" (50). Stories recapture not only personal history but that of a people: "And

Meier tells stories almost as well as Mendel Teichmann and others who have been persecuted for centuries and live in the word" (46). Finally, the narrator needs language to make sense of his suffering and that of his people. If meaning is to come, it must come through the narrator's words, through his own confrontation with a seemingly absurd world.

The Seventh Well is very close in its sensibility to Becker's *Jacob the Liar*. Like that novel, it works as a corrective to earlier Marxist or GDR writing on the same subject—as Peter Demetz notes, such books as Anna Seghers's *The Seventh Cross* or Bruno Apitz's *Naked Among Wolves* emphasize the suffering of communists over that of Jews (*Fires* 49). The reference in Wander's title to Anna Seghers is evident, as are the differences in the books. In Seghers's novel, six recaptured escapees are tied to crosses, but the seventh cross remains empty, a symbol of (political) hope. In Wander's book, the Germans tie six prisoners to only six stakes; the Germans hang the six, however, after *seven* men are arrested.

The number seven repeats throughout Wander's book, generally with a religious significance: a Jew with seven sheep (123); the seven-armed candelabrum, the menorah (136); Tadeusz Moll's rumination on the seventh heaven in Rabbi Löw's writings (105, 109); and, of course, the seventh well. This is also taken from Rabbi Löw and used by Wander as his epigraph: "The seventh well—water of pureness, freed of all impurities; impervious to pollution and turbidness; of immaculate transparence; ready for future generations, that they might alight from the darkness, their eyes clear, their hearts freed." As with Seghers's seventh cross, the seventh well signifies hope. Wander's hope is not political, however, but theological, and his implication of purification through suffering has given some readers pause. Georg Wieghaus balked at the idea of Auschwitz as purgatory (4). Writing in general of the extermination of the Jews, Peter Demetz might have been speaking of Wander's book when he discusses

the theological interpretation of recent history implied in the biblical term "holocaust," which I hesitate to use. It is used more legitimately by those who believe in meaningful suffering, in the presence or absence of the God of Abraham, and the possibility that Hitler or Kaduk, the most brutal among the Auschwitz guards, was the instrument of a higher power. But even if I can see myself less alien to religious thought than I assert in my more secular moments, I cannot under any circumstances accept any explicit or implicit glorification of the Nazis for whatever reason, even mystical. (*Fires* 29–30)

Wander's musing on the salutary aspects of Jewish suffering constitutes the most problematic aspect of his story.

As opposed to what one might expect from a GDR writer, politics do not constitute Wander's main theme. To be sure, they are not absent; in scenes reminiscent of *The Seventh Cross*, Wander's protagonist is helped by common German antifascists as he flees across Germany. After the narrator meets the political prisoner Pépé, he asks: "What had Teichmann done with me? What had Pechmann done with me? And what would Pépé do with me [?]" (81). Significantly, we do not learn what Pépé does with him; compared with Teichmann and Pechmann, the narrator's other two mentors, Pépé remains a shadowy figure. At a decisive moment, however, the narrator reveals that he *has* learned something about politics. Near the end of the war, the Germans call the Buchenwald Jews together for deportation. The narrator thinks of "the gallows in Crawinkel and of the partisan's look, filled with hate, resolute, splendid" (134); he does not follow his fellow Jews, but hides in the childrens' barracks. This small act of resistance saves his life. He has caught typhus, however, and the final scenes of the book—the prisoners' uprising that provides the triumphant culmination of Bruno Apitz's novel—float before him with surrealistic detachment.

Politics, then, are not unimportant, but they do not provide the focus of Wander's book. Instead, he is concerned, as is Teichmann, with the "powers concealed in people" (16), with the surprising and manifold possibilities of human beings (28). Although he shows the brutality of the Germans and the occasional dehumanization of the prisoners, he emphasizes the gentleness, generosity, and solidarity among the latter group; he is not embarrassed by such words as *hope* (39), *dignity* (40), or *soul* (20, 106). Like Primo Levi, he asks if these prisoners are still human (127), and he insists they are. The achievement of Wander's book is its ability to suggest the inner state of the dying Jews, the resources they mobilize to maintain humanity. His best writing describes the perceptions of the typhus-ridden narrator, the "enchantment" provided by "feverish inner images" (28), and the prisoners as a "dream train traveling through somber German forests" (45). With such descriptions, Wander relates something new; as Christa Wolf points out, he supplements the evidence of documents ("Remembrance" 100).

The East German publication of *The Seventh Well* went practically unnoticed in West Germany, and when a small West German press published it in 1972, only alternative newspapers noted it approvingly. In the United States, where most of our reception of East German literature was filtered through the Federal Republic, reviewers also ignored the book. The mainstream West German Luchterhand press finally published the book in 1985, and Samuel Bächli reviewed it negatively in the *Frankfurter Allgemeine Zeitung*. When one discusses the murder of the Jews, Bächli asserts, all artifice, indeed all art, is wrong; one should keep to documents and let screams be screams. He dismisses Wander's book as tasteless (17 April 1985).

In East Germany, critics accorded Wander's book an enthusiastic reception, and the author received the Heinrich Mann Prize in 1972. Author Irmtraud Morgner asserted, "Never have I more impressively experienced the beauty of the human phenomenon than in Wander's book about the daily life of concentration camp inmates" (*Berliner Zeitung* 24 Jan. 1973; my trans.) In *Neues Deutschland*, Werner Neubert compares Wander's book positively with a theater piece playing in West Berlin, George Tabori's "The Cannibals," which is considerably less optimistic regarding the survival of the human spirit in the camps. Neubert finds Wander's book relevant for the contemporary world as well, and he mentions South Vietnam, Greece, and Mozambique (13 Oct. 1971). Wander supported such efforts in an interview: "I see [contemporary connections] in the fact that there are still concentration camps in the Western world and that hundreds of thousands spend their best years in jails" (*Sonntag* 16 May 1971; my trans.). Walter Czollek asserted that the book "awakens unmistakable associations with the injustice that is committed everywhere in the world where imperialists have their hands in play" (158; my trans.).

Although Czollek asserted that "the unholy past is not dead," he insisted that one did not encounter it on the territory of the GDR (156–57). But Christa Wolf, who was writing her own book about the Third Reich, complained that after large printings of such accounts as *Naked Among Wolves* and *The Diary of Anne Frank*, only a few people read new releases, such as *Jacob the Liar* and *The Seventh Well;* she asked whether we really believe we know everything about the camps, the ghettos, and the prisons ("Remembrance" 98). Wolf begins *Patterns of Childhood* with a quote from Faulkner: "What is past is not dead; it is not even past." Unlike Walter Czollek, however, Wolf concerns herself with the presence of the past on the territory of the GDR.

Selective Memory and the Present Past: Fühmann, Wolf, Hermlin

Franz Fühmann, *Twenty-Two Days or Half of a Lifetime* GDR 1973, GDR 1980 (Eng. trans.)

In addition to the works by Jurek Becker and Fred Wander, one book that signaled a changing GDR perspective on fascism was Franz Fühmann's *Twenty-Two Days or Half of a Lifetime,* a remarkable, diarylike account of a trip Fühmann took to Budapest. The dislocation caused by geography, language, history, and culture leads the author to an intensive reexamination of his life. Fühmann takes his title from the Hölderlin poem "Half a Lifetime," which mourns the passing of youth. At the end of Fühmann's book, the narrator, soon to be fifty, writes: "Half a lifetime is long since past. Justify also what you have not written!" (250).

Hence his book contains a relentless, brutally honest self-interrogation, which includes the question "Assuming you had been ordered to Auschwitz, what would you have done there?" (220). He knows it could have been possible, that it was in fact mere chance that he did not join the SS. Yet he adds: "How could I ever say that I had come to terms with my past if I accept chance, which has reigned on it so mercifully, to be my supreme arbitrator? Coming to terms with the past means questioning every possibility, hence also the most remote" (224). Fühmann realizes that as a fascist soldier he allowed Auschwitz to function (222). And he ultimately concludes that if he had been ordered there, he would have acted as did the others, interchangeable like they, and called it his duty (221): "Hence an equals sign between you and Kaduk, that medical orderly of Auschwitz? Yes" (224).

As Christa Wolf later does in *Patterns of Childhood,* Fühmann repeatedly demands what it means to change. He concludes that self-transformation constitutes a lifelong process, one that must be renewed daily. Thus he echoes, in striking fashion, a conclusion reached by Fred Wander in a letter to fellow author and survivor Primo Levi: "There is no purification and no mastery and no 'clearing up the past' through a political act or through decrees or through power. There is only the daily 'wrestling with oneself'—to speak with Goethe, the 'insatiable demand' for purification!" (qtd. in Wieghaus 2; my trans.). Fühmann realizes that one does not transform oneself suddenly like Saul on the road to Damascus (225). His admission contains an implicit repudiation of his earlier *The Car with the Yellow Star*, in which he asserts that after hearing lectures on Marxist economics the scales fell from his eyes.

In *Twenty-Two Days or Half of a Lifetime* Fühmann refers to Marcel Reich-Ranicki, who had asserted that one of Fühmann's early communist poems still exhibited the mentality of the Hitler Youth. Fühmann admits that Reich-Ranicki was correct (213–14). Later, he responds to that critic's rebuke:

> The new social order was the Other as distinguished from Auschwitz; I arrived at it via the gas chambers and had regarded my change as completed when, my will extinguished, I offered myself as a tool to the new social order, instead of being one of its shapers with a contribution which only I could make. All this was contained in that poem pointed to by the sneerer; a bad poem, for all it said was that I was as far as ever from understanding Socialism as a community in which the free development of each individual is the prerequisite for the free development of all. (225)

Fühmann now knows, he asserts, that he cannot "escape the past, not even in a utopia." He compares himself to a leopard, noting that while he cannot change his spots, he can do what is denied those without spots—investigate relentlessly the possibilities of that condition (225).

Readers in East and West Germany commented very positively on Fühmann's book. In the West German *Süddeutsche Zeitung* Fritz Raddatz called Fühmann's prose "masterful" (6 Dec. 1973); in *Die Welt* Peter Jokostra labeled the piece an "event" (27 Sept. 1973); and in the *Frankfurter Allgemeine* Peter Jansen asked what West German author would have the daring to equate himself or herself with Kaduk (27 Nov. 1973). In East Germany Manfred Hahn wrote that Fühmann's book broadened understanding for the power and possibilities of GDR literature, and that it belonged to those books that— even through mediation—were capable of wide effect (23). After Fühmann's death in 1984, Christa Wolf echoed the epigram to her controversial novel *The Quest for Christa T.* ("This coming-to-oneself— what is it?"), asserting that in *Twenty-Two Days or Half of a Lifetime* Fühmann comes to himself ("Worte" 1019).

Christa Wolf, *Patterns of Childhood* GDR 1976, USA 1980, 1984

During the 1960s Christa Wolf's novels *Divided Heaven* (see chapter 3) and *The Quest for Christa T.* (see chapter 2) established her as one of the leading writers of her generation. In 1976 she published *Patterns of Childhood*, an investigation into her childhood in Nazi Germany. Like Fühmann, Wolf concerns herself with the presence of the past, and she attempts to answer the question she poses at the very center of her book, "How did we become what we are today?" (282). Like Fühmann (as well as Becker and Wander), Wolf swerves from the former paradigm, one found in Anna Seghers, Stephan Hermlin, and Bruno Apitz, of heroic communist resistance. As she notes on the cover to the GDR edition, such books tended to view fascism as something external, to delegate it to the others, including, implicitly or explicitly, the West Germans. By recalling her childhood indoctrination under fascism, Wolf searches, like Fühmann, for the fascist within herself. She questions how that early deformation affected her subsequent development and, by extension, the development of her generation and her society.

In July 1971 the narrator, a GDR writer, drives with her husband, her brother Lutz, and her daughter Lenka to her birthplace in G., Poland; before 1945, it was L., Germany (in fact it was Landsberg on the Warthe river; now in Poland, it is called Grozow (on the Wielkopolski). That forty-six-hour visit triggers memories from her childhood (described in the third person with a protagonist called Nelly), from the 1930s through the immediate postwar years. These memories are registered, recorded, interrogated, and analyzed during the period between 3 November 1972 and 2 May 1975, while she writes the book, in part during a stay in the United States (Wolf was at Oberlin College in 1974).

The third stratum makes possible more abstract reflection, for example on the limits of language. We have seen with Jurek Becker that the failure of language to register experience becomes particularly acute when confronting the horrors of World War II. The discourse of Wolf's narrator is often hesitant, her sentences broken; much of the message remain between the lines, unsaid. Rarely does the narrator experience the "pleasure of deploying language for once as a general deploys his troops: logically, forcibly" (282). More commonly we find an almost desperate confession—"this failure of language" (152).

Just as the narrator must struggle for an appropriate language, so must she fight for an adequate form. *Patterns of Childhood* carried no genre designation in the GDR or in its U.S. translation. The West Germans published it, with the author's permission, as a novel, and the disclaimer at the outset insists on its fictionality. At the same time, it is a thinly disguised autobiography, a diarylike confession. The three time levels, interspersed regularly with dreams, blend together without mediation and often provide stark juxtapositions that allow readers to compare the sixteen-year-old Nelly with the sixteen-year-old Lenka, or the narrator with her mother. The three levels can provide an indication of troubling continuities or of positive change. Many words and concepts—ethnic slurs, such as "dirty Polack" (30), or military terms, such as *bridgehead* (294)—are foreign to Lenka. The levels also provide a literary equivalent to the process of remembering; they both reflect and evoke the difficult process of anamnesis.

The narrator knows that her search for a structure, like her search for a language, cannot succeed (22). After a public reading, a member of the audience asks, "And do you believe it's possible to come to grips with the events you write about?" She answers simply: "No. (The death of six million Jews, twenty million Russians, six million Poles)" (334). She is then asked why she worries those issues. Her book suggests several answers. Wolf's groping for language, her at times hesitant, tentative use of a word, and her breaking of syntactical structures represent an attempt to regenerate that German language of Eichmann, "who spoke in slogans until the very end, even about his own death: a master and a victim of the lethal use of language which brings yearned-for absolute political equality to some and annihilation to others—annihilation at the hands of persons who are permitted to commit murder without remorse by a language stripped of a conscience" (237). Wolf and her narrator are searching for that language of conscience.

A second reason for Wolf to address her childhood is her awareness that memory changes. The narrator speculates, for example, about the fashion in which her mother's memories of the prewar years would have developed in the twenty-four years she lived after the collapse of the Reich:

> Prewar times? What happy years! she would have said at first. Later perhaps: A lot of work. And finally: One big fraud. This only to make it clear that memory is not a solid block fitted into our brain once and for all; rather, perhaps—if big words are permitted—a repeated moral act. (143)

Memory, a kind of history, does not remain static. The GDR perception of the Third Reich altered dramatically between 1949 and 1989, and East German literature was in large part responsible for that transformation.

Finally, the narrator believes in the responsibility of the writer, in the efficacy of literature. In a world where objectivity is impossible, the narrator (providing the narrator does not, as in Apitz, pretend omniscience) is not superfluous (69, 321). Writing holds out at least the promise of self-liberation, and books, the narrator asserts, also help develop our capacity to process reality: "How did we become what we are today? One of the answers would be a list of book titles" (369).

How did we become what we are today? The narrator describes her childhood among the petite bourgeoisie—a national socialist stronghold—in a provincial town. There are few ardent Nazis, but no organized resistance exists. Nelly's parents, social democrats, join the National Socialist party, partly out of fear, partly because they possess no good reason not to do so. Two new barracks open in town, and the Jordans open a new store. Business is good, and they build a house. Unemployment drops dramatically.

As Marc Silberman points out, Christa Wolf uses metaphors of dreaming and hypnosis to suggest what a teacher later points out to Nelly—the mass abdication of thought ("Writing" 534). "Hadn't

Hitler demanded more *Lebensraum* for the German people from the very beginning?" the teacher asks; "To any thinking person, that meant war" (391). One of the most striking examples of hypnosis occurs when the photographer Richard Andrack hypnotizes Nelly's cousin Astrid at Nelly's confirmation party. Under Andrack's influence, Astrid insults relatives, does a belly dance, and performs other acts that the spectators find increasingly shameless but do not stop. The scene is surely a citation of Thomas Mann's "Mario and the Magician" (mentioned as one of Lenka's favorite books), in which the magician hypnotizes the Italian laborer Mario, causing him to perform acts he detests. Mario's story, set in Italy during the 1930s, is a parable for fascism—the magician often delivers the Roman salute. But in Mann's story there is resistance: Mario murders the magician.

Nelly believes herself different from Astrid, but she does feel the thrill of seduction. Peter Demetz suggests that Nelly's enthusiastic support for the Führer "was not merely the desire to be somebody, but a kind of exchange transaction in which the young girl offered her submission and her strict performance of duties for the guarantee of being respected by others and for relative freedom from angst" (*Fires* 151). The submission exacted a price, for Nelly must "cheat herself out of her true feelings" (160). And "in those days her fear expressed itself as a continuous penetrating feeling of inner alienation, whose very track consisted in the effacement of tracks. . . . The horrible wish for self-surrender doesn't allow the self to emerge" (231). Nelly does not experience a model childhood; rather, her experience provides a childhood model (the second English translation of the title, *Patterns of Childhood*, is better than the first, *A Model Childhood*, even though *Muster* can be singular or plural, pattern or patterns). Nelly's life, cut from one of the limited patterns available, exemplifies that of a generation.

In her novel, Wolf investigates the psychology of fascism. She quotes the Pole Kazimierz Brandys, who asserted that, while fascism is not peculiar to the Germans, they were its most perfect example (36). Since the concept is larger than the Germans, Wolf is also concerned with ferreting out other examples, and she mentions Stalin's camps. Her refined narrative technique, with its interrelated time levels, also allows her to establish connections with the present and to argue that fascist psychology continues. One example would be in the GDR itself, where others, like Nelly, carry the past within them. An East Berlin taxi driver admits that the Germans started the war and invaded the Soviet Union, but he remains scandalized only by Soviet atrocities committed when the Red Army invaded Germany (360). Elsewhere in the text, East German tourists in a Czechoslovakian beer hall sing anti-Polish songs (286–87).

Other parallels are directed at the West. The narrator notes, in quotation marks, that the West Germans were "liberated" from fascism, thus implying either that they do not perceive it as a liberation or, the more orthodox view, that capitalism, which brought fascists to power, continues unabated in the West (394). She speaks of German concentration camps and of those established in Chile by Pinochet (248). Leaving Poland and memories of the German fascist past, she encounters unlikable citizens from the Portugese dictatorship (404).

The narrator directs much of her unease at the United States. She shows in her book the fashion in which Americans accept Nixon's hypocrisy (70); then she demonstrates how the Germans lied and yet managed to believe their lies (391). After speaking in detail about hypnosis in the Third Reich, she mentions the trancelike state induced by American consumer society (259). She speaks of World War II atrocities committed by Germans and shows Lenka's disgust and outrage at a photograph of an American soldier with his rifle to the head of an elderly Vietnamese woman (157). She argues that racism is one cause of U.S. involvement in Vietnam, telling Lenka that a rich, white American president automatically hypostatizes his values. That in turn echoes the German disdain for "inferior" Poles, Slavs, and Jews. Indeed (and this echoes Eichmann's language without conscience), she finds racism in the language itself, which can equate "fairness" and "fair" skin (254). She also compares U.S. black ghettos with the Jewish ghetto in Warsaw.[2]

Wolf does criticize her own society in *Patterns of Childhood*. As we have seen, she implies a continuation of fascist psychology in East Germany. Additionally, she speaks of "antagonistic" contradictions engendered by the continuation, even in socialism, of the dichotomy between rewarding mental work and generally unrewarding manual labor (274). She also regrets, as in her earlier *The Quest for Christa T.*, the continual difficulties in developing the self (339). But she leaves no doubt of her country's superiority to those in the West; she believes especially that it is the better Germany (282, 310, 324, 394).

Perhaps for that reason, Hermann Kant, the influential head of the Writers' Association, reviewed the book positively after its publication (*"Kindheitsmuster"* 137–44). That was important, for Wolf had just signed a petition protesting the coerced expatriation of the dissident writer Wolf Biermann, a petition that created a scandal and briefly made Wolf persona non grata. As Alexander Stephan points out, critics feared that an attack on Wolf's book would classify them with the hardliners, while a too positive response might have raised suspicions that they wished to express solidarity with Wolf (49). As a result, the GDR reception remained predominately lukewarm, and the real provocation of the book for a GDR audience, the concept of a daily fascism within socialism, was generally ignored.[3]

West Germans objected with some justification to Wolf's emphasis on "fascism" in the Federal Republic, Portugal, Chile, and South Vietnam—and of course in the country supporting those governments, the United States—as opposed to her silence about events in Czechoslovakia (the Prague Spring occurred three years before the narrator's visit to Poland) or in Poland proper (where workers' unrest and anti-Semitic purges took place in the late 1960s). Rather than criticizing Soviet rule in those and other Eastern bloc states, she emphasizes German-Soviet friendship.

U.S. reviewers did not appear as troubled by Wolf's politics, and they read the book approvingly as a German's attempt to come to terms with her past. The *Atlantic Monthly* thought that Wolf may be underestimating what the Reich did to her (Sept. 1980), but reviews in the *Nation* (6 Dec. 1980), the *Saturday Review* (Sept. 1980), and the *New York Review of Books* (5 March 1981) were quite positive. In the *New York Times Book Review* (12 Oct. 1982), the British poet Stephen Spender admits that he is somewhat dubious regarding Wolf's view of history, but he suggests that the book possesses political balance by citing Wolf's references to Stalin. She indeed mentions Stalin's purges (147) and his camps (277). More significant, however, is her dream in which people are confused as to whether Stalin is in fact dead, in fact buried. It is a recurring dream. The narrator asks her brother: "When will we start speaking about that, too? To get rid of the feeling that, until we do, everything we say is temporary, that only then would we really begin to speak" (245).

The text contains gaps, then—gaps of which the narrator remains painfully aware. Peter Demetz believes that Wolf's "memories are a tragic book which, given her circumstances, has to repress a good deal about contemporary problems in order to reveal the forgetfulness of others in another age" (*Fires* 156). That is true, with the exception that Wolf is also writing about *contemporary* amnesia regarding the Third Reich, and with the additional exception that the *Soviet* past remains taboo. The book's gaps undercut its moral indignation about contemporary politics, and some repeated utterances about the need for honesty subsequently ring hollow.

In *Patterns of Childhood* a Soviet historian tells the narrator that she will "live to see the day when one would be able to speak and write about everything, openly and freely. That time will come, he said. You'll live to see it, I won't" (362). Wolf's book demonstrates that in 1976 the time had not yet come. Less than a decade after the publication of *Patterns of Childhood*, Mikhail Gorbachev assumed power in the Soviet Union; his program of *glasnost* made it increasingly possible to speak of Stalin and his crimes. In the wake of their quiet revolution from November 1989, former GDR citizens can now, in fact, "speak and write about everything, openly and freely."

Stephan Hermlin, *Evening Light* GDR 1979, USA 1983

Together with Christa Wolf's *Patterns of Childhood*, Stephan Hermlin's *Evening Light* undoubtedly constitutes one of the most important GDR literary achievements during the 1970s. A poetic autobiography, the text consists of short "chapters" that deal primarily with Hermlin's youth in the Berlin of the 1930s. *Evening Light* describes the fashion in which Hermlin at age sixteen joined the Communist party, and it concentrates on his experiences in the communist underground resistance during the period of German fascism.

Utilizing dreams and stream-of-consciousness techniques, Hermlin presents what GDR literary popes would have condemned ten years earlier as "modernist" writing. Apparently fragmented, the text is in fact structured in several ways, since Hermlin, in recounting his life, wishes to bestow that life with meaning. His signature on the application to the Communist party, a signature he never retracts, symbolizes a continuing commitment that unifies the book.

Arguing for the unity of his text and hence his life, Hermlin employs rhetorical devices designed to bring the reader to his point of view. His devices are, literally, forms of persuasion. Hence he remembers the communists as having "a certain enthusiasm and confidence" (29), while the fascists often evince demonic characteristics. The narrator idealizes his brother as confidant, protector, and "only friend" (66), then confides to him the secret that he has become a communist. The brother, who has been reading Lenin, "praised me wholeheartedly. 'They're the only people you can really trust,' he said, returning the copy of *State and Revolution* I had lent him" (63).

Hermlin also structures the text with Christian theology. The final line of the first episode is "Abide with us," a sentence cited in its entirety during the fourth episode: "Abide with us, for it will soon be evening, and day is nearly done" (16). The references are to Bach's sixth cantata, written for the second day of the Easter holidays, and to the Emmaus story from Luke 24:13, in which Cleopas becomes convinced that Christ has indeed risen. Thus, as Bernhard Greiner correctly notes, *evening* and *evening light* suggest not only twilight and death but new beginnings, rebirth, and resurrection ("Autobiographie" 234). The text hence offers us a grand drama of death and rebirth, referring not only to the communist movement (crushed by the fascists, disfigured by the Stalinists) but to the narrator. After speaking of the defeats characterizing Stalinist cultural politics during the 1950s, he asserts, "The workers' movement has considerable regenerative power, which has also played a role for me, and in me" (40).

Hermlin's forms of persuasion do not always succeed. As with his story "The Time Together," *Evening Light* contains gaps, especially regarding the Soviet Union. The narrator describes the exhilaration and hope he felt during the building of the white, shining Soviet cities in the 1920s (45). He mentions Soviet support of the republicans in Spain and notes that Moscow transported some of the wounded to the Soviet Union for medical treatment (87). His brother, as we have noted, assures him that communists alone are trustworthy (63). There is, however, no mention of the forced collectivization or the Terror in the Soviet Union during the 1930s.

Hermlin generally avoids the subject of Stalin (whom, in the late 1940s and early 1950s, he occasionally celebrated in his poetry), and he prefers to leave some related matters ambiguous, as evidenced by his discussion of Sergei Kirov's assassination in 1934. Many Western historians, notably Robert Conquest, believe Stalin initiated the murder to further his political purposes, a thesis Trotsky suggested already in 1935. Until quite recently, official Soviet historiography advanced a variant of the explanation given in *Evening Light* and accepted by the youthful narrator, maintaining that disaffected revolutionaries, in conspiracy with Zinoviev, plotted the murder. From his current perspective, the narrator criticizes his former, more innocent certainty of belief (89), and by projecting his current knowledge into his former naïveté, he infuses the final sentence of the passage with an ominous irony: "Stalin's eye was unerring; he would expose everyone who stood in our way" (90). An East German reader without access to Western historiography might well have missed Hermlin's irony, and the passage remained obscure for some in the West as well. In fact, West German scholar Beate Ehlert accused Hermlin of heroizing Stalin (81).

According to Robert Conquest, Kirov's murder provided an excuse for the Great Purge, but that event, in which numerous German communists died, remains unmentioned in Hermlin's *Evening Light*, except in the narrator's oblique reference to his youthful confidence that Stalin would uncover all traitors. The narrator does not note that Karl Radek, whose *Moskauer Rundschau* he read every week (43), died in a Soviet prison. Also absent are the infamous show trials, even those of Zinoviev and Kamenev, both of whose names appear in the text. Finally, the narrator ignores the Hitler-Stalin pact signed in 1939. That pact fits precisely into the historical framework of Hermlin's text, and its omission hence creates a particularly striking silence.

Hermlin may, however, be indirectly criticizing East bloc practices in his passage describing German workers who present a quiet act of resistance in the 1930s by sitting on benches reserved for Jews. The narrator concludes the scene:

> In Lenin I had read that even the slightest trace of anti-Semitism is evidence of the reactionary character of the group or individual that exhibits it. I could see this remark contained a kind of formula, a quasi-mathematical equation. Wherever the cowardly pestilence raised its head, there could be no socialism, all noble words to the contrary. (94)

Although this passage, in context, clearly refers to the national socialists, it contains a subtext. Speaking with his West German publisher in 1979, Hermlin asserted, "The Jewish question, which for a number of years in our country was repressed under the influence of certain developments in other socialist countries—let us say repressed, for anything else would be unjust to the GDR, which up to now has behaved honorably regarding this matter—is now being quite consciously examined again" (Hermlin, "Wo" 400; my trans.). In an interview that Hermlin held in 1983 with Silvia Schlenstedt, an interview that in many instances reads as a gloss on *Evening Light*, he registers his abhorrence of anti-Semitism and notes that "certain occurrences in socialist countries have made not only me uneasy, they are an occasion for disquiet for every single socialist or communist" (Schlenstedt, *Hermlin* 22; my trans.).

These "certain occurrences" include anti-Zionist persecution and trials during the 1940s and 1950s in Bulgaria, Hungary, Czechoslovakia, the GDR (notwithstanding Hermlin's protestations regarding honorable conduct), and the Soviet Union. Thus Hermlin indirectly revises the rather optimistic picture of Jewish-Gentile relations he had presented in his story from the 1950s, "The Time Together." In his 1983 interview with Schlenstedt, Hermlin noted that he had long been afflicted with certain blindspots regarding anti-Semitism, expecting it to vanish with the abolition of capitalism. During the interview he admits that view to have been naïve and premature (Schlenstedt, *Hermlin* 21).

Although Hermlin had been outspokenly critical of GDR cultural policies during the 1970s, *Evening Light* was published in his country, where, led by a glowing review written by Hermann Kant (*"Abendlicht"*), the reception was very positive. Noting Hermlin's frequent avowals of communist principles in *Evening Light*, Klaus Werner rather smugly challenged Western critics to transform the avowals into oppositional statements (486–87).

Most West German critics ignored Werner's challenge and praised *Evening Light* as a work of considerable literary merit. Karl Corino proved an exception in the *Stuttgarter Zeitung*, accusing Hermlin of employing a splendid prose to distract from what he left unsaid (1 Dec. 1979). In the United States, Joel Agee, a knowledgeable observer of the GDR, wrote in the *New York Times Book Review* of a "beautiful memoir." He discusses Hermlin's "telling pages" regarding the damaging effects of Stalinism, but he notes, as Hermlin does not, that the GDR government quickly silenced critics of such policies. He adds,

"I am more moved by Mr. Hermlin's instinctive rallying, when he was a child, to the side of the poor and the oppressed than I am by his mature political thought, which betrays its unease—or perhaps the inner and outer structures under which it must operate—by rhetorical and tautological arguments" (18 Sept. 1983).

Writing/Righting the Past

In their attempts to write/right the past, GDR authors produced texts of ever greater subtlety and sophistication. Through the end of the 1970s, however, these texts remained disrupted by censorship. Following Anna Seghers, Bruno Apitz celebrated communist resistance and martyrdom in Buchenwald, but his stereotypes and melodrama convey a skewed image of the camps. Christa Wolf writes in *Patterns of Childhood:*

> Heroes? It would be better for us, it would be more bearable, if we could think of the camps as places where the victims necessarily turned into heroes. As if it were contemptible to break down under no longer bearable pressure. One should also, you think—again unrealistically—talk in the schools about those millions who gave themselves up, and who were given up by their comrades: "zombies." One should also, you think, teach the horror of the results of man's hatred of man; it would only increase the admiration for those who resisted. (339)

Jurek Becker and Fred Wander, both Jewish survivors, present a picture of Jewish suffering that departs from the previous GDR prescription of heroic communist resistance (although Becker's Jacob is a hero). Christa Wolf reviewed Wander's book very favorably, and it may well have influenced her work on *Patterns of Childhood.*

The SED employed books by Seghers, Hermlin, Apitz, and others to legitimate its dictatorship. As the East German writer Helga Königsdorf asserted in 1989, the Party's "abuse of an imposed anti-Fascism" had in fact "threatened to produce a new Fascism" (qtd. in Jarausch 85). Franz Fühmann's *The Car with the Yellow Star* also supported the aims of the Socialist Unity party. Utilizing the genre of the nineteenth-century *Bildungsroman*, it traces a man's development from a convinced fascist to a committed socialist, but the transformation remains unconvincing from a psychological and a literary point of view (among other things, it is not dialectical). In later works, *Twenty-Two Days or Half of a Lifetime* and *Patterns of Childhood*, Fühmann and Wolf investigate more convincingly the fashion in which the past continued to inform the present. These stages in the development of GDR literary history are heuristic and certainly not rigid: Stephan Hermlin's *Evening Light*, published in 1979, reaffirms the heroic perspective from the 1950s, though using narrative techniques made available to GDR writers in the 1970s.

Hermlin and Wolf remained handcuffed by the taboo regarding Stalin, and they appeared unable to continue the limited discussion begun by Anna Seghers in *The Decision* (1968). In the 1980s such GDR writers as Christoph Hein, Volker Braun, and Heiner Müller published increasingly critical investigations of Stalinism. But issues that might embarrass the SED, such as the Stalinist past of the KPD or the Party's behavior during the Hitler–Stalin pact, remained extremely delicate and, until November 1989, subject to censorship.

An increasingly differentiated approach to the phenomenon of anti-Semitism marks a further development in the East German reading and writing of the past. Orthodox Marxist thinking locates the cause for anti–Semitism in economics. As a Nazi thug prepares to plunder a Jewish villa in Anna Seghers's *The Dead Stay Young*, we learn that "most of all, he looked forward to the fulfillment of his secret desire: confiscation of the owner's property" (349). In "The Time Together," Stephan Hermlin advances an ideal of Jews and Gentiles working together to create a world free of capitalism, fascism, and anti-Semitism. And for all its distance from the prescriptive forms of socialist realism, Johannes Bobrowski's *Levin's Mill* demonstrates that Grandfather's motivation, including his anti-Semitism, is basically economic. Becker and Wander, two concentration camp survivors, do not challenge or confirm this thesis; they simply ignore it. Becker and Wander would, I suspect, agree with Jean Améry that "all attempts at economic explanations, all the despairing one-dimensional allusions to the fact that German industrial capital, concerned about its privileges, financed Hitler, tell the eye-witness nothing" (*Mind's Limits* viii).

In the 1970s, GDR writers, spurred by anti-Semitism in the East bloc, more openly questioned the Marxist thesis. In his biography of the eighteenth-century philosopher Moses Mendelssohn (*Herr Moses in Berlin*, 1979), Heinz Knobloch pointedly refers to Mosche Kulbalk, a Jewish writer murdered in the Gulag. In 1979 Stephan Hermlin warned, as we have seen, of "certain occurrences" in socialist countries, occurrences that should disturb every socialist or communist. Stefan Heym's *Collin* (1979) deals cautiously with anti-Zionism in connection with Stalinism; the novel was only published in West Germany, as was his 1988 autobiography, which speaks openly about East bloc anti-Semitism during the 1950s (*Nachruf* 368–69, 451–52, 507, 528–29, 563, 678, 680). As GDR writers continued, haltingly, to come to terms with the fascist and Stalinist past, they became increasingly aware that classical Marxist categories were (and are) insufficient to explain the continuing phenomenon of anti-Semitism. In that realization, they repeated a process undergone some thirty years earlier by such Western leftists as Theodor Adorno and Max Horkheimer of the Frankfurt school.

NOTES

1. One of the first acts of the new, democratically elected GDR parliament in 1990 was to recognize its share of responsibility for World War II crimes against the Jews and to promise reparations.
2. Marcel Reich-Ranicki correctly notes that such a comparison trivializes the Jewish ghettos ("Zettelkasten" 216).
3. An exception to the cautious reaction was Annemarie Auer's angry "Gegenerinnerung" in *Sinn und Form*.

2

Forms of Protest: Early Experiments or the Politics of Epistemology

"Each word had the hollowness of lies."
—Uwe Johnson, *Speculations about Jakob*

During the decades of the 1950s and 1960s, not all writers allowed restrictive GDR cultural policies to straitjacket their prose. Three of the more radical literary experiments from that time, Uwe Johnson's *Speculations about Jakob* (FRG 1959), Fritz Rudolf Fries's *The Road to Oobliadooh* (FRG 1966), and Christa Wolf's *The Quest for Christa T.* (1968), provide the focus in this chapter. These works suggest an underground movement, one counter to GDR aesthetic orthodoxy. It is a movement concerned with formal and linguistic experimentation, a movement that, following the preoccupation of nineteenth- and twentieth-century modernist writing, queries language—its potentiality and inevitable limits. Additionally, these three texts experimented with narrative perspectives and techniques, thus undermining the authority of an omniscient narrator who provided certainty of perception and a reassuring totality. Inquiry into the epistemological possibilities of literature was, however, unwelcome in the GDR.

The GDR campaign against modernist art commenced in the decade that culminated, ironically enough, with the publication of Johnson's *Speculations about Jakob*. The administrators of the Soviet Zone of Occupation and of the fledgling GDR originally wished to attract artists of repute and hence permitted a range of artistic forms. Soon, however, the cold war and Stalinization of the country began to strangle diversity. In March 1951 the Party officially began its campaign against ostensible formalism in art and literature, asserting that formalism privileged form over content and was hence antihumanistic. Marxists located the engine for formalism in capitalism and imperialism, held to be inimical to art.

A leading opponent of artistic modernism was the brilliant Hungarian Georg Lukács, who wrote on philosophy, literature, and aesthetics. Grounded philosophically in Hegel and aesthetically in German Classicism and nineteenth-century bourgeois Realism, Lukács argued that literature should mirror those elements that "objectively" determine the depicted reality, thus becoming itself a "totality of life" (*Essays*). Formally, the artistic totality should be organic and "closed." Lukács and his GDR followers damned as "formalist" ("modernist," "cosmopolitan," "decadent") works that contravened those practices through the use of montage, alienation effects, narrative interruptions, or parabolic form. Lukács participated as cultural minister in Imre Nagy's short-lived Hungarian reform government, hence after 1956 he abruptly became a nonperson in the GDR. Nonetheless, his influence lingered, and it was not until the 1970s that GDR writers began to discover an affinity for the experimental literature of German Romanticism, a literature always favored by Anna Seghers but neglected by Lukács in favor of Classicism and Realism.

To accompany the campaign against formalism, GDR cultural politicians imported and wholeheartedly embraced the Soviet doctrine of socialist realism. Formulated in 1934 by Andrey Zhdanov, socialist-realist art was expected to demonstrate the revolutionary possibilities of reality while educating the reader or viewer to a socialist perspective. Socialist production sites (e.g., factories) constituted the preferred subject matter, and socialist-realist workers were to embody positive, exemplary heroes who functioned as identification figures for the reader.

GDR cultural bureaucrats amalgamated Zhdanov with Lukács to create a dogmatic cultural policy whose results for GDR literature proved not at all felicitous. Stephan Hermlin, one of the grand old men of East German letters, described his country's early cultural politics in *Evening Light* (1979):

New exegetes were at work trying to outdo each other with condemnations and newly devised restrictions. The art of this century became more and more a slough of perdition; the great names of literature, music, and painting were made to personify all sorts of evils; third-rate academic epigones were promoted to geniuses. Theorists sought the root causes of this ruin; one zealot had already worked back so far that he was able to declare Flaubert and Baudelaire decadent. (39)

Within this atmosphere, Uwe Johnson did not attempt to publish *Speculations about Jakob* in his country; he once noted that authorities would have perceived his "description" as an "attack" (Neusüß 48).

During the 1950s and 1960s, the GDR cultural climate alternated between wintry gusts and moments of fragile thaw. But in essence the hostility to formalism, as defined by East German cultural authorities, remained unchanged. In 1963 a breakthrough Kafka conference was held in Liblice, Czechoslovakia, where the Western Marxist Ernst Fischer suggested that Kafka's theme of alienation might have relevance in the East bloc as well. But also in 1963, GDR Party Secretary Walter Ulbricht refused to entertain the idea of cultural coexistence between East and West, and he warned against those who would employ Khrushchev's revelations about Stalin against the doctrine of socialist realism (Emmerich 126).

East Germany reached one of its cultural-political nadirs in December 1965, during the Eleventh Plenum of the Central Committee of the Socialist Unity party, when the Party condemned several GDR writers and intellectuals for their "modernism," "skepticism," "anarchism," "nihilism," and "pornography." This proved no atmosphere for Fritz Rudolf Fries's *The Road to Oobliadooh*, which, had it been able to appear in the GDR, would have been subjected to each of those adjectives.

After 1965 the SED position appeared to harden further. Wolfgang Emmerich notes that *Neue Deutsche Literatur*, the journal of the GDR Writers' Association, carried no more contributions from Western writers, though it had previously published such authors as Martin Walser, Peter Weiss, and Heinrich Böll. In 1968 the Socialist Unity party warned against modernist tendencies in Czech art, tendencies it believed paved the way for counterrevolution (Emmerich 127–28).

Also in 1968 Christa Wolf's *The Quest for Christa T.* was scheduled to appear in the GDR, but it was 1969 before a severely limited edition, for a select audience, could be published. Even so, Heinz Sachs, the editor of the publishing house that dared to print the novel, lost his position, and the novel disappeared underneath a wave of hostile criticism, not to reappear until 1973. In the interim Erich Honecker had succeeded Ulbricht as Party chair, and in December 1971 he proclaimed: "When one proceeds from the firm position of socialism, there can be in my opinion no taboos in the realm of art and literature. That concerns questions of content as well as style—in short: the questions of that which one calls artistic mastery" (Emmerich 178; my trans.). GDR writers, who long had written for their desk drawers, began to open those drawers. But Honecker arrived too late for Uwe Johnson, who had been living in the West since 1959.

Uwe Johnson, *Speculations about Jakob* FRG 1959, USA 1963

West German literary historians usually claimed Uwe Johnson for their country, an undertaking simplified by the fact that in East Germany—where Johnson went to school and to the university, and where he wrote his first two novels—he remained, until after his untimely death in 1984, persona non grata. Although Johnson's first published novel, *Speculations about Jakob*, appeared only in West Germany, it was written in East Germany, about East Germans, by an East German citizen. The novel points to a road GDR cultural authorities consciously decided not to travel.

Born in 1934 in the German (now Polish) province of Pomerania, Johnson spent the first ten years of his life in the town of Anklam on the Peene river. He went to a Nazi school in Kascian for one year. After the German defeat, he attended a socialist *Gymnasium* in Güstrow. From 1952 to 1956 he studied German literature, first in Rostock, then in Leipzig with Hans Mayer. During this time he worked on his first novel, *Ingrid Babendererde*, which publishers in East and West rejected. The confidential GDR reader's report concluded with the recommendation: "Author needs a brainwashing" (*Spiegel*, 6 Jan. 1992; my trans.).

After graduation Johnson could not find steady work, since his writing and his conversation had marked him as politically unreliable. He survived doing literary odd jobs—he translated Melville's

Israel Potter—and he worked on *Speculations about Jakob.* In 1959, the year Suhrkamp published *Speculations about Jakob,* Johnson left the GDR for West Berlin.[1] It proved a triumphant year for German literature: Heinrich Böll's *Billiards at Half-past Nine* appeared, as did Günter Grass's *The Tin Drum.* Like the novels by Böll and Grass, Johnson's book soon attained the status of postwar classic.

Seemingly chaotic, Johnson's novel is in fact carefully structured. In part 1, we learn that in 1945 Jakob Abs came with his mother from Pomerania to Jerichow, a small city in what would become the north of the GDR. Cresspahl, a cabinet maker, took in the refugees. Jakob found employment with the German railways, and in 1956 he works as a dispatcher in a city on the Elbe river. Cresspahl's daughter Gesine has left for West Germany, where she earns her living as a translator for NATO. In October 1956, Rohlfs, a captain in the GDR State Security Service, receives orders to enlist Jakob and his mother in convincing Gesine to work for the East bloc. Mrs. Abs flees West on 17 October, after State Security speaks with her; Rohlfs keeps Jakob under surveillance.

In part 2 Jakob makes the acquaintance of Jonas Blach, an assistant professor at the university in East Berlin. They meet in Jerichow, where Jonas, who loves Gesine, is staying with her father to prepare an oppositional essay for publication. Part 2 takes place between 23 October and 4 November 1956.

In part 3 Gesine enters the GDR illegally and visits Jakob in the city on the Elbe. The Hungarian uprising begins the same day. To hide Gesine, Jakob takes her to Jerichow. Rohlfs, aware of Jakob's maneuvering, allows them to travel unhindered. During the trip, Gesine realizes she loves Jakob, not Jonas. Rohlfs visits Cresspahl's, where he attempts to convince Gesine of the rightness of his cause. Gesine requests time to think and arranges a meeting in West Berlin. Rohlfs brings her to the border.

In part 4 Jonas, returning to East Berlin, discovers he has lost his position (Rohlfs has assumed responsibility for his case). He visits Jakob at work, just as the latter is actively helping the railroads transport Soviet troops to Hungary, where they will suppress the uprising. Jonas gives Jakob the manuscript of his political essay, which Jakob in turn gives to Jöche, a railroad engineer from Jerichow. Jakob then travels to West Berlin (31 October) and meets Gesine; they visit his mother in a refugee camp. Meanwhile, the English bomb Egypt in the Suez crisis. After Jakob returns from West Berlin, he is killed by a locomotive as he crosses the tracks at work (probably 8 November).

In part 5 Jonas learns from a railroad employee of Jakob's death, and he travels to Jerichow to retrieve his manuscript from Jöche. The following day (9 November), Jonas returns to the city on the Elbe. He calls Gesine to tell her of Jakob's death, and during the call, he is arrested by Rohlfs. Soon thereafter (10 November), Rohlfs meets Gesine in West Berlin, where they speculate about Jakob. The story lasts one month.

The reader must glean the story from a multitude of competing perspectives that include the narrator's voice, dialogues, and monologues from Rohlfs, Jonas, and Gesine (in the English version, the translator has supplied the names of the monologuists, an advantage denied the German reader). Hansjürgen Popp notes that part 5, narrated without dialogue or monologue inserts, functions primarily to establish the speakers of the earlier dialogues and their locale (56). The dialogues in parts 1 and 2 are between Jöche and Jonas, spoken when the latter visits Jerichow to retrieve his manuscript. Jonas and Gesine participate in the telephone conversation of part 3; one of Rohlfs's assistants, who wishes to arrest Jonas, stops the call with a "technical disturbance." The dialogue in part 4 records fragments of the conversation between Rohlfs and Gesine in a West Berlin wine bar. The monologues, more difficult to fix spatially, occur after Jakob's death; they result from conversations between the characters involved, or from agreement or disagreement with the narrator's version. Dialogues and monologues attempt to solve the enigma of Jakob's life and death.

The speculations about Jakob are also speculations about language and ideology. Johnson's figures repeatedly debate how they should characterize the action of Jakob's mother, who, after being interviewed by Rohlfs, leaves the GDR. Was she simply "going away," "fleeing," or "deserting"? (e.g., 44; Johnson characterized his own departure as "going away" [Neusüß 48]). Gesine, who works for NATO, finds English words surfacing during her stream-of-consciousness monologues or in the narrator's version of her thoughts; when she returns to the GDR, she feels as if she is speaking a foreign language (114). Rohlfs, of the State Security police, often employs Russian phrases.

In contrast, Cresspahl hovers between silence and an insular dialect, a kind of pure German discourse untouched by the conquerors. As Peter Demetz notes, Johnson's sympathies seem to be with Cresspahl (*Postwar* 212), and one thinks of the more recent and extremely popular German television film *Heimat*, with its celebration of rural German virtues and its condemnation of shallow American materialism. It is important to remember, however, that Cresspahl is also—like the inlays he carefully inserts—an anachronism (144). A bit like Thomas Mann's Peeperkorn in the *Magic Mountain*, Cresspahl senses the loss of magic and the coming of alienation in the world; Jonas notes "the painful dignity, the grand gestures and motions Cresspahl uses for the little things, because the precious contents have been lost" (140). Cresspahl, Gesine, and Jakob communicate in dialect. Through their language, Gesine and Jakob maintain contact with a vanishing culture, but they must still choose between the United States and the Soviet Union.

A crucial element in Bertolt Brecht's theory of non-Aristotelian drama was the *Verfremdungseffekt*, or alienation effect, with which he attempted to uncover the artificial, human-made—and hence changeable—aspects of a society concerned with appearing "natural" or "normal." In a sense, as Bernd Neumann points out, Johnson transfers the alienation effect to the novel, exposing the skeleton, the framework that other novelists cover up (38–41). Hansjürgen Popp asserts that the very structure of the book supports that argument: the author forces us to read slowly, to question and think, to work with the narrator (52–53). Johnson's repeated and extended descriptions of mechanical processes also alienate and interrupt reading. Examples of that are his descriptions of the postal service (26–28), of the telephone (50–53), of geology (145–47), and of the jukebox (220).

Most importantly, however, Johnson alienates through his use of language that calls attention to itself. We have noted the intrusion of Russian, English (in the German text), and German dialect into the narrative. Italian is used to recall Gesine's sojourn in the south: "But I never drank anything so cool and clean as a DRY MARTINI in an atezza su livello del mare metri cinquencento cinquanta" (165). Here the block letters suggest the materiality of advertisements in capitalist Italy (Christa Wolf and Erwin Strittmatter employ similar techniques in the early 1960s); elsewhere Johnson uses them to record a telegram, a slogan, or an announcement. In the following passage, capi-

talization emphasizes the ambiguous language of Jonas's oppositional essay:

"But we are incorrigibly dedicated to the notion of progress."
Cresspahl saw no reason to defend the notion of progress (what
did it, after all, mean?), but the INCORRIGIBLY DEDICATED
stopped him. INCORRIGIBLE was the term the socialist government used for its enemies, it implies quarrelsome superior fool-
ish useless, whereas DEDICATED applied to the opposite side,
to the international working class, UNERRINGLY convinced of
the one and only path that led to socialism, to the indefatigably
willing executors of party instructions, and what did INCORRI-
GIBLY DEDICATED mean (Cresspahl thought) coming from
Jonas? (136)

Usually, however, the intellectual Jonas remains very much aware
of his language, especially during those moments when it proves
insufficient. Recalling his initial encounter with Jakob, Jonas muses:
"If I remember correctly, I immediately began searching for words.
Which I discarded again, one after the other" (59). He finally decides
that Jakob is "like a cat," but he knows the description is wrong
(59–60). Later "he had the impression [life] was passing him by. To
use an imprecise circumlocution, he couldn't find the proper word
for it" (85). When he meets Gesine for the first time, he feels that
"each word had the hollowness of lies" (86). For his professor "words
were not enough too polished threadbare to express the giant maze
of proved and assumed facts" (211).

In *Speculations about Jakob* a fundamental divergence of perception
apparently renders agreement or truth impossible. "What is a market
place?" Rohlfs asks his assistant. "For everyone it's something different," is the answer, and Rohlfs responds, "Precisely" (65). Gesine
tells Jonas: "As long as nobody can get up and say: This is how it was
and no other way" (132). And Jakob thinks: "They saw Cresspahl get
on the train, but not off, now they're weaving the whole story around
Cresspahl, as though things were the way a man sees them" (49).
Jonas says of Gesine and Jakob, "Even if they had seen something,
it couldn't be told" (150). When Jonas realizes Gesine's feelings have
changed, he notes: "She no longer needed to tell anybody: something
has changed. (Because it can't be told)" (153).

Johnson's concern with epistemology informs the structures of his novel, for he often offers us several differing, sometimes irreconcilable, points of view. The description of Cresspahl provides an early example of this. He is mentioned in the conversation between Jonas and Jöche (8), then by Gesine (8), then described, in alternation, by the narrator (8–9, 13) and Rohlfs (9–13), who are in turn interrupted by Gesine (13). When Gesine travels to the GDR and sits in the restaurant of a Dresden hotel, the narrator introduces the scene, after which we encounter Rohlfs's description of Gesine and hers of him. These are punctuated by the narrator's reporting of short, declarative sentences—"Good evening. How are you?"—as if those are the only "facts" of which he can be sure. These examples are the most evident ones, inasmuch as Johnson supplies the differing points of view one after the other, but the author also uses his polyperspectivist technique at a greater remove. Gesine's and Jakob's taxi ride to Jerichow, for example, is first described by the narrator (125–26) and then, shortly thereafter, by Gesine (129–31); Jonas's meeting with Gesine is described by Jonas (86–88), and then, seventy pages later, by Gesine (156–58).

Scholars sometimes mention Uwe Johnson in connection with the French *nouveau roman*. One thinks as well of the film *L'année dernière à Marienbad* (1961), written by Alain Robbe-Grillet, a pioneer in the *nouveau roman* movement. In the film, released soon after Johnson's novel, we are privy to various perspectives recounting an affair a man and a woman (perhaps) had had the previous summer. At the conclusion the viewer is unsure whether the woman seduced, was seduced, or was raped; indeed, it remains unclear whether the man and the woman in fact slept together, or whether they even knew one another at that time.

Johnson's novel utilizes similar techniques (montage, flashback, and stream-of-consciousness) to a similar end, for several important questions remain unanswered. The novel is narrated after Jakob's death, so we do not possess his stream-of-consciousness reports, and the narrator only very rarely reveals to us what Jakob was thinking. Thus, in contrast with the other characters, Jakob remains a rather shadowy persona, and the conflicting memories the surviving figures have of him only exacerbate the problem. The West German scholar Bernd Neumann sees in Jakob the communist ideal; Jakob is at one with his work—he is not alienated. Neumann argues that the Hungarians fought for that kind of communism in 1956 (52), but his interpretation ignores the fact that Jakob lets the Soviet troop train through to suppress the revolt. Peter Demetz sees Jakob as an orderly German who, in allowing the trains to pass, does his work and his duty (*Postwar* 208). I think that we should ascribe some kind of socialist leanings to Jakob: he does, after all, return from West Berlin, even though Gesine, whom he loves, asks him to remain. It appears as well that he agrees to work with Rohlfs, although that, too, remains unclear, and Jakob furthermore attempts to outmaneuver Rohlfs by traveling with Gesine to Jerichow. Neumann rightly sees symbolic significance in the "parable" Jakob uses to calm Gesine after she dreamt she was trapped in a room with no exit:

> Jakob put an arm around her shoulder and pulled her toward him and said: "See that grey thing on the left, know where left is? that's the door, then out into the hall and down the stairs with the light switches glowing red in the dark so you know where they are." (230–31)

This may well be a declaration of loyalties, though it is vague enough and cannot help overly in an interpretation.

Ultimately, the questions as to who Jakob was, whether he worked with Rohlfs, and why he died (suicide, accident, or political murder?) remain unanswered. The narrator, who, in charge of the various reports, has the most information, does not divulge the answers if indeed he or she possesses them. The two characters who know most can only, as Gesine says, "speculate"—thus echoing the title and our efforts (191). (Molinaro translates *mutmaßen* here as "assume," though the reference to the title's *Mutmaßungen* is unmistakable.) The novel both demands and resists interpretation, and to insist on one—as does Rohlfs in a conversation with Gesine—is to risk Gesine's retort, "But can't you see that you are belittling reality?" (224).

East Germans ignored the publication of Johnson's novel in the West, though after the author published *The Third Book about Achim* (1961), Aron Hochmuth and Horst Kessler wrote a polemical attack in *Sonntag*. They accused Johnson of purposefully creating difficulties in the GDR so that he might pose as a defender of literature against state interference while marketing his political martyrdom in the

West. Hochmuth and Kessler, who spell Jakob with a "c," note disapprovingly that Johnson has learned from Joyce, with his inner monologues and stream-of-consciousness "chaos" (*Wust*), and they criticize the book's debt to "bourgeois philosophies, according to which it is no longer possible today to adopt a secure ideological position" (qtd. in Riedel 50; my trans.).

West German reviewers, though often puzzled, frustrated, and/or irritated by Johnson's purposeful opacity or his irregular use of language and grammar, almost uniformly recognized the novel as powerful and important. Marcel Reich-Ranicki, for example, characterized *Speculations about Jakob* as a "provocation and an unbelievable imposition," while characterizing Johnson as "a great hope" (qtd. in Riedel 60; my trans.). Hans Magnus Enzensberger, the angry young man of West German letters, praised the book as the first "Pan-German" novel since the war, asserting that it possessed the "inestimable advantage of belonging neither here [West Germany] nor there [East Germany]" (qtd. in Riedel 79; my trans.). West Germany had been waiting for an author to treat the sensitive theme of German separation (Enzensberger noted that Germans had written more good books about Alaska and Eskimo than about the two Germanys). With *Speculations about Jakob* and with his subsequent writing, Johnson obtained the reputation as the novelist of divided Germany.

His work reached American audiences with that appellation as well. The *Saturday Review* contended that Johnson inspires "the reader to his own speculation—not only about Jakob, but about the divided world in which we live" (6 April 1963), and *Time* wrote approvingly that "the reader is forced to feel and appreciate the equivocal human concerns and rival pulls between East and West in intimate human terms that propaganda clichés used by both sides too easily dismiss" (12 April 1963). U.S. reception of the novel ranged from cautious acceptance to vehement rejection. In the *Atlantic Monthly* William Barret confessed that he was unsure what precisely was taking place in the book, but he asserted that "one has no doubt of the talent of the author or the merit of his book" (May 1963). In the *New Republic*, however, Hilary Corke complained of monotony, and avowed: "I would do almost anything rather than have to read through [this book] again" (25 May 1963). The *New Yorker* denounced Johnson's "slipshod and opaque writing" and asserted that "style, motivation, coherence, and meaning are missing" (18 May 1963). The

Nation chastised Johnson for refusing to recognize differences between East and West Germany (6 April 1963). In a front-page review for the *New York Times Book Review*, M. J. Lasky calls Johnson's book a "fascinating anti-ideological novel," but Lasky proceeds to criticize the clichéd description of West Berlin during Jakob's visit there: "A little more cool tentativeness here too would have been in order" (14 April 1963).

Fritz Rudolf Fries, *The Road to Oobliadooh* FRG 1966, USA 1968, GDR 1989

The back cover of a small GDR paperback containing Fritz Rudolf Fries's stories, published in 1983, can serve as an introduction to the author. In Emily Dickinson's words, it tells the truth but tells it slant:

> Fritz Rudolf Fries was born in 1935 in Bilbao, Spain. In 1942 his family moved to Leipzig. From 1949 to 1953 he studied English and French in Leipzig. Afterward employed as a free-lance translator and interpreter. 1960–66 research assistant at the Academy of Arts and Sciences of the GDR. First literary work: *The Road to Oobliadooh* (Novel, 1966). In the same year became free-lance writer. 1979 Heinrich Mann Prize. (Fries, *Leipzig;* my trans.)

Those practiced in reading between the lines will understand that *The Road to Oobliadooh* had not yet been published in the GDR, and that its appearance in the West occasioned at least a minor literary sensation, causing Fries to lose his job at the East German Academy of Arts and Sciences. The prestigious Heinrich Mann Prize, awarded in 1979, helped consolidate the hesitant, uneasy rehabilitation of this writer who, as Friedrich Albrecht noted in 1979, maintained more admirers abroad than at home ("Schaffensentwicklung" 64–65).

Fries sets his novel in the GDR between the summers of 1957 and 1958—Johnson's book concluded in late 1956, after the Hungarian uprising. This was the period of Fries's early twenties (his protagonist, Arlecq, possesses many autobiographical traits). It was the time of the "heroic building up of socialism" celebrated in many novels, but we see little of that heroism here. Instead, we meet two cynical and bored young men, Arlecq and his sidekick Paasch, who experience the GDR as bleak and dull. It is a time of "demarcation" (*Abgrenzung*) from the West, when the great authors of modernism—Kafka, Joyce, Faulkner, Hemingway, and Proust—were forbidden; when, in response to the jitterbug, the GDR tried to develop its own folk dance (a failure); when dance halls and radio stations were limited to 40 percent Western hits and 60 percent indigenous music. Earlier in the 1950s GDR authorities had viewed jazz and blues as expressions of American decadence, until GDR supporters of such music argued that it was in fact the creation of poor American blacks.

Fries's novel contains three parts, the first including a stream-of-consciousness prologue that relates Arlecq's summer affair with Isabel, a Spanish actress, in Dresden. Part 1 recounts the adventures of Arlecq, a translator and would-be author of a novel, and Paasch, an alcoholic dental student. Both are firmly resolved to flee the unimaginative GDR quotidian, and they escape into music, alcohol, movies, and sex. The latter proves counterproductive, for they impregnate their girlfriends, and Paasch greatly fears having to marry and set up a prosaic dental practice. The cipher for their utopia is Oobliadooh, supposedly based on a jazz song by Dizzy Gillespie: "I knew a wonderful Princess in the land of Oobliadooh" (45). The title, then, refers to American music, and also to American movies: Fries told me in conversation that the title was in part inspired by a spate of such movies as *The Way to Morocco*.[2] In 1990 the GDR scholar Jürgen Grambow also suggested that Fries may have been influenced by American literature, such as Kerouac's *On the Road* ("Zur Prosa" 1312).

In the second part of the novel, the two protagonists flee to West Berlin, where they thrill to quality tobacco, good films, and a Count Basie concert. Nonetheless, Paasch finds the commercialization disgusting (and the competition a bit frightening), hence the two hold a news conference at which they assert they were kidnapped by Western agents and brought to West Berlin against their will. They return as heroes to the East, but in part 3 they smuggle their way, like Günter Grass's Oskar Matzerath, into an insane asylum (where a friend of theirs named God also lives). In an interview with Friedrich Albrecht, Fries argued against those who see that conclusion as pessimistic. Arlecq's pregnant lover discharges him from the asylum, and we are to assume he will begin life as a productive citizen and father; Paasch will remain until his alcoholism is cured (53). This is a possible reading, though a somewhat disingenuous one—an interpretation having to do, perhaps, with Fries's desire to publish the book in the GDR. Arlecq will reenter society, but the novel has repeatedly disparaged that society as a banal one; that is why, after all, Arlecq and Paasch have struggled so hard to escape it. Additionally, Paasch makes Arlecq promise to smuggle him a bottle from time to time. The ending remains open, as does the (dialectical) last sentence, "The questions, the answers, the questions."

Barbara Einhorn points out that the book's structure creates an acceleration toward the conclusion. Each section becomes noticeably shorter, and while part 1 contains chapters referring to the past, the two remaining segments take part entirely in the present. The awaited birth of two children supplies a future-oriented perspective as well (Einhorn 484–87). The novel's very form collaborates in the project of returning the protagonists to the quotidian.

Einhorn also notes that Fries leaves the question open as to who actually narrates the novel. It may be Arlecq, reflecting on his life, but it may be someone else (Einhorn 479–80). In any event, the narrator does not appear entirely reliable, and one occasionally encounters sentences such as this: "If there is any harmony at all, thought Paasch or Arlecq, it is only in music, a masculine art" (27).

Rich in association, the prologue anticipates many of the subsequent themes and developments. Fries makes frequent reference to blue flowers, thus evoking the German Romantic author Novalis (1772–1801). The blue flower, which functions as a leitmotif in Novalis's *Henry von Ofterdingen*, symbolizes the power of the creative imagination; Arlecq is a latter-day Romantic who searches out blue flowers within the drabness of the GDR. The prologue also invokes forbidden heroes of modernism (Benn, Picasso, and Gertrude Stein), references that will accumulate as the novel progresses. Fries presents a tribute to Proust, Arlecq's favorite author: eating blackberries, Arlecq finds they trigger a maelstrom of association, as did Proust's famous madeleine (9).

As the title of Fries's novel suggests, music is his major metaphor, and music serves at least three functions within the text. In a first, most obvious sense, a preference for Western music, during a time when GDR authorities were attempting to suppress it, signals an oppositional political statement. Popular music also provides Arlecq and his friends an escape, a refuge from the banality surrounding them. Finally, music presents a utopian moment that contrasts with an ossified reality and the degraded language that both constitutes and mirrors that reality. In this last function, music becomes a blue flower representing creative fantasy in all its manifestations, including Fries's literary text—a challenge to the language of propaganda and to the restrictive tenets of socialist realism.

The attempted interdiction of jazz (as well as other art, such as literature) provides ample opportunity for social criticism. Arlecq for example suggests parallels between Nazi and SED cultural politics when he speaks of the prohibition of jazz during the Third Reich—"The Road to Oobliadooh was overgrown with barbed wire" (57)—and when he notes that not much changes thereafter: " . . . stayed up till midnight listening to the new sounds from the non-denazified propaganda box that was still, with Nazi pigheadedness, hostile to the new wave lengths" (62–63). With the satisfaction of the insider, Arlecq reports the fashion in which jazz aficionados circumvented bureaucratic hurdles by changing song titles: "The combo was now playing 'St. James' Infirmary.' Except that, to avoid trouble with the management, the musicians called it 'The Negro Slaves' Lament'" (35–36). The important thing, Arlecq remarks wryly, is that the titles sound as though they came from the Party newspaper. During periodic prohibitions of American music, he recounts, audiences would still gather to listen to jazz or blues, but they would speed up the music to more acceptable waltzes when the police arrived (115).

Jazz serves as a political signpost. Riding to Rostock with a pompous SED official, Arlecq whistles a few bars from George Shearing's "Lullaby of Birdland." The escort reacts negatively, and the political lines are established (193). During that trip to Rostock, Arlecq employs music as metaphor to suggest liberation from the Soviets during the workers' uprising of June 1953. He tells a visiting Latin American revolutionary priest of a piano in the marketplace:

Paasch had run with him to the broadcasting building, may even have thrown a stone too while the tanks were still approaching the city, before they demolished the placards with their slogans in childish lettering, such as DOWN WITH PARTY PRIVILEGES. . . . Someone had stood at the battered grand piano and hammered out a ragtime, long before the Youth Club

reached the point of discussing ragtime as a form of expression
of the Negro proletariat. (206)

Arlecq then indicates that boring bureaucrats, such as their SED
guide, took command and restored order.

Fries does not, however, utilize music merely as a weapon of political satire directed at fatuous SED cultural policy. It also provides
Arlecq and Paasch a means of inner emigration, of eschewal. Confronted with a GDR reality that incessantly diminished opportunities
for "poetic confusion" (108), Arlecq flees into a world of the imagination defined by sex, literature, movies, and above all music; Paasch,
no reader, prefers schnapps, but otherwise he shares his friend's
tastes. Two particularly striking examples of their retreat into jazz
occur when Arlecq surrenders to "the exalting power of music" (39)
while Paasch plays piano at the beginning and, with structural neat-
ness, at the conclusion of the novel.

Imagination possesses, however, a double edge in *The Road to
Oobliadooh*, serving not only as escape but as the generator of a utopian alternative against which one can measure the present. Language structures the "real"; hence, Fries's text moves beyond a satirical critique of GDR cultural politics to an interrogation of language
itself, especially GDR officialese. The martyrdom of Arlecq's friend
Stanislaus presents an epigrammatic illustration of the depreciation
of life in fustian society. Stanislaus enjoys a comfortable position as
a librarian when, in a manner reminiscent of existentialist plots from
the 1950s, the meaning of his life collapses. He can no longer bear to
work with "strangely mutilated newspapers" and forbidden books
that lead to the falsification of history (131). His existence has grown
intolerable, he admits to himself. Whereas he had formerly protected
himself with satire, parodying with great skill GDR propaganda at a
New Year's Eve party (119), he now moves to active opposition and
is arrested for placing political leaflets in library books. Arlecq believes his friend acted thus "so that a fresh start in an entirely new
direction could be made, so that word and reality would coincide
again" (210). In GDR society the cleft between the lived "text" and
the official one had grown unacceptable.

Arlecq's experience resembles Stanislaus's. He dismisses the language of official "newspapers and magazines containing official information that became the subject of derisive whispers, mocking disre-

gard" (85). The "Rhapsody of Work" which swells the *People's Daily* amuses him (136), and at one point he shows a foreign visitor an eight-year-old paper to demonstrate that the information it contains does not differ from that morning's news (208). He indicates to the same visitor that the bombastic idiom of the official guide, who speaks the newspeak of the newspapers, provides no place to search out nuance (205). As a simultaneous interpreter, Arlecq ignores an official speech and substitutes one of his own, using official clichés. No one notices (195).

Arlecq's estrangement from language appears primarily, but not exclusively, political. Making love to a woman, he fills "a few word-husks with love" but ultimately lapses into an alienated silence (121); at a funeral service, he mutters: "words words words," as a comment on the efficaciousness of the sermon (98). Arlecq maintains a vision of a new language: "In Arlecq's dream the letters whispered a sophisticated language that made the censors turn crimson when their brains soaked up the disquieting phraseology like blotting paper" (86). If Stanislaus's reaction to the alienation of words from "reality" lies in overtly political protest, the picaresque hero Arlecq mobilizes fantasy. He counteracts the *Peoples' Daily* with illicit editions of Proust, Apollinaire, T. S. Eliot, Hemingway, and Truman Capote; his revolutionary cry sounds: "Readers of the World unite" in a bond of the imagination (136). The exchange of literature can be interdicted or at least hindered (Arlecq's friends steal Western books from the Leipzig Book Fair), and the best movies are in West Berlin. But the airwaves prove difficult to censor: music, a metalinguistic form, becomes the most effective medium for Arlecq's metalanguage.

Music serves as an international esperanto that breaks down borders. American jazz signals Arlecq's childhood awakening from Hitler's fascism (62), and a Schumann festival demonstrated that music "knew no frontiers, wiped out international differences" (142). Arlecq prefers pop music to Schumann (just as Ulrich Plenzdorf's Edgar Wibeau prefers "real music" to "some Händelsohn Bacholdy" in *The New Sorrows of Young W.* [13]). Arlecq asserts that it, like the picaresque novels he translates and of which he himself figures as hero, contains latent social criticism and overt sexuality (86). Music provides communication, authentic language: Paasch meets Arlecq at a jazz concert (63), Arlecq's lover Isabel emanates a Gypsy rhythm (20), and jazz connects Arlecq with a Latin American revolutionary just as it separates them both from a GDR functionary (205). Filled with the "exalting" (39) and "orgiastic" (40) power of music, Arlecq hallucinates that "Stanislaus wrote his radio play which, when produced simultaneously in all languages, would be instantly understood, and tyranny and despotism, for those were his targets, would creep like worms into the deepest crevices of the earth" (38).

Utilizing an open form with abrupt transitions in mood, style, and time, Fries approximates in his novel the improvisational form of a jazz composition: music functions in the work as a metaphor for Fries's own project of reviving language. Like Uwe Johnson, he "foregrounds" or "alienates" through the insertion of French, Spanish, English (in the German text), or Russian words and sentences; or with the preciously Biblical language spoken by the escapee, one whom Arlecq calls God, from an insane asylum; or with his satire of GDR propaganda. Again like Johnson, Fries capitalizes such words as CHAMPS ELYSEES or WEST HITS to convey the magical mystery such words denote. Fries's utilization of these strategies, together with a denial of traditional narration, constitutes more than a rejection of Lukács's theory of the novel and its vision of totality; it represents an attack on the official self-perception of GDR society as structured in its language. Against a rational, antipoetic polity determined to overtake the West in per capita consumption, Fries sets his vision of a more spontaneous, individually oriented alternative.

With *The Road to Oobliadooh*, Fries anticipated at least two developments in GDR literature. One was formal: after the change of government in 1971, GDR writers were allowed to rediscover modernism and to experiment with form. Thus the stylistics of such a novel as Christa Wolf's *The Quest for Christa T.* were the subject of an intensely concerned discussion in the GDR during the late 1960s, whereas Stephan Hermlin's *Evening Light* (1979), which also employs modernist techniques, could appear about a decade later without controversy. With the exception of works by Uwe Johnson, who was not published in the GDR until 1989, and possibly those by Johannes Bobrowski, Fries's novel constituted the most radical experimentation in GDR prose to that date.

Fries also anticipated the rediscovery of Romanticism in the GDR. In the 1970s many writers rejected Lukács's models of Goethe and Classicism, turning instead to Romantic writers: Bettina von Arnim,

Karoline von Günderrode, Hölderlin, Jean Paul, and, to the extent that he can be termed Romantic, Heinrich von Kleist. Gerhard Wolf published *Poor Hölderlin* (1972), and his wife, Christa Wolf, wrote *No Place on Earth* (1979) about Günderrode and Kleist. In 1975 Günter de Bruyn published a biography of Jean Paul, whom Fries quotes in the epigram to his novel. GDR writers discovered in the Romantics an appealing sense of experimentation in literature and life. Patricia Herminghouse asserts that "the trace which . . . led writers of the 1970s to writers of the Romantic era [was] less the vision of a better future than dissatisfaction with present reality, a belief in certain ideals which [made] it impossible to affirm the present as being in harmony with them" ("Rediscovery" 2). In this, Arlecq and his quest for the blue flower proved a leader, as Bernhard Greiner has demonstrated ("Sentimentalischer" 282–301).

It is not difficult to discern why the book could not be printed in the GDR. There is a frank discussion of the 1953 workers' uprising, and at another point, Arlecq wonders, "How can you tell one dictator from another?" (205). The novel lampoons stupid and restrictive GDR cultural policies and officious GDR functionaries, and it condemns censorship. We have mentioned the comparison of Nazi and SED cultural politics; later, when Stanislaus is arrested for political reasons, Arlecq compares the internment with fascist concentration camps by noting that "work doesn't only make a man free, it also makes him hungry" (214). Earlier in the story, Arlecq insists on confusing Stanislaus's name with that of Paasch's father (30–31); the latter was in a Nazi concentration camp (103, 189). After Paasch and Arlecq escape to the West, they return to the GDR, but Arlecq later suggests that it was primarily on Paasch's account; Paasch, with his alcoholism and his nonexistent work ethic, would not have survived in the competitive West. That is hardly a ringing endorsement of the SED state, and Arlecq muses that were it not for Paasch he might have remained in the West: Isabel lived in Paris, and the movies were better in West Berlin (196, 136).

In the West, feuilletonists at times objected to Fries's extravagant and often difficult language (Uwe Johnson's style had also proved irritating to many); nonetheless, they accorded the book a uniformly positive reception. In the right-wing *Die Welt*, Günter Schlichting wrote that he was fascinated by this novel from the "Zone" (8 May

1966). But the left-wing paper *konkret* asserted approvingly that Fries's novel was the first from the GDR that betrayed in its content, but not in its form, its country of origin (8 Aug. 1966).

After *The Road to Oobliadooh*, however, Fries's writing changed. Subsequent collections of stories, *The Television War* (1969) and *Sea Pieces* (1973), are formally accessible. Fries's themes changed as well: he no longer advanced viciously vehement attacks on GDR cultural policy, instead criticizing U.S. policy in Vietnam or Latin America. The West German critic Jürgen Wallmann characterized Fries's writing as dutiful socialist-realist exercises ("Fantasie" 870–71); in *Die Zeit* Dominik Jost wrote that Fries had become "conformist to such a degree that it is simply embarrassing" (5 Oct. 1973; my trans.). Fries's second novel, *The Air Ship* (1974), received mixed, but generally favorable, reviews in the West, although in *Die Zeit* Fritz Raddatz called it a debacle and asserted that Fries had accommodated himself to the point of speechlessness (7 Feb. 1975). In his "rehabilitation" interview of 1979 with Friedrich Albrecht, Fries jokingly noted that, were we in the sixteenth century, he could claim he had seen the torture chambers (Albrecht, "Interview" 55). In a 1986 conversation with me, Fries insisted he had maintained his independence, noting for example that he had never joined the Party. He claimed that his books were not widely reviewed (beyond the scholarly journals, such as *Weimarer Beiträge* and *Sinn und Form*), and that he continued to experience difficulties publishing some of his work. However, he noted to me that he did want to be published in his country.

Indeed, Fries published several novels and collections of stories in the GDR. *The Air Ship* was filmed (the result, one of the first experimental films in the GDR, quickly disappeared from East German cinemas), and I espied the difficult *Alexander's New Worlds* (1982) for sale in newspaper kiosks, next to penny novels containing far less challenging material. Fries was a member of the GDR Academy of Arts and Sciences, he wrote regularly for *Sinn und Form*, and he received the Heinrich Mann Prize in 1979. He was allowed to travel regularly, and he published collections of travel anecdotes.

In the 1970s his journeys took him to St. John's University in Minnesota, where he lived for a time as writer in residence. Fries wrote a gentle report of his experiences, and I suspect he composed the concluding paragraph with *The Road to Oobliadooh* in mind:

Later we go to a party that the Dean of Arts and Sciences . . . gives for [me]: he has picked out his loveliest jazz records, because he has been informed of the musical interests of the guest. . . . I experience a curious return to the artificial paradises of the postwar period, when the voices of the speakers from Armed Forces Radio suggested to us an America that probably never existed and never will, and yet that survives in jazz: this unconcerned melancholy, this weary optimism, these metaphors of love, drawn with lipstick, from Billie Holiday. Bob, as the dean is called by everyone, fills the glasses; his wife refuses to go into the kitchen as long as Billie Holiday is singing. For the others, we freeze into a picture, the initiated collectors who consummate a sacred act, recognizing each other in the magic of this music—and for one evening awakeners of the American dream. (Fries, "Kloster" 130; my trans.)

Fries's title *The Road to Oobliadooh* is, we recall, inspired by American art. In a sense, Oobliadooh *is* America, though not a "real" America. As Fries writes, it represents an America "that probably never existed and never will," a poetic space of the imagination, not dissimilar to Brecht's America of tigers and moonshine. This America lives on in Fries's book, which, written in the 1960s about the GDR of the 1950s, remained until the late 1980s an embarrassment for East Germans who wished to honor him.

Prodded by creeping *glasnost*, Fries's GDR publisher announced in the later 1980s that it would print *The Road to Oobliadooh*. Fries prepared this development by proleptically distancing himself from his book in the past twenty years. He told the American scholar Richard Zipser that, in his youth, the open border in Berlin made clear the sensual enticements of the West (e.g., jazz concerts) over the rather dry Marxism-Leninism in the East. If at first the theory embarrassed itself, Fries added, it was only for a time (Zipser, *DDR-Literatur* 3:63). In 1982 he published a short epilogue to *The Road to Oobliadooh* in *Sinn und Form* (an epilogue really comprehensible only to those who have read the officially nonexistent novel), which can be read as a disavowal of the book. The narrative tone is more distant; and Paasch and Arlecq murder their wives, attempt to escape the GDR, and are arrested by the People's Police ("Frauentags").

Translated by Leila Vennewitz, *The Road to Oobliadooh* appeared in the United States in 1968. It was noted in such publications as *Kirkus, Book List,* and *Publishers Weekly;* the *New York Times Book Review* and *Time* reviewed it in more detail. The *Times* printed a piece by Mary Carter who complains about the "explosion of proliferating data," the effect of which "is to obscure whatever movement or central idea the book is intended to illuminate." Carter finds the quest of youth as depicted in the novel "curiously languid and directionless." That, plus the relentless stream of allusion, generates

> an equal languor in the reader—who, to be fair, must conclude that the idea of fragmentation and randomness is, indeed, central to our time. It may be significant that what does emerge from the book is the sense of overwhelming proliferation of available data and the hopelessness of attempting to synthesize it all into some entity of heft, direction and meaning. (9 Feb. 1969)

The tentativeness of Carter's conclusion is striking, as is her evident bafflement regarding Fries's project.

An unsigned review in *Time* rated the novel considerably more favorably, noting that the "people's republic of East Germany" had produced one gifted novelist, Uwe Johnson, and that in Fries it had "the makings of another." The reviewer objects that the novel is at times "ultra-literary in just the wrong sort of way," but he or she also notes that "moments of fiction materialize, cooly precise, sharp and fresh." Praising Fries's "crisp humor," the reviewer rightly places its source in a parody of the "pretentious twaddle of all establishments, whether founded upon outworn socialist unrealities or rampant democratic rhetoric" (10 Jan. 1969).

Concerned with introducing a foreign book to Americans, the reviewers tend to decontextualize the novel and to emphasize what is "universal." Writing amidst the youth rebellion of the 1960s, both reviewers see Fries's novel in that perspective. *Time* asserts that Arlecq and Paasch have "much in common with youth everywhere," while the *Times* speaks of "young East Germans, whose pursuits and attitudes seem to be identical with those of the young everywhere." The reviews do not emphasize that Fries sets his novel in the 1950s, not in the 1960s, or that his protagonists want to be not like youth "everywhere" but like youth in the West, something that the GDR did not allow in the 1950s. In a different but related vein, the "ultra-literary" aspect of Fries's book, a quality that irritated the reviewer from *Time*, makes more sense when one knows that many of Arlecq's favorite books were unavailable in the GDR of that time. To speak with David Bathrick, these readers recontextualize (and misread) a GDR novel for a U.S. audience, but the misreading is not a productive one.

Christa Wolf, *The Quest for Christa T.* GDR 1968, FRG 1969, USA 1970

Born in 1929, Christa Wolf, like Uwe Johnson and Fritz Rudolf Fries, studied German literature with Hans Mayer in Leipzig. Also like Johnson and Fries, she demonstrated an early interest in matters of form and language. In her novel *Divided Heaven* (1963; see chapter 3), she modified the prescriptions of socialist realism while experimenting with narrative perspective. In *The Quest for Christa T.*, the novel that brought her recognition in the West, her experiments became radical.

In the early 1960s the narrator attempts to reconstruct the life of her friend Christa T., who has recently died of leukemia. She uses her friend's letters, papers, and diaries to supplement her own memories and her own fantasies about Christa T. The narrator recalls her first acquaintance with Christa T., when they were both schoolchildren in the Third Reich, and then the reestablishment of their friendship as students during the early 1950s in Leipzig. The book recounts Christa's experiences as a schoolteacher, her marriage to the veterinarian Justus and the birth of their children, her subsequent affair with a forester, her role in the planning and construction of a home on a lake, and her final illness and death.

During the Sixth GDR Writers' Congress, held 28–30 May 1969 in East Berlin, Max Walter Schulz, the influential director of the Johannes R. Becher Writers' Institute and a vice president of the GDR Writers' Association, attacked *The Quest for Christa T.*:

We know Christa Wolf as a talented fellow fighter for our cause. Precisely for that reason we are not allowed to hide our disappointment about her new book. No matter how partisan the subjectively honest intention of the book may be, the fashion in which the story is narrated is designed to call into doubt our life goals, to shake our mastered past, to create a broken relationship to the here and now and tomorrow—whom does that profit?

Who profits from Wolf's subjectively honest intention and partisan commitment, when she here and there in the literary text and in one's general impression so obviously emphasizes the ambiguity of her message, that the other side need only choose what it wants, need only read out of it what it would like. We are not alone in the world, we socialists. (71; my trans.)

Schulz's prose is turgid, but his message is clear: Wolf may have meant well, but her book endangers the GDR. It would take over four years, a change of government, and a more liberal cultural policy before the novel became available in GDR bookstores.

Schulz's reference to the "mastered past" indicates that Wolf swerved from the paradigm established by many of the writers we have examined in chapter 1. Her novel describes no communist-led antifascist resistance. It does mention the 1944 assassination attempt against Hitler, in response to which Christa T. and the narrator put on their Hitler Youth uniforms to demonstrate solidarity with their government. Christa T.'s father is a socialist, but his daughter and her friend appear to have been ardent young fascists. After the war, the narrator and Christa T. experience difficulty finding the language to express their naïve illusions and beliefs during the Third Reich. Following GDR policy, they know what they must do: "But to make the precise and sharp cut-off separating 'ourselves' from 'the others,' once and for all, that would save us. And secretly to know: the cut-off very nearly never came, because we ourselves might well have become otherwise" (27). The narrator implies that only accident—of birth, sex, or locale—may have preserved them from participation in Nazi atrocities.

In her later *Patterns of Childhood* (1976), Wolf investigated in more detail that "mastered past" of fascism that, in *The Quest for Christa T.*, represents merely a subtext. In *The Quest for Christa T.*, Wolf, like Uwe Johnson and Fritz Rudolf Fries, concentrates her attention on East German life in the 1950s, another aspect of the past hardly "mastered" by East German historians or authors. In the summer of 1953, the time of the workers' revolt in the GDR, Christa T. writes a letter in which she struggles with the thought of suicide (70–71). The book also discusses the Hungarian uprising in 1956 and the "dark night" it occasioned (133).

More important than specific references to historical events (Khrushchev's secret speech revealing some of Stalin's crimes may or may not be implied in the passage discussing Hungary) is the general mood the novel evokes. The narrator says little specifically describing the repressive measures that lead to the *Gleichschaltung* of intellectual life (50–51)—though there is a description of the public humiliation of Günter, a student who defends subjective causality rather than objective, economic factors when discussing Schiller. But one result—the choking of individuality—is apparent.

The text does present eloquent defenders of the GDR during the 1950s, when, despite great odds and with no Marshall Plan assistance, the country attempted to become an industrial power and a socialist society. Christa T.'s former schoolmate Irene Dölling has little patience for individual vagaries:

Wanted? Did we ever have any choice? Weren't we forced to do the first things first, as well as we could, and to ask for nothing more, over and over? Haven't the results been astounding achievements? (49)

One could, however, read of the "astounding achievements" of the GDR in the newspapers and in the official histories. Wolf's narrator wishes to demonstrate the devastating results for individuals.

The text examines the nefarious effects of the public propaganda, the fashion in which students eager to transform society internalized the increasing regimentation, comparing themselves with the idealized superpeople in the newspapers (56). Abandoning the ego—the self—as bourgeois nonsense (173), they eagerly integrated into the socialist "we." Christa T., however, could not, and one of the central themes in the novel is the difficulty of saying "I," of becoming an individual, within a socialist society.

"Accommodation" (*Anpassung*) serves as a leitmotif in this regard. Irene Dölling thinks Christa T. is "endangered" because she cannot recognize limits (49). In June 1953 a doctor diagnoses Christa T.'s "deficient capacity to adapt oneself to existing circumstances" (72).

A former student of Christa T.'s lectures her confidently that "the essence of health is adaptation or conformity" (111). (In an extreme but related example, some Soviet citizens who could not "fit in" were committed to mental institutions.) Christa T. never asked herself, the narrator notes, whether it was indeed she (and not her society) who needed to adjust (74); hence she was ill. Marcel Reich-Ranicki is thus perfectly justified in viewing Christa T.'s illness as metaphor: "Christa T. dies of leukemia, but she is suffering from the GDR" ("Christa Wolfs" 62; my trans.).

Despite her difficulties in the GDR, however, Christa T. remains a convinced socialist who "identifies deeply with her time" (71). She realizes that socialism presents her with the long sought "way to herself," allowing her to merge her own longing for wholeness into a larger movement for social justice. Indeed, she knows that she cannot be whole or complete in isolation, without social activity. The text presents the requisite distance from West Germany and from West Germans, who are depicted as cynical, condescending, and materialistic. Christa T. also spits on a West German monument commemorating German territory incorporated by Poland and the Soviet Union at the conclusion of World War II (125). She does not, it is true, succeed in finding that "way to herself," and some West German commentators have seen her emphasis near the conclusion of her life on her house and family as a retreat from societal commitment, at least as defined in the GDR. But Christa T. also knows that time is on her side: "For she knows that before long people won't still be dying of this disease" (182). The narrator, too, has earlier asserted that "the times were working for [Christa T.]" (87). The novel presents loyal criticism.

We recall that Max Walter Schulz acknowledged Wolf's "subjectively honest" intentions and her "partisan commitment." He chastised her, however, for her depiction of GDR failures, a depiction that he believed West Germans would use for their own purposes. He was correct, but GDR officials often employed that argument to muzzle criticism; it encouraged self-censorship and justified state censorship. Schulz was upset not only with *what* Wolf wrote but with the fashion in which she wrote it. Along with Johnson and Fries (and, to an extent, Johannes Bobrowski), Wolf served as a pioneer in bringing modernist techniques to GDR literature.

Wolf fashions a complicated narrative technique to deal with her difficult project—that of remembering. As Heinrich Mohr has pointed out, the narrator is remembering for the future (198); Christa T. is dead and does not need us. "But it seems that we need her," the narrator remarks (5). Christa T. believed that one had to work on one's past as on one's future (143), and the narrator works on the past. In so doing she is of course concerned with "facts," but not in a positivistic sense; facts, we hear, are the traces events leave in us (172). "And doesn't thinking create facts?" the narrator demands (58). In referring to her title (in the German, Wolf uses "*nachdenken*" for thinking, as she does in her title), Wolf underscores the creative aspect of her remembering: she is (re)creating Christa T. and her history.

Like Christa T., the narrator knows the power of *Erfindung* ("fantasy, invention"). At the outset she insists that one cannot cling to (positivistic) facts, "which are too mixed up with chance and don't tell much" (23). She notes in her story: "So much for the action, and doing justice to the facts. But it isn't the truth" (67). She asserts that she will have to invent for the sake of truth (23). Thus, when she narrates her first postwar encounter with Christa T., she describes it twice, each time differently (27). After recounting a summer love of Christa T.'s, the narrator concludes, "It was like that, or maybe it was different" (41). The narrator's conversation with Irene Dölling is purely fictional. Christa T.'s visit with the General, a fortune teller, is twice invented: Christa T. writes down her experience, hence (re)creating it, and the narrator then decides to "correct" her (80). In the ensuing text, the narrator speaks of "her General" and of "my General." A school director with whom Christa T. talks "will have to be invented here" (103). Describing a New Year's Eve party, the narrator emphasizes that she is "correcting" the "facts": "We all drank to her—or I very much wish we had" (165). In this fashion, the narrator underscores the fictionality of her undertaking: she is not showing us the "real" Christa T. (whatever that might mean) but, quite consciously, her picture of Christa T. Just as Christa T. tries to set her fiction against Stalinist regimentation determined to stamp out the individual (56), the narrator dares to set her fiction of Christa T. against the "new world of people without imagination," the "factual people," the bureaucratic planners who, during Ulbricht's New Economic System of the 1960s, manage the revolution (51).

The difficult narrative techniques Wolf develops to transport her act of creative remembering contribute to the ambiguity Max Walter Schulz so regretted. They also have ramifications for the theory of language implied in the work. Like Fritz Rudolf Fries and Uwe Johnson before her, Wolf alternates in this work between *Sprachkritik*, which, criticizing language clichés and bombast, contributes to greater exactitude, and *Sprachskepsis*, a recognition of the seemingly inevitable frustration of attaining satisfactory precision in language.

Heinrich Mohr has demonstrated the fashion in which Wolf attempts to renew the exhausted topos of the idyll. Describing Christa T.'s summer lover, the narrator writes: "Best thing would be for them to run across the fields and for the spread hay to give off its fragrance. So off they run, and there's the fragrance of hay, everything's just as it should be" (39). Mohr correctly argues that the narrator intends not to destroy the scene with her distancing irony but to make the idyll possible again in literature, to rehabilitate it (213–14).

Language criticism becomes social criticism when Wolf directs it at the bureaucratic officialese that, especially in the 1950s, characterized GDR reality. Christa T. "was doubtful, amid our toxic swirl of new name-giving; what she doubted was the reality of names" (35). Later the narrator comments sardonically on Christa T.'s reaction to her society's vehement, overplayed words: "She felt how words began to change when they aren't being tossed out any more by belief and ineptitude and excessive zeal but by calculation, craftiness, the urge to adapt and conform" (56). Near the end of her life Christa T. finds herself disintegrating amidst "banal actions and clichés" (157). She has always attempted to resist banality, in part by writing, by creating her own, more authentic discourse: "Write poems, 'dichten,' *condensare*, make dense, tighten; language helps" (16). The narrator pursues the same task. As we have seen, she alienates hackneyed tropes. Additionally, her emphasis on fictionality and ambiguity causes the reader to slow, to question, to work with her. Finally she, like her mentor Christa T., foregrounds language with wordplays and ostensible etymologies, both of which are of course more apparent in the German text.

Even as Christa T. and the narrator attempt to counter the entropy of discourse, they remember the limits of language. The narrator says of Christa T.: "She must have realized early in her life that we aren't capable of saying things exactly as they are" (33). Later the narrator asserts programmatically, "It didn't happen the way one can tell it;

but if one can tell it as it was, then one wasn't in on it" (64). Throughout the text one finds such sentences as *"hard to put a name to it"* (174). Some experiences, such as life under fascism, can only be related in broken sentences. Undeterred, the narrator attempts to "speak different words, finally find the courage to make whole sentences out of the broken ones, to eliminate the vagueness in our talk" (27). The text's concern with etymologies implies a prelapsarian myth of a "purer" language. The narrator also projects a utopian future during which the current lack of precision will vanish from discourse: "Words, too, have their time and cannot be tugged out of the future according to need. It means much to know they are there" (185).

In an investigation of Christa Wolf's theory of language, Manfred Jäger asserts that her skepticism remains fundamentally conservative, that she draws back from the more radical implications of her insights (158). We should not, however, expect from Wolf the requisite modernist protestations of despair regarding the "impossibility" of narration and the "necessity" of silence. Her narrator recognizes her inability (at least currently) to describe things as they are; she accepts it and makes it productive. After recounting Christa T.'s visit with the school director, the narrator comments, "Their conversation might have been like this, but I won't insist that it was" (106). Similarly, she notes of Christa T.'s writing that "it's not important whether it happened exactly as she described it or not" (107).

By evincing a sovereign indifference to the "disheartening pressure of facts" (37) and to chronology (110), the narrator can elide the knotty problem of the inevitable semiotic gap between signifiers and signified. For her, as we have seen, facts are those traces events leave in us, and that of course exposed Wolf to charges of bourgeois relativism and subjectivity, terms not well liked by GDR cultural functionaries. Nonetheless, events will leave different traces in different people (64). The narrator accepts this, too. In a sense, it is the structural principle of her book, for she unabashedly shows us her own subjectivity, the traces events left in her. She is creating a reality, and she knows that each reader, encountering her fictional construct, will in turn create another reality. She does not, however, see that as contributing to isolation and fragmentation, charges leveled by Lukács against Western modernism. Rather, she views it as socially productive.

Some members of the GDR cultural establishment were evidently prepared to accept Wolf's novel in that spirit. In 1968, *Sinn und Form* printed roughly three chapters, and excerpts appeared in *Sonntag*. The Munich journal *Kürbiskern* published other excerpts, and Wolf appended a proleptic "Self-Interview," in which she anticipated and attempted to counter GDR criticism. The GDR Mitteldeutscher Verlag printed twenty thousand copies of the novel at the end of 1968, sending five thousand to West Germany, where they were sold with a West German cover and a 1969 publication date. The remaining copies were sent primarily to GDR critics, functionaries, and library officials (Schmitt 30). Fritz Raddatz called it a "printing for the wolves" ("Mein Name" 73; my trans.).

In January and April of 1969, *Sinn und Form* and *Neue Deutsche Literatur* published reviews that contained some of the very objections Wolf had foreseen. Their tone was reserved but generally negative. Working with the prescriptive categories of socialist realism, they could not identify in Christa T. a positive hero or a role model for GDR readers. In late April 1969, at the Tenth Plenum of the Central Committee of the Socialist Unity party, Heinz Adameck, director of television and a member of the Central Committee, attacked the novel. Heinz Sachs, the director of Mitteldeutscher Verlag, underwent the humiliating process of self-criticism in *Neues Deutschland*, then lost his position. At the Sixth GDR Writers' Congress (28–30 May), Max Walter Schulz and others rejected the novel. While often recognizing the book's considerable literary merit, critics feared it would lead to resignation and to bourgeois individualism. The official attacks had the desired effect: public discussion of the novel ceased, at least in the East.

West German reviewers of course emphasized many of those elements East German critics found so troubling: Christa T.'s difficulties as an individual in a regimented society; the criticism of Stalinism; and Christa T.'s death. As we have noted, some readers argued that Christa T.'s emphasis on her house symbolized an inner emigration. While West Germans noted the utopian qualities of Christa T.'s (and the narrator's) quest, they also emphasized the glaring gap between contemporary GDR society, which was suppressing the novel, and Christa Wolf's socialist ideal.

The scandals surrounding the novel helped bring it to the attention of U.S. critics, who treated the book as an experimental text that harkened to Uwe Johnson. They also emphasized the dissident qualities: the *Christian Science Monitor* noted the "sensational controversy" (4 March 1971) and the *New York Times* the "grim fury" (31 Jan. 1971) that the slender book aroused. *Library Journal* urged both academic and public libraries to purchase the novel (1 Dec. 1970). The *Christian Science Monitor* spoke of "a serious literary work. An artist has struggled to master the over-worked medium of the novel, and a voice has made itself heard through the Iron Curtain." The *New York Times Book Review* praised Wolf's "muted brilliance." In the *New York Review of Books* John Willett lauded Wolf's "sensitivity, commitment, and independence of mind," as well as her "Johnson-like technique of narration." He termed it a "small masterpiece," adding, "More than any other work of art to date, it seems to open up the Wall" (2 Sept. 1971). In the *Saturday Review* Peter Moscoso-Góngora called Wolf a "brilliant writer." He noted with regret, "*The Quest for Christa T.*, a milestone in many ways, points up the sad fact that the profoundly innovative [writing] being produced in East Germany, with its paradoxical exploration of social issues through the nexus of a seemingly subjectivist probing of personality, is largely unknown to American readers" (8 May 1971).

Between 1968 and 1973 Christa Wolf's *The Quest for Christa T.* constituted one of the most sought-after pieces of contraband in the GDR, one that Western visitors smuggled to GDR relatives and friends. In 1973 and 1974, after the change in government and Erich Honecker's more liberal cultural policy, eighty thousand copies of the novel could appear, although for many GDR literary scholars it remained an uncomfortable theme, if not a taboo (Behn 7). Meanwhile GDR writers, particularly younger women writers, profited from Wolf's literary and personal example. One sees the influence of Wolf's style in the work of Helga Schütz, who in her writing has attempted to remember the German past. One also discerns it in the title and style of Gerti Tetzner's *Karen W.*, which deals with a woman's attempts to loosen the constrictions of patriarchy. And Wolf served as mentor to Maxie Wander, whose *Good Morning, My Lovely* (1977), a book of interviews with GDR women, created a literary sensation in both Germanys; Wolf wrote the foreword.

In one of the final GDR evaluations of *The Quest for Christa T.*, Therese Hörnigk classified it as a central work in the creation of a new self-understanding within GDR literature, and she noted some of the leading GDR authors—Franz Fühmann, Günter de Bruyn, Jurek

Becker—who have acknowledged the importance of Wolf's book (131–32). The narrator of *The Quest for Christa T.* asserts that time would have worked for Christa T. It has worked for Christa Wolf's novel.

Forms of Protest

Speculations about Jakob, The Road to Oobliadooh, and *The Quest for Christa T.* deal with the 1950s, an arduous time for the GDR. Imposed on a conquered people by the Soviet Union, the Socialist Unity party confronted difficulties of tremendous magnitude: a workers' revolt in 1953; Khrushchev's partial condemnation of Stalin in 1956; the Hungarian uprising that same year; and the massive hemorrhage of labor as every year thousands of East Germans, voting with their feet, left for the Federal Republic. GDR newspapers and other sources of official propaganda noted with pride that despite these obstacles a new society was created, one that, in the 1960s, the government officially termed socialist. Johnson, Fries, and Wolf demonstrate the cost that new society exacted from some of its citizens. For that reason alone, their books proved unwelcome.

At least as important as any social critique, however, were the forms in which the authors presented that critique. Johnson had learned from Faulkner and the French *nouveau roman;* Fries had studied Proust and the pre-Realist German writer Jean Paul; Marcel Reich-Ranicki discerned traces of Uwe Johnson, Heinrich Böll, Max Frisch, Günter Grass, and Wolfgang Hildesheimer in Wolf's *The Quest for Christa T.* ("Christa Wolfs" 64). In other words, these writers drew on literary traditions considered anathema by GDR cultural bureaucrats, who had hypostatized German Classicism and bourgeois, nineteenth-century German Realism as timeless models and standards. A novel by Balzac, according to GDR arbiters, still describes a world that is whole, that can be understood, analyzed, and changed. A novel by Kafka, they argued, depicts a fragmented reality, and inculcates in the reader feelings of alienation and pessimism.

Thus for Johnson, Fries, and Wolf the very choice of form is a political act, a "form of protest" against prevailing cultural orthodoxy. Johnson's narrative strategies create and reinforce his theme of the fundamental elusiveness of reality. Fries's narrative techniques—his abrupt shifts and changes of perspective, his untrustworthy storyteller—point in a similar direction. Christa Wolf acknowledges these difficulties of perception and of narration, but unlike Johnson, she refuses to resign herself to the impossibility of knowing. Instead, she takes the very elusiveness of reality and makes it work for her.

Wolf's book hence conveys more optimism than the novels by the skeptical Johnson and Fries. The utopian dimension in her theory of language demonstrates that as well. Wolf's hopefulness may have helped her novel into print, as opposed to the decadence and pessimism (by GDR standards) of Johnson and Fries. The historical moment also aided her: *The Quest for Christa T.* appeared about a decade after Johnson's *Speculations about Jakob,* and even so, it needed an additional four years, a change of government, and a more liberal cultural policy before it could become generally available. Wolf's social criticism remained more discreet and less parodistic than that advanced by Johnson and Fries. Additionally, Wolf had performed long and reliable service for the Party: between 1963 and 1967 she was a candidate for the Central Committee. All these elements helped *The Quest for Christa T.* to press, while *Speculations about Jakob* and *The Road to Oobliadooh* lingered in the obscurity of official nonexistence.

In the more liberal cultural climate of the later 1980s, Jürgen Grambow could publish a plea for a more differentiated understanding of Johnson's work, which he views in connection with books by Bobrowski, Fries, and Wolf ("Heimat" 139). An East German collection of Johnson's stories appeared in 1989. Fries's novel was also published in the GDR in 1989, twenty-three years after its debut in West Germany.

From an East German perspective, the novels by Johnson, Fries, and Wolf contain a feature that ultimately might have helped even Johnson past the censor's desk: the protagonists visit West Berlin or West Germany, and they return to the East. Despite the sometimes vehement criticism these novels direct at the GDR, the protagonists ultimately demonstrate solidarity with their country. Yet even in the later 1980s, as Gorbachev-inspired *glasnost* vanquished Stalinist-inspired socialist-realist chimeras, GDR publishers did not publish *Speculations about Jakob,* a landmark experiment in East German literary history. Until the end, Johnson's investigation into the politics of epistemology remained unwelcome.

NOTES

1. In 1961 Johnson's wife began a liaison with a Czech secret agent, and for approximately fifteen years she supplied East bloc intelligence agencies with information on Johnson's activities in the West (*Der Spiegel*, 6 Jan. 1992).

2. Personal conversation with Fritz Rudolf Fries, Berlin-Friedrichshagen, July 1986.

3

Adjustment to the Quotidian: The Literature of Reform

"I . . . didn't have anything against Communism and all that, the abolition of the exploitation of the world. I wasn't against that. But against everything else."
—Ulrich Plenzdorf, *The New Sufferings of Young W.*

U.S. citizens familiar with former East bloc propaganda might well envision a similar literature, one celebrating parades of heroic workers or glorifying bustling collective farms under a shining noonday sun. Much East German writing, especially the "boy-meets-tractor" variety from the 1950s, helped create such stereotypes. Nonetheless, GDR literature displayed a perhaps surprising diversity and subtlety.

Certainly there existed, at least until 1989, cultural apparatchiks who desired East German writing to resemble the happy picture of government propaganda, and not a few hack writers hustled to do their bidding. But since the birth of the GDR, more discerning authors, including socialists, chafed under the restrictions and prescriptions imposed on them by their government; in the 1950s Bertolt Brecht asserted, "It is not the duty of a Marxist-Leninist party to organize the production of poems like a poultry farm; otherwise the poems will resemble each other just like one egg and another" (qtd. in Flores 64). The best and bravest East German writers pressed relentlessly for more autonomy, and we should view the history of

GDR literature as one of growing emancipation from governmental restraints. Especially in the later 1960s and beyond, writers successfully utilized literary form and language (with the resulting gaps, ambiguities, and paradoxes) to wrest space for the discussion of topics censored in the more straightforward prose of journalism.

I do not wish to underemphasize past restrictions on GDR authors: writers there were too often driven to despair by interior or exterior censors. Nonetheless, many GDR writers received inspiration from their sense of mission. After receiving the U.S. National Medal for the Arts in 1987, Howard Nemerov (who subsequently became poet laureate) commented to the *St. Louis Post Dispatch* on the pleasures of writing poetry in the United States, where "poets are for the most part a harmless impertinence like birds at an airport" (19 June 1987). Precisely that sense of the poet's marginality in the West, the seeming public irrelevance of literature here, disturbed East German writers. For better or worse, they argued, GDR authors were taken seriously.

The Socialist Unity party always expected its writers and artists to help implement its program (and it sometimes understood that role quite narrowly). It wanted them to break fascist or capitalist thought patterns, educate socialist citizens, and facilitate an acceptance of the GDR state. In turn, it rewarded writers with travel and financial privileges. The dangers of sycophancy, opportunism, and complacency were patent, but some GDR writers always found the courage to swerve from the Party line, oftentimes with dramatic results. The five works in this chapter were published during the 1960s and 1970s, in the GDR, by committed socialists. All introduced new elements into East German literature, all pushed limits and challenged restraints. Three of them, *Divided Heaven*, *Ole Bienkopp*, and *The New Sorrows of Young W.*, unleashed far-reaching extraliterary debates that spread from academic journals to newspapers, magazines, factories, and government circles. In a society that censored writers, literature was not just the affair of professional readers, such as professors and critics. Even after the publicity surrounding Salmon Rushdie, it is hard to envision such a debate in the United States.

In the future, such debates will grow increasingly rare in Germany as well. With the collapse in 1989 of the SED dictatorship and its censorship, writers have obtained the freedom to write as they please. So have journalists and historians, two formerly muzzled groups whose work found expression between the lines of GDR poems, plays, and novels. As democratic institutions develop, with an independent press and a vigorous historiography, literary writers will find themselves less exposed but less privileged—and less read. In fact, they may well become more like birds at an airport—a harmless impertinence. However—as the former bomber pilot Nemerov surely knew—such birds can occasionally bring an airplane to crash.

Erwin Strittmatter, *Ole Bienkopp* **GDR 1963, GDR 1966 (Eng. trans.)**

Born in 1912 in Spremberg, Erwin Strittmatter grew up between coal mines and potato fields. His father, a baker, also owned a small farm, and Strittmatter worked it while completing an apprenticeship as a baker. He labored variously as baker's helper, waiter, chauffeur, servant, stable boy, and factory worker. Arrested briefly in 1934 by the Nazis for insubordination, Strittmatter nonetheless went to war when drafted, though he later deserted. After the war, he worked first as a baker. On account of the GDR land reform, he received a farm and did well with it, carrying out successful experiments to increase productivity. Strittmatter meanwhile strived to educate himself. He obtained work as a newspaper correspondent, later becoming an editor. In 1951, after the publication of his first novel, *Oxcart Drivers,* he became a free-lance writer. He has written copiously, publishing several novels, plays, and essays, but his most controversial novel remains undoubtedly *Ole Bienkopp.*

The novel describes the development of Ole Hansen, a forester's son who grows up in a German village called Blumenau. As a youth he builds a beehive in a wagon and wanders with his bees, hence the nickname Bienkopp (Bee-Head). The forester and communist Anton Dürr attempts to convince Bienkopp that happiness cannot be found in isolation. Only after Bienkopp returns from the war and receives, like Strittmatter, a farm due to land reform does he become more receptive to Dürr's program. Bienkopp and Dürr work in Blumenau to restrain the influence of such men as Julian Ramsch, the sawmill owner, and Serno, a farmer with large landholdings. Ramsch maintains contacts with Western agents who promise him assistance on "Day X" (e.g., 17 June 1953), and he will stop at nothing to further his business interests. When Dürr dies in an "accident" staged by

Ramsch, Bienkopp vows to institute Dürr's idea of a "new peasant community"—a collective farm.

Serno and Ramsch endanger Bienkopp's experiment, but ironically the greatest threat derives from Communist party functionaries, notably Mayor Frieda Simson and District Secretary Herbert Wunschgetreu, who accuse Bienkopp of anti-Party activity. Enraged, Bienkopp withdraws from the Party, but soon thereafter, in June 1952, the SED decides to introduce collective farms as national policy, and Bienkopp becomes a hero. By 1958 (and part 2 of the novel), Bienkopp's New Peasant Community has become Flowering Field, with 25 members. Ramsch has left for the West, followed by Ole's wife Annagret, who had become his lover. Serno's influence diminishes as his workers become increasingly assertive of their rights.

Simson, Wunschgetreu, and Wunschgetreu's subordinate, Kraushaar, continue to create bureaucratic difficulties for Bienkopp, who for example cannot obtain an excavator for the plentiful marl he wishes to utilize as inexpensive fertilizer. In addition, the Party wishes to raise meat production, leading Simson and Kraushaar to bring expensive imported cattle to Bienkopp's collective. The Party cannot, however, provide grain or adequate stalls, a contingency that Bienkopp had foreseen, and that had caused him to resist the Party initiative. When some cattle die, Simson and Kraushaar blame Bienkopp and remove him as director of the collective. Bienkopp then makes a frenzied attempt to unearth the marl, alone, with only a shovel. In an effort to compensate for his lapses and intrigues, Wunschgetreu finally brings an excavator to the village, but Bienkopp has died of exhaustion and exposure.

Strittmatter asserted that he wanted to explore in his novel how a socialist society could harness the potential of the creative, if eccentric, individual without allowing that individual to swerve into anarchy (Emmerich 144). Hence the book features a movement between Bienkopp's productive activity within a social community and his isolation. At the beginning that isolation is "regressive"—Bienkopp has no political consciousness—but later his solitude is that of the progressive avant-garde. He proves a pioneer at collective farming, and he correctly predicts problems with stalls and fodder when the Party does not. Strittmatter, who has always insisted that literature constitutes a productive force, clearly intended Bienkopp's clash with the Party bureaucracy, and his ultimate death, as a provocation.

An impatient dreamer and activist, Bienkopp constantly struggles with Party officials more concerned with protecting their comfortable desk jobs than with assisting him in implementing his revolutionary ideas. Bienkopp represents grass-roots socialist-activist democracy (he shocks many when he insists *he* is the Party [176]). His ideas and needs conflict with directives issued by centralized planners who have lost touch with their constituencies.

The second part of Strittmatter's novel takes place after 1956, after Khrushchev's denunciation of Stalin. Although GDR citizens did not know the extent of Stalin's crimes, they had learned something:

> The year nineteen hundred and fifty-six had come and gone. Herbert Wunschgetreu knew now that a good comrade does not carry out directions blindly, but thinks about what he is doing. A comrade who packs away all hesitation, and above all his active understanding, in awe of experienced old Party members, is not necessarily acting in the best interests of the Party.
>
> But insight was one thing and putting it into practice another. (300)

Through his investigation of language, Strittmatter identifies and characterizes those who have abandoned their "active understanding." When a well-meaning city poet reads at Bienkopp's collective, the farmers find his poetry "naïve," "ignorant," "impossible," and "thought-up" (336–37). They invite him to come spend time on the farm, thus anticipating the Bitterfeld Program.

As Fritz Rudolf Fries, Christa Wolf, or Volker Braun do later (and as Uwe Johnson did earlier), Strittmatter interrogates and parodies the stilted bureaucratic officialese that both represents and constitutes the GDR's "revolution." For example, the narrator describes the transformation farmer Bullert undergoes when he speaks as a Party functionary:

> Gone the free, natural, humorous Bullert-talk of village, street and field. In its stead a kind of linguistic stilt-walk . . . .
>
> Those comrades who used to belong to the Church are familiar with this kind of hocus-pocus. Liturgy it's called in the service. Opium for the people. (171)

GDR newspapers functioned as repositories of such language, and the narrator parodies a newspaper editor's "good idea he'd had before." After the Party decides to collectivize, making Bienkopp a famous pioneer, the editor interviews Ole and asks why he had established the New Peasant Community. Bienkopp explains that he had vowed to carry on Anton Dürr's dream after the latter's death, but the "editor balks at this—too opaque for his paper, too mystical, not optimistic enough." He prefers slogans and wants Ole to proclaim that he created his farm for "the good of the community" (218).

The narrator reserves his strongest satire, however, for Frieda Simson, mayor and would-be Party star: "Frieda, Frieda! The dogmatitis is eating her joy in life. Maybe she ought to go to the doctor's and get some new slogans prescribed" (271). Simson hides behind Party jargon, thus avoiding the burden of thought, and she censors the farmer Wilm Holten for attempting to explain the Party classics in his own words: "Where will it end when every ignoramus of a Party member pollutes the words of the classics with his tomfoolery?" (129). The former mayor, Adam Nietnagel, for whom Simson worked as secretary, found that when he dictated to her, his "living words" became "transformed into a stiff, bureaucratic, refrigerator German" (129). Even her acknowledgement of fault consists of clichés, from which the narrator turns with disgust: "We will go too, Comrades. We'll spare ourselves Frieda Simson's stereotyped self-criticism" (215). During World War II Simpson maintained a fascination with the military, especially with military men; she later views Party directives as military orders to be carried out blindly, and her language contains a "tough militant note" (129). Other functionaries, Kraushaar for example, share her dogmatitis. Karl Krüger, who on the contrary remains skeptical of many Party directives and slogans, loses his position.

The narrator actively practices language criticism, italicizing or capitalizing hackneyed words or phrases to alienate them from the text, causing the reader to pause and consider the categories such words represent. Thus, when the "lively wit" of Frieda Simson creates a new slogan, the narrator prints it as a verbal icon, suggesting the omnipresent GDR political banners: "EVERY HAMMER-BLOW FOR THE PLAN IS A NAIL IN THE COFFIN OF THE WAR-MONGERS!!!" The narrator then provides a curt afterword that emphasizes Simson's hyperbole: "Three exclamation marks" (170). With italics he exposes a slogan with which Simson attempts to denounce a popular teacher: "The new teacher is a *social loss* as far as Frieda is concerned" (270). Kraushaar must contend with "the *open-stall campaign* and the *cattle stock increase plan*" (279). The narrator parodies communist bureaucrats who are shocked by Karl Krüger's indifference to jargon, or by his readiness to consult experts, not ideologues: "As if it wasn't enough that Krüger left the question of the *yarovisation* of their grain crops to the decision of the peasants themselves— these experts had got Krüger to the point of grossly underestimating the almost life-and-death question of the *square-nest-potato-planting-procedure!*" (228). Krüger loses his position, but he notes that with time the *"travopolnaya system,* the *Michurin gardens, yarovisation,* and the *square-nest-procedure* all went out of fashion" (228).

The narrator does not restrict his language critique to the Party. He italicizes Ramsch's Americanisms (which Ramsch in turn often mispronounces) to underscore the businessman's ostentatious attempts to appear educated. Ramsch's language also functions as an obvious ideological signpost: Westerners or Western sympathizers speak of the *"Free World"* (364) and the *"iron curtain"* (353), while dismissing the GDR as the *"Zone"* (356). The narrator also alienates Western advertising and consumerism—for example, Ramsch's work with *"Hula-Hoop"* (356). Strittmatter neatly combines his critique of language abuse in East and West (although he never leaves doubt that his sympathies reside firmly with the GDR) as Ramsch rides the subway from East Berlin to West Berlin, a passage still available to East Germans before the building of the Wall. On the walls of one station one sees the exhortation *"First more work, then a better life!"*; the walls of the next station read, *"Give yourself a treat, you've earned it—have a Camel!"* (151).

As opposed to the language of ideologies in East or West, Bienkopp's speech is often laconic, biting, or ironic, though he can attain a biblically tinted lyricism and elegance when defending his programs (175). The narrator, too, constantly looks for fresh expression, and he unmasks frozen thinking by demystifying clichés, employing neologisms, and revitalizing archaic expressions. The GDR scholar Reinhard Hillich rightly sees that not as a mere formal device, but as the linguistic expression of the novel's thematic project, which is to activate readers to consider their socialist environment from a new perspective (102–4). "Change a man and you change his talk," is

Anton Dürr's opinion (129), and that characterizes the narrator's undertaking as well. He invites his readers to assist him—and intimates the utopian quality of Bienkopp's personality, one that present language cannot contain—when he has the good Party man Karl Krüger eulogize the deceased Bienkopp as a person possessing "self-will without self-interest—we've still to find a word for that" (392).

Strittmatter's insistence on the tragic death of his protagonist presented a rupture with GDR literature of that time, literature in which authors often conjured away conflicts and contradictions with the twist of a pen. Other services of *Ole Bienkopp* include its criticism of the Party bureaucracy and its insistence on grass-roots, socialist democracy. In retrospect we can also identify in Strittmatter one of the first authors to concern himself with the environmental issues that today plague the former GDR. He describes, for example, the fashion in which long-term matters of soil conservation and renewal are sacrificed to the Party's desire for immediate results (300–302). Wolfgang Emmerich has characterized GDR literature of the 1960s as a seismograph that registered unrest before it could be discussed at Party meetings or in Party newspapers (143). Strittmatter and his novel contributed to that development.

Emmerich also notes some weaknesses in the novel, and there are more than a few. The symbolism is often obvious, the attempts at humor are not always felicitous, and the satire is sometimes primitive. Emmerich and others, such as Patricia Herminghouse ("Wunschbild" 409–12), point out the stereotypical aspects of the characterizations, especially when the novel sets the "bad" Annagret against the "good" Martke, Ole's young lover. The book unwittingly reveals a good deal regarding the fashion in which a male GDR author writing in the 1960s viewed women in his country. Emma Dürr continues her husband's work for the Party, and Frieda Simson serves as mayor; both they and their society take that for granted. Also taken for granted is the fact that the women will continue to cook, keep house, iron shirts, hang out the wash, darn socks, and mend children's pants. "Equal" rights mean two jobs for women.

Translated into English by the East German Seven Seas Press, Strittmatter's novel was not reviewed in the United States, although an essay on GDR literature in the *Nation* did mention that the book possessed more literary merit than most contemporary East German writing (17 April 1967). In West Germany most critics sniffed at

Strittmatter's stylistic limitations, though in the *Frankfurter Allgemeine Zeitung* Marcel Reich-Ranicki praised the author's "amazing richness of imagination" (15 Feb. 1964; my trans.). Some critics dismissed the book as recycled national-socialist blood-and-earth prose, socialist style, but Wolfgang Emmerich argues that such comments result from ignorance regarding a tradition of socialist village novels (145).

In the GDR, initial negative reviews in *Neues Deutschland* and *Sonntag* were countered by an unexpected and spontaneous wave of support for Strittmatter. The debate, which turned on the question as to whether Strittmatter should have allowed Bienkopp to die, raged for weeks in newspapers, journals, and Party discussions. The more unbending GDR critics decried the death as unnecessary and pessimistic. They also took umbrage at the caricature of the newspaper editor. And they of course bristled at the characterization of some Party functionaries as corrupt, lazy, or stupid, regretting Strittmatter's failure to emphasize that such officials as Kraushaar or Simson were not in the majority. In addition, they remained suspicious of a literature that posed questions instead of presenting answers (Hillich 70–71).

Strittmatter defended himself by asserting that literature should not function as a history book, sociological reference book, or textbook (Hillich 89). Writing in 1984, GDR scholar Reinhard Hillich emphasized the fashion in which Strittmatter's narrator addresses the reader as "Comrade," and he underscores the narrator's important question regarding Frieda Simson: "Is she guilty, Comrades, or are we?" (389). Hillich admits that people like Simson indeed existed, but accepting Strittmatter's argument regarding *Ole Bienkopp* as a poetic construct, a poetic provocation, he can then insist, "In fact, reality was not so" (89; my trans.).

Strittmatter's book is nonhistorical in other ways as well, for the author presents a benign view of GDR land collectivization (1952–60) as a voluntary and salutary process. After World War II, the Soviets and then the new East German government expropriated the large estates of the Junkers and other land holders, redistributing them in smaller parcels to former peasants and to refugees. In 1952, however, the GDR government deemed small farms economically inefficient (in Strittmatter's book, Bienkopp wants collectives because he sees new class antagonisms developing). The government began to encourage farmers to pool their holdings into collective farms, and by 1960 all

East German farms were collectivized. As opposed to the land reform of 1945–51, farm collectivization was not popular, and in the end the government forced it. The British historian David Childs writes:

> Between June 1958 and June 1959 the area of GDR agricultural land belonging to collective farms increased from 29 per cent to 40 per cent. In the following year virtually all the remaining land was collectivised. About 250,000 peasants were forced into collective farms during this period. . . . Cardinal Julius Döpfner, the leading representative of the Catholic church in the GDR between 1957 and 1961, attacked the inhuman methods used to recruit the peasants into the collective farms. (59)

In part due to this, the exodus to West Germany accelerated. In Strittmatter's novel, only a capitalist murderer, an adulterous wife, and a greedy dairy man leave for the West. But in reality 143,000 East Germans left their country in 1959, 194,000 in 1960, and 30,000 in April 1961 alone (Demetz, *Fires* 115). In August 1961 the GDR government erected the Berlin Wall.

Christa Wolf, *Divided Heaven* GDR 1963, GDR 1965 (Eng. trans.)

With the Wall built, the GDR could allow publication and discussion of more controversial books, such as Strittmatter's *Ole Bienkopp* (1963). Christa Wolf's *Divided Heaven*, a book whose subject is the Wall, although that structure is never explicitly mentioned, also appeared in 1963. The widely debated novel represents Wolf's declaration of loyalty to the GDR. Whether it also presents an apologia for the Wall remains an open question.

The protagonist, Rita, is nineteen when she meets Manfred, a Ph.D. candidate in chemistry and ten years her senior. They plan to marry. But two years later, in 1961, Manfred has left for West Berlin, and Rita lies in a sanitorium, recovering from a suicide attempt disguised as a factory accident. Convalescing, she attempts to "read" the events of the past two years.

Inspired by the pedagogy teacher Schwarzenbach, Rita had left her small village in 1959 and moved to a city to train as a teacher. Manfred also studies there, and she takes a room in his parents' house. Before beginning her course of study, Rita had pursued an internship at a factory that manufactures train cars. There she had worked in a crew with Ralph Metternagel, an impressively self-sacrificing worker, and she had met Ralph's former son-in-law, the equally impressive Wendland, manager of the factory.

Despite his love for Rita, Manfred grows increasingly disillusioned with conditions in the GDR. The text advances sociohistorical causes: Manfred had grown up in a loveless, petit-bourgeois family; he had experienced the nihilism of World War II; and his scientific colleagues in general maintained an arrogant and cynical view toward East German society. Manfred leaves for West Berlin, and after he is settled, he asks Rita to join him there. She visits him for a day but returns to the GDR. A week later, on 13 August 1961, the East German government constructs the Wall, irrevocably separating the two lovers, and Rita attempts suicide. As she recovers in the sanitorium for a period of approximately two months, she reflects on her story and begins to give it meaning.

Joan Becker's translation of the novel serves Christa Wolf very poorly. As Charlotte Koerner points out (*"Divided Heaven"*), Becker shortens the book, eliminating motifs and symbols. She edits two pages from chapter 13 of the German text, and combines chapters 13 and 14. The entire English version is narrated in the past tense, whereas Wolf often uses the present, especially when the narrator speaks of "us" to construct a sense of community and identification. Perhaps most troubling is Becker's elimination of Wolf's experiments with narrative perspective. Writing once of the nineteenth-century German author Georg Büchner, Wolf asserted that his experiments with point of view—his unmediated movement from "he" to "I"—cause irritation even today ("Reader" 198). She employs the same method in *Divided Heaven*, irritating Becker to the point where she substitutes instead an omniscient narrator throughout, thus—for American audiences—bringing the novel more into conformity with the formal prescriptions of socialist realism.

Divided Heaven derives in part from the Socialist Unity party's Bitterfeld initiative. (Scholars sometimes place *Ole Bienkopp* in this category as well, although Strittmatter already had had ample farming experience.) In 1960 Christa Wolf had worked for a time in a factory in Halle. Her experiences structure Rita's, who follows Schwarzenbach's advice to work in a factory before becoming a teacher. The novel's language, for the most part simple and at times reproducing workers' slang, results from the Bitterfeld directive, as well as from an attempt to fulfill the socialist-realist demand for popularity and accessibility. Other socialist-realist elements include the positive heroes—Metternagel, Schwarzenbach, and Wendland—and the narrator's partisanship: he or she at one point speaks (in the German version) of the year 1961 as a "difficult test" confronting "us," a test not easy to pass (136).

In important respects, however, Wolf expands the formal possibilities of socialist realism with her narrative technique. The (German) text alternates, often without transition, between the omniscient narrator, who refers to Rita as "she," and the inner monologue of the "I": "And at the place where [the two train cars] will meet, there she is lying. There I am lying" (*Der geteilte Himmel* 12; my trans.). Also innovative—for GDR literature of the time—was Wolf's construction of two temporal planes within her story. Rita's recollections commence in late August 1961; the story begins in the "present," from which she remembers the period between her first meeting with Manfred in summer 1959 and their parting in West Berlin a week before construction of the Wall. In German, both temporal planes are narrated in the present tense. Wolf manipulates these techniques to create, when convenient, an ambiguous and elusive text. As Dieter Sevin points out, she hence renders the censor's work difficult, while also inviting the reader to participate in solving some of the unanswered questions posed by the novel (19).

The novel traces Rita's development from village dweller to city denizen, from girl to woman, from apolitical naïveté to political savvy. If the first of those movements brings her closer to Manfred, the latter two result ultimately in their separation. Following her need for self-fulfillment, for example, Rita decides to become a teacher. It irritates Manfred that she does not consult him regarding her decision, and he feels secretly threatened by her plans. He desires a traditional wife who will subordinate her life to his, and governed by wishful thinking, he predicts the failure of her endeavors in the factory and the academy (19).

Fresh from the country, a female, and ten years younger than Manfred, Rita is at the outset very dependent on her fiancé: "He liked to give her a blouse which suited her, or to show her how she should do her hair, and she accepted all his suggestions without hesitation" (30). Before long, however, she feels, at least in the German text, "equal to him" (*Der geteilte Himmel* 96; my trans.). The decision to become a teacher was one she had made with the assumption that Manfred could have no objection; later, however, she continues to act as she thinks right, even though she suspects Manfred would not approve. She has dinner with Wendland, of whom Manfred is jealous, and she defends the Party official Rudi Schwabe against attacks from Manfred's colleagues, without asking Manfred his opinion (115).

The latter example indicates that for Wolf, Rita's political development has surpassed Manfred's. Rita proceeds from unspoken disagreement with him (96) to open contradiction, as when she supports Wendland against Manfred, whose arguments fill her with "shame and anger" (151). She also defends a classmate whose parents have fled to the West. That intercession threatens her career and brings her to a confrontation with Mangold, an outspoken and dogmatic pedagogy student who intimidates even his teachers.

The differences between Rita and Manfred are representational and epochal. Fascism and war have had a crippling effect on Manfred, who muses: "It's a queer thing, the new generation starts somewhere between us. She can't possibly understand that we were all injected early with this cynicism that's so hard to shake off" (42). Whereas Manfred's cynicism leaves him distrustful and ultimately alone, Rita maintains a more open and hopeful view of the world. Riding in a railroad car to whose construction she has contributed, she feels a sense of purpose, of place, of belonging: "She felt a thrill at being a part of the whole thing" (150). Significantly, during a moment of societal crisis—the building of the Berlin Wall—she, as well as others, is drawn to her factory, though it is Sunday. Manfred, however, feels "out of place and unwanted" (110), and he leaves for the West.

Rita's successful integration into the collective provides her with a sense of security and mission; Manfred's isolation breeds despair. These diametrically opposed experiences inform their weltanschauung. Manfred believes that "history is built up everywhere on individual misery and fear" (136). Rita, speaking with Schwarzenbach of her return to the GDR, smiles at the latter's bombast when he mentions the "attraction of a great historical movement" (192–93). But she, or the narrator using free indirect speech, admits that she may have entertained similar feelings in West Berlin.

Rita's decision to leave Manfred and return to East Germany is, whether or not consciously reasoned, a political one, and for it to be meaningful, for her sacrifice to have sense, she must believe that she returns to a society with history on its side. Hence the book defines her choice of ideologies as one between good and evil. The novel implies that life in the West is materialistic, pleasant, and empty; in the East, life is "harder, sterner" (192), but it is more moral, more "noble" (191), because GDR society is actively engaged in an experiment to root out evil from the world (191). Manfred does not believe this possible, and Rita does, though doubts at times unsettle her:

> "I sometimes wonder whether we ought really to judge the world by our standards—of good and evil, I mean," Rita went on. "Shouldn't we just take it as it is?"
>
> But if that were really true, she thought, it would have been silly not to have stayed with Manfred; any sacrifice would be silly. (196)

Despite her doubt, or perhaps on account of it, Rita reestablishes her belief in the superior morality, the superior purpose of the East. When she moves to Manfred's city in 1959, she is puzzled by the numerous impressions she receives, and she lacks "the clue which would link up these fragments into a complete play" (30). Speaking of his own life, Wendland suggests, "Perhaps it's impossible to see the logic of things from above or below, but only later on, looking back" (105). When the Soviets send the first cosmonaut into orbit, Rita finds in that event, at least in the German text, precisely that ex post facto justification that renders meaningful her endeavors, struggles, and sacrifices: "Everything that had occurred up to now received its meaning through that" (*Der geteilte Himmel* 227; my trans.). Looking back on her story from the sanitorium, Rita begins to make sense of it. In her political maturity, she assembles the fragments of her life into a complete play.

Committed to the "better Germany," Rita works to reform it. As in *Ole Bienkopp*, the text presents a struggle between those who are communists in spirit and those communists—such as Mangold—who, through their unimaginative orthodoxy, destroy that spirit. In a daring analogy, Wolf equates the dogmatists with bourgeois enemies, such as Manfred's mother: "Rita wondered why she had never noticed how much alike Mangold and Frau Herrfurth were; was it possible for people to fight for quite opposite things in the same narrow-minded, selfish, nagging way?" (125). The novel stresses the parallels in other ways as well: Schwarzenbach notes that Mangold speaks of the Party line like Catholics of the Immaculate Conception (132); and Frau Herrfurth receives her "inspiration" (a more accurate translation of the German *Evangelium* would be "gospel") from Western radio broadcasts (155). Manfred leaves the GDR because of bureaucratic interference in his scientific project and because he receives a promising position in the Federal Republic, but his alienation begins earlier. He tells Rita that he too once possessed youthful idealism and reformist zeal. After he had made a speech condemning Party abuses, however, a "friend" denounced him in a newspaper article that characterized his talk as the bourgeois errors of an isolated intellectual (133–34). The denunciation becomes a self-fulfilling prophecy.

In the 1960s, the text notes, GDR newspapers printed the very things for which Manfred was attacked in the 1950s. By analogy, Khrushchev publicly criticized Stalin in 1961. Christa Wolf's novel condemns those who, like Manfred's "friend," self-righteously refuse to entertain necessary criticism, but it also judges harshly those who, like Manfred, lack the courage (and the political acumen) to persevere. Thus Rita, when threatened by the dogmatic Mangold, has confidence that, over time, he cannot prevail (131). Schwarzenbach, a fellow reformer, provides Rita timely assistance against Mangold, and Rita in turn inspires Schwarzenbach at the conclusion of the text, when his confidence flags (196–97). Manfred's idea for a spinning jenny is blocked by bureaucratic intrigues (perhaps directed by the West), but later we learn that the Party may develop it (137). Martin, who defends his friend Manfred, is expelled from the university, but "only" for eight months. Similarly, Christa Wolf proved one of the few writers to defend beleaguered colleagues from a particularly philistine Party attack in 1965. As a result, she lost her candidacy for the SED Central Committee.

Courage, solidarity, perseverance—these are the qualities demanded of a GDR reformer in the struggle against the dogmatists, and these are precisely the qualities Manfred lacks. In *Divided Heaven*'s most explicit apologia for the Wall, Martin—a positive character—regrets:

There's a commission looking over our works just now. They're asking about our machine. Couldn't Manfred have held out just these eight months? That's what bothers me most of all. If only he had hung on, *even if we'd had to keep him here by force* [my emphasis]. If he were here now he would simply have to face up to things. (137)

The U.S. scholar Anna Kuhn notes that Wolf's "mentor figures, imbued with her own ideals about socialism, believe they have access to truth and come perilously close to imposing their views on others for their own good" (35). Martin clearly advocates such methods in the passage above.

Implicitly or explicitly, *Divided Heaven* argues for the Wall as a response to the Western threat. The West lures the trained and talented technical elite, represented by Manfred, as well as precious labor and management, such as the director of Metternagel's factory (51). Martin holds the West responsible for blocking development of Manfred's invention and for cutting off production materials to the factory in which Rita works (173). The narrator wonders when Western radio will move from promises to threats (155). There is talk of war (169), and the narrator uses the weather and the sky as metaphors for political conditions. The atmospheric tension of the prologue finally disappears in the epilogue, after construction of the Wall. By building the Wall, then, the GDR blocks Western aggression, removes the threat of war, and applies a tourniquet to its bleeding economy.

Nonetheless, the novel evidences a certain ambiguity regarding the divided Germany. Before the Wall is built, Rita visits Manfred in West Berlin and is unsure whether she will return to the GDR (169). While with Manfred, she asks herself: "Why must she be forced to make this choice? She would lose a part of herself whatever she decided" (190; a more precise translation would begin, "Who in the world had the right to place a person, even a single one, before such a choice?"). To be sure, Rita still possesses a choice in early August 1961, and she chooses her country. Dieter Sevin argues that her decision at that point remains tentative, if only because she can still return to West Berlin (51–52). On 13 August, however, she cannot, and soon she attempts suicide. In late August 1961, as she recovers from a nervous collapse, she speaks with Schwarzenbach about her feelings then and now:

"You know, a year ago I would have gone with Manfred anywhere he wanted. But now . . . ."
That was what Schwarzenbach had been waiting for.
"And now?" he asked.
"The Sunday after I'd been to see Manfred was August 13th," she said after a long pause [a better translation: " . . . she said, without directly answering Schwarzenbach's question"]. (192)

Readers in East and West are as interested in Rita's answer as is Schwarzenbach, but she responds only that the Wall has rendered moot such choices.

Beyond its discussions of flight to the West and sealed borders, Wolf's novel discreetly touches other controversial topics. Although the narrative attributes some production problems to Western sabotage, it also recognizes systemic deficiencies (51–52). Additionally, when Rita returns to her village, she sees the results of the recent collectivization: "Rita could feel [the farmers'] anxiety, their fear of losing something, and their still vague hopes that they might gain something from the changes which cooperative farming was bringing to their lives" (128). The story mentions the Twenty-first Party Congress of the Soviet Union, during which Khrushchev publicized some of his anti-Stalinist accusations from 1956. Manfred writes his friend Martin, "I know one must deceive oneself about many things for a long time (you must, if you want to go on living), but it's hardly possible that you don't feel some horror at what human nature is capable of after what came out at the last Moscow Party Congress" (136). The indirect fashion in which Wolf broaches the subject of Stalinism—and from the point of view of Manfred, a negative figure living in West Berlin—indicates its explosive and semitaboo quality.

Textual silences betray other taboos. In Erwin Strittmatter's *Ole Bienkopp*, only negative characters, such as an adulterous wife or a conniving capitalist, fled West. Wolf's novel, though less stereotyped, evinces a similar structure. Manfred's worldview turns increasingly cynical and politically incorrect before he leaves; his mother, a bitter, bourgeois, hysterical woman, one irrevocably opposed to the GDR, wishes to follow. An authoritarian father takes his family West, abandoning one daughter (122). A factory director who desires to evade his responsibilities leaves for the West and then works for the enemy by sending seditious broadcasts (51). A man suspected of working as a spy also flees West (137). Martin asserts that all who leave feel a sense of shame and try to justify their decision, "because they know in their hearts that it wasn't right" (136).

In retrospect Christa Wolf would see that her optimism regarding the prospects for reform had been misplaced. In 1989 she published a letter in the GDR *Wochenpost* (no. 43) in which she noted with dismay but not surprise the fact that GDR schools had never taught or encouraged independent thought. Hundreds of citizens answered her letter. Reading their often emotional responses, one sees that the Mangolds had defeated the Schwarzenbachs, and that Manfred's bitter sense of betrayal was shared by many (Gruner, *Angepaßt*).

Despite all it did not, could not, or would not say, *Divided Heaven* ignited a lively discussion in the GDR, and in 1965 the Mitteldeutscher Verlag published a separate volume of selected reviews, primarily from the GDR. The East German critics in that volume generally attempted to view the novel in a positive light, although from their socialist-realist standpoint, they noted its defects: it discusses the division of Germany more from a subjective rather than political perspective; it allows a negative hero, Manfred, too much space and does not contradict him firmly enough; and it does not illustrate clearly enough the tenet that only in socialism can one achieve personal happiness. However, in one of the most positive GDR reviews, Günther Dahlke argued that Rita knows her longing for love, and for a unified Germany, becomes unfruitful if she must pay too high a price; if she were to stay with Manfred in West Berlin, she would have to deny part of herself as well as her country. Dahlke suggests that the reader can reach those or similar conclusions (Sevin 58–60).

Such arguments as Dahlke's overcame a not inconsiderable number of political reservations, and the German Academy of Arts accorded Wolf the most prestigious literary award of the GDR, the Heinrich Mann Prize. Dieter Sevin believes Wolf received the award at least in part due to the considerable interest her novel stirred in West Germany, where some critics labeled it the beginning of a discrete GDR literature (60–61). Writing for the *New York Times Book*

Review, a West German critic in fact asserted that there was no "female novelist of her generation . . . of equal literary standing in Western Germany" (12 Sept. 1965).

Nonetheless, the English translation was not well received. David Caute wrote in the *Nation* that, although "*Divided Heaven* is only mildly didactic, it never travels far from a familiar formula," and he asserted that "Christa Wolf is not a writer who penetrates deeply." Reading Becker's translation, which, as we have noted, destroys Wolf's formal experimentation, Caute is "struck by the fatigued traditionalism of style and structure which stands between so much Socialist literature and real artistic achievement." He did note that Western novelists have

> always found it easy to ignore work, particularly proletarian work. . . . It is therefore hardly surprising that in the modern Socialist novel the intrusion of this theme appears gratuitous and false. Even so, the effort is rewarding. (13 Feb. 1967)

As Christa Wolf's reputation grew, the translation was reissued, and it has had four printings. The American version carries an introduction by Jack Zipes, who argues that the positive heroes "project themselves on the course of history, and in that they do this to eliminate exploitation and oppression, they endow their acts with a moral quality" (xxxvi).

Günter de Bruyn, *Buridan's Ass* GDR 1968, GDR 1973 (Eng. trans.)

Born in 1926, Günter de Bruyn became a flak helper in 1943 and then a soldier. After a period as a prisoner of war, he worked as a farmer in what would become West Germany. In 1946 he moved to Berlin and, after a brief period of training, served as a teacher for a village in the Soviet Zone of Occupation. Between 1949 and 1953 he studied to be a librarian, and he worked in that capacity until 1961, when he started his career as a free-lance writer. In 1963 he published *The Gorge,* a lengthy novel of development describing the awakening to communism of a misled German youth who, like de Bruyn, becomes a teacher after the war. Although the Academy of Arts awarded de Bruyn the Heinrich Mann Prize in 1964, *The Gorge* is an unwieldy work with a lumbering gait and numerous stylistic infelicities. De Bruyn himself has since repudiated it for its rigid schematism.

In *Buridan's Ass* de Bruyn finds his style, which becomes light, elegant, and ironic. If *The Gorge* is a novel of development, *Buridan's Ass* describes the lack of it in its protagonist. Forty-year-old Karl Erp, director of an East Berlin library, falls in love with the student librarian Fräulein Broder (we never learn her first name) and arranges for her permanent employment on his staff. She at first resists his advances, but they then begin an affair. Erp leaves his wife, Elisabeth, and two children in their comfortable suburban villa and moves into a dilapidated, nineteenth-century, inner-city tenement, in which he shares Broder's room. Like Buridan's ass, which in a medieval fable cannot choose between two hay bundles and hence starves to death, Karl cannot decide on a divorce.

For reasons of workplace morale, either Erp or Broder must leave the library. Broder sacrifices her promising Berlin position for one in the country, hoping Erp will follow (his youthful dream was to do revolutionary cultural work in the countryside). Erp meanwhile has been offered a ministerial post, thus making it possible for both him and Broder to remain in Berlin. He does not tell her that, however, and when she has left for the countryside, he returns to his wife, who is not delighted.

The East German scholar Karin Hirdina rightly noted that *Buridan's Ass* introduces several themes into GDR literature, themes that gained importance in the 1970s: the unheroic quotidian, the ossification of engagement into comfortable accommodation, and the investigation into socially differentiated life-styles—one lives differently in a nineteenth-century tenement than in a single-family suburban home. De Bruyn also examines the mid-life crisis of men between forty and fifty, and the changing relations between the sexes (32).

Indeed, Günter de Bruyn was one of the first GDR authors, male or female, to take seriously the discrepancy between patriarchal reality and East Germany's legal commitment to gender equality. Karl and Elisabeth maintain a traditional marriage, and Karl, exercising the right that men have long reserved for themselves, takes a younger mistress. Neither Elisabeth nor Fräulein Broder satisfies him fully, and in his fantasy he combines the two: "Fräulein Broder's voice naturally, but in this wishful dream she would have much of Elisabeth in her: reserve, lack of ambition, adaptability, or put more crudely: readiness to serve" (218). When Elisabeth troubles Erp, he thinks that "she lived at his expense, and not badly. He did not reproach her for it (at least not aloud), but she could really think of it for herself once in a while" (149). In the nineteenth century, Karl Marx and Friedrich Engels discussed the economic basis of bourgeois marriage, but remnants of that basis clearly lingered in twentieth-century GDR socialism. As de Bruyn pointed out in an interview, however, it does matter that the story takes place in the GDR, where no one starved and all had work—where the woman did not need to be financially dependent on the man (Plavius 12).

As a contrast to Karl's marriage and to his fantasies of subordinate women, de Bruyn describes the marriage of Fred and Ella Mantek (Fred Mantek, Karl's mentor, friend, and professional predecessor, works in the Ministry of Culture and functions as one of the positive heroes who surround de Bruyn's antihero): "Community without dependence; the co-existence of two sovereign personalities without a power struggle, a pleasant balance of forces; two centres with circles that overlapped without complication; two suns in one sky; two trees intertwined that steal no light one from the other and which grow together tall and strong" (163–64). Fräulein Broder desires that arrangement for herself, and she adopts Ella Mantek as a role model. Both Manteks have their own work and their own lives. They practice what Baumgärtner, a bestselling author in the story, disdainfully labels "married democracy" (164). Baumgärtner believes that "from a wife one must demand uncritical admiration, a talent for home-making, and, if possible, a knowledge of typing" (164).

Buridan's Ass can and should be read as an early work in the literature contributing to the GDR women's movement, a movement that attained prominence in the next decade. De Bruyn himself described the novel as one in which two women find their way, leaving a man behind (Reso 757). Erp functions as catalyst, causing Broder to refine her values and act on them, while Elisabeth rediscovers a sense of self, finding work and independence. At the novel's conclusion Karl wishes to return to his former life, but that is no longer possible, and it is unclear how, or even if, his marriage will continue to function.

GDR critics accorded the book a warm welcome. They enjoyed the style, sometimes comparing it with that of the nineteenth-century Realist author Theodor Fontane, and they noted the emphasis on the quotidian and on the antihero. In a literature that had until then stressed the positive hero functioning in a social role, de Bruyn's Erp presented a new character. Beyond that, the book appeared, at least on the surface, to present little that was threatening to GDR cultural politicians. The narrator mentions the Berlin Wall on numerous occasions, but Erp also makes the requisite statement that it forms the dividing line between two epochs (98). America's bombing of Vietnam finds (rather forced) mention (132). The positive heroes, Mantek and the librarian Hassler, are both certified antifascists, and they do their best to help and advise Erp. In fact, society as a whole appears remarkably accommodating. With an ironic gesture toward the king's messenger who brings a last-minute reprieve in dramas (225–26), de Bruyn has Hassler find a potential solution that allows both lovers to remain in Berlin—a promotion to a ministerial position for Karl.

Hence, although some Western literary critics viewed the treatment of a love triangle as a retreat into the private, and thus, within a GDR cultural framework, as a message of political protest, de Bruyn always emphasized the *social* aspects of his novel, and GDR critics followed his lead. The lack of societal opposition may, according to de Bruyn's novel, prevent great and tragic love affairs of the Romeo and Juliet variety; however, it leaves space for individual development and responsibility. De Bruyn's narrator muses:

> If it is true that greatness arises from opposition, then our understanding society would be no soil for great romances. Possibly. But that speaks for society. (214)

De Bruyn's novel proved popular—and unthreatening—enough to be filmed in the GDR, and Ulrich Plenzdorf adapted it for the stage.

U.S. reviewers ignored de Bruyn's novel, which was printed by the Seven Seas Press. West Germans praised the author's style, but they also emphasized Erp's political cynicism and hypocrisy. Wolfgang Emmerich wrote that de Bruyn used the hackneyed love triangle to unmask the lies and methods of accommodation widespread in GDR society (154). Fritz Raddatz saw novelty in the depiction of moral baseness and political opportunism not as criminal outsider situations but as a "natural," routine part of the quotidian (*Traditionen* 346). These are valid observations, and I would suggest further that the "good society" of this novel, the benevolence of which de Bruyn and GDR critics underscored, appears rather too benevolent; it has something artificial, something of a fairy tale about it. The positive heroes—the wise Mantek, the salty Hassler—are stock characters in GDR fiction; they are clichés. Clichéd, too, is the deus ex machina at the conclusion, when Hassler, representing society, functions as *der reitende Bote*, "the mounted messenger," to bring a solution. It is as if de Bruyn were admonishing us not to take these conventions overly seriously, and telling us that we should concentrate instead on the most interesting character in the novel, the antihero Erp.

In this novel, de Bruyn makes several references to Adalbert Chamisso, the nineteenth-century German author whose Peter Schlemihl sells his shadow to the devil in exchange for riches: Erp is a GDR Schlemihl. Before she falls in love with Erp, Fräulein Broder perceives him as a "sated prosperity-communist who had a home and a car and now wanted to add a mistress" (130). Erp lives smugly in his villalike house and garden (inherited from his capitalist father-in-law who lives in West Berlin) and takes special pride in his car. Even in the 1980s an East German often had to wait twelve years to obtain an automobile, and in the 1960s, the time of de Bruyn's story, a car represented a striking status symbol. It is Karl's "biggest treasure" (151). Not surprisingly, the more idealistic Broder finds it superfluous (160). De Bruyn brings together Karl's bourgeois values with the Chamisso theme as the lovers make an outing to the small town of Nennhausen. Broder remarks to Erp:

"Nennhausen was the place where Chamisso had the idea for his Schlemihl." . . . [Broder continues:] "Would you sell your shadow?" — "Never." — "Not even if it meant that you had to sell the car?" — "There! Did you see, a deer. It could have been nasty." — "When you're driving you have another face, a strange one." —"A concentrated one." —"A snobbish and power-hungry one." (187–88)

Erp elsewhere mouths ideological slogans that for him have long become empty, and he feels threatened when Broder takes him seriously (160–61). Similarly, he provokes an ideological fight with his Western in-laws primarily as an excuse to leave his home and visit his mistress (134–35). In his short story "Approximation" (1977), Hans Joachim Schädlich also examines the theme of politics as a cover for self-interest, but Schädlich, a dissident author writing in the mid-1970s, presses his theme further than does de Bruyn, a reformist author in the late 1960s. It is nonetheless telling that de Bruyn rewards his antihero with a promotion to a government post.

Our evaluation of the social-critical dimension inherent in de Bruyn's novel will hinge ultimately on our estimation of Erp's typicality, and here the novel leaves the question tantalizingly open. Writing in *Sinn und Form*, Martin Reso admits that Erp possesses a certain representational function, especially regarding an existing tendency toward "bourgeois philistinism" (*Verspießerungstendenz;* 760), and it is intriguing to posit Erp's development as synonymous with that of the GDR, as a metaphor for his society. Fräulein Broder terms Karl's situation "revolutionary: he had broken with the old conditions and what was needed now (against resistance, without experience) was to create new ones" (169). Erp's new liaison would enable him to fulfill his "dream of living and working in the countryside, where the revolution in culture really had something revolutionary" (160), but the novel exposes the dream as armchair philosophizing, the empty rhetoric of a complacent forty-year-old man. Karl's father remembers that even his son's adolescent "revolt" contained "more accommodation than rebellion" (198). This phrase suits the GDR as well, which never made its own revolution, but rather adopted the imported one of an occupying force. Karl's father, and I suspect this applies to de Bruyn himself, remains suspicious of a revolution made by men like Karl, who moved effortlessly from the Hitler Youth to the blue shirts of the GDR Free German Youth (199).

After the governmental change in 1971, de Bruyn could publish his more critical *Presentation of a Prize* (1972), which describes the quandary of a GDR Germanist who must honor the worthless production of a once promising writer whom he himself has helped co-opt. In 1975 de Bruyn published a biography of the late eighteenth- and early nineteenth-century German novelist Jean Paul Friedrich Richter; his comments on censorship and state interference were widely read as being directed toward the situation of writers in the GDR as well. Both these books from the 1970s are more honest regarding censorship than is *Buridan's Ass*, which though written about librarians by a man trained as one, only speaks of banned books with regard to the Nazis.

In 1978 de Bruyn boycotted the Eighth GDR Writers' Congress

because several critical writers (e.g., Christa Wolf and Stefan Heym) were not invited. In West Germany in 1984 he published *New Splendor*, a novel detailing the exploits of a GDR official's vapid son. Like *Buridan's Ass*, it deals with connections, privilege, and corruption, but the tone is angry, and the irony by turns bitter and savage. The novel provoked considerable controversy with its devastating attack on the treatment of the elderly in the GDR, and despite the fact that de Bruyn had become a prominent GDR writer with an international reputation, East German publishers delayed the release of the book for a year. De Bruyn's prominence did provide a degree of protection and privilege; if *New Splendor* had been written by an unknown author, it most probably would not have appeared in the GDR. With that caveat, one can compare *Buridan's Ass* with *New Splendor* to gauge the increased readiness both of de Bruyn to criticize and of his society to accept that criticism. At the Tenth GDR Writers' Congress in 1987, de Bruyn attacked East German censorship practices. Although the Party newspapers suppressed de Bruyn's speech, the journal of the GDR Writers' Association published it in 1988, thus demonstrating once again the tension between the Party and the critical intelligentsia.

Ulrich Plenzdorf, *The New Sorrows of Young W.*
GDR 1972, USA 1979

When *Sinn und Form* published Ulrich Plenzdorf's *The New Sorrows of Young W.* in 1972, it presented its readers an enormously important cultural document. In its incarnation as theater piece, *The New Sorrows of Young W.* proved a sensational success in the GDR, at one point playing simultaneously to sellout crowds in two East Berlin theaters. Featuring a disaffected GDR teenager who drops out of society, the play sparked a vigorous debate pro and contra, which soon included the highest echelons of East German government. As literary text, it provokes all the thorny questions of reading involving GDR literature: Is it "good" art, and why? Can it only be appreciated in the West by adopting the perspective of a reader/viewer in the East? Are the text's numerous deferences to East German authorities the result of compromise or commitment? Is its triumph (and, by some, condemnation) in the East due to the fact that readers disregarded Plenzdorf's disclaimers, reading between the lines?

Born in a working-class section of Berlin in 1934, Plenzdorf grew up in a communist family during the Third Reich. He finished his *Abitur* and proceeded to Leipzig to study Marxism-Leninism in 1954, but after one year he left the institute to work as a stagehand in the East German Deutsche Film AG (DEFA) film studio. After a period in the army, in which he voluntarily enlisted, he studied film and began to support himself writing filmscripts (among them an adaptation of Günter de Bruyn's *Buridan's Ass*). Already his second script, *Karla*, in which he begins to probe the contradictions between propaganda and reality in a GDR school milieu, proved controversial, and the authorities suppressed it.

Plenzdorf wrote the original version of *The New Sorrows of Young W.* in 1968–69, but as he noted during a discussion in 1973, he composed the piece for his desk drawer.[1] He added that due to "outside pressure" (read "censors"), he had not been able to work entirely as he had wished for many years; additionally, publishers rejected *The New Sorrows* several times (Weimann 178; my trans.). After the change in government, however, a revised version appeared in *Sinn und Form* (1972). Plenzdorf adapted it for the stage, and the work received its premier the same year in Halle. In 1973 the author published a further revised version, a so-called novel, which provided the basis for the English translation. Translated into fifteen languages, *The New Sorrows of Young W.* has become synonymous with the GDR cultural thaw between 1971 and 1976.

In Plenzdorf's story, young apprentice Edgar Wibeau tires of his life as model student and flees his provincial town for Berlin, where he lives in a dilapidated summer cottage. He spends his time listening to tapes of rock-and-roll music, lounging, attending rock concerts, musing about his two favorite books—*The Catcher in the Rye* and *Robinson Crusoe*—and reading *The Sorrows of Young Werther*, a book published in 1774 by Goethe. Edgar knows neither title nor author, for he has used the cover, title page, and afterword as toilet paper. After initial difficulties with Goethe's eighteenth-century style and language, Edgar grows increasingly fond of the tale, parts of which he commits to memory.

Goethe constructs his story around letters that the painter Werther writes his friend Wilhelm. Werther has fallen in love with Charlotte, who is, however, engaged. In an attempt to flee his passion, Werther leaves and takes a government position, where he is humiliated due to his bourgeois background. He returns to Charlotte's vicinity and, lapsing into deep despair, ultimately commits suicide.

Edgar identifies ever more closely with Werther; in a sense, Werther's story becomes Wibeau's. Edgar falls in love with a kindergarten teacher whom he calls Charlie. He attempts to reenter society by working with a painting crew, but his unconventional ways endear him to no one, and he is fired. Though Charlie marries a rather staid fellow named Dieter, Edgar manages to consummate his passion with her (the text implies a rape); after this, she rejects him. Edgar tries to trump the painting crew by constructing an electrically powered spray-paint machine—the crew had previously attempted to invent such a machine but had failed. Edgar fails too, for he accidentally electrocutes himself, and he narrates his story from the "Great Beyond."

Plenzdorf noted that he wrote the text "expressly for interpretation" (Weimann 178; my trans.); journalists and scholars from East and West hurried to supply theirs. In the East the reception proved on the whole favorable, and the Academy of Arts and Sciences awarded Plenzdorf its Heinrich Mann Prize in 1973. In general, GDR literary critics agreed that Plenzdorf's piece met Erich Honecker's recently formulated guideline allowing artistic experimentation providing the author proceeded from the standpoint of socialism, and that it offered a socialist contribution in the form of a challenge to integrate youths like Wibeau into GDR society.

Nonetheless, the text made some GDR literary arbiters nervous. For Friedrich Plate, Wibeau's conflict with society remained unmotivated and unexplained (227–28). (Recall that Erp, in *Buridan's Ass,* had no overt conflict with society.) Plate, upset by attempts in the West to read Plenzdorf's text as an oppositional one, quoted August Bebel: "When your enemy praises you, consider what mistake you made" (Plate 224; my trans.). The text's open conclusion—is Wibeau's death an accident or, as with Goethe's *Werther,* suicide?—especially disturbs Plate, who would have preferred more clarity. He finds that the reader must work rather hard to supply the socialist standpoint the author neglected to include. Hopefully, Plate added, Plenzdorf did not omit it purposefully (228).

In the West literary critics searched for an oppositional text or subtext. Fritz Raddatz emphasized the Goethe quotations Plenzdorf inserts into the text, for example, "I return into myself and find a world," or the twice-repeated attack on dehumanizing work. The shock effect for GDR readers, Raddatz asserted, results from a confrontation with a text about alienation, which, theoretically at least, should not exist in their country ("Flucht" 37). Marcel Reich-Ranicki wrote that the book could be read as an "apolitical" youthful revolt, but in a GDR context, where the state attempted to regulate and observe the private life of individuals, any criticism aimed at the world of adults must take on an eminently political character ("Fänger" 226). Similarly, Wolfgang Werth claimed that GDR readers felt "shocked" or "liberated" because they could read between the lines (284).

Other reviewers noted the fashion in which Plenzdorf diluted his criticism, and Wolfram Schütte characterized the mentality of the piece as "petit-bourgeois" (278). Such objections did not take into account the particular conditions under which GDR artists produced. Additionally, Western critics often overlooked the fashion in which form and language can also function as protest. In its intertextuality, its irreverent dialogue with Goethe's *Werther*, Plenzdorf's book comments on GDR cultural policies. The work must be read within the context of East German respect for the German Classicism of late eighteenth- and early nineteenth-century Weimar; East German cultural popes always asserted that the GDR, and not the Federal Republic, inherited and continued that heritage. Some GDR critics felt Plenzdorf's handling of Goethe to be parodistic and provocative: a prominent lawyer pronounced himself "disgusted" by the equation of Werther and Wibeau (Mews 51).

Conservative GDR readers also protested against Wibeau's ebullient discourse, modeled on Holden Caufield's youthful slang and labeled "sewer language" by one reader (Mews 50). Wolfgang Emmerich correctly observes that the numerous linguistic levels—Goethe's language, the slang of working-class youths, the polite language of adults, and the newspaper propaganda—serve to break apart the one-dimensionality of reality. Emmerich asserts that it is especially the "jeans-language" that questions the frozen, uncreative language of the political quotidian. It is the language of youthful comrades, not that of those over twenty-five who have accommodated themselves. As such, Emmerich asserts, it functions as protest (181).

Wibeau's slang contains numerous Americanisms. As he waits for a jeans sale, he speaks of his "Bluejeans Song," notes that he feels "high," and characterizes the whole affair as a "happening" (59). This "linguistic imperialism" parallels Wibeau's general fascination with Western music, dress, and literature. His cultlike celebration of those things, his programmatic declaration that "jeans are an attitude and not just pants" (14) made GDR cultural functionaries nervous. The East German editor Werner Neubert complained that Wibeau had received more, intellectually, from "them" than from "us" ("Niete" 218). In the 1950s and 1960s there had been periodic attempts to prohibit "decadent" American jazz, blues, and rock music, to reintroduce folk dancing (de Bruyn mentions that in *Buridan's Ass*), and to discourage other manifestations of Western popular culture, such as blue jeans. In the later 1960s, prohibition, a hopeless task, yielded to *Abgrenzung* (demarcation): the SED urged GDR citizens to limit their contact with Westerners and with Western influences, such as West German television broadcasts. In Reiner Kunze's dissident *The Wonderful Years* (FRG 1976), such chapters as "Wine," "Schoolmates," and "Pardon" ridicule these policies, and Plenzdorf's text (a spiritual descendent of Fritz Rudolf Fries's *The Road to Oobliadooh*) clearly attacks them as well.

Plenzdorf's work also criticizes the constrictive prescriptions of socialist realism. In a subtle reference to the socialist-realist demand for "useful" art, Wibeau remarks: "A pair of pliers is good if it grabs. But a picture or something like that? Nobody really knows whether it's good or not" (24). Dieter, for Edgar a negative figure, parrots another tenet of socialist-realist art—that it be for workers and about them—when he recommends that Edgar abandon his abstract painting and orient himself more "toward real life, . . . toward the life of the construction worker, for example" (41).

Plenzdorf's most sustained and obvious attack on socialist realism comes with the description of a didactic entertainment film Wibeau must watch in school. The film depicts the story of a young man who is at first a criminal and politically suspect, but whom GDR society ultimately integrates as a useful citizen. Edgar does his own deconstructionist viewing, identifying not with the protagonist but with the protagonist's brother, who refuses to accommodate himself and joins a circus to "see the world" (22; in an indirect reference to the Wall, Edgar insists that everyone wants to see the world, and that whoever denied it was lying). Siegfried Mews and others correctly interpret the scene as a polemic against *Ankunftsliteratur* or "Literature of Arrival," a GDR genre taking its name from Brigitte Reimann's short novel *Arrival in the Quotidian* (1961), which describes the difficulties three high school students encounter attempting to reconcile their ideals and illusions with the GDR reality. As with the film described in Plenzdorf's book, Reimann's young people successfully integrate themselves into their society. The film has some similarity with Plenzdorf's earlier work, and Siegfried Mews sees a Plenzdorf self-portrait in the filmmaker of the *New Sorrows* (45). Wibeau tells the filmmaker that he finds the film didactic, boring, and useless. The filmmaker admits he had suspected that was true, but that "it had to be that way" (22; a more explicit translation: "otherwise it would not have been possible").

With the very important exception of Wibeau's death at the conclusion, however, Plenzdorf, like de Bruyn, tends to place his criticism within an affirmative framework. Although the form of Plenzdorf's work parodies Goethe and hence the GDR cultural politicians whose Goethe is museal and forbidding, Wibeau does defer to the GDR respect for German Classicism, specifically terming Goethe and Schiller "worthwhile people" (48).

Similarly, although Wibeau polemicizes against socialist realism, his own narrative contains nonironical, prescriptive elements of that mode in the figure of Zaremba, the heroic worker who acts as a counterweight to Wibeau, and who attempts to integrate him into the collective (curiously, GDR critics often complained of the absence of such a counterweight). Zaremba is an excellent worker and a convinced communist (his chest is covered with tatoos of communist icons to prove it) who fought in the Spanish civil war. Wibeau is additionally impressed that Zaremba, although older than seventy, remains sexually active (50), and Edgar accords Zaremba the greatest honor by asserting that jeans would become him (14).

Wibeau attacks the Stalinist practice of public self-criticism, finding it degrading. But addressing us from the "Great Beyond," he spends much of the book practicing self-criticism, and he blames only himself for what occurred (Wibeau is a first-person narrator presenting his subjective point of view, which we are not necessarily obliged to accept at face value).

Wibeau's fascination for the West sends a subversive signal, but Plenzdorf limits that as well. Wibeau asserts that when he sees pictures of Vietnam he forgets his pacifist leanings and feels ready to become a soldier for life (42). For all of Wibeau's criticism of the GDR, Plenzdorf wants it clear that the criticism is coming from the left, and Wibeau presents an unambiguous ideological confession:

I didn't have anything against Lenin and the others. I also didn't have anything against Communism and all that, the abolition of the exploitation of the world. I wasn't against that. But against everything else. (44)

This passage is not, I suspect, a red herring designed to move Plenzdorf's text past the censor's desk but a statement of the author's own credo—Plenzdorf calls himself "red to the bone" (qtd. in Brenner, "Einleitung" 40; my trans.).

Plenzdorf wrote his text, as we have noted, to provoke interpretation. What he did not say is that although the book invites, indeed demands, interpretation, it also stubbornly rejects it. The most controversial aspect of Plenzdorf's text, the most resolutely "open" space, is Wibeau's death at the conclusion. The book version of the *New Sorrows* breaks adamantly with the coerced resolution from the first, unpublished version, in which Wibeau survives a suicide attempt, his invention of the painting machine proves successful, and in a scene typical of (though at the same time parodying) the "Literature of Arrival," he returns to his hometown a hero. In the *Sinn und Form* version, Wibeau dies by accident, but his invention can be reconstructed and will probably be patented. In the final, book version, Wibeau dies by accident, and his invention cannot be reconstructed.

Death remained an unwelcome element in the optimistic GDR literature of the 1950s and 1960s. Only Erwin Strittmatter in *Ole Bienkopp* and Christa Wolf in *The Quest for Christa T.* had dared to conclude their novels with the protagonist's death, and both novels unleashed explosive discussions. Plenzdorf's book proved no exception. The GDR critic Peter Biele found Wibeau's fate the consequence of certain Western leanings, the final result of his individualism. Biele believes Wibeau dies not because of society but because of his disturbed relationship to it (205–8). Some West German critics agreed, though less approvingly. Wolfram Schütte termed it a secularized sacrificial death (279), while Karl Corino thinks Wibeau must fail because the government demanded it: "Obviously that stubborn, individualistic inventiveness had to fail by higher command" (253; my trans.). Other Western critics read differently. Fritz Raddatz spoke of a societal killing ("Flucht" 308). Wolfgang Emmerich found that Wibeau, like Christa T., had to perish, because GDR society provided him no opportunity for self-fulfillment (181).

The text thus supports diametrically opposed readings, as the GDR critic Friedrich Plate ascertained with some exasperation:

> Some say, and this alone still leaves open many possibilities: Edgar Wibeau dies because of the conditions surrounding him. Another opinion is already more precise: he dies because no one understands him and because no one wishes to. It has additionally been asserted: Wibeau dies on account of GDR reality. To be sure, the speaker polemicized against the characterization of Wibeau which would have to lead to that conclusion; nonetheless the interpretative possibility appears to me worthy of concern. Another opinion: Edgar dies because of his own self-declared individualism. That seems to me to be the most correct interpretation. With much irony the following interpretation has been suggested: Edgar dies of work. As long as he lazes about, he at least exists; when he begins to work productively, to supersede the borders of his egocentrism, that leads to his death. The nuisance is, this interpretive possibility can also not simply be dismissed. (225–26; my trans.)

Clearly, the conclusion to the *New Sorrows* presents the most telling example of the text's ability simultaneously to demand and to resist interpretation. That, in turn, represents its most subversive aspect.

We should note that Plenzdorf's book does swerve from its Goethean paradigm. Unlike his model Werther, Wibeau does not commit suicide, and he claims that he never would have freely ended his life. However, he states that he never would have really returned to his home in Mittenberg (83). Trapped between accommodation and rebellion, Wibeau has no exit. Yet if one agrees with Wolfgang Emmerich that Wibeau, like Christa T., had to die, one must note that Plenzdorf, like Christa Wolf, cushions the effects. Christa T. lived too soon, we are told; people will soon no longer die of her disease. In Plenzdorf's book Wibeau dies while working on a painting machine; he wishes to be a creative individual *and* a contributing member of society. He is not successful, but the extended questioning, the "Quest for Edgar W." that his death unleashes within the novel, signals a hopeful attitude. Similarly, Plenzdorf's own conscious attempt to write a book that would spark an extraliterary discussion demonstrates his own optimistic assessment regarding the possibilities of literature to reform society.

A fascinating epilogue to the *New Sorrows* occurred when Plenzdorf held a news conference during a visit to Switzerland. Recalling Wibeau's statement that jeans represent a point of view, Peter Zeindler observed that Plenzdorf wore jean pants and a jean jacket. When Plenzdorf insisted that he did not show negative qualities in his work merely to be negative, as he was sometimes accused of doing in the GDR, Zeindler noted the theatrical, posed quality of Plenzdorf's delivery. Finally, Plenzdorf answered questions by quoting from his own film *The Legend of Paul and Paula*, in which a young woman proves willing to pay any price, including her life, to realize her individuality and her happiness. Zeindler concludes by questioning which Plenzdorf one should believe—the wearer of jeans, ready to pit his whole self against society, or the rhetorician, who ostensibly wishes merely to discuss that attitude ("Glück"). Plenzdorf himself becomes an ambiguous text that Zeindler "reads." As text, Plenzdorf raises some of the questions of reading involved with GDR literature: does he say what he wants or what he must? By quoting his own texts, he makes a self-referential gesture toward the indecipherability of his own work, while also calling attention to the fundamental intertextuality—and perhaps ultimate indecipherability—of all literature.

Ambiguous literature also does not translate easily, and Kenneth P. Wilcox's attempt received mixed reviews. Paul F. Dvorak asserts somewhat surprisingly that "Plenzdorf's linguistically uncomplicated work about the 17-year-old Edgar Wibeau should present few major stumbling blocks for the translator, with the possible exception of the vulgarities and colloquialisms of today's younger generation" (519). While pointing out some translation problems, Dvorak believes that in general "Wilcox has done a fine job," and that he has made *The New Sufferings* "a very readable work." Like Dvorak, John Neubauer thinks the English reads smoothly, but he finds that problematic: "The earthy German slang, which defies both GDR and bourgeois morals, repeatedly becomes either bland and polite or inaccurate"

(125). Neubauer also predicted that unfamiliarity with Goethe's *Werther* would "greatly reduce the reading pleasure of most American readers," and indeed, the only reviews of this translation were printed in scholarly journals.

In December 1971 Erich Honecker had announced that for artists proceeding from the firm position of socialism, there should be no taboos. In May 1973, however, he spoke critically in *Neues Deutschland* of attempts to "force one's own sufferings onto society" (28 May 1973; my trans.). He added that the anonymity and isolation of individuals depicted in some films and theater pieces were signs that these works did not correspond to the demands that socialism placed on art. Plenzdorf was not specifically named, but Honecker's reference to "sufferings" (*Leiden*) was clear. The thaw had barely begun, but it was already drawing to a close.

Volker Braun, "Unfinished Story" GDR 1975, USA 1983

In 1968 Günter de Bruyn declared that in his society, which had eliminated such hindrances as class, there could be no more great tragedies of love. In *Buridan's Ass* de Bruyn demonstrates how the state actually assists the protagonist with his love affair. In 1975, after a change of government and the resulting cultural-political liberalization, Volker Braun's "Unfinished Story" takes issue with de Bruyn's antiseptic view. Braun describes a teenage love affair that encounters numerous obstacles, including a massive assault by the state.

Volker Braun (b. 1939) was politically outspoken as a high school student, and he narrowly escaped suspension; after graduation he could not at first study (Hollis 5). Between 1957 and 1960 he worked as a printer, an excavator, and a machinist's apprentice. From 1960 to 1964 he studied philosophy in Leipzig, and he moved to East Berlin in 1965, where he worked at the Berliner Ensemble theater and, beginning in 1972, the Deutsches Theater. In the 1960s Braun's poetry— fresh, boastful, vigorous, and provocative—burst upon the GDR literary scene. Together with the poetry of Wolf Biermann, Sarah Kirsch, Karl Mickel, and others, it announced in no uncertain terms that a talented new generation of socialist poets had arrived. Braun also wrote plays, many of which orient themselves toward the Bitterfeld Program and Braun's experience with manual labor.

Braun's writing often explores the contradiction between the needs of the individual and those of society, between the socialist promise of liberation and the reality of enervating work. He has won numerous literary prizes, but his plays have not always been welcome on GDR stages, and two critical plays from the 1970s, *T* (for Trotsky) and *Lenin's Death*, could only be published in the later 1980s, after *glasnost* allowed a more differentiated view of the Soviet Union. In the 1970s and 1980s Braun also established himself as an author of prose that, as Bernd Allenstein and Manfred Behn point out, makes a program of breaking taboos (2). "Unfinished Story" provides an example of Braun's grimly optimistic reformism.

A Party official and his wife, a newspaper editor, admonish their teenage daughter Karin to end her relationship with Frank, a former delinquent who, according to the father, is planning additional illegal activities. Karin breaks off with Frank. That action does violence to her feelings, however, and when she begins a newspaper internship in the neighboring town of M., which is also Frank's town, her relationship with him revives. Eventually she moves in with him and his mother. That brings renewed and relentless pressure from her parents as well as from her superiors at the newspaper, and although she has become pregnant, she moves out. Frank attempts suicide. As he lies in a coma, Karin learns that the authorities suspected Frank was preparing to escape to the West. Their suspicion was based on a suggestion a former GDR citizen, now living in the West, made to Frank in a letter. Frank maintained no desire to leave, however, and the authorities must ultimately concede that as well. Karin revolts against her parents and the world they represent. Unlike Christa T. or Edgar Wibeau, Frank survives, and he and Karin prepare to "finish" this story.

Braun refers to literary works by Georg Büchner, Brigitte Reimann, Ulrich Plenzdorf, Bertolt Brecht, Christa Wolf, and Johannes R. Becher to establish a conscious intertextual dialogue. When Karin finishes school and travels to M. to begin an internship at a newspaper, the narrator says "she had arrived" (18), thus evoking Brigitte Reimann's *Arrival in the Quotidian*. The reference to "Literature of Arrival" also recalls the didactic film in Ulrich Plenzdorf's *The New Sorrows of Young W.* In the movie a young man who is a former delinquent falls in love with a young female student. Her parents first oppose the relationship, but they relent after realizing how well-integrated the young man has become. Braun's story presents a rather different paradigm.

Discussing Karin, the narrator recalls the pattern characterizing the "Literature of Arrival" and also echoes a poem by Brecht:

> Perhaps it wasn't a case which belonged in a special chapter of history books. She experienced more urgently—like a shock—what happens to every person who is growing up—when he sees his lofty ideas of a new society go up in smoke. Once he finally forces himself into the existing possibilities. For society isn't new for him, and as opposed to the happy OLD COMRADES, he no longer sees the changes and breakthroughs as an enormous contrast to the dark past.[2]

In Brecht's poem "To Those Born Later," written during World War II, a communist addresses posterity from his "dark times." There are several other allusions to Brecht's poem in Braun's story—for example, when Party officials regret that they cannot act as humanely as they would wish (59), or when Karin discerns that political development does not necessarily entail human development (69). Brecht's communist recognizes and acknowledges similar faults, attributing them to the difficult times. He also believes they will disappear in a more humane, socialist society of the future. Braun's story demonstrates that these flaws continue to exist, blocking that more humane state in which Brecht placed his hopes. As the dissident poet Wolf Biermann noted bitterly in his poem "Brecht, Your Posterity," the East German rulers used the excuse of "dark times" to rule more comfortably (Nachlaß 1, 409). Yet the attitudes and values of those Braun calls the "OLD COMRADES" became increasingly foreign to GDR young people like Karin or Edgar Wibeau, children who, to use the phrase of the young GDR poet Uwe Kolbe, were "born into" GDR socialism and could not compare it—at least experientially—with those former dark times. For the old comrades the GDR represented a long-awaited and dearly purchased victory. For Karin and Frank it functioned as a leviathan.

In the course of the story, Karin discovers that "two worlds exist in the same land" (26, 34, 46)—the integral, politically correct world of her parents, and another world, one replete with contradictions. The narrative describes her increasing alienation from the world of her parents. Braun utilizes the concept of alienation to refer indirectly to Christa Wolf's *The Quest for Christa T.*, whose protagonist founders on the contradictions of GDR society. Wolf takes her epigram—"This coming-to-oneself—what is it?"—from Johannes R. Becher, poet and first GDR Minister of Culture. In "Unfinished Story" the father reads a posthumously published poem by Becher, one in which he lauds his liberation from public service, which he had experienced as alienating. Echoes of Becher's "coming-to-oneself" abound in Braun's story. A worker complains of the enormous difficulties during the years of reconstruction, a time in which one could not "come to oneself" (25; translated by Fiala as "one could never relax"). Later, Karin attempts to comprehend her own almost unquestioning obedience: "What was this something inside her that allowed her to forget herself? That something that prevented her from coming to herself?" (61; trans. by Fiala as "from being herself?").

Karin's alienation from society is more profound than Edgar Wibeau's. She explicitly mentions Plenzdorf's text, of which she has heard through Honecker's criticism that the author attempted to foist his own sufferings onto society as a whole (41). Although she finds Plenzdorf's book accurate (her younger brother has read it enthusiastically), she also thinks Wibeau too young and his problems too superficial. She asserts that Werther, Wibeau's literary role model, was far more conscious of, and affected by, the misery of his times:

> The enormous significance in *Werther* was that a rift [*Riß*] went through the world and through himself. . . . W. just didn't penetrate it—the deeper contradiction—which one should find! How would a book be—how would a book affect her—a book in which someone would come to that rift . . . into which one would have to fall." (41–42)

With his mention of a "rift through the world," Braun signals yet another intertext, *Lenz*, a story by the nineteenth-century author Georg Büchner. In *Lenz*, the tale of an eighteenth-century German author who becomes insane, Büchner writes that "the world [Lenz] had wished to serve had a gigantic crack [*Riß*]" (156). "Unfinished Story" contains several other disguised linguistic echoes from *Lenz*, as Charlotte Koerner and Dennis Tate have demonstrated (Koerner, "Brauns 'Unvollendete Geschichte' "; Tate 177–226). By comparing

Karin with Lenz, who, Marxists argue, was in part driven insane by his unresponsive times, Braun makes a provocative gesture toward his own society (Tate 182). He later cites Büchner explicitly: "'What a powerful thing it is, the State!' (Georg Büchner)" (67). The quotation is from Büchner's revolutionary leaflet *The Hessian Messenger*, in which Büchner urges Hessian peasants to revolutionary action. (In "Little Lessons in Prosody" [FRG 1977], a dissident text by the GDR writer Hans Joachim Schädlich, a young poet is arrested after citing the *Hessian Messenger*.) In 1978 Braun published, only in the West, his essay *Büchner's Letters*, in which he states that when reading Büchner one must forcibly remind oneself that one is not reading a contemporary. As Dennis Tate notes, "In Büchner's critique of the apparatus of German state repression, the self-perpetuating nature of bureaucracy, the hypocrisy of officially fostered affirmative literature, and the bloody excesses of the French Revolution, Braun recognizes historical problems as yet unremedied in the post-1917 socialist era" (212). Braun clearly intends some approximation of these significances in "Unfinished Story."

That "powerful thing . . . the State" functions in this story as a mechanism that intercepts mail (both Karin and Frank appear to find that natural), censors newspapers, and invades the most intimate spheres. Worried by their difficulties with the state, Frank and Karin experience sexual difficulties (21). The state twice sunders their relationship, and it drives Frank to a suicide attempt. In Karin's dreams she frequently feels herself under surveillance, a feeling often combined with a sense of violation by men. In one dream, her father, a state official, has his hand over her eyes, while later in the dream a man clings to her like an insect and rapes her with his snout (62–63). In her final dream she realizes that almost all the factory workers are women, while the managers and engineers are men (73).

When Karin asks herself, then, what it is that makes her forget herself, that prevents her from coming to herself, the answer is clearly the patriarchal state. With his critique of GDR officialese, Braun demonstrates the fashion in which Karin and the other characters have internalized the state's authoritarian structures. As representatives of the state, the parents speak its language. Directly in the first sentence, when the father commands his daughter to desist in her relationship with her friend Frank, the narrator calls attention to the language: "He had to inform her (he *did* say inform) of certain things which he had learned" (13). Similarly, after the parents have initiated the events that lead to Frank's suicide attempt, the narrator demonstrates the fashion in which the father distances himself with his language: "One evening after these incidents, Karin's father drove to the gardens on the outskirts of M." (57). The narrator comments in a parenthetical aside, "(You could call it incidents if you wanted to keep a clear mind.)"

As did Fritz Rudolf Fries, Erwin Strittmatter, and Uwe Johnson before him, Braun emphasizes various clichés by capitalizing them. This technique serves at least three functions. Using the terminology of the Czech linguist Mukarovský, we can view Braun's use of capitalization as an example of "foregrounding," of language calling attention to itself (similar to Brecht's alienation effect). As a second function, one bound up intimately with the first, the capitalized words or phrases serve as verbal icons, suggesting the omnipresent political banners of the GDR. Finally, Braun indicates the fashion in which such clichés enter the subconscious, operating there as superego. Thus the father's use of *informed* in the first sentence recurs two pages later in Karin's reflections: "She also had grown uncertain. . . . Her father had been INFORMED" (15).

Such foregrounding emphasizes not only the banality of the clichés but their danger, for the language of the state forms a prisonhouse for Karin, controlling her reactions. After leaving the hospital where she has seen Frank in a coma, she characterizes herself using the discourse of the newspapers; she staggers, she thinks to herself, as if she were "DRUNK" (52). She even dreams in the state's language: the narrator tells us "she knew the terms in her sleep" (73). What the narrator of *The Quest for Christa T.* says of GDR political banners, with their "new words," applies here as well: "Who'd call them back to mind today if they'd really stayed outside and hadn't infiltrated among us in so many and devious roads?" (56).

As with Ulrich Plenzdorf's *The New Sorrows of Young W.*, Braun's text is open-ended, "unfinished"; the author wants the reader to contribute creatively to a solution. Braun advances his harsh criticism to help reactivate what he considers a stalled revolution, and the text contains a number of hopeful moments. As Karin reaches a point of maximum confusion and despair, the narrator asserts, "Her story couldn't end here" (71). Braun then allows Frank to recover and to be reunited with Karin. Thus the author swerves from his model,

Büchner's *Lenz*. Whereas the conclusion of Büchner's text finds the protagonist catatonic, Braun positions Karin and Frank at the beginning of "new stories" (Tate 208).

The story contains other important signals of Braun's optimism regarding reform. Karin has a revolutionary dream in which the workers really capture power. Socialist democracy and genuine communication are suggested as the means to mediate and perhaps resolve the contradictions that nearly destroy Karin (and we have learned earlier that her "story is our history—and it is that of the whole land" [60]). When Karin awakens from the dream, she can "not yet" remember it. Her father, meanwhile, has begun to practice that democratic communication suggested in the dream. Much to the distress of Karin's mother, the father has started visiting taverns, "where he sits around and talks with all sorts of people" (79).

Despite his criticism of the Party and its servants, Braun does include a positive Party official to whom Karin's father turns for advice. In another of Braun's provocative gestures, the official implicitly compares the GDR with a polluted, stinking river. At the same time, the official points out a water-reprocessing plant and asserts: "The worst pollution is over now; it will certainly not get worse. In the future it could even improve" (60). Braun could not know that the worst was still ahead. In 1976, one year after the publication of "Unfinished Story," GDR officials expatriated the dissident poet Wolf Biermann. In the ensuing scandal and protest, numerous GDR writers left their country, as Georg Büchner had done 142 years earlier.

Like Ulrich Plenzdorf's *The New Sorrows of Young W.*, "Unfinished Story" first appeared in *Sinn und Form*. Unlike Plenzdorf's text, however, "Unfinished Story" could not appear as a book. It is a sign of the more constrictive cultural climate that Braun's work, though at least as provocative as Plenzdorf's, could not unleash a similar debate in official circles. In fact, it was greeted with almost total silence.

The West German Suhrkamp Verlag published "Unfinished Story" in 1977. West German newspapers had already commented on the text; following its earlier publication in the GDR, Nikolaus Marggraf had called it an "astonishing, courageous piece of prose" (*Frankfurter Rundschau* 2 Dec. 1975; my trans.). In 1977 Karl Corino termed it "Braun's most convincing prose to date" (*Deutsche Zeitung* 11 Nov. 1977; my trans.), and the slender volume became a best-seller in the

Federal Republic, where it has remained one of the most widely discussed pieces of East German literature (Hollis 2).

In England, Manchester University Press has published Braun's story as a college text. In the United States, the piece has been translated as B.A. and M.A. theses but has not found a commercial publisher. In the GDR, the growing impact of Gorbachev's *glasnost* led to the publication of "Unfinished Story" as a book in 1988.

On the Way to Glasnost

The five examples in this chapter demonstrate the increasing formal independence of GDR literature. The omniscient narrator and relatively traditional narrative techniques characterizing *Ole Bienkopp*, for example, yield in the 1970s to the highly subjective, idiosyncratic, first-person narration of Plenzdorf's Edgar Wibeau. All these texts (including Strittmatter's) were innovative for their time, and if they remain recognizable socialist-realist literature—even the more recent pieces by Plenzdorf and Braun maintain vestiges of such prescriptive elements as a heroic worker or a wise Party official—they bring to that literature new, more aesthetically satisfying formal structures: they have re-formed socialist realism.

All the texts provided their society with a challenge, one meant as a contribution to discussion and to reform. In no small part, the provocative element in these texts results from their insistence on "open spaces," on the creation of ambiguities that simultaneously demand and resist the hermeneutic act. The deaths of Bienkopp and Wibeau; the near-deaths of Rita and Frank; Christa Wolf's experiments (in the German text) with perspective; Günter de Bruyn's elusive irony; and Ulrich Plenzdorf's and Volker Braun's intertextuality—their dense weave of allusion and echo—these thematic and formal elements render the books more difficult to interpret, and hence to control. Not incidentally, they "open" the texts, protecting them from the closure of censorship.

On a thematic level these books expose errors committed by the Party, but they carefully balance any mistaken, inept, or corrupt official with one who, at the very least, is capable of learning from past mistakes, one who is capable of reform. The texts avoid systemic criticism—for example, the suggestion that the Party may have forfeited its "right" to lead, or that socialism itself may be the root of the problems discussed. As Plenzdorf's Edgar Wibeau states:

I didn't have anything against Lenin and all. I also didn't have anything against Communism and all that, the abolition of the exploitation of the world. I wasn't against that. But against everything else. (44)

Strittmatter, Wolf, de Bruyn, Plenzdorf, and Braun all protest, like Wibeau, against that "everything else," insofar as it represents a smugly complacent "revolution," one managed from above. Against bureaucratic ossification, they set a vision of grass-roots, socialist democracy, one that takes note of the individual and his or her needs. In four out of five of these texts, that becomes, quite literally, a matter of life and death.

Although the texts by Plenzdorf and Braun are by GDR standards "difficult" and "open," they remain quite accessible in comparison with Western avant-garde literature. The theory of language implied in these texts is also relatively conservative. Strittmatter, Plenzdorf, and Braun practice language criticism, attacking or parodying the linguistic "dogmatitis" exemplified by Strittmatter's Frieda Simson. Wibeau's ebullient slang represents a protest against the norms of conformity, and Braun develops sophisticated narrative techniques to demonstrate the fashion in which invidious officialese can colonize the unconscious. None of these texts, however, demonstrates a concern with *Sprachskepsis*, that radical doubt one finds in more experimental texts, such as those by Uwe Johnson or Fritz Rudolf Fries. In *Divided Heaven*, Wolf in fact tells us that Rita had regained "the strength she needed to call things by their right names" (202).

GDR reformist texts demonstrate that hopeful attitude toward language and the possibility of communication, including narration. Near the conclusion of another, more sophisticated reformist text, Wolf's *The Quest for Christa T.*, the narrator notes that "words, too, have their time and cannot be tugged out of the future according to need. It means much to know they are there" (185). Similarly, we are told that a word does not *yet* exist to describe the utopian dimension in Ole Bienkopp's personality, or that Volker Braun's Karin can not *yet* remember—that is, verbalize—her utopian dream.

The reformist confidence in the power of language and of literature to effect change appears to be well-founded, since thematically and/ or formally, these five texts all contributed something novel to GDR literature. The passionate debates surrounding publication of *Ole Bienkopp*, *Divided Heaven*, and *The New Sorrows of Young W.* attest to the impact of these works on GDR society. *Divided Heaven*, *Buridan's Ass*, and *The New Sorrows of Young W.* have been filmed, and hence they have reached an even wider audience.

Western readers can find much in these texts to irritate them, and that is surely one reason the translations—three of them from the East German Seven Seas Press—have had little resonance in the United States. Strittmatter's description of collectivization remains rather benign. With some justification, one can read *Divided Heaven* as an apologia for the Wall. Peter Demetz objects to de Bruyn's use of the diminutive when describing the "little watchtowers" along the German-German border, where "barbed wire peacefully rusted away": "For de Bruyn's sake, I hope that he is telling us what the silly lovers see, rather than what he himself as narrator wants us to perceive" (*Fires* 124). Wolfram Schütte characterized Plenzdorf's strategy of throttling his own criticism as "petit bourgeois" (278). Volker Braun's story, the most recent of the five discussed here, presents perhaps the most relentless political criticism, but it lingered for many years in the shadow of semirepression. Nonetheless, these five texts expanded the limits of the sayable in the GDR, even when, for reasons political if not epistemological, they left some things unsaid.

NOTES

1. The original version was published in West Germany in 1982.
2. "English Translation" 78. I have altered the translation slightly.

4

Beyond the Limits of the Permissible: The Literature of Dissent

"In a discussion about [*Sleepless Days*], I heard a cultural function-ary claim that my book transgressed the boundaries of the cur-rent East German cultural policy. I replied that the book was indeed an expression of my dissatisfaction with these bound-aries. I told him I thought it necessary to extend these bound-aries, and that my book should be understood as an attempt to do so. In all probability, it only makes sense to write books of this sort."

—Jurek Becker, Interview with Richard Zipser

An ill-defined and variable border exists between a literature of re-form and one of dissent. In the pre-1989 GDR, the historical moment (the world situation, the prevailing East German or Soviet cultural policy), the taboo-breaking contents of a work, a writer's national and international reputation, and his or her perceived political depend-ability could delimit that ambiguous grey area of the politically ac-ceptable. In the GDR, as opposed, for example, to the Soviet Union, much criticism came from the left: writers held existing GDR social-ism to an idealized conception of what they believed socialism could or should be. In those instances the difference between reform and dissent became one of degree, although Roger Woods noted in 1986 that "those who advocate a socialist market economy, a system of strict socialist legality, creative freedom or any other kind of genuine

147

autonomy of social function or of a group from the total control of the parts are objectively striving for 'system-rejective' change, although they may think they want 'within-system change' " (19).

Some dissidents lost hope that East Germany could or would change, and they despaired of GDR socialism, though not, perhaps, of socialism entirely. Such writers often left their country, and as self-styled realists, they characterized those who remained as naïve dreamers or as sycophants. Yet the reformers who remained, and who were sometimes disdainful of those who left to "market" their dissidence in the West, believed they themselves were realists working within the realm of the possible. The issues were neither simple nor clear-cut, and a writer could be stamped a dissident *malgré lui:* the GDR poet Wolf Biermann, regarded by many in both East and West Germany as *the* dissident writer, always considered himself a reformer. For the purposes of this chapter, we can define a literature of dissent as one that not merely expanded limits but exceeded them. This literature irrevocably crossed the borders of the permissible, and East German authorities suppressed it.

The youthful GDR state rejected—at least in its propaganda—the "bourgeois" antagonism between political power and critical intellect, between rulers and the intelligentsia. Wilfried van der Will notes the symbolism involved in the autumn 1948 invitation to Heinrich Mann, Thomas Mann's brother and a famous writer in his own right, to serve as president of a newly founded academy of the arts in East Berlin (32–33). In 1910 Mann had published his programmatic essay "Geist und Tat" ("Intellect and Action"), in which he calls on the intelligentsia to oppose power and privilege. The East Germans wished to demonstrate with Heinrich Mann that socialism had transcended that divide. Mann agreed to take the post, but he died before he could travel to the GDR.

Subsequent events demonstrated that the marriage between power and intellect, if ever it existed, was short-lived. The Soviet Zone of Occupation and the early GDR provided some room for artistic freedom, but in 1951 the East Germans imported the Soviet dogma of socialist realism and issued a resolution against "formalism," which in practice soon came to mean just about everything the authorities did not like. During the next twenty years, amidst long freezes and fragile thaws, these conditions created a host of dissident intellectuals. One of the most important contemporary Marxist philosophers, Ernst Bloch, returned from his World War II exile at Princeton to Leipzig University, where political pressures forced him into retirement in 1957; he emigrated to West Germany in 1961. His colleague Wolfgang Harich, an important young Marxist theoretician, taught philosophy in Leipzig until 1956; in the wake of the Hungarian uprising the SED arrested Harich as a counterrevolutionary and jailed him until 1964. In 1959 Uwe Johnson left Leipzig with two manuscripts in his suitcase and went to West Berlin, where he soon ranked among the most important postwar German writers. Hans Mayer taught literature in Leipzig until 1963 (among his students were Uwe Johnson, Fritz Rudolf Fries, Christa Wolf, and Volker Braun), then he went West. Authorities dismissed the distinguished poet Peter Huchel from his duties as editor of *Sinn und Form* in 1962, and after nine years of inner exile, he emigrated to West Germany.

Wolf Biermann triggered undoubtedly the most infamous cultural-political scandal. Biermann was born in 1936. His father, a communist and a Jew, was later murdered at Auschwitz. Raised by his communist, working-class mother in West German Hamburg, Biermann emigrated to the GDR in 1953. He studied political economy in East Berlin and worked for two years at the Berliner Ensemble's theater. He began writing poems, ballads, and political songs, accompanying himself on guitar. The SED supported his songs about Vietnam, the Spanish civil war, or U.S. civil-rights workers murdered in Mississippi; when he turned his critical gifts toward the GDR, however, attacking bureaucratic inertia, complacency, and dogmatism, he encountered strong opposition.

In 1961 Biermann lost his candidacy for Party membership, and he was forbidden to perform until June 1963. In 1965, after successful appearances in East and West and after the West Berlin publication of his poetry volume *The Wire Harp*, the SED moved to end his career. *Neues Deutschland* attacked his "skepticism," "self-complacent egotism," and "bourgeois individualism" (5 Dec. 1965; my trans.). The Eleventh Plenum of the Central Committee included him, together with writers Stefan Heym and Heiner Müller, in its numerous condemnations, and in February 1966 the government issued the "lex Biermann," forbidding him from playing in the GDR. In his 1971 study of East German poetry, John Flores explains the basis for Biermann's impact:

Both "partisan" and "popular," [Biermann] meets precisely the qualifications of "people's poet of the nation" set forth by East German cultural authorities. Yet Biermann, their most faithful pupil, has brought them little comfort because his realism is not only socialist, and readily accessible to the masses, but also truthful. In fact, it is precisely because his poetry is so obviously that of a true believer, and so highly contagious, that its "realism" represents such a threat to the establishment. (312)

During the next decade Biermann lived the life of an outcast in East Berlin, publishing his books in West Berlin and recording his records for CBS in his apartment. Erich Honecker's new course from 1971, which helped such writers as Christa Wolf, Ulrich Plenzdorf, and Stefan Heym, did not avail Biermann. He remained, as John Flores noted, "a living defiance of society in the GDR. An outgrowth of its values and all it represents, he [was] the glaring antagonism born of its own dialectic, its own child who [lived] to haunt it and terrify it into a realization of its promises" (312).

Somewhat surprisingly, the SED allowed Biermann to accept an invitation from IG Metall, West Germany's largest trade union, to perform a series of West German concerts in November 1976. At a concert in Cologne, Biermann displayed solidarity with his country (accepting, for example, the Soviet suppression of the 1953 workers' revolt), while subjecting it to his usual stinging critique. After the concert, the SED, citing laws preventing slander of the state, announced that Biermann would not be allowed to return to the GDR. Twelve prominent GDR artists published a letter, refused by *Neues Deutschland* and hence printed only in the West, protesting the decision and inviting the government to reconsider. In the following days and months, over 150 artists and intellectuals signed the letter, thus presenting a confrontation of unprecedented proportions. An international outcry supported the GDR protesters: Western labor organizers and writers' organizations, the communist parties of France, Italy, Spain, and Sweden, and such left-wing intellectuals as Jean-Paul Sartre and Simone de Beauvoir, condemned Biermann's expatriation.

The SED did not retract its decision and attempted to bring its house in order with various forms of harassment. It arrested some writers and expelled others from professional organizations or even from the country. In the ensuing years, numerous artists and intellectuals, several extremely prominent, left the GDR. The SED also marshaled loyal supporters, such as the playwright Peter Hacks, for a counteroffensive. Hacks characterized Biermann as a talentless poet who attracted attention by provoking scandals and marketing his opposition (Roos 46). Hacks thus employed a standard GDR argument to defame its domestic opposition, an argument that ignored the fact that for political reasons East German publishing houses regularly printed bad literature by Party loyalists.

The publication dates of the works I examine in this chapter cluster around that decisive caesura of November 1976. All four authors (Reiner Kunze, Hans Joachim Schädlich, Jurek Becker, and Rolf Schneider), though not all four works, were involved in the events surrounding Biermann. Reiner Kunze and Wolf Biermann were friends in the GDR, and Kunze had defended Biermann in his "Song: The Biermann Cometh":

> Biermann is their man?
> What pus!
>> A man's a man beer is beer
>> Biermann came from there to here
>> You did not want to drink.

> (Hamburger 163)

Kunze's book *The Wonderful Years* appeared in West Germany in September 1976, and Biermann supported Kunze during his Cologne concert in November, singing his "Kunze-Song" (*Nachlaß* 465). Introducing the song, Biermann proclaimed his solidarity with Kunze, emphasizing however that Kunze was his friend, not his comrade. Biermann insisted Kunze had not composed "fascist" literature, as some GDR critics claimed, and asserted that everything his friend had written was true. At the same time, Biermann noted with dialectical flair, "we communist writers" believe that with "sad truths" one can lie about the reality of life in the GDR. In April 1977 Kunze left for West Germany.

Like Kunze's *The Wonderful Years*, Hans Joachim Schädlich's *Approximation* (FRG 1977) was written during the "thaw" before Biermann's expatriation. Kunze's and Schädlich's investigations of the darker sides of GDR existence provide a contrast to the generally optimistic mood between 1971 and 1976. After protesting Biermann's expatriation, Schädlich lost his position at the East Berlin Academy of Sciences. In 1977, shortly after publication of *Approximation* in West Germany, he left the GDR.

Biermann's friend Jurek Becker published *Sleepless Days* (1978), a book demonstrating the anger and rebelliousness many East German artists felt at the time, only in West Germany. Granted a long-term visa, Becker had left the GDR in December 1977, retorting, "If it is a question of keeping my mouth shut, then I would rather keep it shut in the Bahamas" (*Der Spiegel* 18 July 1977; my trans.). Rolf Schneider's *November* (1979), which deals directly with the Biermann scandal, also appeared only in the West. Schneider left the GDR in 1979 with a long-term visa. The most loyal of the four writers discussed in this chapter, Schneider continued to maintain a residence in the GDR, dividing his time between East and West Germany.

Reiner Kunze, *The Wonderful Years* FRG 1976, USA 1977

Reiner Kunze is a son of the working class, and for a time it appeared that the GDR, the land, he once wrote, that he would "choose over and over again" (*Sensitive* 19; my trans.), provided him a congenial home. Born in 1933 as the son of a miner, Kunze later studied philosophy and journalism in Leipzig. He wrote poetic apologias for the GDR, and in 1962 he became a free-lance writer. He then published, only in the Federal Republic, the poetry collections *Dedications* in 1963 and *Sensitive Ways* in 1969.

As Wolfgang Emmerich points out, many poems in *Sensitive Ways* were influenced by the Soviet suppression of the Prague Spring, and Kunze composed some critical pieces before 1968, indicating that his disillusionment had begun considerably earlier (170). In 1960 Kunze wrote "The End of Art," translated by Boria Sax for Amnesty International:

> You must not, said the owl to the rooster
> You must not sing praises of the sun
> The sun is not important
> The rooster took
> The sun out of his poem.
> You are an artist,

Said the owl to the rooster;
And it was very dark.

("Laws" 1)

The SED placed a publication prohibition on him, although after the change of government in 1971 he was allowed to publish the poetry collection *Letter with a Blue Seal* (1973). Even in the more liberal atmosphere of the thaw, however, many of Kunze's poems remained too controversial to print.

Kunze's bitterness became fully apparent in 1976 with the publication, in West Germany only, of *The Wonderful Years*. Utilizing a minimalist prose schooled on Brecht, he mounted a frontal attack against the regimentation of GDR society and the accompanying devaluation of the individual. The book appeared in West Germany with a foreword by the Nobel Prize laureate Heinrich Böll. It quickly became a best-seller and was filmed in 1979.

The difficulties of self-realization within socialist society, a society that often viewed subjectivity, individualism, or nonconformism as negative traits, had become an increasingly urgent theme in GDR literature during the 1960s, and stories of the conflict between the individual and society often centered on youthful protagonists. Arlecq, the young picaresque hero of Fritz Rudolf Fries's *The Road to Oobliadooh* (FRG 1966), complains that the GDR offers increasingly less opportunity for "poetic confusion." The protagonists of Christa Wolf's *The Quest for Christa T.* (1968) and Ulrich Plenzdorf's *The New Sorrows of Young W.* (1972) die, some critics argue, because they cannot survive as individuals in East Germany. Volker Braun's "Unfinished Story" (1975) establishes an analogy between interfering parents and the state, a situation one finds in Thomas Brasch's collection of stories *The Sons Die before the Fathers* (FRG 1977). Brasch left the GDR in December 1976, much to the embarrassment of his father, an important cultural functionary.

Stephan Hermlin's *Evening Light* (1979) summarizes the problems of the individual in societies professing to adhere to Marxist tenets. Hermlin's narrator recalls a sentence from Marx's *Communist Mani tfesto* that posits the development of society as the basis for the development of the self. The narrator had read the sentence many times, and it accorded well with the weltanschauung to which he adhered for much of his life. Thus he is shocked to discover that he had read the sentence backwards; according to Marx, the development of the individual provides the basis for the healthy development of society (20).

That jarring cleft between the promise of wholeness in Marxist thought and the repressive, disfiguring reality of the GDR informs Reiner Kunze's writing in *The Wonderful Years*. Kunze cites Kurt Tucholsky, a leftist writer from the Weimar Republic: "What counts is not that the State live—but that Man live!" (57). Thus Kunze holds left-wing theory up as model and critique. The daughter in his narrative longs for a book by Herbert Marcuse, whose vision of socialism *and* personal liberation appeared as subversive in the GDR as it proved to be in the United States during the 1960s (56).

Taken from Truman Capote's *Grass Harp*, Kunze's title refers to the years of experiment and self-discovery that characterize adolescence. Inexorably, in almost every snapshotlike vignette, Kunze demonstrates the fashion in which the GDR destroys that sense of wonder in its young people. The book cites numerous causes: a lingering tradition of repression deriving from both the Prussian and the Nazi inheritance; widespread petit-bourgeois morality that, in a seeming paradox, blossoms in GDR socialism; fear and cowardliness, especially among teachers who further their career at their students' expense; and a repressive, insecure state that politicizes every facet of life.

The state turns innocents into enemies. It brands the honor student Michael as an "uncertain element" when he attempts out of intellectual curiosity to read the Bible (42–46). Following a late night jazz concert, police send teenagers from a train station into the rain because they are resting their heads on each others' shoulders (41). And after a music festival in Berlin, the police clear the street of teenagers, whom they consider "youth-litter" (47). Kunze delights in taking a minor incident and depicting an absurdly inappropriate response on the part of the state or its authorities. When teachers denigrate pupils who wear wire-rimmed glasses (which signal "Western imperialist fashion and decadence"), the narrator notes that his daughter's grandfather and great-grandfather, miners, wore wire-rimmed glasses (34). Similarly, a teacher accuses the daughter of maintaining sympathies for the United States when she uses an infantry trooper's kit as a book bag; the teacher does not understand the English written on it: "Fight for peace and do not fall except in love" (62). Even death is politicized: when pupils wear black arm-bands to mourn the suicide of a classmate, school authorities view it as an expression of opposition (66).

The first section of Kunze's book addresses the regimentation occasioned by the militarization of GDR society, and as with the title of the entire work, the heading of this section, "Peace Children," provides a bitterly ironical orientation. On 1 September 1978 the GDR made *Wehrerziehung* ("defense education") a compulsory subject for the ninth and tenth grades; in September 1981 it became compulsory in the eleventh grade as well. Although those developments post-dated Kunze's book, the mentality that occasioned them did not. David Childs wrote that *Wehrerziehung*

> caused quite a stir, and rightly so, in the Western press, but the outcry tended to give the impression that something totally new had started. What was new was the official, compulsory element. In fact the GDR had been trying to get its youth to "play soldiers" almost from the time it was founded. (188)

Kunze's description of a militarized society emphasizes the development of *Feindbilder* ("images of the enemy"). These are part of the government's campaign of *Abgrenzung*, or fencing itself off from the West, and are thus related to the harassment involving the wire-rimmed glasses or the U.S. infantry kit. As with the infantry kit episode, Kunze emphasizes stupid, antirational, or absurd elements to create his parody. A child, for example, knows nothing of Lenin as ideological leader but considers him an army captain (14). Other children know that Americans are to be hated but are unsure how they must evaluate Angela Davis:

> First pupil: She's not American. She's a Communist.
> Second pupil: No, she's not! She's black. (16)

Like their teachers, children learn to work with simplistic categories, categories often formed by ignorance. Hence the narrator exhorts his daughter to learn, to acquire knowledge with which to confront the authority of the state (84–85).

Nonetheless, "Open Fire," the conclusion to "Peace Children," surprises. We hear not of a perfectly indoctrinated, militaristic youth but of one who, shortly before his period of obligatory military service begins, attempts to flee to the West. According to GDR authorities, he is caught and imprisoned, where he commits suicide. The mother receives only her son's ashes in an urn, and we can assume that the boy, in attempting to escape his own order to open fire, was shot at the border by those who had not. The mother asks how her son could inflict such suffering on her; but the question is wrongly put, Kunze implies, and should be reversed, for military service represents the culmination of the regimentation and hatred inculcated as part of childhood training. In his protest, despair, and death, the son steps into individuality. He, Gerhard, is the only figure in "Peace Children," and indeed one of the few in the entire book, who has a name.

The second part of Kunze's book, "Café Slavia," deals with the suppression of the Prague Spring in 1968 by troops of the Warsaw Pact, including those from the GDR. Kunze has a Czech wife and has translated Czech poetry, receiving a Czech literary award in 1968. The Soviet bloc intervention in Czechoslovakia contributed much to his disillusionment with socialism and with his own land. The stories in *The Wonderful Years* suggest several parallels between the Third Reich and the GDR, and when East German troops invade Czechoslovakia, Kunze's text evokes comparisons with the earlier Nazi occupation (98).

Kunze provides transitions from the first half of his book to "Café Slavia." For example, an East German adult seems to be suggesting Jaroslav Hašek's Schweik, a Czech literary hero, when he describes the narrator's son: "A real soldier, because he carries out the most idiotic order. And a brilliant soldier, because he carries it out in such a way that the idiocy of the order becomes obvious" (24). More explicitly, in the penultimate scene of the first part, the narrator speaks in praise of the only teacher at his daughter's school who refused to sign a proclamation supporting the invasion of Czechoslovakia, and who suffered a nervous breakdown thereafter (85). (The government arrested many citizens, especially young people, who protested the invasion either by displaying Czech flags or by passing out leaflets.)

Readers of Milan Kundera will recognize the atmosphere of Kunze's Czechoslovakia, in which the government sends dissident intellectuals to work at menial tasks or undertakes tawdry attempts to turn people into informers. Kunze emphasizes small acts of

Schweik-like resistance: postcards showing (medieval) Prague under siege or depicting the battle of the White Mountain in 1620, after which Bohemia was re-Catholicized and much of the intelligentsia, as in 1968, left the country. The narrator receives no service in a Prague café, because he checked a coat made in the GDR, whence came troops (92). After an evening funeral, Czech authorities practice petty harassment by extinguishing the lights; the people form a chain and help each other down steps in the dark—a symbol of solidarity (105). Once again, as so often in Kunze's book, death is politicized.

Kunze also draws attention to the anti-Semitic undertones in the events of 1968. In 1952 the Czechs had staged a show trial against Rudolf Slánský, a prominent communist and the country's former vice-minister. The government tried thirteen other Party members, most of them Jews, and executed eleven, including Slánský. William Korey, an American who has studied Soviet treatment of Jews, believes that the Soviets exerted strong pressure on the Czechs in 1968 to stage another Slánský-like show trial. In the GDR, *Neues Deutschland* wrote that "Zionist elements have taken over the leadership of the [Czech] Party" (qtd. in Korey 151). Against that background, Kunze wrote his "Pasturella Pestis" ("Plague Bacillus"), which except for the title consists entirely of a quote:

At the very start of the new year, 1945, Beneš assembled his people in London. Doctor Ducháček . . . suddenly became one of the leading politicians in the People's Party. The same holds for the Trotskyite Pavel Schönfeld-Tigrid (a Jew—Editor's note). *General Practitioner, Journal for Continued Medical Education,* Prague, April 20, 1975, page 233. (109)

The editor of the *General Practitioner* employs Nazi methods in an attempt to defame Schönfeld-Tigrid, a man perhaps of Jewish descent, who was not a communist or a Trotskyite but a liberal close to the Catholic Party. What in fact provoked the Czech communists was the fact that Schönfeld-Tigrid later worked as editor in chief of the Czechoslovak Division of Radio Free Europe.[1]

Numerous thematic parallels and references join the Czech and East German parts of Kunze's book. The Czech experience with a repression more open, more crass, illuminates similar structures in the GDR. For example, the narrator receives a letter from a blacklisted

Czech friend whose talented son cannot attend the university. Thus Kunze returns to the irony of the wonderful years and mirrors his own rage as a father.

Another theme unifying both parts of Kunze's book, and indeed a theme that implicitly or explicitly stands at the center of almost any work of dissident literature, is the role of the writer. In "Clown, Bricklayer, or Poet," a poet is described, only in part ironically, as someone who "dares to do the unheard of," who "connects things in astonishing ways," and who "has creative stamina" (24). At the same time, Kunze's book argues that the GDR state crushes precisely those qualities in its young people. For an insecure government, such qualities cannot be desirable attributes in a writer.

"Visit" describes in detail the vicissitudes of a dissident GDR writer. The story relates the attempt of a young woman, who works under duress for the state security police, to seduce the young poet Jürgen and to frame him by involving him in the exchange of stolen Western literature. The fictional Jürgen resembles Jürgen Fuchs, a GDR writer arrested in the automobile of human-rights advocate Robert Havemann after the Biermann expatriation in 1976. Both Biermann and Havemann figure in "Visit," and Jürgen uses a Biermann song satirizing the state security police to expose the female informer.

In "Mail from Bohemia" the narrator commemorates a Czech friend who has translated over fifty books of literature into Czech and has been instrumental in disseminating Czech writing abroad. After he protests in 1968, the government muzzles him. As if in response, Kunze translates poems from several Czech poets who vanished from Czech literary history between 1968 and 1989, (just as Kunze's name practically disappeared from GDR literary history).

Kunze's final vignette, which he inserts in lieu of an afterword, features a worker who demands of the narrator, a professional writer, "Do you write what's in the newspaper or what's in real life?" (124). GDR newspapers presented in words the propaganda advanced by a Czech postage stamp described by Kunze: "*Czechoslovakia—Liberation by the Soviet Army 1945–1975*, and under it: dancing Soviet soldiers amid Czech and Slovak children, women, and men, all dancing, cheering, and waving bouquets of flowers" (108). The GDR papers wrote of Zionist elements seizing control of Czechoslovakia, and Kunze wrote of anti-Semitism. The GDR papers portrayed their land as peaceloving, and Kunze wrote of militarization. For him, the role of the writer is to contradict, to satirize, and demystify; he "dares to do the unheard-of" (24).

Astonishingly, the East German Copyright Bureau provided Kunze permission—without examining his manuscript—to publish in the West. After *The Wonderful Years* appeared in West Germany, the GDR Writers' Association evicted Kunze, and its future president, Hermann Kant, attacked him publicly in primitive terms. Heinz Kamnitzer, president of the GDR-PEN association, ridiculed Kunze in a poem. Kunze's telephone was often blocked, books from the West were confiscated at the border, his friends and acquaintances were interrogated, and ministers and priests were fined for allowing him to read in their churches. His wife and daughter also encountered numerous personal and professional hardships. In 1977 Kunze and his family left the GDR.[2]

The scandal surrounding Kunze assured *The Wonderful Years* a sympathetic reception in West Germany. Nobel Prize laureate Heinrich Böll, who had hosted Solzhenitsyn after the latter emigrated from the Soviet Union, wrote a strongly favorable review in the influential *Die Zeit* (Wallmann, *Kunze* 176–80), and Kunze's book was very widely discussed. Some critics, such as the former GDR citizen Hans Mayer, asserted that the environment of lies depicted by Kunze could also occur in the West (Wallmann, *Kunze* 183–87). In the *Frankfurter Allgemeine Zeitung* Volker Hage noted that the chapter "Organ Recital" named organs in West Germany as well, and that Kunze warned against authoritarian behavior in both Germanys (2 Sept. 1976). Nonetheless, Germans on both sides of the border rightly considered the book a vehement attack on the GDR, and when Wolfram Schütte termed it one of the most courageous books from East Germany, one could ascertain that nonliterary criteria—how could it be otherwise?—proved important in the reception (Wallmann, *Kunze* 187–91).

West Germans often attempted to make banned GDR books available to East German audiences through television, and a filmed version of *The Wonderful Years* appeared in 1980. Interestingly, the unanimously positive reception of the book transformed itself into an equally negative reception for the film. Although aesthetic criteria and Kunze's inexperience with film certainly played a role in the negative reviews, Sabine Brandt speculated that West German leftists could only allow criticism of the GDR from the GDR ("Politische").

When it came from the West, they dismissed it as cold war propaganda.

Although German literature does not possess a particularly large audience in the United States, a well-written book by an East German dissident had, as in West Germany, favorable prospects. Various U.S. bibliographical organs recommended *The Wonderful Years*, and before its appearance, Herbert Mitgang of the *Times* was frank about the politics of translation: "The fact that a New York publisher has taken it on is more than a literary act; it sends a message across the Wall" (17 Dec. 1976). When the book appeared, John Leonard wrote in the *Times*, "The years may not have been wonderful, but the book is" (21 April 1977). In *Newsweek* Peter Prescott noted that Kunze "illuminates by understated eloquence the daily abrasion of the human spirit under Communist regimes." In an infelicitous but revealing formulation, Prescott asserted that Kunze also presented grounds for hope: "In youths' persistent indignation, in its fecklessness, in its conforming to American taste in clothes and music, is the state confounded and man's future preserved" (9 May 1977).

Writing a positive and thoughtful review for the *Christian Science Monitor*, Alexandra Johnson notes that after she had finished her draft she learned that Kunze had been expelled from his country (actually, he left "voluntarily"). Did that, she wonders, change her perception, "making the book more a political than a literary achievement?" She rejects this notion, though she questions whether that will be possible for first-time readers. She nonetheless indulges in some literary hyperbole, calling *The Wonderful Years* a "communist version of *La Comédie Humaine*" (4 May 1977). Writing a favorable and sensible review for the *New York Times Book Review*, Martin Greenberg had cautioned against such excess:

Reiner Kunze's book is an act of heroism. As a piece of literature, it is quite modest, and modest in its manner. It is not entirely free from sentimentality about the young. Perhaps a certain delicacy it has suffers in translation, but it will not do to overpraise it, as Heinrich Böll is already overpraising it in the jacket blurb. How one hates the roar of publicity which envelops these heroic works. I think of the overpraised *Dr. Zhivago*, of the overpraised novels of Solzhenitsyn. By all means let us praise the courage of these writers. But literary truth is important too. (24 April 1977)

Hans Joachim Schädlich, *Approximation* FRG 1977, USA 1980

Born in 1935, Hans Joachim Schädlich studied linguistics in East Berlin and Leipzig, finishing a dissertation on phonetics in 1960. Between 1959 and 1976 he worked at the East Berlin Academy of Arts and Sciences. In November 1976 Schädlich signed the petition protesting Wolf Biermann's expatriation, causing him to lose his position. Thereafter, he worked as a free-lance translator.

Schädlich published his dissertation in 1966 and another scholarly book on linguistics in 1973. In 1969 he began writing fictional short stories, only one of which, "Auntie Loves Fairy Tales," appeared in the GDR. In August 1977 he published a collection of stories, *Approximation*, with the West German Rowohlt Verlag. A month later he applied to leave his country, a request his government first denied, then granted in December. Until 1989 he lived in West Germany, primarily in West Berlin, and has published the novel *Tallhover* (1986), about the history of the German political police, and *Eastwestberlin* (1987), a collection of prose.

Unlike *The Wonderful Years*, the stories in *Approximation*, written between 1969 and 1977, do not present an immediately obvious thematic or structural unity. Most have a dark side, describing misunderstanding and alienation ("Himly and Himly" and "Auntie Loves Fairy Tales"), or forms of asocial behaviour such as patriarchal abuse of women ("Come, My Sweetheart"), the corruption of money ("Apple in a Silver Bowl"), a robbery ("Crime Story"), and violent frustration ("Nowhere a Place" and "Dobruska"), including an attack on a deformed young man. The locale is clearly the GDR, though the events might occur anywhere—which is Schädlich's point. He wishes to unmask the socialist paradise suggested in the newspapers and the trivial literature, and he displays the new socialist human being (not coincidentally, several protagonists are workers) as still very much capable of brutish behavior. As such, these stories become political.

If stories of asocial behavior are only "newsworthy" within a GDR context, in which they assume a political significance they might otherwise lack, Schädlich's collection also includes a number of more precisely political narratives that carry the satirical thrust one finds in *The Wonderful Years*. His prose proves particularly adept at revealing the various mechanisms through which power was exercised in the GDR. In the title story, Schädlich demonstrates the fashion in which leaders identified with the ideology of their country to further their own careers:

> There is to be a speech; that is the custom, and an ambitious associate, recently co-opted into the intimate circle, steps to the microphone. The speaker says what he [the ruler] too would have said, namely, that thanks are due to the toilers for what they have done.
>
> Not done for his good or that of the speaker, but for the good of the toilers themselves, and of the grand design. If any thanks are to be given, it is the design that gives thanks, acquiring speech in the speaker's mouth, and the toilers thank themselves in the speaker's words of thanks. (5)

Masquerading as servants, GDR bureaucrats utilize the cause of the people to cover their own ambition and hypocrisy. In "Posthumous Works" a government official who wishes to obtain potentially embarrassing papers from a dead poet's lover so that he may suppress them tells her that "if she gave the notes to him, and so to everyone, the poet's words would be returning to her" (65).

The hypostatization of "the design" entails the devaluation of the individual. Through Schädlich's at times very refined use of free indirect discourse, we experience the thoughts of a government official: "But it was not given to the individual, however stalwart and well-meaning, to see what was best for the whole. And the whole was what mattered" (61-62). Many stories address that disregard for the individual, most evidently in the recurring image of the GDR as a prison.

In an article published by *Die Zeit* (17 Oct. 1977), Schädlich compared paragraph 213 of GDR criminal law, which forbade East German citizens to cross their border without permission, with the GDR signature on the International Pact for Civil and Political Rights, which guarantees freedom of travel, and which the GDR ratified in 1973. In the story "Tibaos" Schädlich utilizes Brechtian alienation techniques to write an allegory that satirizes the absurd fictions and condescending justifications surrounding the former GDR prohibition on travel. Tibaos wishes to tour abroad but finds guards at the border, ostensibly to protect the country (officially, the GDR termed the Berlin Wall an antifascist protection wall). Tibaos knows that he would be shot were he to attempt to leave (50). But if he can find powerful monied allies abroad, he might be allowed to depart—this is a reference to the former West German practice of "buying" GDR citizens from GDR prisons. An expert warns Tibaos of a foreign plot to depopulate his country, and he furthermore predicts that Tibaos would probably be unhappy abroad. Tibaos responds that if he is unhappy it is no one's business but his own, exposing the patriarchal character of much GDR propaganda (53). After applying to leave his country, he suddenly finds it impossible to sell his work and earn his living there. His room is searched, and his petition is ignored for a year. When he inquires, it is denied. His experience parallels that of many GDR citizens who applied, as permitted by law, for an exit visa, and who then waited for an unspecified, seemingly arbitrary period during which they could not work in responsible positions, were harassed by the state in petty and not so petty ways, and coped with ostracization by acquaintances and, sometimes, friends.

Several stories deal with entrapment. In "Parts of the Countryside" the narrator suggests that the problems of a psychologically disturbed young woman who dies of exposure result in part from her sense of imprisonment:

> She travels to the northern end of the country and to the southern end. . . . Later she returns to the interior of the country. . . . She stays clear of the remaining borders of the country. Must let the small clarity of the lake outside the town stand for great expanses; must see the hill as a mountain. (17)

In "Barely Legible Letter" a worker renounces his citizenship after GDR authorities ignore his request to visit his dying father in the West (numerous families were split by the Wall). The worker insists he is "not the country's property." He has lost confidence in his government and does not ask questions because he no longer believes the answers (55). In "Search for a Sentence" an author watches a tourist encounter the Berlin Wall and attempts to imagine his feelings.

Schädlich's stories demonstrate other governmental modes of manipulation. An ambitious politician is "co-opted into the intimate circle" (5). A dissident writer softens his opposition when confronted with the implicit threat of imprisonment and with the more pleasurable sensation of official favor and of seeing his (admittedly self-bowdlerized) work in print. (By way of comparison, Schädlich describes in another story the imprisonment of the sixeenth-century writer Nikodemus Frischlin, who refused to cooperate with the government and lost his life.) The woman who possesses the embarrassing posthumous papers of a poet is promised a house and an income (66–67). The government can use the stick as well, and in "Under the Eighteen Towers of the Tyn Church," Schädlich describes the massive police effort to track down two GDR high school students who, while vacationing in Prague, make oppositional statements to Western reporters.

Like Kunze, Schädlich utilizes history to make his point, but whereas Kunze employs historical allusion within a contemporary scheme, Schädlich often moves back in time, depicting events from the past and allowing his readers to establish parallels with the present. In "The Emperor of Russia's Visit to the Emperor of Germany" and "Last Honors," he evokes remarkable similarities between nineteenth-century imperial courts and modern socialist political practices. Schädlich gains additional satirical force by narrating the stories in the style of a report in *Neues Deutschland*, a style replete with bombast, titles, and trivial detail. In "Stand up and Be Counted" Schädlich reveals only at the conclusion of the story that the speaker is a German emperor and not a GDR statesman, as the author has lead his reader to believe. "This Statue Slightly Larger Than Life-Size" again plays with reader expectations, at first suggesting that the statue represents a ruler from classical antiquity, and only gradually revealing that it is Walter Ulbricht, the SED First Secretary from 1953 through 1971. Ostensibly written in 2976, the text displays Schädlich's satirical use of style, for it mimics the harmless, well-combed prose of a text "designed for use in the schools" (125).

Despite all ideological differences, the similarity between past and present forms of repression becomes clear in Schädlich's treatment of the writers' role. As with Kunze, that represents a central theme. In "October Sky" a nineteenth-century journalist reflects on the censorship that affects his work. Reading a newspaper, he finds "that the finest trait in the character of the urban and rural inhabitants of the country was their boundless enthusiasm for the ruler" (129), an impression one formerly received from GDR newspapers. "Little Lessons in Prosody" describes the fashion in which the government transforms a young dissident writer into a sycophant. As we have noted, Schädlich's "Brief Account of the Death of Nikodemus Frischlin" reads as a counterpoint to "Prosody," for as Frischlin asserts, it is the "poets and learned men" who provide a danger to despots. The sixteenth-century efforts to co-opt Frischlin are crasser than those described in "Little Lessons in Prosody," but the principle remains the same. In a story that evinces the same verve, if not the same humor, as Stefan Heym's *The Queen Against Defoe* (Switz. 1970), Schädlich's Frischlin defends with spirit his right to freedom of expression: it is the poet as hero. The story contains one of the most important declarations in Schädlich's collection: "The poets have power to condemn the knavery of . . . despisers of the people, and they are not bound to make an accounting to each and every swaggerer. Such are the liberties of a poet, and where such do not exist, no one has any liberty" (151).

"Posthumous Works," another story concerning writers, describes the combination of idealism, naïveté, and loyalty that caused some authors, especially those who had spent World War II in exile and had hoped to find a home in the GDR, to suppress their doubts or dissent for fear that their criticism would be trumpeted in the West:

> But the poet balked when it came to accepting [his friend's] judgment of the work of other writers. The abbreviated yardstick was all too familiar to him. He did not like dividing opinions into pros and cons, and did not want to use his friend's words: useful or useless. Then again, but even more sharply, the poet detested the element of haste, rejected the arbitrary phrases written for rapid consumption. But because he did not want to provide the wrong people with language to be used against his friend, he kept his objections to himself. (62)

In this passage Schädlich describes with considerable acumen the invidious and formerly widespread process of self-censorship in the GDR.

Like Reiner Kunze, Schädlich devotes his last story to the role of the writer. His "Search for a Sentence" implicitly investigates the differing functions of authors in East and West. At least since the Austrian Hugo von Hofmannsthal's famous "Chandos Letter" (1902), in which an author explains why he feels he can no longer write poetry, Western writers have grown increasingly aware of the insufficiency of language to express experience. There exists an inevitable gap between objects and words, which are signs and not the "thing in itself." Writers labor under the knowledge of the impossibility of precise description, and perhaps of narrative itself. Self-reflexive verbal constructs that draw attention to their own inadequacy, to their own inevitable failure, are hallmarks of modernist literature.

The boundaries of narrative ran differently in the GDR. Words attain a different meaning and value when some are forbidden and others must be weighed and rationed. In Schädlich's "Search for a Sentence," the GDR writer Scarron has "created an imaginary authority whose business it is to search through all written matter for offenses against the authority's aesthetic principles; should it come upon any displeasing word, it can impose penalties on Scarron. Since the authority has been conceived on the basis of imagined and real experience, it is not hard for Scarron to draw up the list of penalties" (156). Scarron later notes that he utilizes a "self-chosen censoring authority" (164); Schädlich thus attacks not only governmental censorship, but also, as in the example from "Posthumous Works," the self-censorship it helps engender. From his window seat high above the street, Scarron attempts to describe the experience of a foreign traveler who is about to encounter the Berlin Wall: "But does one, even here, anticipating or meeting objections from a censoring office, already have to exercise nicety in choice of words?" (157).

The text utilizes various metaphors of vision and vision blocked. Scarron, for example, has attained a certain height. He maintains a literal overview and can see farther than the traveler on the street, but he remains hampered. His problem is not, however, so much the linguistic and epistemological one of multivalent words, whose meaning oscillates; his problem is rifles. He cannot decide whether he sees a wire or a wire fence beyond the first wall, and he is unsure of "the correct technical terms for fence and for the small white bulbous things fastened between the various parts of the fence" (162). Scarron concludes that he might receive additional information from the border guards: "But such relations with army soldiers would be frowned on by the examining authority, Scarron tells himself. So he must give up the idea of arriving at higher precision of description, with which the soldiers might have been able to help him" (162).

Scarron struggles to find the proper language to render the traveler's astonishment and horror at the Wall, as well as the meaning of a sentence a passerby shouted to the traveler as the latter prepared to photograph the Wall. After much reflection Scarron chooses an ambiguous double entendre that, though it expresses his meaning and will annoy the censoring authority, will probably be allowed by that authority (160). Schädlich thus underscores the difficulties involved in reading, as well as writing, a GDR text—a text the GDR public, censors, and Western critics carefully examined between the lines. Such care with words can enhance literature, but it can also obstruct it, and Scarron takes "himself to task for speaking unclearly for listeners who are strangers in town, so that the visible recedes in the course of elaborate explanations of the boundary of narrative" (163). A reader of GDR texts must be especially equipped with a knowledge of history and of the GDR context; otherwise, a story may appear meaningless.

As with many of his other stories, Schädlich's "Search for a Sentence" contains numerous literary references. Paul Scarron was a seventeenth-century French author who lived in Paris and Rome. He was paralyzed for the final twenty-three years of his life. His story formed the basis for "Scarron at the Window" by the German author Karl Friedrich Kretschmann (1738–1808). Kretschmann's story in turn inspired E.T.A. Hoffmann's "The Cousin's Corner Window" (1822), which relates the fashion in which an invalid cousin, sitting in his window above the street, infuses the bustling events below him with his imagination. Such use of literary citation, allusion, and echo was widespread among GDR authors; in *The New Sorrows of Young W.* Ulrich Plenzdorf skillfully utilized a text from Goethe to create ambiguity and, not incidentally, additional leeway with the censor. By consciously evoking the ancestry of Scarron, Kretschmann, and Hoffmann, Schädlich underscores the interdependence, the intertextuality of all literature, and hence the absurdity of attempts to censor that literature.

GDR critics ignored Schädlich's book, which Western critics greeted with uniform approbation. Günter Grass championed the stories, reading them during his own tours and recommending them to a U.S. publisher. He also wrote a jacket blurb for the West German publisher, asserting that Schädlich was the first writer since Uwe Johnson to bring the essence of GDR reality to such literary *niveau*. In *Die Zeit* Fritz Raddatz called *Approximation* the most important work of GDR prose literature in a long while (19 Aug. 1977). Marcel Reich-Ranicki praised it highly in the conservative *Frankfurter Allgemeine Zeitung* (11 Oct. 1977), as did leftist authors Nicolas Born in the *Frankfurter Rundschau* (17 Sept. 1977) and Hans-Christoph Buch in the *Süddeutsche Zeitung* (20–21 August 1977). In *Der Spiegel* Jurek Becker celebrated Schädlich's language, his use of Brechtian alienation techniques, and his courage in breaking the "unwritten rules" to which GDR writers were subject (17 August 1977). Becker knew of what he wrote, for he was himself under attack in the GDR and was preparing to publish his dissident novel *Sleepless Days*.

Becker's axiological criteria suggest that, as with Kunze, nonliterary categories played a not inconsequential role in the West German reception of Schädlich's book. Reviewing that reception in 1978, the West German literary critic Hans-Peter Klausenitzer asserted that after the Biermann scandal and the escalating confrontation between the East German government and its intelligentsia, the interest of the West German public centered more on the writer than on the written. Klausenitzer thought the various analyses of Schädlich's style represented indirect, aesthetically coated expressions of sympathy for the author, and he noted that the unanimous approval of Schädlich's difficult texts placed the autonomy of West German criticism into question ("Der Erfolg").

With more distance, John Updike asserted in the *New Yorker* that, although "all honor is due yet another writer who struggled against the inane censorship of a communist state," the translation of Schädlich's "brave work . . . may afford its American readers satisfactions more political than aesthetic; Mr. Schädlich's style is as bleak as his themes, and the ingenious strategies of expression under tyranny can seem rather spindly out in the open" (21 April 1980).

In the *New York Times Book Review* Richard Eder advanced a far more positive assessment of the book. Eder noted that, although European writers have in general exhausted alienation as a theme, in "the particular conditions of Eastern Europe a writer's sense of estrangement can have the effect of the most direct and moving testimony." He helps contextualize those "particular conditions" with reference to Wolf Biermann and Jurek Becker. Eder also recognizes, even in translation, one element of Schädlich's prose that fascinated West German critics—his language. Eder describes a "tone of deliberate, bureaucratic coldness and evasiveness," such as one would find with a hack reporter or plodding policeman: "It is through this imprisoned language, used to force us into the silence and evasions of his society, that the author conveys emotion" (27 Jan. 1980).

Jurek Becker, *Sleepless Days* FRG 1978, USA 1979

Karl Marx wrote eloquently in his *Economic and Philosophical Manuscripts* of the threefold alienation affecting human beings in capitalism. People experience a sense of alienation from their work, the product of which does not belong to them; they grow alienated from others, with whom they must compete; and they are alienated from themselves, for the consequences of the first two forms of estrangement leave no room for development of the self. Jurek Becker's fourth novel, *Sleepless Days,* demonstrates that these three forms of alienation continued to exist in East German socialism as well.

The novel begins with a mid-life crisis, a venerable topos in Western letters. In postwar German literature one finds the theme prominently represented in works by Max Frisch, Martin Walser, Günter Grass, or Ingeborg Bachmann; Peter Handke's Gregor Keuschnig (*A Moment of True Feeling*) awakens at mid-life and realizes, "All at once he had ceased to belong" (9). A few weeks before his thirty-sixth birthday, Becker's Karl Simrock, a teacher, feels a pain in his heart. He dismisses his class and returns home, where he informs his rather unsympathetic wife that the incident, which has made him acutely aware of his mortality, will have far-reaching consequences of which he remains as yet unaware.

In the following days Simrock examines his life and finds it empty. He sets out to correct that: he separates from his wife, begins a love affair, and becomes more outspoken at work. Attempting to escape to the West, his lover, Antonia, is apprehended and jailed for seventeen months. These events accelerate Simrock's own political malaise. Hence when an army officer visits Simrock's class to describe the advantages of a military career, Simrock embarrasses him with unexpectedly direct questions. A small scandal ensues, and Simrock loses his position.

In the course of the novel, Simrock recognizes the unfortunate consequences of his former teaching methods. Near the end of a semester, with the curriculum completed and the grading done, he decides to spend the remaining few sessions reading aloud from books that might provoke his students:

> Simrock was shocked to note how the verses and phrases bounced off the deaf ears of his students and shattered. He told himself that neither the words nor the holiday mood could be responsible for this, the youngsters' indifference must be due to something else. I have a deplorable share in this myself, he thought, for I have been teaching them to close their minds to anything unsettling. (70)

Similarly, when the military officer visits the class and invites questions, Simrock's students remain silent, and Simrock admits with chagrin that their reticence to probe and challenge results from his own example and his own teaching (116).

Simrock concludes it is necessary to change the curriculum, which allowed no space for the imagination of the individual teacher. By allowing the instructor more freedom, an atmosphere might arise "in which children would grow into true individuals and not be doomed to resemble one another the way their teachers did" (112). Simrock knows, however, that he has no allies, and that to suggest curriculum modification is to invite a disciplinary proceeding. After additional thought, he begins to suspect a reason for the tightly crammed schedule:

> The ballast in the programs, he thought, is there deliberately and calculated to a hair; its purpose is to prevent the very thing that seems to me so important: for teachers to find time to teach and educate students according to their own beliefs. From one class to the next, the suspicion grew in him that there was a pretty obvious lack of confidence in his teaching personality; it was regarded as an incalculable risk, and that was why conditions had been created that would prevent its development. (112)

A feeling of paralysis begins to affect Simrock as he becomes aware of the seeming hopelessness of his situation, where even a moderate show of independence, he correctly speculates, would lead to his dismissal. As with the school described in Reiner Kunze's *The Wonderful Years*, a high and apparently unchangeable degree of regimentation informs Simrock's institution, where he constantly receives "well-meant" advice from Kabitzke, the administration sycophant; where Ines Wohlgemuth, a colleague, most probably functions as a Party informant (51); and where students will denounce their teachers (96–97). Kunze and Becker display considerably less optimism about school reform than did Christa Wolf in *Divided Heaven* (1963); in the 1970s, the dogmatic Mangold-types unquestionably rule. In 1990 Petra Gruner edited a revealing collection of 170 letters from GDR students and teachers who documented how accurately Becker and Kunze had portrayed the atmosphere in East German schools (*Angepaßt*).

Alienated from his working environment, Simrock is also alienated from other members of his society. In part that derives from the uncertainty characterizing personal relationships in the novel. Simrock considers an affair with Ines Wohlgemuth but rejects the thought since he finds her politics suspect. In addition to the spies who inhabit Simrock's workplace, GDR society consists of people who, to gain some advantage or merely to be left alone, practice a refined hypocrisy: "And really, how can you persuade a person who isn't happy in a country that the only correct thing is to remain there: That person only will stay out of fear of the risks involved in escaping; that's why we are surrounded by people who apparently fully endorse the system" (100). Simrock's personal relationships are nonfulfilling. He has no friends (106), and his marriage has become an empty ritual. After he leaves his wife, he begins to love Antonia, but she attempts to escape to the West without revealing her plans to him. Although Simrock resolves to wait for her release from prison, he will be living with a woman for whom, in a larger sense, the GDR represents a prison, and who was prepared to leave him in order to leave it.

Ultimately, Simrock discovers his alienation from himself. At first he cannot articulate his dissatisfaction; he knows only a vague unhappiness (4, 7), a lack of concentration (17, 39). His disquiet evolves into disgust (23). Near the middle of the story, Simrock realizes in an epiphany that the origins of his discontent are political, just as the alienation from his work and from others is political:

He was struck by the suspicion that all his unhappiness arose from a pitiful lack of opinion. Whenever he had been obliged to voice an opinion, he had always—he was bound to admit—chosen the one expected by the others, thus gradually losing the capacity to form his own opinions. . . . He felt as if he had fallen deeply and unconditionally into a creed, and as if this creed had stopped his mouth for all time, leaving him only with the choice of constantly repeating it or of exposing himself as a defector. It was this unconditional aspect that accounted for his unhappiness, a disregard for himself as an individual that for many years he had not admitted to himself. (53)

This "lack of regard for himself as an individual" presents the crux of Simrock's dilemma, and the story records his efforts to change. He notes at the conclusion: "What probably disgusted me most was the fact that I never resisted. . . . I did not believe in being responsible for myself" (131).

Simrock's musings echo Kafka's parable of the doorkeeper in *The Trial*, where a man waits in vain for permission to enter a door that, as he lies dying, the doorkeeper shuts. Simrock reflects: "I have been waiting for the door to be opened behind which the action is taking place. I never asked myself whose hand was supposed to turn the doorknob" (19). Becker's novel may share some characteristics with Kafka's, but Becker's Simrock is a socialist in a socialist country. He understands that his dissatisfaction has political roots, and he adopts political action as a corrective.

He begins by attempting to combat the hypocrisy that surrounds him. As a weapon, he employs the most elegant method available to dissidents, East or West: he takes ideology seriously. Hence he does not implicitly or explicitly order his students to attend the May Day parade, for it is nowhere written that attendance is mandatory. He receives a rebuke for that: "voluntary" attendance is in fact a code, one known to all mature GDR citizens, for "obligatory" attendance. In an assertion at once ludicrous and ominous, Kabitzke tells Simrock that various authorities view the latter's emphasis on the voluntary aspect of attendance "as an act of defiance" and warns him that he is acting in a self-destructive fashion (44).

Simrock believes genuine socialist sentiments can develop without coercion. He "wished for a closer relationship to Communism than merely a strict adherence to his country's prevailing rules" (54). Like Wolf Biermann, he is a committed, even fervent socialist, but his very commitment causes him difficulties. He knows that his society needs the dialectic of dissent rather than mechanical agreement (21). Hence he reads to his class a poem by Bertolt Brecht, "In Praise of Doubt." As a result of Simrock's action, an irate father writes a censorious letter, asserting that doubt is not at all what GDR children should be learning. The parent thinks his child should acquire not doubt but "revolutionary patience," an amusing oxymoron that in its irony signals a structural principle in the novel (with its paradoxical title), and indeed in GDR society, where "voluntary" attendance meant the opposite.

Simrock's willingness to doubt puzzles some colleagues and infuriates others. Kabitzke, who actually seems to like Simrock, complains: "I can see that you are growing more and more inflexible. But I can't get to the bottom of your defiance." Simrock replies, "That doesn't matter, as long as the defiance is there" (99). The inevitable explosion occurs when Simrock confronts the visiting army officer with seemingly harmless questions regarding restrictions to which soldiers are subject. Dismayed and speechless, the officer leaves the classroom, and Simrock is dismissed soon thereafter. He takes a job delivering bread.

School authorities allow Simrock the opportunity to return if he confesses his "error." They demand that ritual of "self-criticism" in which communist states indulged since Stalin, and which Ulrich Plenzdorf's Edgar Wibeau found so distasteful. Simrock refuses:

How can you hope for me to apologize for an injustice done to me? How can you expect me to feel gratitude for a humiliation? And above all: How can you want a teacher who is prepared to go along with such a proposition? (130)

Simrock has gained a measure of independence and established a degree of moral integrity, no small victories; he has also lost his ability to influence GDR youth. The West German literary critics Sigrid Lüdke-Haertel and W. Martin Lüdke see in the conclusion a retreat from the political into private existence (7), but the authorities in the novel think differently. Simrock believes they wish to bring him back as a teacher, because "a teacher who had been fired was a potential troublemaker" (130). The state can better control teachers, and authors, when it provides them a comfortable living.

Becker's fourth and last novel from the GDR, *Sleepless Days*, presents his most radical confrontation with East German society. *Jakob the Liar* (1969), Becker's first novel, does not deal with the GDR, and *Leading the Authorities Astray* (1973), his second book, brims with criticism but advances it indirectly—the protagonist declares, "I live [in the GDR] of my own free will" (39; my trans.). Some Western critics dismissed Becker's third novel, *The Boxer* (1976), as an apologia for the GDR. Even assuming the injustice of the latter charge, the change of sentiment in *Sleepless Days* appears abrupt.

Becker's impatience with "revolutionary patience" comes in no small part from his involvement in the scandals surrounding Reiner Kunze and Wolf Biermann. Becker was the only GDR author to object publicly to Kunze's exclusion in October 1976 from the GDR Writers' Association. Then, as one of the original twelve signatories of the famous letter protesting Biermann's expatriation in November 1976, Becker, who in 1975 had received the prestigious National Prize of the GDR, found himself with sudden leperlike status. The Socialist Unity party expelled him in 1976. In 1977 he withdrew from the Writers' Association when the majority refused to support the Biermann petitioners. That year he left the GDR—with the permission of the SED, which supplied him a long-term visa—and he lived in the West, including a semester at Oberlin College and one at the University of Texas, until the demise of the GDR.

Becker wrote *Sleepless Days* in the GDR but published it only in the West, for obvious reasons. He breaks numerous taboos in his novel, which, like Kunze's *The Wonderful Years* or Hans Joachim Schädlich's *Approximation*, describes the regimentation of life and the pervasiveness of hypocrisy and censorship (Simrock's illegal copy of a book by Max Frisch is confiscated) in the GDR. The novel debunks the myth of the heroic worker by demonstrating that dirty, boring work remains dirty and boring even in the workers' state. Becker attacks the GDR legal system as a cynical facade: the trial of Simrock's friend Antonia represents a mechanical exercise that is "prefabricated, predetermined, and tragic" (103). And after Simrock is dismissed from school, the superintendent tells him that "needless to say, he had a legal right to appeal—but in a tone that made it very clear how unwise such a course would be" (121). Additionally, Becker's book deals with GDR travel prohibitions and, like Kunze's book, questions the attractiveness of a military career at a time when the state, over the objections of the Protestant church, was establishing mandatory military training courses in the public schools.

Finally, Becker establishes parallels between the methods of GDR "cultural" authorities and earlier authorities. Simrock attends a new movie that is interrupted by an obviously orchestrated cacophony of catcalls. The film is withdrawn, with the explanation that it had met with the disapproval of the public. These were methods used by Nazi thugs.

Politically brisant, *Sleepless Days* provides Becker's disappointed reckoning with his country. It was written hurriedly, under the pressure of events, during an unsettled time in the author's life. The novel's flaws reflect that, and the *Frankfurter Allgemeine Zeitung* pointed to various grammatical irregularities or infelicitous formulations (25 March 1978). Leila Vennewitz smooths these somewhat in her translation. She cannot, however, change Becker's at times rather awkward manner of rendering dialogue:

> He said: "I suppose you're ashamed now."
> Antonia: "I couldn't tell you before."
> Simrock: "Did you know before we left home?" (92)

Becker's method of putting sentence on sentence without transition leaves a sense of narrative embarrassment, resulting perhaps from the haste in which the author wrote. The most unsatisfactory aspect of the novel derives from the fact that Becker presents an argument, an experiment called Simrock. The development has a somewhat mechanical aspect to it—for example, when Simrock sits down to draft a plan for his new start in life (20–22) or to list the qualities of a good teacher (46–48).

Most West German literary critics did not overlook the novel's stylistic difficulties, but they preferred to emphasize Becker's courage and the book's political importance (an exception was *Die Welt*, which actually accused Becker of a whitewash concerning the GDR [8 April 1978]). Writing in *Die Zeit*, Fritz Raddatz called *Sleepless Days* Becker's "most vehement, most bitter book, the evidence of the integrity of a noble man." He also characterized the novel as Becker's "weakest, most unartistic" one, but he placed more blame on the GDR than on Becker; in the absence of a free press, he asserted, literature must air public issues, often to the detriment of literature (10 March 1978; my trans.). In the *Süddeutsche Zeitung* Wolfgang Werth emphasized the considerable information the novel made available to West German readers. Playing on a famous sentence by Brecht ("Unhappy the land that needs heroes"), Werth asserted that Becker's book demonstrates why the GDR belonged to those unhappy countries (11 April 1978).

Some of that information also reached GDR citizens, though via a different medium. Most East Germans could and did watch West German television, and some West German programming specifically addressed an East German audience. Given the positive *political* reception of Becker's novel, it proved hardly surprising that West Germans filmed it for television in 1982. Thus many East Germans could at least *see* Becker's story. Much to the displeasure of *Die Welt* (26 April 1986), the West German filmmakers tried to de-emphasize somewhat the GDR-specific aspects of Becker's story, instead suggesting that his central confrontation, the praise of doubt against authority, contained relevance for other societies as well.

Ironically enough, translation into English helped Becker's novel. Though German critics had objected to his rather awkward language, the English critic Paul Bundy, writing in the *New Statesman*, lauded Leila Vennowitz's "beautifully and limpidly rendered" translation; he found the novel "deeply impressive" and "the work of an obvious master, whose name will surely be as familiar to us in the near future as those of Heinrich Böll and Uwe Johnson" (30 Nov. 1979). In the United States Dorothy Wickenden wrote a review for the *New Republic* in praise of the "spare, beautifully crafted novel" (3 Nov. 1979), while Irving Howe in the *New York Times Book Review* admires Becker's "beautifully made fiction." Howe correctly perceives Becker's "tone of hovering anxiety, as if somewhere in the background lurked the ghost of Kafka," and he asserts that the "book tells us what it is like to live in the airless world of authoritarianism, the costs of obedience, and possibilities of resistance" (16 Sept. 1979). In November the *New York Times Book Review* included *Sleepless Days* in its "Selection of Best Books of 1979" (25 Nov. 1979).

Rolf Schneider, *November* FRG 1979, USA 1981, GDR 1990

Born in 1932, Rolf Schneider has written numerous works, many dealing with the German past. Some of those works suggested that the past lived on in the Federal Republic, a theme that helped endear him to the GDR government. But Schneider also believed that though it is not the greatest virtue of belles lettres to be controversial it is also not their greatest virtue to be noncontroversial (*Die Zeit* 23 Feb. 1979). One of the twelve original signatories of the letter protesting the coerced expatriation of Wolf Biermann, Schneider was the first of the twelve to integrate that event into literature. Schneider had been neither an apparatchik nor a dissident, but with the 1979 West German publication of *November*, he willy-nilly became the latter.

Schneider's novel centers on the GDR writer Natascha Roth and her family. Roth has a son, Stefan, a daughter, Sibylle, and a husband, Rudolf, who is an art historian. The perspective alternates between Natascha and Stefan, who, at the novel's outset, is hit by a truck and badly injured, so that he limps. The text portrays both characters as alienated. Natascha is neurotic, drinks too much, suffers from an overwrought imagination, and has no friends. Her husband reminds her that due to her privileges as a writer she is completely out of touch with the GDR quotidian. On account of his mother's privilege and of his injury, Stefan also develops a sense of isolation, a sense reinforced when his only friend undertakes a suicide attempt of which Stefan had had no intimation, and when the parents of Stefan's girlfriend forbid her to see him after his mother becomes politically suspect. Both Natascha Roth and her son view the world with melancholy, fear, and often disgust. The narrator registers in minute detail their perceptions, which alienate everyday objects. Both protagonists perceive the established order of things as arbitrary and insecure.

The first half of the book records Stefan's accident and its results, as well as Natascha Roth's paralyzing writing block and her discovery that Rudolf is having an affair. In the middle of the book, a dissident GDR writer (not a singer) named Bodakov is allowed to travel to West Germany for the first time in years; the GDR government does not allow him back. Six artists, including Roth, meet and formulate a public letter of protest. The remainder of the novel deals with

Roth's subsequent difficulties, some real, many imagined. The government subjects all the signatories to similar pressures, causing two to leave the country, two to retract their signatures, and one to retreat into senility. Natascha Roth does not retreat, and she defends her decision to her husband and to her acquaintance Erica Roth with some eloquence.

Natascha and her husband decide to divorce. Natascha fantasizes about leaving for West Germany, but she ultimately remains in the East, where her privileges continue. At the conclusion she departs on a trip to France.

Schneider appends a disclaimer to his novel, asserting that, although he appropriated recent events in a very free form, he wished to write neither a roman à clef nor a documentation; he attempted, he adds, to avoid resemblances with living persons. Western feuilletonists viewed Schneider's disclaimer as at best disingenuous, or perhaps as a proleptic attempt to protect himself. Schneider obviously uses the Biermann scandal of November 1976, in which he was a participant, to attract attention to *November*, and his West German publisher included a pamphlet with documentary material from the affair. Despite Schneider's disavowal of having written a roman à clef, one easily identifies Bodakov as an amalgamation of Biermann and Reiner Kunze; Natascha Roth possesses elements of the cosmopolitan Schneider, who wears Burberry coats, drives a Mercedes, and has a handicapped daughter.

Schneider disappointed Western critics with his treatment of the Biermann scandal. The *Frankfurter Allgemeine Zeitung* found the description anticlimactic: rather than showing the Biermann affair—and its results—as the cultural-political earthquake that it was, Schneider displays it more as a minor disruption. As the newspaper correctly points out, the only concrete result appears to be that the Roths decide to divorce (28 Feb. 1979).

Schneider does de-emphasize the consequences of signing the protest petition. Natascha Roth finds that some acquaintances no longer greet her, and her son loses a girlfriend because the girl's father does not want her associating with someone from the Roth family. The government sends a rather embarrassed agent to talk with Natascha; it also observes her house and intercepts some mail. And someone writes "red pig" (a play on her name: *Rot(h)e Sau*) on the sidewalk (that is reminiscent of Nazi tactics and reflects what actually happened to the poet Sarah Kirsch, who signed the Biermann protest letter). Roth's career continues unhampered, however, and at the conclusion of the novel, she begins a business trip to France. By comparison, after Schneider's decision to publish *November* in the West, he could no longer perform public readings in his country, and publishers canceled two of his contracts; he received threatening letters and telephone calls (although he has an unlisted number), and the government refused his visa application for Austria.

Nonetheless, I think we can take seriously Schneider's claim that he did not wish to write a documentary novel, that his goals were different. In a talk entitled "The Social Revolution in the Modern Novel," a talk that GDR authorities prevented Schneider from delivering in Austria, and which he then sent to *Die Zeit*, Schneider singles out two themes for discussion: the continuation of privilege in the GDR, and the necessity of remembering the past (30 March 1979). These figure as major themes in *November* as well. At the conclusion of chapter 1, as Stefan is transported in an ambulance to a hospital, he hears the medical personnel discussing the fact that, because his mother is a privileged writer, he will go to a clinic that did not usually accept cases like his (9). His mother travels to Paris at least once a year (11), wears leather clothes, and drives a French car (17); she and her husband look younger, less worn, than GDR workers of a comparable age (87). Natascha brings Western clothes and delicacies to her children, either from her trips to France or from the domestic "currency shops," where one could buy Western goods for "hard" (Western) currency (e.g., 23, 25). By contrast, the parents of Stefan's friend Thomas do not possess Western money and cannot make purchases in the special shops (92).

Near the conclusion of the novel, a taxi driver complains to Roth of the currency shops and their corrosive effects:

In clipped sentences he railed against the number and the stock of the foreign-currency stores. He described a case of corruption known to him, caused by the universal greed for West European currencies. "People like us aren't privileged," he growled. *Not privileged.* The driver lapsed into a hostile silence. (234)

In his article for *Die Zeit*, Schneider asserted that Marx's sketch of socialism did not constitute a radical egalitarian fantasy, but that the philosopher did expect a lessening of social differences in the economic realm and in the consciousness of citizens. Schneider's novel demonstrates that this had not occurred in the GDR, and that the government, through its currency shops (born of the need for "hard" Western currency) or its privileging of certain professions, actually contributed to the creation of different socioeconomic groups.

In *Die Zeit* Schneider also discussed the necessity of remembering the past, especially the communist past with its misuse of arbitrary power. Stalin and his legacy remained central problems, but Schneider noted that Soviet bloc communists too often circumscribed Stalinism with terms of embarrassment, such as *cult of personality* or *dogmatism*. If others refuse to investigate the phenomenon, Schneider asserted, then writers must.

In *November*, Stalin hovers in the background, informing the text and governing the actions of the characters. Bodakov once wrote paeans to Stalin. After the revelations of 1956 and an ensuing personal crisis, "he moved away not merely from Djugashvili, but from everything for which, for a long time, Djugashvili stood" (46). Erica Roth, an acquaintance of Natascha's, says that in 1956, when Khrushchev unveiled some of the truth concerning Stalin, her horror was easily eclipsed by the fear that everything might disintegrate, and that all efforts would have been in vain (57). And yet she seems to contradict that statement three pages later, when she compares a nation with the human psyche, speaks of psychosomatic energies, and complains that her society dealt too summarily with Khrushchev's revelations (60).

Erica Roth may believe repression breeds disease, but she supports the expatriation of Bodakov and condemns Natascha Roth for protesting. Natascha, however, perceives the connection between Stalinism and Bodakov's expatriation. Hence she sides with Bodakov against Erica, even though she does not like him or his writing:

> Monstrous things have been done in our name, you know that. I'm talking about the past. That wouldn't have happened if someone had spoken up, perhaps someone like us. Silence is no solution, Erica, and mistakes put into words are better than silence. (160)

Similarly, Schneider wrote in *Die Zeit* that to remain silent would be comparable to lying, and in the West German *Stern* magazine (24 Nov. 1977), he repeated Erica Roth's point that repression breeds illness. Schneider does not know how GDR socialists are to free themselves from Stalin and his legacy (in which he includes Pol Pot), but he insists on the necessity of critical inquiry, in literature and elsewhere.

· Most West German critics remained unimpressed. Joachim Kaiser asserted in the *Süddeutsche Zeitung* that Schneider attempts to show the difficulties of his heroes as the result of private problems (4 April 1979). In the *Frankfurter Rundschau* Yaak Karsunke spoke of the reprivatizing of a state action. He criticized Schneider for underplaying the repressive reality of GDR society; without a clear picture of the outward pressure, the social and coerced element of the escape into scenes from a marriage cannot be recognized (7 April 1979).

Schneider does, however, create a connection between Natascha Roth and her society with his references to speech and silence. For some time before Bodakov's expatriation, Roth's creativity has been dwindling. In an attempt to overcome her writing block, she works on a biography of Rimbaud, who ceased writing poetry after his twenty-first birthday. Here, too, she encounters difficulty putting pen to paper, but Rimbaud's story occupies her thoughts, and she ponders the connection between revolution and poetry, asking whether the collapse of the 1871 commune led ineluctably to the death of Rimbaud as poet (41). Near the conclusion of the novel, she imagines that Rimbaud, in a letter to Verlaine, answers her questions affirmatively. The parallels with the GDR are clear: the suppression of a "revolution" has lamed a writer.

Roth's inauthenticity as an author also paralyzes her. After an Italian truck driver is shot and killed at the GDR border, Roth writes an angry poem that her son discovers: "He would have liked to talk to his mother about why she wrote differently from the way she spoke, why she wrote for herself differently from how she wrote for publication, why she talked to him differently than to other people" (68–69). Roth signs the letter protesting Bodakov's expatriation to free herself from self-censorship: she views it as a vaccine against speechlessness (127). She defends herself to her son by saying that she would have otherwise suffocated (133). With that she unwittingly echoes Klaus Poche, who published a novel, also in 1979, describing a GDR writer and entitled *Choking*. Natascha Roth joins a list of GDR literary figures from the 1970s who suffer from writing blocks; prominent examples from the post-Biermann era include the protagonist of Werner Heiduczek's *Death at the Seaside* (1977) and Stefan Heym's *Collin* (FRG 1979). (Until 1989, only Heiduczek's novel had been published in the GDR, and it was long available only by special permission in many libraries.) The protagonists in these novels all suffer from governmental or internal censorship. Additionally, the Stalinist past weighs on them. Not surprisingly, illness often serves as a metaphor for a more general societal disease born from the repression of which Schneider speaks.

In addition to the obvious references to the continuation of privilege, to Biermann's expatriation, and to Stalinism, *November* broaches several other taboos. It describes officially sanctioned discrimination against a handicapped youth (152–53). It notes parallels between the Socialist Unity party and previous authoritarian German governments (158). It deals with the dissatisfaction of GDR youth raised in socialism but nonetheless (or therefore) longing for Western music and books. The government responds to student protests with arrests and deportations (145, 222). *November* also relates the story of a woman who is arrested attempting to flee West with her three children to join her lover (53).

Thus it surprised no one when in 1978 the East German Hinstorff Verlag refused to publish *November*. (A few weeks earlier Hinstorff had also rejected Jurek Becker's *Sleepless Days*, after which Becker left the country.) Just as the GDR media excoriated Christa Wolf's unpublished *The Quest for Christa T.* in the late 1960s, in the late 1970s the establishment assaulted Schneider's unpublished *November*, and Schneider himself at times encountered vicious ad hominem assaults. At the 1978 Leipzig Book Fair, Vice Minister for Culture Klaus Höpcke labeled *November* an "artistically, politically, and humanly tasteless, inferior book" (qtd. in *Die Welt* 29 March 1978; my trans.). In *Neues Deutschland* a politically loyal writer called Schneider (along with Stefan Heym and Joachim Seyppel) a "bum" (*kaputter Typ*; 22 May 1979). As usual in such instances, Schneider had no public recourse in the GDR. When he published replies in West German newspapers, East German Party loyalists castigated him anew for cooperating with the class enemy and for providing that enemy anticommunist fodder.

After the GDR blocked publication of *November* at home, Klaus Höpcke appeared to threaten economic sanctions against any Western publisher who printed the novel (*Die Welt* 29 March 1978). The respected West German Luchterhand publishing house, which had printed Schneider's previous work, refused to publish *November*, as did the West German Fischer Publishers (which had published Reiner Kunze's *The Wonderful Years* after the book had had difficulty with other West German publishers). The novel eventually appeared with Albrecht Knaus in Hamburg, and it was widely reviewed in the Federal Republic. Günter Zehm of *Die Welt* found it an "impressive piece of literature" (24 Feb. 1979), but he remained virtually alone with his opinion. Yaak Karsunke was closer to the majority when he criticized Schneider's attempt to lift his "superficial prose with metaphorical gymnastics to literary level" (*Frankfurter Rundschau* 7 April 1979; my trans.). *November* does evince numerous aesthetic difficulties, though probably no more than Schneider's earlier books published by his West German and East German publishers. It was *not* published in the GDR for political reasons, and it *was* published in the FRG for political reasons. Such were the realities of the literary market in a divided Germany.

Writing in the *New York Times Book Review*, Joel Schechter noted Schneider's appraisal of a book's political reception: "Mr. Schneider's wry etching of this situation suggests that East Germans find their largest audience when they become involved in political controversy." Schechter sees in the novel "by no means a strident plea," noting that

it is far less direct than a protest letter, perhaps not a protest at all. But *November* offers a pleasurable and timely example of a novel's capacity to resist both state- and self-imposed silence. Like Heiner Müller, Christa Wolf, and other East German writers who objected to Mr. Biermann's expatriation, Rolf Schneider speaks in an inventive, politically conscious voice that should be heard in America as well as in Germany. (21 June 1981)

As with Jurek Becker's *Sleepless Days*, *November* appears to have gained in translation, for some infelicitous aspects of Schneider's language, aspects that disturbed West German critics, have been lost. Instead, Schechter perceives Schneider's voice, political but not necessarily dissident, as one that would enrich American discourse. In the *Nation* Tamar Jacoby similarly praised Schneider's "quiet, thoughtful writing" and "the absence of bitterness or rancor or shrill polemical ideas." Jacoby noted that Schneider "sees clearly enough that 'audacity' and bitterness do not necessarily make for good literature. And yet, as he shows in *November*, it is not impossible to write in a quiet, questioning way about what it is to make a political act" (2 May 1981). In *The Village Voice* Laurie Stone asserted that we "are fortunate to have" Schneider's novel, and that "the claim that it was ever rejected for literary reasons is profoundly idiotic" (3 June 1981). Like the other U.S. reviewers, Stone enjoyed Schneider's brooding, surrealistic novel about alienation; for American sensibilities, it seems so very German.

Thoughtful U.S. reviewers showed themselves aware of the trap of equating the politically dissident with the good. They also proved refreshingly frank in their willingness to recognize openly, as opposed to some East and West Germans, publication (and translation) of some books as political acts, in order, as Herbert Mitgang put it in the *Times*, "to send a message across the Wall" (17 Dec. 1976). We should also note what translation, as well as politics, can do for axiology. Whereas West Germans praised the literary qualities of *The Wonderful Years* and *Approximation*, U.S. critic Martin Greenberg thought Kunze's book "courageous" but "modest," and John Updike found Schädlich's work "brave" but "rather spindly." *Sleepless Days* and *November*, criticized by West Germans as linguistically flawed, appeared in translation to be "beautifully crafted."

After the publication of *November* in the West, Schneider reached a stage of considerable disillusionment. Writing during 1979 in *Die Zeit*, he asserted that a scandal in the GDR literary scene is manufactured through public attacks on an artist—through aesthetic rebukes, personal insult, and political disqualification. He noted dryly that the target of such attacks experiences sundry private and public inconveniences (23 Feb. 1979). Yet in February 1979 he told the *Frankfurter Rundschau* that he had never seriously considered moving to the West, that he was emotionally attached to the socialist experiment called the GDR, and that emigration would symbolize a personal and political defeat (17 Feb. 1979). In that he is similar to his protagonist Natascha Roth. But a month later, after repressive measures against Schneider increased, he commented to the same newspaper:

Naturally I had to reckon with the fact that such things would happen. At the same time it embitters me that they are actually happening. They are not life-threatening, but they achieve their purpose: anxiety and disgust." (*Frankfurter Rundschau* 21 March 1979; my trans.)

GDR authorities eventually awarded Schneider, like Jurek Becker, a long-term visa for the West (another privilege given to selected writers). Unlike Jurek Becker, however, who remained in the West, Schneider quietly returned to the GDR. A bit like Natascha Roth, he commuted between East and West (in the late 1980s he directed theater in West German Mainz), and his writing during the 1980s was published in the GDR. In 1990, after the collapse of the dictatorship, *November* finally appeared in the GDR.

Literature of Dissent, Literature of Reform

The Wonderful Years, Approximation, Sleepless Days, and *November* do more than present attacks on a stupid or self-serving bureaucracy, such as one finds in Erwin Strittmatter's *Ole Bienkopp* or Volker Braun's "Unfinished Story," a bureaucracy that hinders sincere socialists from reaching their goals. The literature of dissent is not content with unmasking such people as Günter de Bruyn's Karl Erp, who mouths revolutionary slogans while attending to his petty bourgeois comforts. The books by Kunze, Schädlich, Becker, and Schneider share an affinity with Ulrich Plenzdorf's *The New Sorrows of Young W.* in their relentless investigation of the position and rights of the individual in the GDR. But whereas Plenzdorf, with his "open" text full of intertextual feints, presents a teasingly ambiguous message—one liberally strewn with declarations of loyalty—these books are angrier, more bitter. With relentless fury they hammer at GDR restrictions on travel and expression, at the regimentation and militarization of life. Are these authors telling sad truths but nonetheless presenting a distorted picture of their society, as Biermann accused Kunze of doing? This is the GDR as *they* encountered it.

Kunze, Schädlich, Becker, and to a lesser extent Schneider experienced a long period of gradual disillusionment with the GDR, but the Biermann expatriation provided a focus for their anger. Like Schneider's Natascha Roth, they expressed professional solidarity with their colleague, regardless of whether they approved of his politics or his person. As with Schädlich's Nikodemus Frischlin, they believed that "poets have power to condemn the knavery of . . . despisers of the people, and they are not bound to make an accounting to each and every swaggerer. Such are the liberties of a poet, and where such do not exist, no one has any liberty" (151).

The post-Biermann era proved a turbulent time in the literary life of the GDR. Werner Heiduczek's *Death at the Seaside* (1977) and Erich Loest's *It Takes Its Course* (1978), a book that contains scenes of police brutality, were published but then suppressed. The four books discussed in this chapter could only appear in the West, as was the case with Stefan Heym's *Collin* (1979) and Klaus Poche's *Choking* (1979), both about writers. Younger authors often experienced extensive difficulties. Monika Maron's novel about industrial pollution, *Flight of Ashes* (1981), Gabriele Eckart's collection of candid interviews, *That's How I See It* (1984), and Anderson and Erb's collection of experimental writing by lesser-known authors, *Contact is only a Peripheral Phenomenon* (1985), could only appear in the West.

Published works by established writers often bore the marks of censorship, self-imposed or otherwise. The narrator of Christa Wolf's *Patterns of Childhood* (1976) refers to the impossibility of discussing Stalinism, and Wolf's *Cassandra* (1983) signals censored sentences with ellipses. Stephan Hermlin admitted that he shortened a book by two pages after discussion with the government ("Hier" 282).

In the wake of the Biermann expatriation, the East Germans tightened copyright restrictions and laws regarding "incitement hostile to the state," "the illegal taking up of contacts," and "public vilification" (Emmerich 88–89; my trans.). Authors Stefan Heym and Wolfgang Hilbig and the dissident intellectual Robert Havemann were fined for publishing in the West without Party permission. The government arrested other, generally less well-known writers, such as Jürgen Fuchs, Lutz Rathenow, Frank-Wolf Mathies, and Thomas Erwin. Faced with prohibitions, expulsions from the Party and/or the Writers' Association, fines, harassment, and arrests, many writers— Kunze, Schädlich, Becker, Günter Kunert, Sarah Kirsch, and Karl-Heinz Jakobs, to name but a few—left, or were forced to leave, their country. Their departure caused the GDR considerable international embarrassment and damaged the cultural life of that small country.

That is one side of the story, the more sensational, more scandalous side. There is another side, and in some ways the process of
liberalization begun by Honecker in 1971 proceeded, despite these
not inconsiderable setbacks. Selected writers, including Günter
Kunert, Jurek Becker, Rolf Schneider, Klaus Poche, and Joachim
Seyppel, received long-term visas that occasionally were renewed.
New books or reprints of older ones by Kunert, Becker, Volker Braun,
Franz Fühmann, Stefan Heym, Schneider, and Christa Wolf appeared, although the government qualified all these authors as "difficult." *Patterns of Childhood* and *Evening Light*, both by writers who
signed the letter protesting Biermann's expatriation, were published
in the GDR. In 1979 the East German Aufbau Publishers reprinted
The Uncoerced Life of Kast, a novel by another Biermann protester,
Volker Braun. The edition contains a new segment that ends with the
apparent suicide of a Party functionary who despairs of changing the
system.

The 1980s brought the publication—a year later than in the West—
of Günter de Bruyn's *New Splendor* (FRG 1984), a novel that criticizes
the treatment of the elderly in the GDR. Other controversial publications included Volker Braun's *Hinze-Kunze-Novel* (1985), an attack on
remaining structures of class mentality in the GDR, and Christoph
Hein's *Horn's End* (1985), a book that depicts the bitter resignation
and ultimate suicide of a former Party official. But these works were
not easily attainable by the average GDR citizen, or even by a student
of German literature. In the library of the Karl-Marx-University in
Leipzig, for example, one needed special permission to read the
Hinze-Kunze-Novel in 1985.

Speech was not free in the GDR, but the borders of the sayable
inexorably expanded there, and the process accelerated under the
influence of Mikhail Gorbachev's *glasnost*. During the later 1980s the
GDR began to print several previously suppressed literary works—
such as Fritz Rudolf Fries's *The Road to Oobliadooh* (FRG 1966, GDR
1989), Volker Braun's play *Lenin's Death* (GDR 1988), or Stefan
Heym's novel *The Wandering Jew* (FRG 1981, GDR 1988)—and East
German society achieved an unprecedented degree of openness.
Nonetheless, until the revolution of November 1989, the four works
examined in this chapter lingered outside the limits of the acceptable.
Now that the dictatorship of the Socialist Unity party has ceased,

eastern German readers can judge for themselves the literary merits and the measure of realism in *The Wonderful Years, Approximation, Sleepless Days,* and *November.*

NOTES

1. I thank Peter Demetz for helping me to clarify this passage.

2. In December 1990 Kunze published a short book with excerpts from his 3,491-page secret police file that he obtained after the collapse of the dictatorship. The book, *Deckname "Lyrik,"* documents the GDR campaign to destroy the physical and psychological well-being of Kunze and his family. The police paid Germanists to denounce his books, harassed his family, kept him under surveillance, paid friends and neighbors to report on him, tapped his phone, opened his mail, offered him bribes, and when that proved ineffectual, threatened his life.

The documentation consists of short but devastating excerpts that echo both the form and the content of *The Wonderful Years.*

5

Socialist Feminism: The Example of Christa Wolf

To what extent is there really such a thing as "women's writing"?
To the extent that women, for historical and biological reasons,
experience a different reality than men.
                                   —Christa Wolf, *Cassandra*

In 1972, GDR author Charlotte Worgitzky penned a satirical story detailing the development of an East German "superwoman." Decorated by her state and praised as proof of East German equal rights, the protagonist is the mother of four children, the director of a school, and a city councilwoman. She does most of the housework, too—an angel has granted her the ability to survive without sleep. Worgitzky's story neatly demonstrates the many advantages, as well as the near impossibility, of being female in the former GDR.

In theory and often in reality, East German women enjoyed rights unavailable to American women. In 1946 the Soviet military government issued order number 253, which insured equal pay for equal work. The first GDR constitution of 1949 contained a clause establishing equal rights for women. A more recent constitution spoke of the "equal standing of man and woman in marriage and the family" (qtd. in Krisch 147).

In 1989, 91 percent of GDR women of working age were employed for pay, studying, or participating in a professional training program

189

(Nickel 99). The work force was 49 percent female. That may have resulted more from economic necessity (the GDR was labor poor) than from dictates of Marxist-Leninist ideology. Nonetheless, the government helped women enter the work force. In 1988, 81 percent of children ages three and under attended a state-subsidized day-care center, and enough preschool kindergarten programs existed for all children who needed them. These facilities were free; the parents made a modest contribution for milk and nourishment. Generous prenatal leaves were available, as were maternity or paternity leaves of one year (eighteen months with the third child). The government paid a high percentage of net income during such leaves, and the parents' jobs were protected. Some privileges did serve to strengthen traditional gender roles: most women (not men) could take one paid day of leave each month, and mothers (not fathers) of two or more children had a slightly reduced work week (Dölling 122–23).

In recent years approximately 30 percent of firstborn GDR children were born to single mothers, and the government provided those mothers 70 to 90 percent of their former net income if for some reason the child could not attend day-care centers. Parents received one thousand marks (roughly one month's salary) after the birth of a child, and the government, which subsidized basic foodstuffs and children's clothes, also paid parents a monthly "children's allowance" for each child. Health care and birth control were free, as were first trimester abortions, which were legalized in 1972 (Dölling 122–23).

Fifty percent of GDR judges were women, and similar numbers applied to doctors. In Parliament about every third representative was a woman. But in pre-1989 politics, few Central Committee members were female, and there was never a woman among the eighteen full members of the Politburo, the most influential organ of the Party. As one West German analyst noted, "Where power is, women are not" (qtd. in Krisch 150).

GDR women went to work like GDR men, but when they returned home, they began a second shift with the children and the housework. In an average East German family during the 1970s, the woman did thirty-seven hours of housework a week, the man five and one-half, and the children four (Sudau 72). Chronic supply shortages and long shopping lines added to the daily frustration and ennui. These irritations played themselves out in the family arena, and sociologists now acknowledge that the high GDR divorce rates—once hailed as evidence that women no longer need depend economically on men—resulted in part from the double burden to which women were subject.

In a GDR text discussing the equality of women, Inge Hieblinger wrote during 1967: "as much and as great as the accomplishments have already been in the GDR in the struggle for the achievement of women's equality in daily life, everyone knows nevertheless that there are still remnants of *de facto* inequality in the position of women" (248). She hastened to emphasize, however, that the "*socioeconomic reasons* for the existence of *de facto* inequality in the position of women under socialist conditions do *not* lie with socialism" (250). But in 1978 the West German journalist Christel Sudau pointed out the fashion in which the GDR government continued to support traditional gender roles: it allocated training slots for secretaries or seamstresses to females, while delegating males to more lucrative careers as roofers, chimney sweeps, glaziers, or electricians (74–75). Some GDR women did make considerable inroads into traditionally male professions, such as medicine or law. Nonetheless, in 1990 the East German sociologist Hildegard Nickel confirmed the validity of Sudau's analysis from the 1970s:

> By the end of the sixties at the latest, economic and occupational structure in the GDR was polarizing according to gender. . . . We can see how precarious the situation is when we consider that 60%—almost two-thirds—of the girls who left school in 1987 were channeled into 16 out of 259 available noncollege training options. . . . There is one common denominator to all these jobs: they are the worst paid. (100)

The East German sociologist Irene Dölling asserted in 1990 that the GDR government had functioned as paterfamilias and thus constituted in its very nature a patriarchal society; if the state had allowed wives to become somewhat less dependent on husbands, it had bound them yet more closely to itself (126). An independent women's movement was forbidden in the GDR. Academic research on women served a legitimizing function. As Nickel pointed out, such research utilized, consciously or not, a male yardstick, focusing on "deficiencies 'still' displayed by women (as compared to men), which they would have to overcome in order to achieve 'higher,' usually economic goals, in most cases by working harder and exerting themselves more" (105). Nickel maintained that it was taboo to discuss the actual conditions under which women were living (105), and that "it was taboo, particularly from the early seventies, to suggest that formal equality by no means erased the social inequalities between the two genders" (100).

As we can see by the example of Charlotte Worgitzky's superwoman satire (written in 1972, published in 1978), the taboos to which Nickel refers were broken by GDR women writers. In the absence of a free press, of academic freedom, and of an organized feminist movement, women channeled their energy and their protest into literature, one of the few spheres that allowed them a voice. Combining feminist and socialist commitments, GDR women writers created a remarkable body of texts not only distinct from Western feminist literature but, somewhat more surprisingly, unique within the Soviet bloc as well (Bammer 19).

Precisely in the early 1970s, the time Nickel perceives as having been particularly difficult for GDR women, Christa Wolf was raising questions of difference and deficiency. She asked whether women, for centuries outsiders, might bring a different memory, a different epistemology, a different set of values into history, which they were entering for the first time in appreciable numbers. In a 1974 interview with Hans Kaufmann, Wolf characterized GDR accomplishments in the emancipation of women as only a preliminary stage, one from which it was necessary to pose far more radical questions. She furthermore asserted that for women, emancipation should not entail becoming "like men" ("Subjective" 71).

The images of women in GDR literature in general mirror the desired integration of women into the work force. In the 1950s women worked as bricklayers and crane drivers. In the 1960s the women often possessed academic degrees, although as Patricia Herminghouse pointed out, female professors, journalists, artists, and especially politicians remained underrepresented ("Wunschbild" 327). Reflecting the Marxist belief that emancipation is primarily a matter of economics, GDR literature rarely examined the patriarchal dynamics of private relationships, and commentators often noted the delicacy, indeed prudishness, of GDR literature with regard to sex.

During the 1950s and 1960s male authors shaped the image of

women in GDR literature, but during the 1970s women began to find their own voice, with which they identified much unfinished business. In 1974 Irmtraud Morgner's *Life and Adventures of Troubadour Beatriz* marked the beginning of a programmatically feminist literary movement. Morgner's novel describes the experiences of a female troubadour who, dissatisfied with the patriarchal conditions in twelfth-century France, sleeps Rip van Winkle-like for eight hundred years, awakening in Paris in May 1968. Comparing twentieth-century Europe with the twelfth century, she finds that conditions have not markedly changed. Two other GDR novels published in 1974, Brigitte Reimann's *Franziska Linkerhand* and Gerti Tetzner's *Karen W.*, also bring a more female perspective to GDR letters. In 1977 Maxie Wander's *Good Morning, My Lovely*, a collection of tape-recorded monologues by GDR women (with a foreword by Christa Wolf), created a literary sensation in West and East Germany.

One of the most interesting cultural documents from this period is the anthology *Bolt out of the Blue* (1975), a collection of stories with the theme of gender transformation. Editor Edith Anderson has recounted some of the difficulties she encountered bringing the anthology to publication ("Genesis"). Searching for contributors, she invited Hermann Kant, who would soon head the Writers' Association, to participate: "He seemed really shaken." Franz Fühmann exclaimed: "A woman! Why, that's worse than Kafka! That's much, much worse than waking up as a cockroach!" (3). The prestigious Aufbau publishing house rejected the idea on the grounds that a majority of female editors found it "too offbeat" (5). Anderson did sign a contract with Hinstorff Publishers, where the director supported her over the objections of the editor in chief Kurt Batt. Two weeks later, however, the director began to equivocate. He did not want male authors in the anthology, asserting that women, not men, needed emancipation. He attempted to censor a sentence from Irmtraud Morgner's story, "The Glad Tidings of Valeska": "The bedding smelled of tobacco and fish" (8). When Morgner refused to cut the line, the director rejected the story without consulting Anderson.

Hinstorff gave the anthology no advance publicity. The editor in chief wrote an article for *Sinn und Form*, in which he attacked literature that fantasized about sex roles. Three more authors were eliminated. The director purposefully stalled publication, claiming a paper shortage. Dismayed by the delay, Sarah Kirsch, Stefan Heym, Christa

Wolf, and Günter de Bruyn published elsewhere. Anderson threatened Hinstorff with a lawsuit for repeated breach of contract, whereupon it published an anthology of four stories by men, three by women, with an essay by Annemarie Auer. The book quickly sold out. When Anderson inquired about a second printing, she discovered the director had resigned, the editor in chief had died, and the rights had been given to the individual authors. There would be no second printing.

"Self-Experiment: Appendix to a Report" GDR 1973, USA 1978

Christa Wolf's contribution to Bolt out of the Blue, "Self-Experiment," first appeared in 1973 in Sinn und Form. It was reprinted in Wolf's three-story collection Unter den Linden in 1974, and finally as one of the finest and most probing stories in Edith Anderson's anthology. In it Wolf defines almost programmatically those issues that subsequently concern her in No Place on Earth, Cassandra, and Accident: the damage occasioned to both sexes through the ontological and epistemological modes that Wolf here for the first time defines as "male."

Written by Wolf in the early 1970s, the story is set in the GDR of 1992. A successful, unmarried, thirty-three-year-old female scientist agrees to test an experimental drug, Peterine Masculinum 199, that transforms her into a man named Anders (Other). Even with a man's body, however, she continues to possess a woman's past, and a bit like the Greek Teiresias, who became a woman and explored women's secrets, Anders feels at first like an interloper among men. Anders's society views him as a man, however, and soon he begins to feel, think, and act like one—at which point he breaks off the experiment. He has himself metamorphosed back into a woman and then writes a scientific report of the experiment. She appends a more personal account to the report, an account written for the nameless, distant Professor who supervised the experiment. That account constitutes the text of "Self-Experiment."

The content is signaled by the form, even by the title—"Appendix to a Report." The report itself is scientific—"exact and correct and unambiguous" (113). In her appendix, however, the protagonist confronts the "unreal neutrality" (113) of the report with a more personal recollection. Thus the narrator challenges and undermines her former tone of scientific "objectivity."

The GDR societal hierarchy of 1992 corresponds to GDR realities in the 1970s. The female protagonist heads the project group that develops the sex change operation, but she has attained her leadership at considerable expense, losing her lover and the possibility of a child she wished to have (117). She suspects that her colleague Rüdiger resents a female superior (120). The person ultimately supervising the project is a man, the unapproachable Professor, who, unnamed, represents a type (Helen Fehervary and Sara Lennox also see him as a representative of the patriarchal Party [111]). The experiment transforms women into men; no one would wish to be transformed into a woman (114–15).

As in Wolf's GDR, women in her future society hold responsible positions but not the most responsible, and even in 1992 mores have not kept pace with changing roles. Hence two other women scientists, Irene and Beate, maintain high hopes for the experiment. Irene believes it will prove valuable for women (124), and Beate, who balances a career, young children, and a demanding husband, wishes to become a man herself (127).

The fashion in which GDR women have internalized male values as "natural" dismays the narrator, although she herself has served as an extreme example of that internalization: "I had to prove my value as a woman by consenting to become a man" (118). The new perspective—a man with a woman's past—serves as a Brechtian alienation device, demystifying and dereifying "natural" societal structures.

The narrator achieves a similar effect when she takes traditionally negative "female" qualities—subjectivity, ambiguity, intuition, and emotion—and infuses them with new, positive force. She accomplishes that by contrasting "female" attributes with "male" qualities—epitomized by science and characterized by the nameless Professor—which she unmasks as sterile and arrogant. Beneath the more evident social criticism of the text—and allied with it—we encounter a probing into differences in male-female epistemological modes.

Men and women live on separate planets, the narrator remarks (121), only to have the Professor accuse her of subjectivity. Yet after her operation she realizes firsthand how gender influences experience. She had been told that women are poor drivers who lose their way, and as a woman she drove poorly. When she is a man and her automobile stalls in traffic, she finds assistance and cooperation from those around her. Soon she no longer loses her way.

The different epistemological modes must be encoded with the same words:

> It would never have occurred to me, Anders, to give familiar objects the same names I had used for them when I was a woman, if only I could have come up with other words. True, I remember what "city" meant for her: an abundance of constantly disappointed hope constantly renewing itself. For him—that is, for me, Anders—it was a tight cluster of inexhaustible opportunities (122).

Informing the text is the frustration that only one system of words exists to express two qualitatively different fashions of being-in-the-world. Indeed, on its most "literary" level the story presents an extended musing on the possibilities of language. In the second paragraph, we already encounter the sentence "Happy to have words at my disposal again, I can't help playing with them and admiring their ambiguities" (113). The use of *again* refers to a three-day hiatus in the narrator's journal when, without identity, she possessed no language at all, but it also suggests that as a man she maintained a different relationship to language. The word *ambiguities* (in the German text it is *Vieldeutigkeit*, "multivalence") is central: this is the aspect of language—in the world of Wolf's story—that men suppress.

Though men and women must use the same words, they employ them differently. The form of the narrative—the struggle between a scientific report and an impressionistic rendering—signifies at least two modes of communication. Scientific language presents one possibility—the dominant one—of structuring the world: "Every word in my report is true. But all its sentences together explain nothing at all" (113).

The narrator rejects the Professor's science as a system that obfuscates truth through a barrage of facts. Indicting the Professor, the narrator writes: "But you, with your superstitious worship of measurable results, have made me suspicious of those words of my inner language which might now help me to contradict the unreal neutrality of this report by confronting it with my real remembrance" (113).

One of the many reversals the narrator presents is that of science as superstition. Against it she defends the words of an inner language, a language in exile before the words of men.

The narrator incessantly ponders the impoverishment of the shared system of communication, presumably through the use of scientific discourse. Etymologies obsess her:

> While the original meaning of *verwegen*, "presumptuous," was simply "to be headed—mind firmly made up—toward a definite goal." (115)

> I looked it up later; naïve used to mean something like "innate, natural." (123)

> Your [men's] involvement in such an endless number of activities hardly seemed enviable, given the fact that you merely looked on idly as the words *menschlich* and *männlich*, "humane" and "manly," drifted irretrievably apart from one another. (123)

In all the above examples, the narrator posits a previous, "purer" language ("original"; "used to mean"; "derived from the same root"), signifying a more harmonious society. She suggests a homology, as well as a causal relationship between the two. The narrator does not, however, despair of a reconciliation; not she but Irene chooses the word "irretrievable" in the third example. Addressing the Professor again, the narrator notes:

> At present I'm having difficulty regaining access to all the buried regions inside me. Language, you'll be surprised to hear, can help me; our language which grew out of an amazing mentality that could express "to judge" and "to love" in one single word: *meinen*, "to think, have an opinion." You always reproved me for mourning what couldn't be changed. But still I am affected by the fates of certain words, and still what torments me most of all is a longing to see *Verstand* and *Vernunft*, understanding and reason, long ago one and the same word in the endlessly creative womb of language but forced apart by our disputes, in brotherly union once again. (122)

The Professor considers reified language as natural and unchangeable. The narrator, on the contrary, believes that in exploring those "buried regions inside" her (an echo of that "inner language" mentioned at the outset) she can reconcile language and, hence, the social relationships it constitutes and reflects. The British Marxist Terry Eagleton asserts that language is not superstructural but the precondition for human production (*Criticism* 343). The narrator's dissatisfaction with words hence functions as an indicator for an entire range of frustration. Discussing "Self-Experiment" with Hans Kaufmann, Christa Wolf remarked: "It's simply a matter of overcoming alienation, no more, no less. And we should be careful not to think we've already done that" ("Subjective" 72).

Christa Wolf believes the establishment of economic equal rights and opportunity for women to be an absolute precondition for emancipation, but she does not equate the two. She notes in her interview with Kaufmann that economic equal rights can be but a preliminary stage. As with the narrator in *The Quest for Christ T.* (1968), the narrator in "Self-Experiment" believes, or at least hopes, that one day the language will exist to overcome the alienation of men and women from each other and from themselves.

Beyond its considerable undertone of anger, then, "Self-Experiment" advances an optimistic program. When Anders visits the Professor's home, s/he encounters three generations of women: the Professor's mother, his wife, and his daughter, Anna. Mother and wife fulfill a traditional female function: self-effacing, they act as the man's magic mirror, returning a heroically enlarged image. "But Anna wasn't ready to settle for that," the narrator remarks (130). Elsewhere in the story, Anna indicates that she, like Christa Wolf, does not equate equal rights with emancipation, and that women should not necessarily strive to become like men (129).

Wolf's final paragraph points toward her utopian goal: "Now my experiment lies ahead: the attempt to love. Which incidentally can also lead to fantastic inventions—to the creation of the person one can love" (130). Wolf has written a story of reversals: a woman changes her sex (but not her gender); science becomes superstition; and "negative" female qualities become positive. As Sigrid Damm and Jürgen Engler point out, the creation of Anders has biblical echoes of Eve's birth from Adam's rib (46). At the conclusion Wolf reverses that, too: now women will make men.

"Self-Experiment" received a muted response in the GDR. Damm and Engler criticized Wolf for shutting out history and for neglecting currently existing societal limitations on men and women (they admitted that women were more affected by such limitations). They asserted that Wolf, in mounting a justified polemic against the oversimplifications of a weltanschauung, created new oversimplifications.

In the United States the Germanist Gisela Bahr found the story antiscientific and antirational, and she criticized Wolf's categories as stereotypical and regressive. Another Germanist, Sara Lennox, recalled Elaine Showalter's warning that the idea of a specifically female imagination "runs dangerously close to reiterating the familiar stereotypes. It also suggests permanence, a deep, basic, and inevitable difference between male and female ways of perceiving the world" (221). (Wolf's story shows, I think, that the male-female divide is indeed deep and basic, but not necessarily inevitable or permanent.) Lennox was also suspicious of any casual equation of the male with rationality and the female with emotion, inasmuch as these very categories have been used to rationalize suppression of women. However, Lennox pointed out that during their long period of oppression women developed certain characteristics, and she cited psychological studies that support Wolf's assertions: instrumental or goal-oriented thinking and action dominated with men, while women tended to emphasize emotions and human relationships (221).

Soon after publication of "Self-Experiment," the machinations of the zeitgeist occasioned Herbert Marcuse to deliver a speech entitled "Marxism and Feminism" to students at Stanford University. In his speech Marcuse advanced ideas strikingly similar to Wolf's, calling for the subversion of capitalist and patriarchal values by what he termed "specifically feminine" characteristics: "Formulated as the antithesis of the dominating masculine qualities, such feminine qualities would be receptivity, sensitivity, non-violence, tenderness, and so on. These characteristics appear indeed as opposites of domination and exploitation" (283). Marcuse believed these values could undermine capitalist structures, but he argued that they would have to alter socialist philosophy as well, changing it to "feminist socialism":

Feminist socialism. I spoke of a necessary modification of the notion of socialism, because I believe that in Marxian socialism

there are remnants, elements of the continuation of the Performance Principle and its values. I see these elements, for example, in the emphasis on the ever more effective development
of the productive forces, the ever more productive exploitation
of nature, the separation of the "realm of freedom" from the
work world. (286)

Marcuse's speech was widely circulated by the underground press
in the United States and in West Germany, and it was hotly debated
by feminists, many of whom advanced objections similar to those
directed by Gisela Bahr or Sigrid Damm at Christa Wolf.

Undeterred, Wolf continued to argue that men's activities cannot
make them happy. As she asserts in "Self-Experiment," men must
be liberated as well (125). For Wolf this was not a matter of sharing
household chores. She began to consider it a matter of human survival.

No Place on Earth GDR 1979, USA 1972

In the 1970s East German authors wrote often of the delicate relationship between writers and the state. After 1976, after the coerced
expatriation of the oppositional poet Wolf Biermann and the resulting
exodus of many East German authors from professional organizations and even from the country, the stories about writers often took
a bitter and aggressive turn. Although set in 1804, Wolf's novella No
Place on Earth, which deals with the playwright Heinrich von Kleist
and the poet Karoline von Günderrode, clearly stands as a mediated
comment on the precarious and often desperate situation of GDR
writers after the Biermann affair. In an interview, Wolf admitted:

At the time, I was living with the intense feeling of standing
with my back to the wall, unable to take a proper step. I had to
get beyond a certain time when there seemed to be absolutely
no possibility left for effective action.

1976 was a caesura in cultural policy development in our
country, outwardly indicated by Wolf Biermann's expatriation.
It led to a polarization of culturally active people in various
fields, especially in literature: a group of authors became aware
that their direct collaboration, the kind that they themselves

could answer for and thought was right, was no longer needed. We are socialists after all; we live as socialists in the GDR because that's where we wanted to be involved, to collaborate. To be utterly cast back on literature brought about a crisis for the individual, an existential crisis. It was the origin, for me among others, of working with the material of such lives as Günderrode's and Kleist's. (qtd. in Kuhn 139–40)

To read the story merely in this fashion is, however, to simplify it. A feminist reading of *No Place on Earth* helps unify its diverse strands: the conflict between the individual and the state as well as the one between men and women; the rediscovery of Romanticism in the GDR; and the theme of alienation.

The story unfolds at businessman Joseph Merten's country estate in Winkel, a town on the Rhine. A gathering of German Romantic luminaries takes place, and the essentially plotless story consists of fragments from their conversations. Attending an afternoon tea party are, among others, distinguished legal scholar, Friedrich Karl von Savigny, poet Clemens Brentano, and Brentano's sister Bettina. After twenty years of marriage to the writer Achim von Arnim, seven children, and her husband's death, Bettina began to write important books of her own, including an epistolary novel about her childhood friend, Karoline von Günderrode. Günderrode is one of the protagonists in Wolf's novella, and it was at Merten's estate that she stabbed herself to death in 1806.

Günderrode's interlocutor in the story is Heinrich von Kleist, who left us some of the most tortured, and most brilliant, German plays and stories from the early nineteenth century. Although no historical evidence exists that Kleist and Günderrode ever met—hence one meaning of the novella's title—Wolf brings them together to have them speak of their deeply rooted alienation from their historical moment and their longing for new conditions, a desire they know to be unattainable, and yet one they cannot relinquish. Both writers, Wolf believes, suffered from their times and were ultimately destroyed by them: in 1811 Kleist committed a double suicide with Henriette Vogel in Berlin.

The form of Wolf's novella pays homage to Bettina von Arnim's Günderrode novel, which, Wolf writes in an essay on Arnim, includes excerpts from a real correspondence, though Arnim does not hesitate to change or supplement them ("Nun" 310–11). It is precisely that use of fantasy, that breaking of old structures in an attempt to create new forms, that Wolf admires about the Romantics, and in *No Place on Earth*, she inserts fragments from the writings of Kleist and Günderrode, while reserving the right to invent, for example, the encounter between her protagonists.

Wolf employs a sophisticated narrative technique in her own search for new form. The text flows between free indirect discourse, conversation, and interior monologues. At beginning and end, it demands, "Who is speaking?" (4, 113), and "Who is 'we'?" (109). The narrative moves without mediation between the minds of Kleist, Günderrode, and the narrator, and it often proves difficult to discern the individual speaker. Late in the text it becomes for a time impossible. After the announcement of the title—"No place on earth" (108)—the monologues of Günderrode, Kleist, and perhaps the narrator merge into a "we." For a brief, utopian moment, they overcome their separation and alienation. The moment does not last, however, and the text reverts to "Kleist" and "Günderrode," "I" and "you," "he" and "she."

Wolf's text participates in the reevaluation of Romanticism that occurred in the GDR during the 1970s. Previous to that time, the East German cultural establishment had harkened to the theories of Georg Lukács, who had perceived in Romantic irrationalism the seeds of national socialism. Already in the 1930s, however, Anna Seghers warned Lukács against a too one-sided interpretation of German literary history. She believed that the lives and works of the Romantics more directly reflect a time of transition, a crisis period, than does the serene sublimation of the German Classicism preferred by Lukács. She named two writers from whom she thought contemporary Germans might learn: Heinrich von Kleist and Karoline von Günderrode (Kuhn 142).

Seghers functioned as Wolf's mentor, and it is no coincidence that Wolf chose Kleist and Günderrode as protagonists in *No Place on Earth*. Although Wolf allows both characters to experience the *nausée* evoked by a glimpse into nothingness—"And what we would see then, Kleist, if we looked through the rents into the abyss behind the beauty: that would turn us mute" (96)—she carefully provides a sociohistorical causal nexus. Anna Seghers had written that the Romantics "beat their brows" against society's walls (Wolf, "Faith" 116).

Wolf's Kleist knows he is "broken by the times" in which he lives (76), and he tells Günderrode that "I and you as well, I think, are suffering from the evils of the new age" (85).

In a long essay on Günderrode published in 1978 ("Schatten"), Wolf establishes parallels between the problems under which the Romantics suffered and her own time. She begins her studies of the Romantics to ascertain whether their lives and works hold the promise of another, more whole way of being, for Wolf believes that those "evils of the new age" are still very much with us. In Wolf's essay, "longing" (*Sehnsucht*) serves as a key word, and it ties Günderrode to Wolf's modern romantic, Christa T., who is also characterized by her longing. GDR society dismisses Christa T. as a dreamer, a belated romantic: "Bettina and Annette, . . . nobody goes by these romantic names any more" (62), she is told by a well-meaning friend, who is referring to Annette von Droste-Hülshoff and Bettina von Arnim. Yet after Christa T. dies, the narrator finds her "failed" life worth examining, "because its seems that we need her" (5).

Wolf's Kleist and Günderrode share the condition of German Romantic poet Hölderlin, whose tragedy, according to Martin Heidegger, consisted of living in the interstices of time, between the "no-longer" and the "not-yet." Like Hölderlin, Kleist exists "in places where [he] does not live, or in a time which is past or yet to come" (27). In Wolf's essay on Günderrode, she calls the latter a stranger in her own land ("Schatten" 228), a reference to Hölderlin's *Hyperion*. Yet Wolf locates the strength of Kleist and Günderrode precisely where the more rational, well-adjusted men in her story, Savigny or Merten for example, believe them to be weakest. Neither writer can separate the realm of ideas from reality, that of philosophy from that of life (49). They wish to reconcile the irreconcilable (86). Wolf sees that as their tragedy and their hope.

In her Günderrode essay, Wolf asserts that Kleist and Günderrode suffer from a condition for which the word did not yet exist—alienation ("Schatten" 238). Both find themselves rent by that threefold alienation described by Marx; Kleist asks himself whether a painter could "capture on paper the separation of each figure from itself, from the other, and from the natural world around it?" (102). Günderrode needs to overcome "the barrier which segregated her innermost soul from the world" (21), and Kleist "has a need to communicate his innermost secrets" (28). Both do so with their writing, the only avenue open to them in their attempt to mediate the contradiction of their times and their lives. "Poems," says Günderrode, "are a balm laid upon everything in life that is unappeasable" (64).

In the course of the narrative, Kleist and Günderrode discover that they share a similar weltanschauung and a similar weltschmerz, though Kleist is both astonished and a trifle miffed to discover such suffering in a woman: "And what gave her the right to sum up the two of them, both herself and him, in the word 'we'?" (86). That sentence hints at Kleist's limits. Though both he and Günderrode live ahead of their time, Kleist remains more of his age than Günderrode. He prefers "women who remain inconspicuously in the background" (115), and he finds it "disastrous" (19) that Günderrode writes. Later Günderrode reads his mind: "You were thinking: So clever, considering she's only a woman" (112).

Whatever handicaps Kleist and Günderrode share, Kleist is at least a man. Trapped in conventions prescribed by femininity (21), Günderrode leads the severely circumscribed life of the impoverished aristocratic female, living in a convent while Kleist travels Europe between Berlin and Paris. Günderrode remains keenly aware of the disadvantages of femininity in early nineteenth-century Germany. When Kleist accuses her of resentment, she responds:

> People have been using that line from the beginning of time. They start early on, forbidding us to be unhappy about our sufferings, which are all imaginary. By the age of seventeen we must have accepted our fate, which is a man, and must learn and accept the penalty should we behave so improbably as to resist. How often I have wanted to be a man, longed for the real wounds to which you men expose yourselves! (112)

Her outburst has its poetic equivalent in "On the Tower" by nineteenth-century poet Annette von Droste-Hülshoff and quoted in Wolf's Günderrode essay:

> If I were a hunter, out in the wild,
> If I were a bit of a soldier,
> If I were at least and simply a man,
> Then Heaven would counsel and hold me.
> But now I must sit like a good little girl,

Sweet, delicate, and fair.
And I have to hide to let the wind
Blow freely through my hair.
                (Droste-Hülshoff, "On the Tower")

Blocked off from universities, travel, and careers, nineteenth-century women compensated by becoming "Angels in the House" or domestic tyrants; by turning, like Charlotte Brontë's Bertha, into "madwomen in the attic," taking to bed or becoming hysterical; or by writing. In a double-edged observation, the German literary historian Robert Prutz suggested in 1859 that there were so many German women writers because there were so many unhappy German women (252).

German Romantic women found themselves in the margin, in a position of total economic dependence. As Wolf points out in her Günderrode essay, however, out of that situation of total dependence grew, curiously enough, independent thought. Freed from the constraints of earning a living, these women, emboldened by the ideas engendered by the French Revolution, could in fact go to the root of things ("Schatten" 255). When Kleist envies Günderrode that "freedom" (for the tragic situation of men is that they can "act wrongly or not at all" [112]), Günderrode replies that, condemned to the irrelevance of the outsider, women can produce only "ideas that lead nowhere. So we, too, help to divide humanity into doers and thinkers" (113). Yet Kleist believes "that which can be thought ought to be thought" (81), "for what we are capable of desiring must lie within the scope of our powers" (99).

Tellingly, Kleist cannot decide how to address Günderrode, nor can he find the language to characterize her: "He cannot dispose of something for which he cannot find the proper word" (18). He ultimately settles on *hermaphroditic*, which in turn unsettles him. Günderrode knows that she is "three people, one of them a man" (117), and she takes each possibility seriously. Kleist is uncomfortable with Günderrode's "masculinity," yet in the course of the narrative, Günderrode helps him to acknowledge his own "femininity." When he complains that he sometimes finds "it unendurable that nature has split the human being into man and woman," Günderrode replies: "You don't mean that, Kleist. What you mean is that man and woman have a hostile relationship inside you. As they do in me" (104).

In her Günderrode essay, Christa Wolf calls that poet's life a "self-experiment" ("Schatten" 237), thus echoing the title of her earlier story and signaling that in *No Place on Earth* her concerns are the same. "Self-Experiment" established a set of binary opposites, with female love and fantasy providing the positive pole and the coldness of male scientific reason the negative one. In *No Place on Earth* we encounter a similar dichotomy. After musing that her personality contains three people, Günderrode asserts:

Love, provided that it is unconditional, can fuse the three separate people into one. The man beside her does not have this prospect before him. His work is the only point at which he can become one with himself: he dare not give it up for the sake of any human being. So he is doubly alone, doubly a captive. Things cannot go well for this man. (117)

The "male" principle of work leads to the specialization and industrialization that, Wolf writes in her Günderrode essay, nineteenth-century women Romantics perceived as a rape of their nature ("Schatten" 254).

In *No Place on Earth* Wolf asserts that men are victims as well, for historical trends "cut [them] into pieces which scarcely bear any relation to each other" (93). Günderrode says of the jurist Savigny that he

sees everything in terms of Either-Or. You must know, Kleist, he has a masculine brain. He knows only one kind of curiosity: curiosity concerning that which is incontrovertible, logically consistent, and soluble. (80)

In response to this, Kleist muses: "This woman. As if she had some special intimation of the hidden contradiction on which the ruination of mankind is predicated" (80). With that, Wolf points back to "Self-Experiment" and ahead to *Cassandra* (1983), a warning against nuclear Armageddon, and to *Accident* (1987), about Chernobyl.

Kleist and Günderrode function, then, as monitory figures, as Cassandras whose warnings remain unheeded, and as examples whose lives and efforts may be understood by later generations (e.g., 101, 110). At the same time, the protagonists recognize the tenuousness of that hope. They call themselves "a rough sketch—perhaps meant to be thrown away, perhaps to be taken up again" (118), and they have earlier discussed the necessity of speaking, even with the knowledge that no one hears (109). In a study of Wolf's language philosophy, Manfred Jäger notes that although Wolf has insight into the inadequacy of words, she insists upon the moral necessity of continuing to speak (150). Kleist and Günderrode maintain a similar stance in this novella that calls attention to the insufficiency of language. Kleist, we recall, could not find words for Günderrode, and repeatedly we encounter such sentences as "Since that time Kleist has known that words are incapable of depicting the soul" (38) or "He breaks off, language forsakes him" (66).

Nonetheless, Christa Wolf, the romantic, maintains a seemingly unshakable faith in the evolution of language, in a refinement that would both signal and constitute a new way of thinking and perceiving. When criticizing the naïve ("male") faith in the salutary effects resulting from the advancement of science, the narrator writes, "There is flaw underlying this thinking, but it is *still* too early to give it a name" (79; my emphasis). Similarly, when Günderrode discusses Guiscard, the protagonist of Kleist's unfinished play, she exclaims, "The drama has *not yet* created a form for a hero such as this" (116; my emphasis). These and other sentences remind us of the hopeful lines from the conclusion to *The Quest for Christa T.*: "Words, too, have their time and cannot be tugged out of the future according to need. It means much to know they are there" (185). We should recall that *No Place on Earth* is the English equivalent of the Greek *ou* + *topos*, "utopia."

The leading feuilletonists in the Federal Republic pointed sympathetically to the contemporary relevance of *No Place on Earth* but scored Wolf's language and style. Reviewers for *Die Zeit* (16 March 1979) and the *Süddeutsche Zeitung* (4 April 1979) thought the quotations rendered the text artificial and stilted. In the *Frankfurter Allgemeine Zeitung* Sibylle Wirsing commented that the reading leaves one cold (24 March 1979), and in the *Frankfurter Rundschau* Wilfried F. Schoeller objected to the "tiresome moralizing" (7 April 1979; my trans.). In the smaller, regional papers, however, Christa Wolf was celebrated as a courageous author experiencing difficulties with the GDR cultural bureaucracy. Presumably, such reviews helped the book to its best-seller status in West Germany.

In the GDR, readers appeared less disconcerted by the story's

formal difficulties, and they accorded it a cautiously critical, but positive, reception. Dieter and Silvia Schlenstedt, for example, praised
the nearly lyrical qualities of the book, while criticizing its exclusivity,
its approachability only for the initiated. They approved the attempt
to alter values, while regretting that the book called all action into
question by reinforcing dichotomies between those who act (and
hence create alienation) and poets who lament that alienation. They
hoped that history would disprove the dictum "no place on earth,"
and that societal self-reflection and criticism would create a situation
that rendered superfluous such stories of elegiac provocation
(Stephan 73–75).

In the United States, *Library Journal* asserted that with this book
Wolf "upgrades an already respectable voice to one of literary distinc-
tion" (1 Sept. 1982), but in the *New Republic* Amity Shlaes complained
that "Wolf concentrates so hard . . . on forging and sustaining a tran-
scendent and allegorical moment that she omits the kind of particu-
lars that make her other novels live." Shlaes noted with some justification that without the appendix of translators' notes, much of the
novel would remain incomprehensible to those who were not scholars of German Romanticism. Even with the notes, Shlaes added, "the
novel is too often vague and tiresomely paradoxical" (4 April 1983).

Writing in the *New York Times Book Review*, Marilyn French displays
more patience with the story, and her analysis is far more sympathetic. French confesses that although Wolf writes prose, she thinks
of her as a poet, "indeed, as *the* poet of starvation." Starvation she
defines as deprivation; Wolf's "theme . . . is the lack of freedom."
French asserts, however, "that the nourishment Christa Wolf seeks
is not to be found in the West either." She believes the story's "concerns are ours: the difficulties of becoming oneself in a world that
demands conformity" (10 Oct. 1982).

Cassandra FRG 1983, GDR 1983, USA 1984

Christa Wolf's growing commitment to a consciously feminist epistemology culminates in her five Frankfurt Lectures on Poetics, delivered at the West German Frankfurt University in 1982. The fifth lecture consisted of her "Cassandra" story, while the first four trace the
development of her preoccupation with the theme. Directly at the
outset of these prestigious lectures, Wolf warns that she will not

present a poetics—that she does not have one. That is not, as Christiane Zehl Romero points out, the usual demurral of the nontheoretical writer before an audience of academics ("'Weibliches'" 20–21). Wolf argues in her lectures that poetics have been created by men for a male literary history that has largely excluded women.

In her five lectures, Wolf continues her project of bringing women into history. Most of her previous literary production had centered around women—one thinks of Rita in *Divided Heaven*, Christa T. in *The Quest for Christa T.*, Nelly in *Patterns of Childhood*, and Günderrode in *No Place on Earth*. With her essays investigating Günderrode and Bettina von Arnim, Wolf also helped recover and reevaluate the contribution of two neglected nineteenth–century women writers. Arnim's combination of forms and genres especially fascinated Wolf, who saw in it the conscious or unconscious refusal of a patriarchal poetics in which a woman cannot find her voice: "This is the beginning of a different aesthetics, whose fragments we should be collecting" ("Nun" 318; my trans.). Just as she paid tribute, with her montage techniques in *No Place on Earth*, to Bettina von Arnim, Wolf follows Arnim's "aesthetics" in her Frankfurt antipoetics, which consist of a travelogue, a diary, a letter, and a story. Even these genre designations remain tentative and problematic: in *Die Zeit* Fritz Raddatz suggested that the "story" resembles an essay, and that the "documentary" parts—travelogue, diary, and letter—possess a fictional feel (25 March 1983).

In "Self-Experiment" Wolf moved ahead in time, in *No Place on Earth* she moved backward, and in her Cassandra lectures she leaps back into the myth of prehistory, to the time of the Trojan War. Aeschylus's *Oresteia* trilogy, from the fifth century B.C., serves as her starting point. The Greek king Agamemnon, who had sacrificed his daughter Iphigenia to bring good fortune in the Trojan War, is slain by his wife Clytemnestra upon his return from Troy. Clytemnestra is in turn murdered by her son, Orestes, whom the Furies, ancient goddesses defending the rights of mothers, pursue to the verge of madness. In the final play, however, Pallas Athena, representing the rights of fathers, saves Orestes; the newer, patriarchal gods supersede the older ones.

In his *Oresteia* Aeschylus speaks of the Trojan princess Cassandra, whose prophecies of gloom no one believed. Agamemnon brings her to Greece as his concubine, and Clytemnestra kills her. This figure seizes Wolf's imagination. Her Cassandra serves as a symbol of the fashion in which men excluded women from history (during Cassandra's lifetime no one heeded her, and after her death, male authors controlled her image) and of the disastrous results.

Wolf's story begins before the Lion Gate in Mycenae. The Achean king Agamemnon has conquered Troy and returns with Cassandra. He has just entered his palace, where, Cassandra knows, he will be murdered by Clytemnestra and her lover Aegisthus. Cassandra knows, too, that she will be killed after Agamemnon. That knowledge triggers an intensive recollection and reexamination of her life in Troy. She reflects on the barbaric war and the events that made it possible, even inevitable. She also remembers her discovery of a counterworld, an underground society outside the palace walls. In caves and in the forests, groups of women continue to worship Cybele, an outlawed matriarchal deity, and to experiment with alternatives to the authoritarian and ultimately destructive society headed by Cassandra's father, King Priam.

In *Cassandra* Wolf continues her critique, begun in "Self-Experiment" and in *No Place on Earth*, of the "male" *ratio*. In the latter book, Günderrode remarks that "Savigny sees everything in terms of Either-Or," for he possesses "a masculine brain" (80). Cassandra perceives that either-or mentality in the Greeks as well: "For the Greeks there is no alternative but either truth or lies, right or wrong, victory or defeat, friend or enemy, life or death" (106). Cassandra asserts that Greeks think differently than Trojans, but the story relates the increasingly successful attempts of Eumelos, head of the palace guard, to inculcate the Greek way of thinking into the Trojans. Christiane Zehl Romero believes the Trojans lose the war because they trail the Greeks in the development of ruthlessness, but I would argue that Wolf and her Cassandra feel the Trojans lost because they eventually approximated the Greeks, thus betraying their selves, their alternative to the either-or (Romero 22; see also Kuhn 197).

The seeds of self-destruction are already planted in Troy. Even Cassandra ultimately recognizes the Eumelos, and the murderous Achilles, in herself (69, 119). The Trojan preoccupation with "male" concepts, such as "saving face" (35, 39) or "honor" (70), allows Eumelos to take hold and create a "prewar" situation. Cassandra muses: "You can tell when a war starts, but when does the prewar start?" (66). Wolf describes in detail the fashion in which the Trojan rulers utilize propaganda and misinformation to create an enemy who does not exist. Cassandra terms that the "language war" (65), and no lack of sycophantic writers prove willing to wage it (94, 101). Wolf consciously breaks her style, inserting modern terminology— "debriefing" (64); "a news report was manufactured" (64); weapons manufacturers "step up production" (66)—to emphasize twentieth-century parallels.

The "male" inflexibility necessitated by honor and saving face makes impossible the negotiations that Cassandra demands. Hence, war cannot be avoided, and once started, it cannot be stopped. Wolf also sees war as a perverted expression of male sexuality. Agamemnon, "exquisitely cruel" in battle, is impotent (10), a "weakling who lacked self-esteem" (52). Eumelos's cruelty is in part explained by the fact that he must force slave women to his bed (91). Achilles prefers men but sleeps with as many women as possible "as proof that he was like everybody else" (83). He does not want to fight, but he fights like Agamemnon, with extravagant brutality, so that he will not be perceived as a coward (83). Achilles appears to achieve sexual pleasure—"naked hideous male gratification" (74)—while killing Troilus, Cassandra's brother. After slaying Penthesilea, an Amazon who dared fight him, Achilles rapes her corpse (120).

Cassandra feels that Penthesilea fights not only the Greeks but all men (117), and Cassandra, too, comes to believe that "the men of both sides seemed to have joined forces against our women" (104). Priam raises his throne above that of the queen, then the men exclude Cassandra and her mother from council; later they imprison Cassandra for speaking against their plans. The Trojans use Polyxena, Cassandra's sister, as barter, offering her to Achilles if he will supply information on the Greeks or make them forget the theft of Helen. Achilles proffers the body of Hector, Cassandra's and Polyxena's brother, for Polyxena. Finally, the Trojans use Polyxena to lure Achilles to Apollo's temple, where they kill him. Polyxena has foreseen all of this in a dream, a dream in which her father Priam rapes her. During the war, Priam also marries Cassandra to a prince to obtain more troops. When Troy falls, the Greek Ajax rapes Cassandra, and she must then serve Agamemnon as concubine, while the other Trojan women become slaves. Cassandra and the women of Troy suffer the ultimate degradation—men, Greek and Trojan, use them as objects.

Cassandra, who in Wolf's story possesses not supernatural powers but the ability to observe clearly and to avoid the wishful thinking and willful blindness of her society (37), knows that the cycle of destruction will not cease. After Troy, Greece will fall, and after Greece, Rome. Awaiting her death in Greece, Cassandra notes that the Greeks resemble her Trojans. She cautions them that they will endure only if they can "stop being victorious" (16), and she already knows that they will not. Her lover Aeneas leaves Troy before its fall and commences a journey that will lead to the founding of Rome. In a clear reference to Bertolt Brecht, who advised us to pity the land that needs heroes, Cassandra warns Aeneas that soon he will become one. She says: "I cannot love a hero. I do not want to see you being transformed into a statue. . . . You knew as well as I did that we have no chance against a time that needs heroes" (138). She has witnessed the fashion in which Eumelos groomed her brother Hector for the role of Chief Hero (91), and she knows it will happen to Aeneas as well—in this she anticipates Virgil's *Aeneid*. War turns men, too, into objects.

Cassandra's rejection of heroes parallels Christa Wolf's refusal of a poetics that valorizes the heroic epic. "To whom can I say that the *Iliad* bores me?" she asks in her lectures (236). Similarly, she rejects Aristotle's *Poetics*, which reserves tragedy for the noble class and comedy for the lower classes. In form and content, *Cassandra* represents a story of rejection and a search for alternatives. Wolf symbolizes the search with Cassandra's movement away from the palace toward the ethnic and social mixture represented by the society in the caves:

The transition from the world of the palace to the world of the mountains and woods was also the transition from tragedy to burlesque, whose essence is that you do not treat yourself as tragic. Important, yes, and why not? But you do not treat yourself as tragic the way the upper echelons in the palace do. The way they must. (54)

Cassandra's attempt to escape patriarchy parallels Wolf's attempt to subvert patriarchal aesthetics.

Cassandra's gradual estrangement from the palace and its privilege, her discovery of the teeming lives of the less privileged, brings a realization that other ways of seeing exist (20, 48). She locates an alternative to the either-or thinking governing the Greeks and, increasingly, the Trojans: "The caves along the Scamander. Between killing and dying there is a third alternative: living" (118). In the caves the women (and a scattering of men) worship Cybele, whom the Romans would call Magna Mater. In the palace, by contrast, patriarchal forces continue to push matriarchal remnants into the margin: Hecuba looses power and, literally, stature vis-à-vis Priam in the course of the war. Male priests still wear women's clothes, but they worship male deities and outlaw Cybele's name.

Cassandra's experience in the caves allows her to dream of an alternative literary history, one generated and transmitted by women, "so that alongside the river of heroic songs this tiny rivulet, too, may reach those faraway, perhaps happier people who will live in times to come" (81). Wolf tries to uncover this countertradition with her writing on Günderrode or Bettina von Arnim, and Christiane Zehl Romero has argued convincingly that Wolf's constant attention to the writing of Anna Seghers also constitutes a search for foremothers in a female literary tradition ("Remembrance").

Christa Wolf delivered her five lectures to overflow crowds in Frankfurt/Main in May 1982. In early 1983 West German Suhrkamp published them in two volumes. The East German Aufbau publishing house scheduled its edition for the time between July and September 1983. However, at the Frankfurt/Main Book Fair in October 1983, one looked in vain for a GDR *Cassandra*. GDR representatives spoke lamely of a paper shortage and promised the book would appear in November. It did not, but a censored version went to GDR stores early the following year.

In West Germany the two volumes appeared during a period of considerable feminist activity, but more importantly, during a time when the NATO decision to station American Cruise and Pershing II nuclear missiles in Europe, coupled with remarks from the Reagan administration concerning a "winnable" nuclear war, had mobilized a large West European protest movement. In that sociohistorical context, the Cassandra story quickly became a huge best-seller.

Almost uniformly, West German critics recognized the two books as an important contribution to public debate, though they disagreed on the literary qualities of Wolf's Cassandra story. In *Die Zeit* Fritz Raddatz confessed he had not for a long time read literature of such import, and he called Wolf's prose "immaculate" (23 March 1983). In *Der Spiegel* Reinhard Baumgart criticized the pathos and the exalted, lordly tone of Wolf's prose, which, he claimed, could not be modulated, and which hence quickly exhausted all suspense. Additionally, Baumgart objected that Cassandra's often violent thoughts and fantasies ran counter to her program of democratization and "feminization." Finally, he pointed out that she desires death and martyrdom—she wants to be a hero (4 April 1983).

Most West German criticism situated itself between the poles established by Raddatz and Baumgart. In the *Frankfurter Rundschau*, for example, Sibylle Cramer praised *Cassandra* as an admirable piece of prose but also noted the contradictions Baumgart mentioned. She characterized Cassandra as a heroine of the resistance. Cramer found the story "closed," not "open," and saw irony in the fact that Christa Wolf, looking for a new way to write, ends very close to iambic rhythms (22 May 1983).

If form is the message, Cassandra remains imprisoned in patriarchal poetics. Wolf attempts to free her in the first four lectures, only to "fail" (heroically?) in the fifth, the story. Wolf is not unaware of the problem. She writes in her third lecture:

Narrative techniques, which in their closedness or openness also transmit thought patterns. I experience the closed form of the Cassandra narrative as a contradiction to the fragmentary structure from which (for me) it is actually composed. The contradiction cannot be resolved, only named. (266)

Authors are not always the best judges of their work, and we need not use Wolf's criteria to judge her *Cassandra*. If we do, however, it appears that the open form of her first four lectures approaches much more closely the "female aesthetic" she wishes to develop.

Sinn und Form—in which politically sensitive works, such as Ulrich Plenzdorf's *The New Sorrows of Young W.* or Volker Braun's "Unfinished Story," were sometimes tested—published Wolf's fourth lecture in early 1983, when all five lectures were being published in the West. In the following issue, editor Wilhelm Girnus published a scathing polemic against Wolf's "naïveté." After some pedantic philological feints and thrusts, Girnus addresses the crux of the problem: Wolf suggests, "perhaps unwittingly," that history is not an economic struggle between exploiters and exploited but a battle between men and women. Even more grotesque, he adds, is her suggestion that there exists a male and a female way of thinking. Girnus concludes, "That such extravagant nonsense could see the light of day in a socialist country—that just cannot be true" ("Wer" 442; my trans.).

Two issues later (at the time the two books were scheduled to appear in the GDR), Christa Wolf published a short rejoinder, defending herself in part with a quote from Friedrich Engels's *Origin of the Family* ("Information" 865). The next issue, which appeared during the West German Frankfurt Book Fair, featured several indignant responses to Girnus's polemic, which one reader compared with the heavy-handed Stalinism of the 1950s ("Zuschriften" 1094). In the same issue Girnus published a final riposte, asserting that Wolf had not adequately maintained a Marxist-Leninist perspective in her West German lectures, and that she had been too anxious to please her bourgeois audience. One could not, he insisted, expect him and others simply to ignore her many troubling statements ("kein" 1102–3).

Girnus thus served, intentionally or not, as the mouthpiece for hard-line ideological reservations (one respondent noted that the issue with the first polemic arrived seven weeks earlier than usual, which may or may not have been coincidence ["Zuschriften" 1089]). Although more balanced reviews appeared, such as Hans Kaufmann's in yet another issue of *Sinn und Form* ("Wider"), the GDR *Cassandra* appeared with approximately sixty-four sentences missing. Here are some examples of sentiments deemed inappropriate:

> The supreme commands of NATO and the Warsaw Pact countries are conferring about a fresh arms race, on both sides, to counter the enemy's presumed weapons-technology superiority with something equally effective. (225–26; in the West German version, the word *enemy's* is in quotation marks)

> In the news, both sides bombard us with the need to make preparations for war, which both sides call preparations for defense. (239)

> How can I rely on the experts who have led us to their desperate pass? Armed with nothing but the intractable desire to allow my children and grandchildren to live, I conclude that the sen-

sible course may be the one that holds out absolutely no hope: unilateral disarmament. (I hesitate: in spite of the Reagan administration? Yes, since I see no other way out: in spite of it!) (229)

Also missing is this sentence from one of Christa Wolf's acquaintances: " 'The dangerous thing would be if the words we cherish most—"freedom," on the one side; "socialism" on the other—were used to justify the preparation for war' " (252). In that same conversation a colleague of Wolf's asserts (but not for GDR readers), "She for her part has recognized that censorship and self-censorship promote war; she has realized that we do not have the time to postpone writing our 'real' books until later; so, she says, she has stopped speaking with a forked tongue" (253). Christa Wolf signaled these acts of censorship by insisting on ellipsis dots in the GDR version.[1]

The English translation received in general very favorable reviews that emphasized Wolf's feminism. In the *Christian Science Monitor* Kenneth Harper asserted that "feminists should hail Wolf's accomplishment as nothing less than a revision of one of the cornerstones of Western civilization" (10 Oct. 1984). In the *Nation* Ernst Pawel praised *Cassandra* as a "magnificent prose poem of a counter-*Iliad*" and claimed that Wolf "has brilliantly rewritten history" (22 Sept. 1984). The Yale Germanist Peter Demetz praised the "poetic beauty" of *Cassandra* and asserted that "old Marxism gives way to new thought" (*Fires* 155)—precisely the aspect that so scandalized Wilhelm Girnus.

However, Wellesley professor Mary Lefkowitz protested in the *New York Times Book Review* that the reader is "asked to react, not think, and to imagine that Mrs. Wolf's random thoughts about life and literature constitute informative discourse, while in reality they represent only the mental anguish of a woman trying to understand the world around her but lacking the knowledge and mental discipline to offer persuasive and practical solutions" (9 Sept. 1984). Lefkowitz is clearly disturbed by Wolf's politics, and a professional classicist, she also criticizes Wolf's knowledge of ancient Greece. Although more civil, Lefkowitz's critique in many ways resembles Girnus's; Christa Wolf's words continued to provoke.

Accident/A Day's News **GDR 1987, USA 1989**

On 26 April 1986 a nuclear reactor fire in Chernobyl, a small Soviet city near Kiev, quite nearly caused a core meltdown. Gorbachev's *glasnost* revealed its limits, for the Soviets did not report the catastrophe until Swedish monitors identified unusually high levels of radiation approaching Western Europe. Several Soviet citizens died in the accident, but the ultimate death count will be greater.

Already in 1987 German writers groped with the meaning and implications of the event, and one finds discussions of the catastrophe in texts by Bodo Morshäuser, Adolf Muschg, André Kaminski, Hans Joachim Schädlich, Ernst Jünger, and Gabriele Wohmann (Hage 12–13). Christa Wolf's *Accident/A Day's News*, published simultaneously in East and West Germany, constitutes one of the most important contributions.

The short book adheres to the classical unities of time and place, describing one day in the life of a middle-aged, East German woman writer. Her husband, or life companion, is away, and she spends a day in the spring of 1986 alone in her Mecklenburg farmhouse, listening to news of the reactor fire. Recounted in the first person, the story documents the ruminations of the protagonist, as well as her conversations with neighbors, friends, and her daughter who, living in East Berlin, fears the radiation will affect her small children. Also on this day the protagonist's brother undergoes brain surgery to remove a cancerous growth. The surgery, which among other things symbolizes the beneficial aspects of technology, is successful.

The narrator attempts to combat a sense of helplessness and to discover the meaning of the accident. Her thoughts take her into anthropology, human evolution, literary history, and psychology, especially the Freudian death wish: "At which crossroads did human evolution possibly go so wrong that we have coupled the satisfaction of our desires with the compulsion to destroy" (65). With that statement, Wolf repeats, mutatis mutandis, the question she poses precisely in the middle of her earlier autobiographical novel *Patterns of Childhood*: "How did we become what we are today?" (209). Later in that same novel she suggests a possible response: "One of the answers would be a list of book titles" (369). Literary history has always maintained considerable importance for Wolf, and quotations from previous texts invariably inform her work. In *Accident*, literary reference and citation constitute essential structural and thematic elements, and, for example, Wolf sees in a fairy tale "the basic pattern of this day" (72). *Accident* records Christa Wolf's struggle to revise previous texts that she regards as patriarchal "plots" and "pre-texts"—texts that both metaphorically and literally have helped make us the way we are today.

Curiously, feuilletonists in East and West paid scant attention to Wolf's feminist project in *Accident*, although Wolf situates the story in her line of thinking that, beginning with "Self-Experiment," views Western civilization as one that has excluded women and that is hence plagued by immaturity, emptiness, an inability to love, and, at its core, a desire for death. To be sure, as William Rey convincingly demonstrates, in *Accident* the female narrator probes her own blind spot, discovering a death wish, an unseemly glee in destruction, within herself. Rey believes that Wolf has abandoned the confrontational politics of gender, and he asserts that she is developing a new anthropology, one indebted to Thomas Mann's Third Humanism, in which rational and irrational elements combine ("Blitze").

Rey's anthropological arguments ignore the insights of feminist anthropology, which has made gender, in other words the social construction of men and women, a central issue. Viewing human nature as a given, Rey slights Wolf's investigation in *Accident* of the fashion in which society engenders us. As one example of Wolf's continuing concern with the issue, we can cite the conversation between the narrator and her daughter concerning the education of male children:

> Little boys, I said. All they have to put them through to toughen them up.
> They got their revenge later, said my youngest daughter, she was sure of it. Whoever had the ability to love beaten out of him would surely prevent others from loving in turn.
> We would have to make sure it didn't happen to the little one, I said. (18)

Despite her discovery of the will to destruction in women as well as in men, Wolf continues to believe in the possibility of changing the world through ways of thinking and acting that have traditionally been characterized as female. She fuses feminism with intertextuality when she examines and revises texts that have made us the way we are.

Wolf's most obvious revision of a patriarchal text is her rewriting of *Faust*. That story has occupied Wolf for some time; in her Büchner Prize speech from 1980, she recalls the aged, blind Faust who, in what she terms "grotesque self-delusion," manages to integrate the shovels digging his grave into his happy vision of the future. She then speaks of us as "contemporaries of that modern Faust, the 'father of the atom bomb'" ("Shall" 4). The Büchner Prize speech anticipates many of the themes of *Accident:* Wolf criticizes a literature whose forms and language reflect the thought patterns of Western civilization; she speaks of Büchner's attempts to make visible the blind spot of that civilization; she writes of the paradox that couples creativity with destruction; and she speaks of "the taboo of taboos: that Leonce [a figure in Büchner's work] under his many names cannot love, that he can only love the dead" ("Shall" 9).

In *Accident* Wolf describes the scientists at the California Livermore laboratories as men without women, men in isolation, men who love only their computers, men who have signed a pact, not with the devil, but with a technical problem. Her new Faust is Peter Hagelstein, a brilliant young scientist; Gretchen is played by Josephine Stein, who leaves Hagelstein when he continues to work on the Strategic Defense Initiative.

A Faust who does not seek to win knowledge but rather fame. A Gretchen who wishes rather to redeem him than be destroyed by him. . . . I would reflect upon the new Faust-Gretchen variation later. (65)

Five months after the Chernobyl accident, Hagelstein leaves the Livermore laboratory, giving Wolf hope that revisions are indeed possible: "Somebody made it. Nothing is final. I'll have to reconsider the destinies and decisions of modern Faust" (93).

Wolf effects a second intertextual revision with the fairy tale "Little Brother and Little Sister." As recounted by the Grimms, the tale describes the travails of Little Brother and Little Sister, who, persecuted by their evil stepmother, run away from home into the forest. The stepmother, a witch, bewitches the brooks from which Little

Brother wishes to quench his thirst. Little Sister, who understands the language of nature, twice prevents him from drinking, thus saving him from transformation into a tiger and a wolf, but he finally drinks and is turned into a fawn. Sister and fawn then live together in a forest cottage. When the fawn hears the king's hunters, he leaves to challenge them, despite his sister's entreaties to remain at home. On the third day he unwittingly leads the king to the cottage. The king marries the sister, who soon bears a child. The witch kills the mother, replacing her with the witch's daughter. The dead mother returns nightly to care for her child and her brother, the fawn. Her visits alert the king to the impersonation, whereupon he has the witch burned and her daughter torn apart by wild beasts. The wife returns to life and the fawn to human form.

In his interpretation of the fairy tale, Bruno Bettelheim thought Little Brother represents id and Little Sister ego, thus that the story serves as a parable of psychic integration (78–83). Some variant of his reading would appeal to Wolf, for that constitutes one theme of *Accident*. She remains troubled, however, by the tale's implications, for she sees that according to the Grimms and Bruno Bettelheim psychic integration is achieved through the murder of two women, and Wolf distances herself from this ostensible "liberation" through "death and destruction" (74).

The narrator demonstrates the fashion in which the fairy tale contributes to engenderment, the fashion in which literature makes us what we are today, by describing herself and her brother as children, enacting the fable and learning their roles. She emphasizes her glosses on the story: that she, unlike the brother, could restrain herself, did not need to drink, or that she, unlike him, was happy in the hut and did not need to participate in the dangerous hunt. She emphasizes her useless resistance to the plot, criticizing her brother for bringing her the king, whom she, rejecting the Cinderella complex, did not even want to marry (73). Wolf discovers in the fairy tale "the basic pattern of this day" (72): it depicts the love between brother and sister, a love that overcomes animal instincts and brings psychic integration, but it also demonstrates the Faustian drives of the brother, and the trouble they provoke. Brother and sister are trapped in the story's plot: "We both knew how the story went, didn't we, and we couldn't do anything to change it" (72). This is why the revision of the Faust story, which occurs *after* the recounting of the fairy tale, is important, for it shows the possibility of breaking with previous patterns, with the patriarchal pre-text.

At the conclusion of *Accident*, the narrator returns to a fairy tale, "The Three Little Men in the Woods." That tale, a variant on "Little Brother and Little Sister," follows a similar story line, though the queen turns into a duck and swims up a gutter in a back alley to warn the palace: "How now lord king, art asleep or waking" (109). Ute Brandes convincingly interprets this return to the fairy tale as a sign of the narrator's continuing preoccupation with the violent end of "Little Brother and Little Sister," and Brandes argues that *Accident* presents an alternative conclusion: the duck is outside the power structure; its voice is that of "reason, peace, concern, and civility" ("Probing" 111–12). In other words, Wolf revises and rewrites the fairy tale for her own purposes.

Wolf's most extensive intertextual revision involves Joseph Conrad's *Heart of Darkness*, a novella she invokes at the conclusion of *Accident*. In Conrad's story a young Englishman volunteers for work with a Belgian trading company in the nineteenth century, and he pilots a boat up the Congo River. He ventures ever deeper into Africa, appalled yet secretly fascinated by the colonial savagery he encounters, and he feels eerily thrilled by tales of the ultimate barbarian, a European man named Kurtz. At the climax of the novella, the narrator confronts Kurtz, a man stripped of all morality, a man who ultimately crawls on all fours, like an animal. The narrator recognizes in Kurtz his own doppelgänger, and this recognition occasions an acute psychic crisis. At the conclusion of the story, we encounter the narrator again in a frame narrative and find in him a supporter of British imperialism. Forced to choose between the barbarism of Kurtz and the evils of colonialism, he aligns himself with the latter, although Kurtz is a product of colonialism, and although the story has provided a shocking indictment of European imperialism under Leopold II.

We can see the manifold appeal of the story for Wolf. As a Marxist, she emphasizes the indictment of imperialism by inserting in *Accident* ostensibly random passages from *Heart of Darkness*. Wolf is also attracted to the theme of a decent man's encounter with his other self, with the dark side of his nature. This is, on one level, the story of "Faust," of "Little Brother and Little Sister," and of *Accident* itself. Most important for our purposes, however, is the fact that Conrad

excludes women. Early in his novella, the narrator comments dispar-
agingly:

> It's queer how out of touch with truth women are. They live in
> a world of their own, and there has never been anything like it,
> and never can be. It is too beautiful altogether, and if they were
> to set it up it would go to pieces before the first sunset. (27)

Yet the narrator contributes to that very marginality of women when,
at the conclusion, he visits Kurtz's fiancée, a woman he describes as
having a halo (90), to tell her of Kurtz's death. He does not tell her
the truth. Instead of revealing that Kurtz's last words were "The
horror," he tells her that Kurtz spoke her name. He lies, although
he has earlier noted: "You know I hate, detest, and can't bear a
lie. . . . There is a taint of death, a flavor of mortality in lies" (91).

That taint of death characterizes the woman, who lives in a "sepulchral city" (87), in a "street as still and decorous as a well-kept alley
in a cemetery" (89), and who, dressed in mourning clothes, receives
the narrator in a tomblike room with a fireplace of cold, monumental
marble and a piano "like a sombre and polished sarcophagus" (90).
Wolf writes in her Büchner Prize speech, "Has Rosetta [a figure in
Büchner's work] under her many names only the choice between
being driven back into the dead space or becoming like [Leonce, who
loved the dead]?" ("Shall" 9). In company with other feminist critics,
Wolf suggests that men "kill" women into art so that they may love
them, for, taboo of taboos, they can only love death. Conrad's evocation of Brussels as a sepulchral city, his description, cited by Wolf in
Accident, of sunset spreading darkness and gloom even as the narrator praises the glory of the British empire, would be read by Wolf as
symbols of the death instinct of European civilization, a civilization
that has shut out women.

In her Büchner Prize speech, Wolf uses the image of the blind spot,
a recurring image in *Accident*, to describe women's place in history.
In *Accident* she removes women from that blind spot and imagines
them in history, whether it be Gretchen influencing Faust, the fairy
tale queen as a Cassandra-like duck that warns the government, or
the female protagonist in a modern revision of Joseph Conrad. As
with Conrad's protagonist, the narrator of *Accident* journeys to the
heart of darkness, and like that narrator, she encounters a vision of

her own evil. Unlike Conrad's narrator, however, who remains trapped between false alternatives and who pens a bleakly pessimistic text, Wolf sees hope in a process of evolution, one signaled by her epigraph from Konrad Lorenz: "The long-sought missing link between animals and the really humane being is ourselves." Her new anthropology views gender as a social construct, hence one subject to change. Literature can assist that process, for it has helped make us the way we are today.

Accident immediately reached the best-seller lists in both Germanys, although its abundant critical reception proved mixed. In the GDR, *Neues Deutschland* praised the fact that the book challenged readers to reflect and to take responsibility, but it regretted that history played little role in Wolf's reflections, and that when she spoke of dangers to humanity she did not make the solutions clear (30 April 1987). (In fact, Wolf does write about history and about possible alternatives, but she does not speak about class struggle or about the guiding role of the Party.) In *Neue Deutsche Literatur* Hans Kaufmann asserted that Wolf had written an important book (138), and in *Sonntag* Rulo Melchert hailed *Accident* as a literary event. In an indirect reference to previous GDR censorship of Wolf, he notes that Aufbau publishers released the book in the fastest possible time, a feat Melchert thought that one should also characterize as an "event" (26 April 1987). A reader later complained in *Sonntag* that his attempts to order the book from East German bookstores had met with absolutely no success (5 July 1987). Clearly, censorship of Wolf continued.

In West Germany *Der Spiegel* praised the book for the questions it raised (23 March 1987). But the *Frankfurter Allgemeine Zeitung* found the book by turns banal, unoriginal, and too mystical (14 April 1987). *Die Welt* accused Wolf of mystifying Chernobyl and its causes (16 May 1987).

In contrast to many West German reactions, U.S. reviewers embraced *Accident* with strong words of praise. In an encomiastic full-page review in the *New York Times Book Review,* Mary Gordon proclaimed that the book "has the grandeur of a noble labor." Gordon admits that Wolf's "books are difficult, like certain kinds of prayer. But finishing them, the reader is covered by a sense of completeness, of having been taken on a journey in the company of a seer who has stared, with attention, mercy, and courage, into the world's heart" (23 April 1989). In the *Women's Review of Books* Celia Gilbert declared:

"I will turn again and again to the beauty and richness of this seam-less meditation. It gives voice to all of us, to our despair and horror; by a miracle that only a great writer can bring about, it comforts without deception" (July 1989). In the *Christian Science Monitor* Michael Huey asserts that

> with her growing international recognition, Wolf is more than ever free to follow her own calling—in this case, confronting double-tongued politicians in both East and West with her personal vision of a nuclear-free, peaceful world.
>
> Taking such a moral stance, Wolf has not only superseded the prescriptions of East German cultural policies, but also reestablished herself as today's most prominent all-German author. (27 April 1989)

Socialist Feminism or Cultural Feminism?

The extraordinary career of Christa Wolf allows us to witness the development and maturation of an East German intellectual and, insofar as her life may be characterized as exemplary, of the East German intelligentsia. In the 1950s the young Wolf wrote orthodox book reviews.[2] In her novel *Divided Heaven* (1963) a positive character regrets that his society had not been able to restrain the antihero Manfred—be it by force—from leaving for the West (137). Twenty-four years later the protagonist in Wolf's *Accident* asks whether the utopias of our time necessarily breed monsters (30).

Wolf's process of disillusionment with her youthful dream proved long and arduous. In 1968 the Party attacked and suppressed her novel *The Quest for Christa T.* In 1976 she again encountered difficulties after protesting the expatriation of Wolf Biermann. Her autobiographical novel *Patterns of Childhood* (1976) betrays the signs of self-censorship. In 1979, as she writes in *What Remains* (1990), she was conspicuously observed by the state security police. Her government censored *Cassandra* in 1983.

In her essays and speeches, Wolf continued to dream of democratic socialism, and she remained a Party member until 1989, but in her most recent literary work, Marxism fades into relative insignificance. Peter Demetz asserts that in *Cassandra* Marxist analysis gives way to new thought (*Fires* 155), and Anna Kuhn believes that in

Cassandra and *Accident* Wolf writes as a woman more than as an East German (211). In those latter books, Wolf begins to view feminism as a revolutionary program perhaps more radical than Marxism. She also edges close to convergence theories, treating themes common to East and West, such as gender, the destruction of the environment, or nuclear armageddon.

Wolf's discussion of gender has had particular resonance among U.S. feminists, both within and without the academy. Broadly speaking, this reception has assumed one of two forms. One consists of what Angelika Bammer calls the "cultural feminist" reading, which emphasizes "essentialist" female traits. According to this view, Wolf is not so much a German (much less East German) writer but a woman writer, indeed a Great Woman Writer who speaks across the borders of culture or economic system to other women victimized by patriarchy (20). Wolf and others have pointed out that such Western attempts to appropriate her work, or that of other GDR women writers, involves a significant act of decontextualization. Yet as David Bathrick writes: "The very moment that a particular reception takes on a kind of significance and profile within the receiving culture is inevitably the moment that it reflects strongly the values . . . of that same receiving culture, and thereby necessarily 'distorts'" (4). The process of translation and cross-cultural reception is not disinterested: readers take what they need.

A second, somewhat secondary American reading of Wolf emphasizes the author's socialist feminism. For these readers the literature produced by Wolf, Irmtraud Morgner, Maxie Wander, Charlotte Worgitzky, and others played an important role, for according to Bammer it "not only described, but imagined, what a synthesis of socialist and feminist visions might be like in practice" (20). Bammer asserts that for some U.S. feminists, "socialist-feminism promised a possible alternative to either bourgeois feminism or male socialism," and she adds: "With her sophisticated and historically sensitive grasp of the need to understand what, in the context of 1970s Marxism, were still commonly referred to as 'material conditions' and forces like desire and language, Christa Wolf was regarded by many not only as the main architect of this 'third path,' but as the principal guide along the way" (21).

Bammer does not see this process of influence as unidirectional. She in fact argues that during the 1970s GDR women writers affected

American feminist Germanists, who then engaged in dialogue with American Marxist scholars of GDR literature, who in turn influenced GDR women writers and feminists (18). (In her *Cassandra* lectures, for example, Wolf describes an encounter with an American feminist.) One result of this circuitous route may have been, ironically enough, that in the 1980s, when cultural feminism no longer represented the dominant force in the United States, GDR women writers published texts dealing with women and myth—Morgner's *Amanda*, Wolf's *Cassandra*—"that to Western feminist ears had a distinctly cultural-feminist ring" (Bammer 22). I have noted in my discussion of *Accident*, a text subsequent to *Cassandra*, that Wolf pays renewed attention to the social factors that "en-gender" us. Nonetheless, one can argue that Wolf's continued emphasis on women as agents of change romanticizes them, making them the site of renewed myth-making. Marcuse's "feminist socialism" encountered similar objections in the 1970s.

The generally positive reviews of *The Quest for Christa T.*, *Patterns of Childhood*, *No Place on Earth*, *Cassandra*, and *Accident* in leading U.S. newspapers and magazines demonstrate that Wolf has joined a select group of postwar German-language writers—Böll, Grass, Johnson, Handke, and Frisch—whose work has echoed significantly in the United States. Wolf's acceptance by the U.S. book-review establishment involves yet another process of decontextualization and recontextualization, for that establishment has for some time (beginning roughly with *Patterns of Childhood*) regarded her simply as a German author. Reviewing *Cassandra* for the *New Republic*, Michael Naumann speaks of "German" anxieties, and when he writes that "this land loves stories of decline," he is speaking not of the Federal Republic or of the Democratic Republic but of Germany (30 July 1984). The reviewer of *Accident* for the *Christian Science Monitor* proclaims Wolf to be "today's most prominent all-German author" (27 April 1989).

Crossing the border from the GDR to the United States, Wolf's oeuvre has been variously received as cultural feminist, socialist feminist, or simply German, and this attests to its richness. Wolf's concerns with alienation and wholeness, with the dream of real equal opportunity, and with the critique of patriarchy are, as Marilyn French noted, our own. Today, as some feminists applaud the deployment of female U.S. soldiers in combat from Panama to the Persian Gulf—a strategy Wolf would perceive as another example of women imitating men rather than changing them—we will want to continue listening to this author's voice.

NOTES

1. In the later 1980s the censored sentences were restored to subsequent editions of the book.

2. In early 1993 Christa Wolf admitted that she had worked as an informant for the State Security Police between 1959 and 1962. In 1968 the secret police turned on Wolf and her husband, collecting 42 volumes of information between 1968 and 1980 (*Der Spiegel,* 25 Jan. 1993).

6

The Artist as Hero: The German-American Writer Stefan Heym

> "We have an obligation. When we pull out of [Germany], finally, we want to leave behind a country minus the bastards who forced this war, their power smashed. A new kind of country. An American experiment."
>
> —Stefan Heym, *The Crusaders*

In the early 1950s the *New Republic* condemned a novel by the U.S. citizen Stefan Heym as "nothing more or less than an extended apology for the establishment of a police state" (16 April 1951). Over twenty-five years later, the official East German Party paper excoriated Heym, who was then residing in the GDR, as a "former American citizen" who "cooperated eagerly with the class enemy" (qtd. in Emmerich 190; my trans.). At an oppositional rally on 4 November 1989 in East Berlin, a rally held five days before the Wall was opened, Heym rose to speak to a crowd of half a million and was introduced as the "dean of our movement."

His novels have been on best-seller lists in the United States and in Germany. They have been filmed by Hollywood and by West German television. The Nobel Prize laureate Heinrich Böll called Heym's *Crusaders*, an account of America's battle against fascist Germany, one of the finest and most lasting war novels (*Der Spiegel* 18 Sept. 1972). Heym has asserted that he finds English a more logical language than German, and he often writes his books first in English, translating them himself into his native German. His literary models, he once told me in perfect English, were "the great American realists: Twain, Hemingway, Steinbeck."

Stefan Heym's personal history made him a uniquely qualified mediator between the United States and the GDR. A Jew and a leftist, Heym fled Germany in 1933 at age twenty. He found refuge first in Czechoslovakia. Soon thereafter he traveled to the United States, where a scholarship from a Jewish fraternity enabled him to study at the University of Chicago. After receiving an M.A. with a thesis on Heinrich Heine, he edited the New York German language communist newspaper, *Deutsches Volksecho*. When the United States entered the war, Heym joined the U.S. Army and served with a psychological warfare unit. After the war he participated for a time in the allied occupation of Germany, but he encountered difficulties with the army when he refused to write an anti-Soviet article, and he was returned to the States.

In 1942 Heym had published the best-selling novel *Hostages*, followed in 1944 by the novel *Of Smiling Peace*. During the later 1940s and early 1950s, he wrote *The Crusaders*, *The Eyes of Reason*, and *Goldsborough*. The growing anticommunist hysteria threatened him, however, as did the Korean War (a reserve officer, Heym might have been required to fight against North Korea, with which he sympathized). He returned his World War II medals, wrote Truman a truculent public letter, renounced his U.S. citizenship, and took asylum in the GDR, where the government welcomed him warmly. He was given a villa in Berlin, and his wife Gertrude Gelbin founded the English language Seven Seas Press (which subsequently published some of Heym's books). Heym received the Heinrich Mann Prize in 1953 and the National Prize of the GDR, Second Class, in 1959.

The same critical perspective that had caused Heym difficulties in the United States, however, occasioned problems in the GDR, and he was denounced in 1965 by Erich Honecker for his inability to learn. Heym became accordingly unpopular with GDR publishers until the 1971–76 thaw (initiated, ironically enough, by Honecker), during which his *King David Report*, *Uncertain Friend*, and *The Queen against Defoe* appeared in restricted numbers. In 1974 the West Germans published *Five Days in June*, Heym's interpretation of the workers' revolt from June 1953, but it remained a nonbook in the East until 1990.

When the GDR expatriated Wolf Biermann in 1976, Heym was one of the original signatories of the protest letter that shook East German cultural and political life (see chapter 4). After that Heym's novels *Collin*, *The Wandering Jew*, and *Schwarzenberg* appeared in the West but were suppressed in the East. Under the influence of *glasnost*, the GDR allowed *The Wandering Jew* to appear in 1988. After the downfall of the SED regime in late 1989, both *Collin* and *Five Days in June* finally appeared in the country for which they were written.

I include Heym's early, pre-GDR novels in this chapter's discussion, because these works provide insight into the development of the themes to which Heym has devoted his life—the meaning of freedom, of democracy, and of socialism. As his difficulties in the GDR increased, another theme assumed prominence in his oeuvre— the role of the writer. *The Queen against Defoe*, *The King David Report*, and *Collin*, among other works, celebrate the writer as a moral force, as a locus of opposition to oppressive government. These works established Heym's reputation as a GDR dissident.

Stefan Heym in the United States

Hostages USA 1942, GDR 1958

After America's entry into World War II, interest grew in Heym's antifascist work, and in 1942 he published his first novel. Writing in a foreign language, the literary novice borrowed the structure of the detective novel, but he reverses the pattern: the detective, a German occupation commissioner in Nazi-occupied Czechoslovakia, does not triumph.

While at Café Mánes in Prague, the German officer Glasenapp mysteriously disappears. After finding his body in the river that flows by the café, the police arrest twenty customers and employees to serve as hostages. The Germans find on the body a letter to a Czech woman, and the Nazi commander Reinhardt concludes gloom-ily that Glasenapp killed himself after being rejected by the woman. Reinhardt decides to turn Glasenapp into a hero, however, and de-clares that the Czech resistance assassinated the lieutenant. If he cannot locate the murderer, he adds, he will shoot the twenty hos-tages. His superior Heydrich (who was actually killed in Prague by Czech partisans in 1942) abets the plan, for one of the hostages is

Preissinger, a Czech industrialist quisling who has profited from the Nazi occupation by appropriating Jewish businesses. Now the Nazis wish to eliminate him and transfer his holdings to Germans. The Glasenapp case provides a convenient excuse.

Another hostage is Janoshik, the hero. Unlettered but crafty, he had worked as the washroom attendant at Mánes and had functioned as a key figure in the Czech resistance. Shortly before his arbitrary arrest, he had received an important address that he must relay to another resistance contact. With Janoshik's message, the resistance will be able to obtain dynamite to explode German munitions barges destined for the Soviet front.

Despite his imprisonment, the wily Janoshik transmits the message, but afterward the Gestapo tortures him. Nonetheless, his joy at having outwitted the Nazis, and his confidence in the future of the movement—one assumes he is a communist although Heym, working in the United States, does not say that—inspires the other hostages. Janoshik assures them that bullets through good peoples' hearts carry a long echo (324). The "echo" of his death is the exploding of the Nazi barges:

> The cackle of shots evoked a tremendous echo. Crashing thunder rose from the river. Yellow, shooting flames crisscrossed the cobalt sky over the yard. Billowing black smoke soon obscured the square of sky. Explosion followed upon explosion, rocking the building to its foundations. (356)

Meanwhile, the resistance learns that Glasenapp was not murdered and that he committed suicide. It broadcasts that information to Prague. Thus the Nazi executions are demonstrated to be arbitrary terror.

Janoshik symbolizes what Heym sees as the best in the Czech people. He is clever, political, courageous, "a poet of the people" (107), and "a son of his people" (356). He is also a variant on Hašek's famous Schweik, who, feigning dullardness, outwits the rulers. Preissinger tells the Nazis:

> But let me warn you—this Janoshik is not as stupid as he acts. He is sly. He uses his moronic appearance to hide his real

thoughts and activities. Among us Czechs, this type of person appears frequently. (251)

The hostage Wallerstein, watching himself and his cellmates devastated by fear, cannot fathom Janoshik's fearlessness: "Knowing that the more primitive the man the more and greater his fears, he could arrive at only one conclusion: Janoshik, instead of being more primitive than himself and others, was more civilized, having reached a state of inner security, of peace within himself—a peace entirely outside Wallerstein's reach" (235). He ends his examination with the admission: "I cannot comprehend a Janoshik. I can only bow my head in humility and admiration, before the advance guard of a new, fearless world" (238). Wallerstein speculates that Janoshik may have knowledge of a future of which his other cellmates know nothing (305). The narrator confirms this for us when he writes, "For the first time [Janoshik] realized how cruel death must be to [hostages] who, despite their surface superiority, could neither see the future as he saw it—bright and worth dying for—nor even up the score with the Nazis" (321).

Heym's first novel became a best-seller. It was chosen by the Book-of-the-Month Club and excerpted by *Readers' Digest*. Most critics praised the book, though they noted its uneven qualities and refused to make exaggerated claims for it. In the *Nation*, for example, Diana Trilling warned that "neither [Heym's] sincere passion against Nazism nor the emotions which his readers will bring to his subject can raise his book to the place claimed for it in the ranks of serious anti-fascist literature" (14 Nov. 1942). The *New Yorker* asserted that the "author is no Koestler or Malraux, but for the minor leagues this is a wonderful book" (9 Nov. 1942), and the *New York Times* called it "good melodrama which need not blush in the company of the season's best fiction" (25 Oct. 1942). In 1943 Paramount Pictures filmed the novel.

Hostages is clearly a very personal book for Heym. After he had fled Germany, the fascists detained his father, who later committed suicide. In his autobiography, Heym notes that he often asks himself if he is responsible for his father's death, and that he wrote *Hostages* in part to deal with his sense of guilt (*Nachruf* 75, 206). The novel's dedication reads: "Because my father was a hostage."

Of Smiling Peace USA 1944, GB 1944

After the success of *Hostages* Heym attempted to publish several pieces, succeeding only with *Of Smiling Peace*. In this novel he writes of World War II combat in North Africa, and he models his protagonist, Lieutenant Wolff, on Hans Habe, Heym's superior officer in the European theater.

In the story the American army overcomes desultory French resistance to land at Algiers, then advances to fight the Germans in Tunisia. During the narrative we learn the history of German-American Lieutenant Wolff, who had been tortured in the Sachsenhausen concentration camp. He later fought in Spain, where, he says bitterly, his side was betrayed.

Wolff's counterpart is Ludwig von Liszt of the German elite General Staff Corps. Together with a Vichy French general, Liszt develops a plan to roll back the allied advance. On 7 December (the symbolism is clear) the Germans will launch a fierce frontal attack while the Vichy French will attack the Allies from behind. The plan fails, however, when the Americans arrest Monaitre, the fascist French general who was to cooperate with the Germans.

Between battle scenes, Heym arranges a number of unlikely coincidences to bring Wolff and Liszt together so that they may articulate their different positions. Wolff understands, as the other Americans do not, that the war represents an *ideological* struggle that cuts across countries—indeed, Heym hints of fascism in the United States as well (102). Heym suggests that Americans do not really know why they are fighting or for what they fight. Wolff knows. "People learn," he answered quietly; "And I believe in the people" (237). At the end of the novel, Sagamond, a French journalist and member of the resistance, tells the U.S. colonel Wintringham: "And a time is approaching in which the common people will come into their rightful place. That's what the whole war is about, whether you like it or not" (361). Wintringham, one of the people, demonstrates that he, at least, has learned in the course of the novel: "And he wondered how, if and when he came back to his home and his town, he would ever be able to explain to the boys what this war was about. They would not understand, though they were his kind. But *he* understood" (361–62).

Of Smiling Peace received mixed, but generally negative, reviews. The *New Yorker* declared that "altogether, Mr. Heym's second try is not anything like as good as his 'Hostages,' either as straight narrative or as political reporting" (11 Nov. 1944). The novel reads in many respects as a prelude to Heym's most important exile novel, *The Crusaders*, in which he differentiates the rather simplistic Manichaean scheme structuring *Of Smiling Peace* and develops his themes in more depth, with more subtlety and sensitivity. That is how Heym himself understands the novel, and although it was printed by the army in a paperback edition for American soldiers, Heym never translated it into German.

The Crusaders USA 1948, GB 1950, GDR 1950

In one of his finest films, the GDR movie director Konrad Wolf depicted the advance of the Soviet army into Germany during the final months of World War II. A young Soviet-German works with a microphone, urging the Germans—with considerable success—to desert a defeated cause and surrender to the Soviet Union. The young hero is strongly autobiographical, for the Wolf family had fled Nazi Germany for Soviet exile, and Konrad Wolf returned to Germany with the Soviet army. In his novel *The Crusaders*, Stefan Heym presents a similar story from the American point of view. Writing a wide-ranging epic, he shows the advance of the American army from Normandy through the Battle of the Bulge and into Germany. He also describes the immediate postwar era in the industrial Ruhr area. One of the most sympathetic of the heroes is Bing, a German-American who serves in the propaganda unit with a well-meaning but somewhat naïve college professor, Yates.

In *Hostages*, a prison cell becomes a microcosm of Czech society; in *The Crusaders*, Heym uses the American army to present a cross section of America. Representing the establishment is Colonel Willoughby, a clever opportunist who maneuvers himself into a position of considerable power so that he may represent his business interests in the States. Willoughby is opposed by Sergeant Bing, who regards the war as an opportunity to build a new political and economic order, and who cannot comprehend America's seeming lack of a program—as in *Of Smiling Peace*, the Americans do not appear to know why they fight. The apolitical college professor Yates dreams vaguely of a third position. He is no match for Willoughby, at least at the outset. Willoughby sees the choice for postwar Europe as that between the unwashed masses and the know-how of management. The United States Army did not come to Europe to install socialism or communism, he pointedly remarks (188, 292).

Sergeant Bing, who (like Lieutenant Wolff) hates the Germans and the "German" in himself, recognizes the need for an ideological justification of the U.S. involvement: superiority in canon is not enough in the struggle for the hearts and minds of the Europeans. On the Fourth of July he composes a propaganda leaflet (similar to one Heym himself composed), with the American Revolution, freedom, liberty, and self-governance as themes. Operations Officer Crerar contradicts Bing:

> "Sergeant Bing, the Revolution is ancient history. Today, if you mention the word, people cry 'Red'! You've written a revolutionary leaflet. . . . Equality before the law! You know as well as I do that millions of men in our country don't even have the right to vote. . . . Determined to govern ourselves! I know something of who's governing our country—I used to be a Big Business executive myself. And the war hasn't changed it a bit. The same type of men run Europe, the same type of men run the show in Germany. And don't tell me the methods are so different. In America, we don't believe at the moment in concentration camps or in the mass extermination of minority groups. But if the men in power found them necessary, we would have them—" Crerar snapped his fingers—"just like that!" . . .
>
> "I am telling you, if ever we have fascism in the States, the German form of it will seem like a pastorale. They won't do anything to me; I'd stand to gain by it. But they sure as hell would get you. You consider this war as a God-damned crusade." (64)

Bing argues with Crerar and continues his crusade. The crusaders will lose.

Yates at first cannot articulate why the Americans are fighting, but Bing's example, plus Yates's own experiences freeing the French or liberating a concentration camp, help him to recognize and value the U.S. contribution. At the conclusion to part 4, Yates

> was very close to his country, then; perhaps for the first time. It was a wonderful, sweeping feeling. And he thought he

wanted to hang on to it; and dimly, he perceived that he might be able to do it. It depended on what kind of country it was and what kind of country you made of it, on whom it belonged to and who formed its destiny. He felt that you could reduce the great slogans, so seductive and yet so empty, to something real and human and warm and genuine, to something profoundly stirring—a call to action. (408)

He also begins to understand that the Americans do have a program—Willoughby's (620). Yates becomes a crusader, successfully unmasking a kickback scheme of Willoughby's, so that the latter must return to the States in disgrace. It is, as Yates admits, but a local victory, and he does not know, though the reader does, that Willoughby has used his rank and influence to erect a conglomerate of the leading steel companies in the United States (represented by his law firm), France, and Germany.

Yates is appalled as displaced persons or former Nazi prisoners are kept in subhuman conditions or sent to work in the mines, as they were under the Nazis. His defeat of Willoughby allows him to expropriate a leading German steel magnate's estate, which the army uses to house the former concentration camp victims. Finally, Yates is also able to disrupt a ring of ex-Nazis who plot to regain power.

Still, these latter two victories have something ad hoc about them and continue to underscore the lack of a defined U.S. ideology. The implied comparison is with the Soviets—it is said several times that they know for what they fight—who will not allow a capitalist restoration in their zone, where the distribution of industrial estates to the people will be policy. Konrad Wolf's Soviet-German had the backing of the Soviet Union in his work, while Bing is left to his own devices. Ultimately—and symbolically—he is killed by a U.S. plane in a strafing raid.

The Crusaders was widely and generally favorably reviewed in the United States. In the *New Republic* Malcom Cowley asserted that the novel "has a thesis and a sound one, namely, that the war was fought against evils some of which exist in our own army and nation. There is only one thing the novel lacks: the respect for his characters and for truth as opposed to bombast that one has a right to expect from a writer of Heym's talent" (27 Sept. 1948).

The Eyes of Reason USA 1951, GB 1952, GDR 1955

With *The Eyes of Reason* Heym returns to Czechoslovakia, the country of his first book, *Hostages*. He situates his novel during the second Czech republic of 1945–48. In the republic, capitalism and socialism uneasily coexisted. The communists were the largest single party, but a coalition of noncommunists blocked many communist initiatives. The country grew increasingly polarized, and when, after pressure from the Soviet Union, the government refused Marshall Plan assistance, both sides appeared determined to effect a decisive change in the status quo. In 1948 twelve noncommunist ministers resigned in protest against the interior minister's practice of hiring a majority of communists for the secret police. The twelve ministers hoped to provoke a parliamentary crisis, bringing down the government and creating an emergency cabinet that they would control. The communists organized armed demonstrations in the streets of Prague. Other ministers resigned, but the social democrats did not; together, the left remained in power and consolidated it. These events provide the background for Heym's book.

Heym, who traveled to Czechoslovakia in the fall of 1948 as a guest of the new government, explicitly links the travails of that country with those of the three Benda brothers. Through nationalization, Joseph, the oldest, loses the glass works he inherited from his father. He enters politics in an attempt to regain them, and although he has fought in the war to restore democracy to his country, we find that he is increasingly prey, on account of his class standpoint, to pseudofascist thoughts: "It occurred to him, once or twice, that what he dreamed of was a kind of dictatorship—but it was a benevolent one, and, after all, whatever names you gave to the outward forms, when had there been a time in history at which the people did not have to be led by their betters?" (151). Joseph wishes he could imprison a communist in order to muzzle him (148), and he fantasizes about influencing an election (185). As the crisis of 1948 looms, he muses, "Democracy was a wonderful thing as long as you controlled it and made it function your way; once it turned against you, it ceased to be desirable" (283). Joseph eventually flees to Munich in a hijacked plane.

A doctor and the positive hero, Karel Benda spent World War II in the Buchenwald concentration camp due to his activities in the communist underground. (Several of Heym's heroes, like those of Anna Seghers, have been in such camps.) Karel has the most personal integrity of the three brothers, and his perspective becomes increasingly tied to the narrator's. After Joseph flees and his brother Thomas commits suicide, only Karel remains to build socialism in Czechoslovakia.

Heym portrays the writer Thomas Benda as an idealist unable to choose between the more materialistically oriented poles represented by his brothers Joseph (235) and Karel (238). Thomas is often contrasted with another intellectual (and former concentration camp inmate), the communist professor Stanek. Listening to Stanek speak, Thomas realizes the differences: "Stanek, like himself, was working in the medium of ideas. But with a difference, he thought; I build on top of other ideas, Stanek bases himself on such disagreeably tangible themes as means of production, control of banks and finances, supply of raw materials, planned housing, planned everything" (158).

Attempting to write an "Essay on Freedom," Thomas is doomed, in terms of the book, to inevitable failure. Like Archimides, he cannot discover a neutral place from which to move the world. Thomas begins to see this himself:

That's what had been his weakness, that's what was at the bottom of his failure with the Essay—he had thought instead of acted, theorized instead of lived. The world of thought could not be divorced from life; theory was a derivative of practice; a good brawl was a lot more useful than a high-level debate. (268)

Thomas cannot change himself, however, for he sees the weakness in both sides of an argument. Although he, like Yates in *The Crusaders*, learns that bias is necessary (265), that there is no absolute truth, he cannot act and increasingly feels that he does not belong (383, 396, 427). Ultimately, he commits suicide. Reinhard Zachau views him as the tragic hero in the novel, suggesting that Thomas's views were not so far removed from Heym's at the time (42–43).

Writing his essay, Thomas attempts to think through the central problem in the novel—that of freedom. Freedom for whom, under what conditions it may be curbed, and to what ends it should be employed are some of the questions that the novel poses. Bourgeois freedoms are attacked as shams. For example, Thomas writes of the press: "If 51 per cent of the people, stimulated by some headline, shout 'Hosannah!' the other 49 must tolerate the nuisance; but let some high-powered source organize different headlines, which move 2 per cent of the people into the opposite column, and the cry of the majority becomes 'Crucify!'" (294). For Heym, the concept of economic freedom is central, and the communist government official Novak asserts that free enterprise takes "the freedom away from everybody else" (46).

The clear and repeated message of the novel is that if Joseph and his ilk are not to attain power, then the communists must seize it, even if that entails a—temporary—loss of freedom (141, 147, 158). Stanek predicts, "that in order to attain the freedom I talked about—that greater freedom—we shall probably have to curb the freedom of those that would use it to maintain their own power and to keep us in shackles to the end of our days" (175). The implied or explicit answer to the repeated question of who possesses the right to decide such things, is variously the people, the workers, the majority, or the Party. In this novel they are synonymous and, moreover, likened to a relentless, natural force: "The people knew that. Standing there on this day, they knew that no one can fight the ocean, the sand, the skies" (370).

The unintentional irony of Heym's book derives from the fact that many of the warnings uttered by his villains proved correct. The American journalist Elinor Simpson, we are repeatedly told, mouths inane superficialities, yet in retrospect her hectoring appears not so silly:

> "I tell you there is no such thing as socialism," she stated firmly. "There is private capitalism and state capitalism. You can't share and share alike, because people won't work if they know that the next lazy fellow is going to get exactly the same as themselves. And if you have state capitalism, you only supplant one group of managers by another, and you lose your democracy to boot." (71)

Later she tells Thomas:

> This whole idea of socialization—not that it will ever work—it's a terrifying temptation! They want to get the people to sell out

their birthright for the pottage of security—jobs, medical care, old-age pensions. In return, they'll demand only one thing: complete subjection. No criticism. Toe the line. Take orders. (74)

The villain Joseph Benda also prophesies fairly accurately: "The defeat of the Nazis and the land reform gave many of the peasants a piece of ground. Now they're deathly afraid that the Communists will take it away again, as in Russia, and communize the land and the cattle and the women and everything" (191). Joseph's brother Thomas fears that in the new Czechoslovakia there will be little room for him, a doubter. During one of the key exchanges in the novel, he tells Stanek:

That's just what I'm worried about—that if you ever succeed in fully establishing the kind of society you dream of, every one of us will have to ask permission on what to write and with whom to consort and where to go! What do your friends know about you, about me, about our work? Who are those people who do, or do not, give permission? (174)

Many of the fears of Elinor Simpson, Joseph Benda, and Thomas Benda were subsequently realized in Czechoslovakia, where the government of Klement Gottwald established a Stalinist dictatorship.

Most American critics rejected *The Eyes of Reason*. The *San Francisco Chronicle* did call it a "fine story" (15 April 1951), and Fredric Morton, writing in the *New York Herald Tribune Book Review*, suggested that although few Americans would accept Heym's version of events, "the significance of the novel is not wholly dependent on the accuracy of its historic framework; nor need the reader agree with all of the author's conclusions to appreciate the impact of a message well worth remembering" (4 Feb. 1951). But the *New York Times* found that "the only sympathetic figures, besides the children, are 'the simple working men' who believe in the all-redeeming power of the official party dogma" (4 Feb. 1951), and in the *New Republic*, Harvey Swados called the novel "nothing more or less than an extended apology for the establishment of a police state" (16 April 1951). Marcia Davenport, who is portrayed as Elinor Simpson in the novel, condemned it in the *Saturday Review of Literature* (10 Feb. 1951). Not surprisingly, when a translation appeared in the GDR during 1955, the novel was generally praised (Zachau 36–38). The cold war of the critics was firmly established.

Goldsborough GDR 1953, USA 1954, GB 1961

Heym's final exile novel, Goldsborough presents his first published attempt to analyze the American quotidian.[1] Anticipating the later GDR Bitterfeld Program (and also imitating Émile Zola, who visited mines to prepare his naturalist novel Germinal), Heym traveled to New Kensington, a mining town in Pennsylvania. New Kensington provides the model for Heym's town of Goldsborough, where a company fires two older miners to avoid paying their pension. The company's action serves as a catalyst for the expression of pent-up grievances, and the miners strike. During the strike, worker Carlisle Kennedy recognizes the corruption of the union leaders, who are pawns of the mine owners. Consequently, he emerges as the leader of a wildcat union, and his strategies—which include violence—bring the miners a limited victory.

One of Heym's major concerns in this novel, written during the McCarthy period, is to suggest the fashion in which the U.S. economic and political system create their own form of fascism. This was, as we have seen, increasingly a theme in Of Smiling Peace and The Crusaders; here Heym unfolds it fully. Indeed, were one to exchange the word Jew with communist, one would locate a number of—intended—parallels between Heym's America and the Third Reich. At one point, for example, a character notes that being a communist puts one in a new form of concentration camp, except that one is branded instead of living behind barbed wire (451). That comparison trivializes the concentration camp experience. In general, however, Heym captures well the hysteria of McCarthyism. In the novel the press institutes defamation campaigns against communists, crude propaganda leaflets agitate against them, and the house of one strike leader, Doc Hale, is smeared with the word red.

The novel presents above all an indictment of the U.S. economic system. Heym describes what amounts to economic murder being committed against the Pennsylvania miners: they live in shacks, their children are undernourished, and during the strike the children begin to starve. Goldsborough possesses the trappings of democracy, little more. Politicians with money run the courts, the newspaper, the thugs (there is a private army of brown shirt types), and the police. The judge is also a mine owner. The police pummel two strike leaders, Hale and Kennedy, then imprison them on false charges. Heym intends this action as an ironic juxtaposition to the immigrant Bilek's recurring nightmare of police brutality against him in Eastern Europe (320) before the advent of socialism there (254).

Heym wishes to demonstrate that Goldsborough is not anomalous, and he emphasizes connections and parallels in an attempt to broaden the scope of his novel. The local attacks on communists in Goldsborough are echoed by mention of the blacklistings in Hollywood and by the statement that "all over this country men are being put in prison" (491). He views the political machine in Goldsborough as merely a smaller, more vulgar version of the machine that governs America all the way to the White House (e.g., 321). The strike begins in Goldsborough but spreads throughout Pennsylvania, assuming national implications. Heym asserts in his afterword that "fundamentally the United States today *is* Goldsborough" (510).

Heym wrote *Goldsborough* with passion and clear commitment. It contains naïveté: the portrait of the Soviet Union and the East Bloc countries appeared too good to be true, and it was. But Heym's ideological perspective allows him insights somewhat unusual in the United States during the early 1950s. For example, he resolutely condemns racism.

Carlise Kennedy functions as the positive hero, but the reserved, intellectual Doc Hale remains in many ways one of the most intriguing characters. Stefan Heym's novels often contain a figure like Hale (e.g., Yates or Thomas Benda), in whom we may see some of Heym's own ambivalence, and these characters at times subtly undermine Heym's own project. Both Hale and Kennedy are frustrated by the workers, who attend only to their momentary concerns, but Hale becomes ever more separated from them. If the workers (except Kennedy) cannot move from praxis to theory, Hale is unable to move the other way, and he is finally isolated and defeated, dreaming, like Yates in *The Crusaders*, of a "third way." GDR critics disliked Heym's portrayal of Hale, one noting that the author's emphasis on Hale's lack of resolution and on his doubts left the impression that Heym had made the character a bit "too complicated" (Zachau 46–47). In his autobiography, Heym admits that in depicting Hale's feelings at the conclusion of the novel (he must leave Goldsborough to escape political persecution) he was attempting to deal with his own situation at the time (*Nachruf* 526).

The GDR critic and author Gerhard Wolf (husband of Christa Wolf) praised *Goldsborough* highly in *Neue Deutsche Literatur* ("Mensch"). Goldsborough, he asserts, could be any town in a country where capitalism had entered its final stages, for example, in West Germany (154). Wolf likes Heym's "hard" American style of writing, though he asserts that Heym does not share the cynicism of the "decadent pseudorealistic literature of the West" (161; my trans.). Heym's novel, he predicts, will count among the important realistic works of our time (154).

Goldsborough was published only after Heym had left America. It appeared first in the GDR, then in the United States, a process Reinhard Zachau finds "absolutely comparable" ("durchaus vergleichbar") to GDR censorship of Heym after 1965 (48). But that analogy is nonhistorical. One should instead compare practices in the 1950s, when GDR authors who wrote oppositional books were not merely "censored."

Nonetheless, *Goldsborough* did not appear with a mainstream U.S. publisher. That, together with the novel's left-wing subject matter, the negative reviews of *The Eyes of Reason* (and political attacks on people who had had anything positive to say about that book), plus the fact that Heym had fled the United States for asylum in the GDR, insured that the novel was not reviewed in this country. American critics would also ignore Heym's following two novels, *The Lenz Papers* and *Uncertain Friend*.

A New Home: Stefan Heym in the GDR

For Heym, a leftist of Jewish descent, the later 1940s and early 1950s in the United States presented unsettling similarities with the Germany he had escaped in the 1930s. As we have seen, he draws parallels in *Goldsborough* between the Third Reich and the United States, and in his autobiography he speaks of Klu Klux Klan violence against leftists in 1949 as state-sanctioned fascism (*Nachruf* 470). Heym also recalls numerous artists who left the country—Brecht, Mann, Chaplin—and those, such as the Hollywood Ten (including

Lester Cole, who wrote the film script for *Hostages*), who were prosecuted, blacklisted, and/or jailed.

Within that atmosphere, two public denunciations of Heym portended no good. Howard Rushmore, according to Heym a specialist in exposing "disguised" communists, characterized Heym publicly as a dangerous German communist with wide-ranging international connections (*Nachruf* 472). In a series of articles, Charles A. Brady not only condemned the author of *The Eyes of Reason* but called for legal action against those who did not attack the novel (485–86). With the outbreak of the Korean War, Heym, a reserve officer, feared he might be sent into battle like Uriah (an episode he will later imagine in *The King David Report*).

Heym's American wife recognized the many differences between America and the Third Reich: "This will not last forever. The Americans are not like the Germans; despite all obtuseness they will realize where this witchhunt is heading with its denunciations and persecutions, and they will, after a while, change things" (*Nachruf* 550; my trans.). But she and her husband feared what might occur before that time, and Heym, recalling the haven Czechoslovakia had offered him in 1933, left the United States, at first only provisionally.

After stays in France, Switzerland, and Poland, Heym was allowed to enter Czechoslovakia, where he assumed his *Eyes of Reason* would assure him a warm welcome. The new Czech government did not, however, appreciate Heym's portrayal of the wavering Thomas Benda in the novel (which would only appear under Dubček), and it furthermore distrusted the author, a former U.S. Army intelligence officer. Heym was ultimately deported, an act he later viewed as a blessing in disguise, since during that time the Czech Party was purging Jewish communists who had spent time in Western exile (*Nachruf* 528–29).

With trepidation, but also in desperation, Heym returned to Germany, taking asylum in the GDR. He published a collection of short stories, *The Cannibals*, which demonstrates great bitterness toward America. He began writing a weekly column for an East Berlin newspaper and received the Heinrich Mann Prize for literature in 1953. In April of that year he wrote Truman a public letter, returning his Bronze Star and denouncing "concentration camps" in the United States as well as that country's "course towards fascism and war"

(*Nachruf* 550; my trans.). He announced that he had become a citizen of the GDR.

Heym's querulousness brought him increasing difficulties in his new country as well. A workers' revolt in June 1953, two months after he had severed his ties with the United States, shattered some illusions. He attempted to write a book on the subject, one that he now finds too apologetic. GDR publishers thought it too critical, and it could not appear. In 1957 his newspaper column was stopped. *Shadows and Lights* (1960), a second collection of stories, was still quite orthodox but contained rather too much shadow for some functionaries. Faced with increasing official resistance, Heym devised a strategy he would maintain until the publication of *Collin* in 1979: he began to write historical novels. We should remember, however, a statement from a figure in *The Lenz Papers*, Heym's first historical work: "The contours of imagination are usually drawn in the perspectives of our own time" (14).

The Lenz Papers GDR 1963, GB 1964, GDR 1968
(abridged Eng. trans.)

Heym's first GDR novel is set in 1848–49, a period of revolutionary upheaval throughout Europe, a time in which Germans assembled at Frankfurt to write a constitution. The events take place in Baden, where soldiers revolted against the royal family and drove it into (temporary) exile. The provisional revolutionary government bifurcated between moderates (who, in the novel, are primarily interested in playing a caretaker role until the return of the royal family) and those who wished to institute radical economic changes. Heym's sympathies lie with the latter, embodied by Corporal Andreas Lenz and, in a lesser role, the peasant soldier Christoffel. The latter's experiences are primarily rural, while Lenz's are urban. Thus, as Reinhard Zachau points out, Heym attempts to illustrate two aspects of the revolution (60).

The disunity within the revolution weakens it fatally. The revolutionaries fail to consolidate gains, and the revolt does not spread into neighboring provinces. The fledgling government watches with growing dismay, then fatalism, as Prussian counterrevolutionary forces gather on Baden's borders. When the final battle begins, the odds are quite hopeless. Besieged in the fortress Rastatt, the army believes half-promises and surrenders, only to be imprisoned under inhuman conditions while its leaders are executed. Lenz makes a daredevil escape engineered by his lover Lenore, and they travel to the United States, where Lenz dies fighting with the Union troops at Gettysburg.

In the novel, Heym advances his by now familiar argument that to achieve greater freedom, one must first curtail it. Comlossy, a Jacobin, tells Christoffel:

> You know that a law is a law only as long as it is convenient to those in power and not a second longer. Only dreamers like us let themselves be hamstrung by constitutions of their own making and by concern for the other fellow's life and rights. We're getting a brutal lesson, Brother Christoffel! (493)

When Rastatt is besieged and the populace grows restless, Comlossy also suggests stronger methods:

> "How far, I ask you, Citizen Lenz, do we want to let things slip?"
> Robespierre, thought Lenz. For a moment he envied the resolve and inner certainty of [Comlossy], and he knew that Robespierre's were the only feasible methods. (423)

At this point, Lenz—poet, intellectual, bon vivant—envies Comlossy only "for a moment." He is in general a rather good-natured dreamer who has difficulty finding that "inner certainty" necessary to guillotine people. Nonetheless, near the end of the revolt, he holds a speech calling for stronger measures, those of Comlossy (424). Heym wants to write a kind of primer, so that future revolutionaries do not commit the mistakes of 1848 (377, 435–36), and after Christoffel has been lectured by Comlossy, the narrator says of the former, "He was willing to learn the lesson" (492).

In this novel, Heym takes up for the first time what becomes his recurring theme—the role and function of the political writer. One responsibility of the writer consists in bearing witness and reporting (412); this motif is especially pronounced in Heym's later novel *Collin*. When Lenore Einstein's father discusses Andreas Lenz in *The Lenz Papers*, Heym amplifies his vision of the author as hero:

"He's an intellectual!" Einstein retorted. "A writer! A spokes-
man! A man who can take people's dumb, shapeless feelings
and put them into words and thereby convert them into a force,
a danger, an explosive under the seats of the mighty!" . . .
"Without him, those feelings would never become the material
power that moves whole armies and gives that twitch to the face
of the Prince of Prussia although he has just beaten the revolution. The word, Lenore, is always suspect! How does a Prussian
official know that a word is just what it says and that no second,
subversive meaning lurks behind it? How can a government
head be sure that a word will stay where it is and not fly off,
sparking all sorts of tinder?" (469)

That is very similar to the language and the theme of Heym's later
masterpieces, *The Queen against Defoe* and *The King David Report*. In
The Lenz Papers we are told that the protagonist controls men's minds
(470), and an inarticulate Prussian officer, vaguely recalling a dossier
on Lenz, mutters: "Lenz, his ilk, literati—like spark to powder
charge—bang!" (530). This cuts both ways, of course, for independent writers are a danger to any repressive government. As Heym's
own conflicts with GDR officials sharpen, he moves the writer-society
confrontation more squarely into the center of his own concerns. In
principle, he establishes suppositions here that he will never relinquish: that the writer must bear witness, and that an author's words
can rock governments.

The Lenz Papers is Heym's only GDR novel that was received in a
completely positive fashion by East German critics (Zachau 58). In
Neue Deutsche Literatur the author Wolfgang Joho especially praised
the proletarian character Christoffel, who made the work, Joho asserts, an optimistic tragedy (132–33). The reviewer for *Der Sonntag*
objected that Heym's Friedrich Engels wears glasses and stutters;
otherwise he lauded the novel and applauded Heym's depiction of
Christoffel (2 Feb. 1964).

Nonetheless, by Heym's own admission the book is overly long,
and even the paperback edition (trimmed by Heym's wife) has five
hundred and fifty pages of small print. As in many of his books,
Heym's characters often seem to be mouthpieces for philosophical
positions. That is particularly clear with Christoffel, who serves
largely as a foil for Marx and Engels, whom Heym inserts so that we

may be given an analytical overview of events. Lenz's common-law wife, Lenore, espouses a number of strikingly feminist positions (e.g., 352), but the structure of the novel has Lenz torn between the higher and the lower, between Lenore, who has the qualities of an angel, and Josepha, most definitely a whore. Heym's writing is in general uninspired (Reinhard Zachau is probably correct when he surmises that the author's heart was simply not in this novel [60]), and Lenz's songs and poems are often not very convincing indicators of the talent everyone claims he possesses. A transfer of media helped: in 1986 West German television filmed the book, and the adaptation was well received.

Uncertain Friend GB 1969, FRG 1969, GDR 1974

Heym's second historical novel, *Uncertain Friend*, portrays Ferdinand Lassalle (1825–64), an early leader of the German labor movement. Lassalle was jailed for his participation in the revolution of 1848, but in his later years he developed a more evolutionary view of political progress. Accordingly, he attempted to work with Prussian Prime Minister Otto von Bismarck while also organizing the General German Workers' Association (ADAV or *Allgemeiner Deutscher Arbeiterverein*). He had met Marx in 1861 but gradually became estranged from the latter due to differences of personality and politics.

After Lassalles's death Friedrich Engels wrote a letter, quoted by Heym as epigram for his novel, in which he noted that Lassalle "was, at the present, a rather uncertain friend and he would have become, in the future, a rather certain enemy." Engels's characterization has informed the Party line of orthodox communists, for whom Lassalle was merely a reformer. (Contemporary German social democrats view in Lassalle a kindred spirit.) Heym's novel emphasizes Lassalle's monomaniacal positions, his dictatorial drive for power. The author sees it as a tragedy of the working-class movement that it needed Lassalle: it could not begin without him, yet it was hopelessly impeded by his leadership.

The plot possesses two strands, one commencing when Lassalle makes the acquaintance of Countess Helen von Dönniges. Notorious for his womanizing and for his liaison with the older Sophie von Hatzfeld, Lassalle becomes fascinated, then obsessed, by the countess. After several intrigues the countess rejects Lassalle, who then challenges her father and her fiancé to a duel. Lassalle dies from the wounds he receives in the senseless affair.

A second strand of plot outlines Lassalle's political platform, the centerpiece of which was universal suffrage. The novel follows his effort to found the first German worker's party and his unsuccessful negotiations with Bismarck. Ultimately, his obsession with Helen distracts him from his political tasks.

In an interview with J. Robert Moskin, Heym discussed his two goals in *Uncertain Friend*. Discussing his first goal, Heym remarked,

> Lassalle is a nonperson of the working-class movement. He had a falling out with Marx. I considered Lassalle on the basis of the question: How [much] can you work together with the enemy in order to achieve your progressive goals? (7)

In answering this question, Heym follows the reasoning of the orthodox Marxists, for Lassalle's negotiations with Bismark fail. Buoyed by a wave of jingoistic popularity after a successful war against Denmark, the Prussian prime minister has no further need of Lassalle's assistance in pacifying the German working class.

Heym's second goal in *Uncertain Friend* is to question Lassalle's rise to power:

> The other thing that interested me was the question of the one-man dictatorship in the working-class movement. Was that just an aberration in Stalin's time? Or was the possibility of a one-man dictatorship built into the structure of the working-class movement? (Moskin 7)

Heym presents Lassalle as a man so egotistical that he does not hesitate to compare himself regularly with Napoleon, Caesar, and even Jesus. Knowing the workers need his name, experience, and connections, he insists on a role as unquestioned leader of the ADAV, considering the "picayune democracy which the little man loved" (57) to be a "formality" (56). He believes "the contradiction between the need for one-man rule and the need for democratic trappings was universal as long as the people were what they were: a lot of contrary, uninformed, unthinking, egotistic louts who had to be forced to their own good and welfare" (61). Heym's Lassalle maintains no respect for those he wishes to lead, and his distaste for the workers is evident throughout the novel. He characterizes them as "that huge, grey, uncouth mass of proletarians" (60), as a "great fickle whore" (75). His public words are different: "A deep instinct of class has arisen among our workers, a new self-reliant way of thinking nullifies the outpourings of the quack writers and the corrupt Press. You have justified my confidence in the intelligence of the working man, and the insight I have gained into the great character of your class is one of my most beautiful, most unforgettable experiences" (105–6).

The Bavarian foreign minister tells Lassalle that his "revolution" is quintessentially Prussian: "Economically, administratively, politically, this state of yours is bound to be one huge bureaucratic machine, grey, boring, deadly; its only interesting feature the dictator at its head—you" (239). Lassalle's assistant, Becker, also sees the leader as a dictator, and he ponders the central question: "But it was a new kind of dictatorship, Lassallean, and he wondered whether it would die with the man or would recur because it was ingrained in this new kind of organization" (182).

Heym told J. Robert Moskin that in his novel the one-man dictatorship presents a possibility, not a necessity. In *Uncertain Friend* the figure of Julius Vahlteich, a worker who helps found the ADAV and who serves for a time as Lassalle's secretary, symbolizes an alternative. Vahlteich entertains misgivings about Lassalle from the outset, and he eventually breaks with him to agitate for more democracy within the ADAV. He insists to his lover (Lassalle's former concubine):

> What haunts you and me, Mathilde, is Lassalle's eternal *I*; the same thing that blights our movement—this dictatorship of one man who thinks he's the greatest, his plans the only ones that will succeed, his mind the only one that can decide, his secret plots correct and justified because they're his. Why should people like you and me, simple people, be sacrificing and organizing and revolutionizing, if we only exchange one kind of tyranny for another? (140–41)

Like many other figures in the novel, Vahlteich was a historical personage, and Heym appends a passage in his afterword from

Vahlteich's *Ferdinand Lassalle and the Beginnings of the German Working-Class Movement*, published in 1904. Among other functions, the postscript indicates that Vahlteich did become a figure of impact in the working-class movement, and it thus suggests that his values—those of grass-roots, decentralized democracy—remain a dialectical, theoretical possibility in that movement.

As in Heym's previous novel *The Lenz Papers*, *Uncertain Friend* is overly long and often plodding. This interior monologue of Helen's reads like a parody of Joyce:

My God, she thought, does he still need to prove himself well I'll let him I'll be better at it than the old hag I'll be Child to him Woman Mother nursing him tending to his needs he needs me needs my love this is love yes? it must be it is. (206)

The two plot strands never mesh in a convincing fashion, and at the conclusion the melodramatic love affair dominates, submerging the political aspects Heym wished to emphasize.

This book was Heym's first GDR novel that could not appear in his adopted country. It may have been blocked because of the—rather mild—investigation of one-man dictatorship, a communist problem not limited to Stalin. More probably the novel's prohibition had to do with Heym's general standing at the time. In 1965 Erich Honecker had denounced him in a speech: "Working people in the GDR have written letters against Stefan Heym, because he belongs to the constantly negative critics of conditions in the GDR. He is obviously not ready to accept suggestions that have been made to him on numerous occasions" (qtd. in Zachau 64; my trans.).

Heym published the novel with the West German Bechtle publishing house, for which he received a minimal three hundred mark fine for ignoring the GDR copyright bureau. As Reinhard Zachau notes, a higher penalty would have necessitated a trial, and East German authorities had little interest in such publicity (64). Nonetheless, Heym stirred some controversy in West German television by calling Lassalle an ancestor of Stalin, and West German reviewers paid attention to that. During the thaw of 1971–76, the novel also appeared in the GDR, where Werner Neubert reviewed it quite negatively for *Neue Deutsche Literatur*. Neubert suggested that Heym maintained a rather superficial relationship to the real workers' movement ("Sinn").

The Queen against Defoe Switz. 1970, GDR 1974, USA 1974

With only forty-five pages, Heym's *The Queen against Defoe* is a small but acerbic piece in which the author discovers his authentic voice. It constitutes one of his finest efforts, continuing and developing a theme from *The Lenz Papers*—the writer as oppositional hero.

Daniel Defoe (1660–1731) remains known to most readers as the author of *Robinson Crusoe*, but he also worked as a pamphleteer, propagandist, and publicist for the Dissenters, a religious group at odds with the Anglican church. His text *The Shortest Way with the Dissenters* takes various Anglican thoughts to extreme conclusions— it argues that the Dissenters should be banished to America or killed. The pamphlet, at first welcomed by the Anglicans, caused them considerable embarrassment when it became clear that Defoe had written ironically. He was arrested, tried, and sentenced to three days in the stocks. Instead of pillorying him, however, the populace of London celebrated him, turning the entire affair into a folk festival.

Heym recounts the story through the diary of Josiah Creech, a clever, corrupt sycophant who, as the right-hand man for the Secretary of State Earl of Nottingham, has access to an army of informants and police. The earl believes Defoe could not have acted alone and insists on searching for a conspiracy. He promises Defoe money and freedom if he will divulge names, yet Defoe, no obvious candidate for heroism, refuses to betray innocent people (and, it is at least hinted, he is too proud of his work to want to share it). Defoe responds to the earl: "Cannot you Lordships understand . . . that a man's free thought is not like the stick which the dog returns at a master's call? Or are you that steeped in the ways of orthodoxy that to your mind any idea not previously approved necessarily becomes part of a seditious plot?" (55).

Heym published the story in Switzerland, together with an attest from an East Berlin professor who certifies the historical authenticity of Heym's book. In an effort to have the piece appear in his own country, Heym was clearly attempting to persuade the censors that his book in fact deals with the eighteenth century. Curiously enough, there was also some debate in the Federal Republic regarding the contemporary relevance of Heym's story. Writing in the *Frankfurter Allgemeine Zeitung*, Konrad Franke thought the story dated, of historical relevance only, and suggested that GDR authorities print it (7

March 1970). Sabine Brandt came much closer to the truth when she asserted in *Die Zeit* that the jacket Heym cut would fit many, but that the SED could wear it (10 July 1970).

Heym's theme—the relationship between the writer and the state—is indeed universal. When Defoe insists that his enemies are hypocrisy, injustice, and intolerance (47), he utters a battle cry applicable to every society and every time. When the government burns Defoe's work, we are reminded of an earlier Germany (36). When Defoe attacks capitalist banking practices (58), Heym is most certainly not referring to the GDR.

The story is no *conte à clef* and will disappoint those looking for parallels between its characters and GDR personages. Nonetheless, assertions that Defoe—like Lenz in Heym's earlier novel—was a master of the double entendre (37), that he is more dangerous than all the armies of France (21), that the secret service must hunt him down (35, 44), and that "a statesman can be toppled by a sharp pen as easily as by gunpowder" (25) were well enough understood in the GDR, where the Eulenspiegel publishing firm rejected the manuscript with the explanation that it could be interpreted in two ways (Zachau 72). In 1974, during the cultural thaw, the slender piece appeared in the GDR, and Hermann Kant, president of the GDR Writers' Association, proclaimed proudly that the East Germans had published *The Queen against Defoe* after they had realized that they were not the queen ("Verantwortung" 220).[2]

In its treatment of class, the story demonstrates its Marxist orientation. Defoe is "of lowly descent and a butcher's son" (28), and throughout the story working people assist him. A weaver hides him (40), and "small people, a shipwright, a baker, a broker, and such," pay his bail (48). At the conclusion "the people" rise up to defend Defoe from Creech and his hired thugs; it is the apotheosis of the writer, the overcoming of the gulf between the intellectual and the masses. After Defoe is free, there is talk that "maybe 'tis time to think of another revolution" (61). Reinhard Zachau points out, however, that the political solidarity Heym portrays results in part from wishful thinking: the real London crowds showed respect for Defoe as a person and pity for his situation, but they did not identify with his liberal political program (73).

With the exception of Konrad Franke, West German critics hailed *The Queen against Defoe*, and Martin Gregor-Dellin called it Heym's most accomplished literary work (Zachau 70). Published with three other short stories by Heym, the piece was reviewed fairly widely in England, and the *New York Times Book Review* took notice of Heym for the first time since the 1950s (8 Sept. 1974). Heym's writing sparkles in *The Queen against Defoe*, and indeed, in his autobiography the author explains that he underwent a process of osmosis with Defoe's language, adopting it as his own. Heym's wife usually corrected his English, but after reading this piece, she asserted that he no longer needed her editorial assistance (*Nachruf* 750).

The King David Report FRG 1972, USA 1973, GDR 1973

The King David Report, Heym's finest novel, was published in the Federal Republic in 1972, and to the surprise of many, it appeared in the GDR soon thereafter during the short-lived cultural-political thaw. In his novel Heym imagines how the biblical King David "report" (1 Samuel 6 to 1 Kings 2) might have originated. In the Bible the story constitutes quite obviously a patchwork job, comprising many sources; it contains evident compromises and downright contradictions. Into the interstices of the report Heym then inserts Ethan, who is actually mentioned in 1 Kings 31 as one of the wisest men in Israel. In Heym's fiction Ethan becomes a historian and the report's author.

King Solomon summons Ethan from a provincial city to Jerusalem to write "The One and Only True and Authoritative, Historically Correct and Officially Approved Report on the Amazing Rise, God-fearing Life, Heroic Deeds, and Wonderful Achievements of David the Son of Jesse, King of Judah for Seven Years and of Both Judah and Israel for Thirty-three, Chosen of God, and Father of King Solomon" (9). Ethan participates as a nonvoting member on a committee of Solomon's sycophants. The report he is to write should allay various unsavory rumors about David and legitimate the rule of his son, Solomon.

A man of conscience who maintains a fondness for the truth, Ethan is not unaware of the risks:

I . . . saw that I might end, as some writers did, with my head cut off and my body nailed to the city wall, but that, on the other hand, I might wax fat and prosperous if I guarded my tongue and used my stylus wisely. With some luck and the aid of our

> Lord Yahveh, I might even insert in the King David Report a word here and a line there by which later generations would perceive what really came to pass in these years and what manner of man David ben Jesse was: who served as a whore simultaneously to a King and the King's son and the King's daughter, who fought as a hired soldier against his own blood, who had his own son and his most loyal servants assassinated while loudly bewailing their death, and who forged a people out of a motley of miserable peasants and recalcitrant nomads. (11)

Narrated retrospectively by Ethan, the novel retraces his detective work, his examination of written evidence, and his interviews with survivors. Ethan labors under the watchful eye of Benaiah ben Jehoiada, head of the secret police, who quickly ascertains that Ethan knows too much (107).

Ethan demythologizes David (the fight against Goliath, he discovers, never occurred), and he uncovers the shadow side of his rise to power. But Ethan fails in his attempt to write discreetly while waxing fat: Solomon "honors" him by taking his beloved concubine Lilith; his wife, Esther, who has a bad heart, dies; and Ethan is judged guilty of literary high treason. Benaiah wishes to execute him, but Solomon instead forbids Ethan to publish, thus silencing him to death.

Numerous noncommunist reviewers have read this novel as a comment on Stalin. Writing in the *Frankfurter Allgemeine Zeitung*, Rolf Michaelis pointed to the show trials, the arrests and executions, and the work camps as parallels with the Soviet Union. He compares David's alliance with Israel's enemy, the Philistines, to the Hitler-Stalin pact, and he sees in David's secret list (whether it really exists or not is left open in the novel), used by Solomon to rid himself of undesirables, a parallel to Lenin's "Testament" and other secret Soviet documents (16 June 1972). However, as Christiane Bohnert argues, one can undoubtedly read the book as an allegory of power in general—as an examination of the corruption bred by unchecked rule and as a condemnation of fascism as well as Stalinism ("Stefan Heym"). Apparently the East German censors agreed, and they allowed the book to appear. Nonetheless, Heym clearly wished to attack practices in contemporary socialism. He says in his afterword that the novel presents a "story of today, charged with political meaning" (254), and Heym often and deliberately departs from his own King James English to employ words from the vocabulary of socialism, for example "unperson" (119) or "rubbish heap of history" (112).

Heym's investigation of censorship is not limited to an attack on former GDR practices, but it clearly implies them. At the outset of the novel, Solomon tells Ethan that he will help him should the historian falter or become unsure of what the truth might be (10), and the committee he appoints to aid Ethan gives the scholar guidelines not dissimilar to some tenets of socialist realism:

> But contradictions are there to be smoothed over, Ethan, not to be stressed. Contradictions puzzle and embitter the heart; but the Wisest of Kings, Solomon, wishes all of us, and especially the writers of books, to accentuate the more edifying aspects of life. We are to strike a happy medium between what is and what we want people to believe, and to reflect the greatness of our epoch. (42)

Solomon praises Ethan for his cunning with words and his ability "to direct thereby the thinking of people" (85).

In a further reference to the writing of history in communist countries (or under totalitarian regimes), the court recorder notes:

> In books which are published in certain foreign lands, word about those who displease the eye of their king is frequently reduced from several pages to one miserable line, or stricken out, so that the person thus treated becomes an un-person and his sons are the sons of nobody. But these be the ways of the uncircumcised, and also unwise, for a complete perversion of facts fools but complete fools and renders the entire book unbelievable; and as soon as another king ascends the throne, he orders the book rewritten, whereby the previous king's un-persons are resurrected and his favorites correspondingly demoted, so that the history of a people comes to depend on which edition of it you read. (138)

Ethan's middle-of-the-road course proves ultimately impossible. As Benaiah growls, "We can read . . . even between the lines" (244). The court recorder gives Ethan some collegial advice: "A scribe should write, not think" (149). And in the center of the book (the structural location emphasizes the importance), Amenhoteph the eunuch warns, "You had better castrate your thinking, Ethan" (122).

Ethan refuses that advice, and only once, when Solomon directly threatens his life, does he compose a propagandistic lie (245–46). His desire to write between the lines represents a strategy thematized elsewhere in Heym's work. Thus when Benaiah complains of Ethan and his "words which have more than one meaning," the reader recalls Defoe, who had "a mastery of the double meaning; he took back with one word what he conceded with the other" (37). In *The Lenz Papers* Lenore's father lectures her: "The word, Lenore, the word is always suspect. How does a Prussian official know that a word is just what it says and that no second, subversive meaning lurks behind it?" (469). That, in turn, sounds much like Ethan: "But words have their own life: you cannot trap them or hold them or rein them in, they are of many hues, they both conceal and reveal, and behind each line that is written, lurks danger" (117–18). Ethan demonstrates here an almost mystical reverence for the power of the word. Near the end of the novel, he insists to the court, "As the sun breaks through the clouds . . . thus the truth will break through words" (245). His belief in the word ultimately transforms the Pauline tenet of "love, hope, and faith"; in the novel an angel speaks to Ethan, telling him, "All this will turn to dust, says the Lord; but the word, and truth, and love, these shall remain" (251).

As in *The Lenz Papers* or *The Queen against Defoe*, Heym fills *The King David Report* with references to the danger that writers and scholars represent to despots. Nathan the prophet repeats a familiar theme of the novel when he notes, "But as knowledge of the facts may lead a person to dangerous thoughts, the facts must be presented so as to direct the mind into the proper channels" (82). Later, after Ethan is arrested, bound, and physically maltreated, the policeman responsible reports, "We treated him according to the deserts of a person in the category of a learned man holding questionable thoughts" (220). Benaiah warns Ethan not to write or *harbor* displeasing thoughts (28).

Ethan, however, entertains no such grandiose schemes as toppling a king with his words. As Heym's Collin does later, Ethan discovers another power in his language. Amenhoteph tells him: "But you Ethan, and all those in your trade make men immortal by your words, so that the names of men you wrote of will be remembered thousands of years hence. Therein lies your power" (60). For Ethan, writing constitutes memory; erase the writing, and one extinguishes history (17).

David Roberts sees the novel as "totally pessimistic" ("Heym" 208), but it seems to me that Ethan's power proves far stronger than Solomon's. Despite Solomon's measures against him (in Heym's book), Ethan remains mentioned in the Bible, Heym's intertext, as one of the wisest men in the kingdom of Israel, second only to Solomon. In a fine twist, Heym also credits Ethan with authorship of the Song of Solomon and Solomon's aphorisms (in the novel, Solomon plagiarizes them), thus demonstrating the subversive power of language and the truth of Ethan's dictum that, indeed, the word will remain. Finally, we should consider what is not included in Heym's novel, but what Heym may well assume his readers know: in the Bible Solomon increasingly turns away from God, breaking the covenant. After his troubled reign, the kingdom breaks into ten parts, and the tribes that, to Ethan's grudging admiration, David molded into a people, return to their former state of fragmentation.

West Germans accorded Heym's novel a warm welcome. The right-wing *Die Welt* called it "brilliant, amusing, elegant" (22 June 1972; my trans.), but Heinrich Böll also praised it in the liberal *Der Spiegel* (18 Sept. 1972).[3] In December 1973 the novel appeared in the GDR. Though not unfriendly, reviewers there distanced themselves from Heym's treatment of power and history. They also criticized the fact that the parable character of the book had been exploited in the West to demonstrate ostensibly "timeless truths" about the fashion in which power corrupts.[4] In the United States, Alvah Bessie lauded the novel and Heym in the *Nation:*

> In the telling of this tale Stefan Heym demonstrates not only his diabolical ingenuity as a satirist—he is of the order of Defoe and Swift—but also as a stylist in English who is a match for those other foreigners, Joseph Conrad and Vladmir Nabokov the Russian, who abandoned their native tongues to write in ours.

Bessie admires the fact that Heym has been a "nonperson in two countries" but has succeeded in being rehabilitated in his lifetime without undergoing the humiliating process of "self-criticism" demanded by "the Establishments of this world—Socialist, capitalist or in transition" (19 Jan. 1974).

Five Days in June FRG 1974, GB 1977, USA 1978, GDR 1989

The narrator of *Five Days in June* often employs a terse, factual style reminiscent of a reporter or indeed of a historian, for it is history, or the semblance thereof, that Heym is concerned with writing. The chapters begin with precise information as to the time and the day; the novel commences on 13 June at 2 P.M., four days before the 1953 workers' uprising that the Soviet Union suppressed with tanks.

Characteristically, Heym has personified the forces or positions that he wishes to examine, and directly at the outset of the novel we encounter the dogmatic Party secretary Banggartz in debate with Witte, the trade union representative at the People's Plant Merkur. The opening sentences make clear the confrontation as Banggartz threatens Witte:

> "Either you stick to the party decisions, Comrade Witte, or you face the consequences. It's as simple as that."
>
> Witte felt sorry for his party secretary. Banggartz believed in what he said; but what Banggartz said was too often what he wanted to believe.
>
> "I'm afraid, Comrade Banggartz," he replied, "for me it's not as simple as that." (9)

Witte is the only character of rank in the novel who realizes that the Party's attempt to raise the work norms by 10 percent constitutes the wrong decision at the wrong time. Events ultimately vindicate him, but first he must plead with numerous officials, none of whom assists him, be locked out of his plant and be isolated from the workers he represents, and suffer a police interrogation. In the course of the story, he learns that Party bureaucrats habitually refer to the workers as "their workers"; that his trade union has become a fifth wheel, a society for mutual backslapping; and that the Party, whether it consists of dogmatic socialists like Banggartz or critical ones like him, is isolated indeed.

Heym began work on this novel after his own experiences with

17 June. Newly arrived in the GDR after having fled the United States, he found the workers' revolt against "their" state an unwelcome dilemma. He attempted to work through his conflicting emotions in a novel with the provisional title *A Day Marked X*, the name given to the hoped-for revolt by a number of West German politicians. This original version has never been printed, but those who have seen the manuscript indicate that it remains very close to the official GDR view of the uprising as a Western-sponsored, counter-revolutionary putsch (Zachau 82). In the 1960s and 1970s Heym revised the work, in his words, from an "apologia" to an "analytical account" of events, which became *Five Days in June* (Zachau 82).

Reinhard Zachau finds even the revised manuscript too apologetic because Heym (like Anna Seghers in *Trust*) continues to cleave in good part to the "infiltration theory" whereby the SED attempted to delegate all responsibility for the uprising to Western—read fascist—agents (82). The author inserts as montage, for example, various (true) reports indicating the extent of the West's involvement (119, 335), and he invents figures who act as agents provocateurs: Heinz Hofer, who had left the GDR, but who returns as a pistol-toting Western agent; two thugs, one harelipped, the other effeminate, the former with a criminal record; a young man in a T-shirt displaying a lasso-swinging cowboy; many agents disguised as workers; and Mr. *Quelle* ("Source"), a prominent West German politician who is deeply involved in the ferment.

Nonetheless, Heym also indicates that although Western politicians and agents take full advantage of the communist blunders, and although they are responsible for the escalation of demands from a mere redressment of the norm increase to calls for free elections and the resignation of the GDR government, the communists themselves are to blame for the original uprising. Through montage he documents the unwillingness of Party officials to retreat from the decision to increase the norms, despite worker unrest. On 28 May the Party raised the norms, leading to protests. On 11 June a communiqué from the Council of Ministers ignored the issue. On 16 June the *Tribüne*, the organ of the trade union, defended the correctness of the raises, which in turn incited the walkouts. Heym inserts these documents into his narrative, and he constructs his story so that the errors and ultimately the stupidity of the Party's stubbornness become—to him—tragically apparent.

Heym furthermore has his characters admit the mistakes they committed (93), and when one Soviet commander, worried about the "necessity" of Soviet intervention, forecasts the propaganda victory the West will enjoy, another Soviet remarks, "I'm afraid, Michail Petrovich, this is a situation into which we were manoeuvered by ourselves" (140). Michail Petrovich then looks at a portrait of Stalin. At an important junction in the novel, Witte, positive hero and, as Zachau correctly points out, mouthpiece for Heym (87), realizes that in light of the Party's inflexibility the workers are striking with justification (182). Like Wolf Biermann and other socialist critics of the SED, Heym sees the uprising as one with a Janus head—at once a fascist coup and a justified expression of workers' outrage. Western agents do play a role in Heym's novel, but the Party itself allows them a foothold.

Heym's solutions to the problems he raises in his text are those of a committed Marxist-Leninist, and they are not unproblematic. Witte takes some comfort in his hope that the Party can learn from its mistakes, and he asserts that after today (17 June 1953) people will have to learn to think for themselves or cease to call themselves communists (214). At the conclusion of the narrative, Witte speculates that the Party needs a statute encouraging criticism. In 1954, as a result of the events in June 1953, the Party did indeed so amend its bylaws, and Heym places the relevant citation at the outset of his novel:

> It is the duty of the member of the party . . . to develop self-criticism and criticism from the ranks, to uncover without fear or favour shortcomings in the activities of the party and to help eliminate them; to struggle against gilding the truth and against the tendency of getting intoxicated with success, and to fight all attempts to suppress criticism or to gloss over criticism by apologies or false praise. (5)

Heym failed in his obvious attempt to protect and justify his book, which could only appear in the GDR in 1989, the year the Wall opened.

Witte ventures some cautious speculation concerning the role of the Party: "But who is to prevent these representatives from one day representing merely themselves?" (347). Earlier he had asked himself: "The holy grail, for whom were they guarding it? And who had named them guardians of this grail?" (257). Witte does not tread further than that. He does not question that the "logic of history" is on his side (257, 347), and though he refers indirectly to Brecht's sardonic résumé of the uprising—"that the Government [should] choose another people" (346)—he also states that there is no alternative to the unpopular government: "Despite its mistakes and shortcomings . . . there is only this one party, this one flag" (346). Witte acknowledges that the Party erred with the increase in the wage norms, but he will not acknowledge any validity in further demands for free and secret elections. Instead, he holds Western agents responsible for that "escalation." After the Party rescinds the norm increases, Witte is prepared to lock the workers in their factory to prevent them from striking.

Five Days in June evidences several artistic weaknesses, especially regarding characterizations. Witte, who like many of Heym's positive heroes is a former concentration camp internee, looks with prescient exactitude into the sands of time and finds the right answers. One of his opponents, widow Hofer, is shrill and ugly. Her husband worked for the SS, she enjoyed the so-called *Kristallnacht*, longs for former times, and listens to RIAS. Her son, a Western agent, has "shifting eyes" in a "jaded face" with an "indifferent mouth" (141). Confident of success, he struts, swaggers, and rapes his wife. When the Soviets crush the uprising, he cries with his head in his mother's lap. As opposed to the many corrupt American officers in *The Crusaders*, Heym's Russian officers are specialists in German Romanticism, quote Shakespeare, and drink tea.

The characterization of the worker Kallmann partakes less of cliché. Heym does equip him with a leitmotif reminiscent of popular nineteenth-century novels, but he allows Kallmann's portrait more shadow and light. Kallmann maintains vague socialist leanings, but he believes such a society should develop "naturally," without revolution. Kallmann proves capable of action both heroic and dastardly: he protects the Party secretary but beats his own wife. He occasionally attempts to think for himself, without notable success; he tends to be carried by events and, after much wavering, he ends on the "wrong" side. In Kallmann, Heym has created, probably against his intentions, the most differentiated, and hence the most interesting, character in his novel. When, at the conclusion, Kallmann throws a portrait of Marx into a canal, the symbolism is not necessarily felicitous for Heym's own project.

Five Days in June was reviewed negatively in England and hardly at all in the United States, perhaps because *Library Journal* characterized it as a "well-written political document rather than a piece of remarkable literature" (15 June 1978). In West Germany reviewers compared *Five Days in June* unfavorably with *The King David Report*, which, though written much later than *Five Days*, appeared shortly before it. Fritz Raddatz, who had worked in a GDR publishing house during the 1950s and who had read Heym's earlier version *A Day Marked X*, wrote probably the most balanced and perceptive review in *Der Spiegel*.

Raddatz asserts that Heym's book can be read on three levels: as novel, as history, and as an exploration of conflict management in socialism. As literature, Raddatz notes, the novel fails. As history it says some things for the first time, but in general, argues Raddatz, the literary clichés are not separable from the political ones. In Heym's novel, for example, the Soviets kill only one person, and only accidentally with a ricocheting bullet. In reality they aimed at people. Ultimately, Raddatz asserts, this is not a book about 17 June but an exploration, disguised in prose, about the ability of socialism to mediate disagreements. That, he believes, provides the truly explosive potential of the novel (18 Nov. 1974).

Other West German critics analyzed only the first two levels and found them wanting. *Die Welt* (23 Oct. 1974) and *Der Spiegel* (15 Aug. 1975) criticized the novel as apologetic. Writing in the *Frankfurter Allgemeine Zeitung*, Marcel Reich-Ranicki announced that Stefan Heym possessed more intelligence than taste, and more courage than talent (21 Dec. 1974).

Collin FRG 1979, USA 1980, GDR 1990

Until the later 1970s Heym had cloaked his growing criticism of the GDR in historical novels that dealt in general terms with the problems of writers: *The Lenz Papers, Uncertain Friend, The Queen against Defoe*, and *The King David Report*. With *Collin* Heym resolved, as he noted in an interview with *Der Spiegel*, to stop "beating around the bush" (12 Feb. 1979; my trans.).

Heym sets the novel in the GDR during the 1970s. Celebrated GDR writer Hans Collin is recuperating in an elite hospital. His friend Pollock, a literary critic, had urged Collin to write his memoirs, but for a writer disciplined in self-censorship, the examination of his past has occasioned a breakdown. Also in the hospital is Urack, the gravely ill chief of secret police. The two men enter a grotesque competition, each determined to outlive the other. Collin is befriended by the young doctor Christine Roth, who sees in Collin's suppression of his past the root of his disease. With her assistance and against Urack's opposition, Collin renews his confrontation with the Stalinist 1950s, including his own passive acquiescence in political trials.

Christa Wolf's quote from Faulkner—"the past is not dead, it is not even past"—with which she opens *Patterns of Childhood*, represents a recurring theme in *Collin* as well. Christine Roth listens to a victim of a political trial and muses, "And though the thing had happened long ago, it lay like an iron collar around the present, choking the new life; the sins of the fathers were still unredeemed, the biblical curse still held" (243). Collin thinks of "this past which, never quite buried, sat like an incubus on this country and everything in it" (218).

Collin lives in a society that forbids doubt because it views it as a weakness that aids the class enemy. Urack lectures Dr. Gerlinger, the head of the clinic in which both Collin and Urack are patients:

We are right, historically. We are acting for the working class, even though this class might not always understand us. The worst for us is to doubt. Doubt means defeat. A person who doubts removes himself from the struggle. (44)

One sees the development of Heym's thinking here, for in *Five Days in June* (published five years before *Collin* but begun in the 1950s) the hero also acts on behalf of the working class and the historical cause; in *Collin* the words come from a Stalinist.

Christine Roth joins the Party with an attest from her former father-in-law (a communist who served time in a concentration camp, and whose words, therefore, we are to take seriously): "[She] questions things and seeks to examine them on her own, but once she has found a cause to be right, she will support it from her whole heart (20)." The battle lines, then, are drawn between Stalinists and non-dogmatic communists—one thinks of Jurek Becker's Simrock in *Sleep-*

less Days (FRG 1978), who read in class Brecht's poem "In Praise of Doubt," only to be reprimanded by school authorities. Roth's goal will be to revive doubt in Collin's mind, doubts that his books implicitly contained, but that he suppressed.

Censorship is hence a dominant theme in Heym's novel. Theodor Pollock is instructed how to review a play (90). Peter Urack, a young oppositional poet and the grandson of Urack, is told by his grandfather: "We're against words which make sense" (98). Through a combination of outer and inner pressure, Collin so censors himself that his production suffers, and he finally lapses into silence, then illness.

Discussing his novel, Heym noted that we should read Collin's illness as a more general metaphor:

> [There are] of course things in our society and in our time which—if they do not come to the surface and are not analyzed and correctly treated—make people ill: this eternal schizophrenia of saying one thing and thinking another is not only unhealthy for the individual, but unhealthy for the entire society. ("Über" 376; my trans.)[5]

Indeed, the theme of disease pervades Heym's novel. Havelka, who was imprisoned during the 1950s, is ill. Collin is ill, but so is his nemesis Urack. In a curiously moral twist, Heym shows Urack tormented by the ghost of Faber, another innocent Party comrade whom Urack brought to fall. "We are all trapped in our past," Roth notes; "we are all seeing ghosts" (226).

In an interview, Heym contemptuously dismissed the question as to whether *Collin* is an anti-GDR book ("Über" 376–77). Nonetheless, his description of that country is hardly flattering. He includes show trials and Stalinist thugs who use the same tones that the Gestapo had formerly (129). He shows a society in which the most sensitive do not survive (181), a society of "sullen, barely hidden discontent" (234). He characterizes East Germany as a land of "general servility" (17), in which the Party attempts to co-opt independent thinkers, such as Roth, with privileges. Heym compares the GDR alternately with a feudal court (43, 90–91) and with a tribe practicing voodoo (133). Small wonder that many youths and trained professionals, such as doctors, flee (22).

Despite this rather grim picture, Heym advanced what he (not his government) considered positive criticism, and his book does contain a number of hopeful elements. Christine Roth successfully resists pressures from Gerlinger and Urack, two representatives of Party authority, and helps Collin surmount his creative block, an act that is tantamount to overcoming her own history as a communist. Collin does write his memoirs, and though he will die at the task, Pollock secures the manuscript from the authorities. Above all, the novel demonstrates yet again Heym's confidence in the importance of the writer, in the ability of the word to effect change. Collin, too, realizes this in the course of the novel. For all Urack's power—spies, prisons, intimidation—Collin, with only his words and, finally, his courage, is the more powerful.

Collin represents an important political document and an important personal one as well. With it Heym asserts his right to criticize existing GDR conditions in an open fashion. Although readers should not posit a rigid parallel between Collin and Heym, it is clear that in writing the novel the author confronted some of his own ghosts. Reviewing the book for *Die Zeit,* Wolf Biermann reported that in 1965, after various writers and intellectuals (including Biermann and Heym) fell into disfavor with the Party, Heym cut himself off from the blacklisted ones in an obvious and disturbing fashion. With surprise and admiration, Biermann remarked, "I didn't think old Heym had a novel like *Collin* in him" (3 March 1979; my trans.).

Heym did not attempt to publish the book in the GDR, sending it instead to his publisher in Munich. Its appearance caused a scandal in the East. Heym was fined nine thousand marks (more than nine months income for the average East German) for violating copyright laws (the fine for publishing *Uncertain Friend* without permission was much lower), and he was threatened with imprisonment. He was ejected from the Writers' Association—thus losing privileges including a regular income and a pension—and was vilified in various forums by official spokespeople, such as Hermann Kant ("Zu wissen"). In a venomous ad hominem attack in *Neues Deutschland* (22 May 1979), the writer Dieter Noll accused Heym, along with Rolf Schneider, of cooperating eagerly with the class enemy and of being a "bum" (*kaputter Typ*). West Germans responded by filming the novel (the former GDR writer Klaus Poche wrote the screenplay) for television. Since most East Germans were within West German broadcasting range, a great many at least *viewed* Heym's story.

Collin thus became a succès de scandale, although West German reviewers were in general not enamored of its literary merits.[6] The confrontation between the two central figures, Urack and Collin, remains somewhat mechanical; the protagonists represent ideas and do not come alive in any meaningful fashion. As usual, Heym's women are particularly unconvincing characters. Additionally, his language remains rather flat. In an article published by the East German *Sonntag*, West German Oskar Neumann isolated various particularly infelicitous sentences from Heym's novel, holding them up for his disdain. That demonstrated the kind of cynicism one encountered often in GDR cultural politics: Neumann reviewed and condemned a book the GDR reading public could not obtain, just as Dieter Noll and others attacked Heym in newspapers that did not allow him to respond. The effort the GDR cultural establishment undertook to discredit Heym's *Collin* underscored the threat it felt. For all its flaws, *Collin* is one of the first GDR books that so uncompromisingly confronts the Stalinist 1950s, and Walter Janka's autobiographical *Difficulties with the Truth* (1989) corroborates many passages from Heym's novel, in which the figure of Havelka represents Janka. After the fall of the SED government in 1989, *Neues Deutschland*, the paper in which Heym was denounced as a "bum" and a class traitor, began to serialize *Collin*. The novel appeared with a GDR publisher in 1990.

The Wandering Jew FRG 1981, USA 1984, GDR 1988

In *The Wandering Jew* Heym returns to the techniques that had proved so successful in *The King David Report*, reinterpreting legend to his ends. He writes of the Jewish shoemaker Ahasverus, at whose door, according to Medieval myth, Jesus Christ paused when carrying his cross to Calvary. Ahasverus refused Christ his request to rest and was hence condemned to remain on earth until the second coming.

Heym's novel actually operates in several different times. During a prologue in Heaven, the angels Lucifer and Ahasverus, whom the narrator calls revolutionaries, protest God's will that they worship man, and they are hence cast out. Several scenes take place in the interspace of their fall to earth. Heym sets the major part of the story in the sixteenth century, where the novel traces the rise of the Lutheran minister Paul Eitzen. This narrative is interspersed with Ahasverus's memories of Christ's passion and crucifixion. Finally, there is contemporary time, consisting primarily of letters between Jochanaan Leuchtentrager (Carrier of Light, or Lucifer), ostensibly a professor at Hebrew University in Jerusalem, and Professor Siegfried Beifuss of the Institute for Scientific Atheism in East Berlin. That story culminates as Beifuss leaves the GDR on a broomstick with Ahasverus and Leuchtentrager.

Lucifer and Ahasverus quickly part ways due to an ideological disagreement. Lucifer prophesies to God that man "is like vermin and will multiply like lice and will turn Your earth into a stinking mire, he will shed the blood of his brother and spurt his seed into the lowest animals, into donkeys and goats and sheep, and will commit more sins than I could ever invent, and will be a mockery of Your image, o Lord" (9–10). While not disagreeing, Ahasverus believes that "everything can be made to change" (10); he embodies the spirit of revolution. Leuchtentrager later notes the symbolic character of Ahasverus as "unrest personified; any fixed order exists for him only to be put into question and, depending on the case, to be over-thrown" (222). Ahasverus wants Jesus not to turn the other cheek but to take up the sword and combat injustice in the world. In Heym's retelling, Ahasverus sends Christ from his door when Christ insists on making his sacrifice. The sacrifice, Heym wishes to demon-strate in the novel, has been in vain (198). When Jesus returns to earth in the twentieth century, Heym employs an alienation effect (a bit like Buñuel in *Viridiana*) by showing Christ's horror at the nuclear arsenals of the superpowers.

In Heym's novel God is a dictator and a symbol for order, though Ahasverus insists that "His much-praised order is as full of contradic-tions as He himself" (124). God's arbitrary order functions as a meta-phor for earthly order, maintained by the cooperation between the Lutheran church, represented by Eitzen, and worldly authorities. Eitzen travels to Schleswig-Holstein to work for Duke Adolph and his secret police in "the establishment of the kingdom of God in Sleswick" under Adolph's "benevolent" dictatorship (233–34). Both Adolph (204–5) and Eitzen know "how one thing depends on the other, to wit, an orderly government on the right faith" (241). Thus Eitzen presides over a show trial of dissidents, and he has Ahasverus, in one of his incarnations, tortured to death.

Heym's novel takes place in the wake of the German peasant re-volt from the early sixteenth century, a revolt in part inspired by the liberating, even revolutionary, implications of Luther's new theology. Luther himself condemned the uprising in the strongest terms, and it was suppressed with much bloodshed about a generation before Eitzen's time (14). Eitzen asserts that "Doctor Luther confirmed that no rebellion was justified however just its cause, and that it was forbidden by God, and that the worldly authorities were instituted and armed with the sword so that uprisings and rebellion might be nipped in the bud" (202). Ahasverus had participated in the rebellion in one of his incarnations, and, a master dialectician, he praises Luther, for he knows the theologian's thought has helped smash outmoded systems, even if Luther himself will try—unsuccessfully—to undo what cannot be undone (47).

In addition to emphasizing Luther's condemnation of the peasant revolt, Heym underscores the religious leader's anti-Semitism. His Luther roars:

I shall give you my true advice: first, that you burn their synagogues and Jewish schools to the ground and take away their prayer books and their talmudic scriptures and forbid their rabbis to teach, and second, that you hand to all young, strong Jews flails and axes and spades and make them work in the sweat of their noses; but if they refuse such work, drive them out of the country along with their Wandering Jew. (43)

These words have a particularly ominous ring given the development of subsequent German history, as the Israeli professor Leuchtentrager reminds the German professor Beifuss (226).

Heym employs a Marxist analysis of anti-Semitism, pointing repeatedly to economic causes. Thus Luther's pupil Eitzen preaches a fiery anti-Semitic sermon that culminates in a condemnation of Jewish usury practices: "With this assertion he has come to a matter which, as he well knows, is moving his congregation a lot more deeply than does Pilate washing his hands, or the Jews' racial pride, or their alleged election by God" (85). The narrative makes other references to the economic basis of anti-Semitism (e.g., 17, 152, 180), climaxing with the Israeli professor's contention that after the Reformation, when the Catholic banking houses of Fugger and Welser were no longer available, and when Protestants returned to biblical law (Deuteronomy 23:20 forbids usury), they found themselves without bankers, a role the Jews then filled. With that, anti-Semitism acquired an economic foundation (226).

Heym's political project becomes clear when we recall that in 1983 the GDR celebrated with great fanfare the five hundredth anniversary of Luther's birth, declaring 1983 a Luther year. Luther was born in Eisleben, he studied in Erfurt, preached in Wittenberg, and translated the Bible into German in Eisenach. All these sites lay in the GDR, but through most of the 1940s, 1950s, and 1960s, GDR scholarship had excoriated the older Luther as a reactionary and celebrated Thomas Müntzer, a leader of the peasant revolt. In 1980, however, Party Chairman Erich Honecker hailed Luther as "one of the greatest sons of the German people" (qtd. in Büscher 244). In the later 1960s and 1970s, the GDR view of Luther had grown more differentiated, as reflected in Heym's novel by Ahasverus's own remarks concerning the progressive implications of Luther's thought.

Nonetheless, Heym clearly relishes the task of reminding the GDR, in the midst of the hyperbole surrounding the Luther year, of the religious leader's more embarrassing features. Mr. Würzner of the GDR's Thought Police warns Beifuss that professor Leuchtentrager (a citizen of Israel, with which the GDR had no diplomatic relations) is maneuvering Beifuss into positions "contrary to the positions of state and party":

This refers especially to the Luther discussion into which your "dear Colleague" would like to inveigh you. In view of the approaching Luther year of 1983 which, as you very well know, is being sponsored by the highest representatives of your state and party, such a discussion is by no means in our interest. If Herr Joachanaan Leuchtentrager is reminding you today of Luther's anti-Semitic speeches and writing, he will tomorrow quote to you what Luther, during the peasant war, said against the "thieving, murderous gang of peasants" that ought to be "smashed, choked, and stabbed to death just as you kill mad dogs," and he would thereby place into a most awkward position not only your own person but everybody else who is trying to make a resounding success of our planned Luther celebration. (228)

It is precisely Heym's intention to "place into a most awkward position" certain GDR dignitaries. Heym is an artist, and as Luther remarks in the text, "with painters and stone carvers and suchlike people you can never be sure if their hand was directed by one of the good angels or, rather, by Satan" (44).

Heym's critique of the GDR does not stop with his satire on the Luther year. The ultimate irony of the novel is that the "revolutionary" GDR remains unwilling to admit the existence of Ahasverus, champion of the underprivileged and spirit of revolution. Leuchtentrager, who quite literally plays *advocatus diaboli*, criticizes not merely the Catholic church when he asserts that "as any organization founded on dogma it forgives no one who places even a title of its doctrine in question" (58), or when he notes that Beifuss reminds him "of those Vatican astronomers who refused to admit the existence of the moons of Jupiter because these moons refused to fit into their Aristotelian *Weltbild*" (144). Beifuss, meanwhile, is admonished by his superiors that scholars cannot remain aloof, that they must take a decided stand in support of the Party line (95), even if that entails a *sacrifizio d'intelletto*:

> I would suggest your giving some thought to the preparation of a project through which . . . you might prove the close interaction of religion and imperialist expansionism, particularly in relation to Israel. I am stressing Israel because we observe similar tendencies in Islamic countries as well; these, however, we will disregard in view of the political aims pursued by our Soviet friends and ourselves. (94)

Truth defers to political expediency.

The Wandering Jew refers not only to the GDR Luther celebration but also to an international context—that of the European peace movement during the early 1980s, a movement that developed partly in response to the NATO decision to deploy U.S. Pershing II and Cruise missiles in Western Europe. Stephan Hermlin organized the "Berlin Conference for Peace" in East Berlin in 1981, inviting East and West German writers representing a range of opinion. The conference was repeated in West Berlin in 1983, at Günter Grass's instigation. During this period, an unofficial, independent peace movement developed in the GDR. Its motto was "Swords into Ploughshares," the biblical expression that is, not accidentally, cited in Heym's novel (198). The words are also engraved on the memorial the Soviet Union gave the United Nations, but that did not prevent GDR police from arresting some East German citizens who wore buttons displaying the motto.

Heym leaves little doubt, when his Jesus condemns the nuclear age, that he is siding with the unofficial GDR peace movement and criticizing the strategy of mutual destruction utilized by both sides (GDR propaganda attacked only the Western armament policy): "The entire hellish force was in the hands of just a few rulers, men of limited mind, who proclaimed at every opportunity that they needed their arsenals exclusively for the defense of peace, because peace required a balance of horror" (262). In *Cassandra* (1983) Christa Wolf assumes a similar position.

The West Germans greeted Heym's novel with respect, though some reviewers, such as Peter Pawlik in *Die Zeit* (16 Oct. 1981), appeared a bit confused as to what the novel was about. Writing in *Der Spiegel*, Jurek Becker accorded the novel the most unreserved accolades, terming it a "splendid [*großartiges*] book." Becker suggested that Heym is himself the Wandering Jew, a man who never found a comfortable home, and who has created difficulties in every society in which he has lived (2 Nov. 1981).

American reviewers generally ignored the Marxist aspects of the novel (Ahasverus as revolutionary) and applauded its language, imagery, and satire. In the *New York Times* Eva Hoffmann wrote that Heym achieved "moments of poetry and moral passion" (23 Feb. 1984). In the *New York Times Book Review* Ernst Pawel first attacked Heym's earlier political stances and then praised *The Wandering Jew* for its "highly effective satire." He asserted that the novel presents an "often brilliant, always imaginative journey through millenniums of bigotry and greed" (26 Feb. 1984). The *West Coast Review of Books* spoke of "a deliciously biting satire about dogmatic obscenity" and added that the "novel is quite splendidly a work of fantasy which contains remarkable verve and vitality as well as poetry and biting wit" (July 1984). In an encomium published by the *New York Review of Books*, D. J. Enright lauded "Heym's brilliant theological fantasy, simultaneously profound and comic, spiritual and fleshy" (26 April 1984).

The 1988 GDR publication of *The Wandering Jew* signaled an increasing willingness to "rehabilitate" Heym under the sign of *glasnost*. Ursula Reinhold reviewed the novel carefully but positively in the *Weimarer Beiträge*. She also commented on Heym's other writing, including *Five Days in June* but omitting *Collin*. Reinhold praises Heym for attempting to make "really existing socialism" approximate more exactly its ideal, and she writes that although *The Wandering Jew* presents no answers to the problems it raises it nonetheless constitutes a constructive contribution to the debate. Still, she finds the contemporary scenes (i.e., the criticism of the GDR) incommensurate with the legend and hence damaging to the aesthetic construct ("Stefan Heym").

No Place on Earth. Stefan Heym in Schwarzenberg

> It is with the greatest concern and apprehension that I make the confession that the future belongs to the Communists—and this is not merely a pretense! Indeed, only with horror and disgust can I think of an epoch in which these sinister iconoclasts will come to power; with their callused hands they will smash mercilessly the marble statues so dear to my heart; they will break all the whimsical toys and fragile works of art so beloved by the poet; they'll cut down my laurel groves and plant potatoes in their place.
>
> And yet, I'll also confess quite openly that this same Communism, so inimical to my interests and inclinations, exercises a fascination on my soul against which I cannot defend myself; a voice rises up inside of me in its favor, a voice which I cannot silence.
>
> It is the voice of Logic. I am caught in the web of a terrible syllogism, and if I cannot disprove the premise that all men have the right to eat, then I am forced to subject myself to all its consequences.
>
> —Heinrich Heine

Stefan Heym, who wrote his M.A. thesis on Heine, cites the passage above in *The Eyes of Reason* (420–21), published in the early 1950s, and in his autobiography, published in the late 1980s (*Nachruf* 602). Heym early adopted Heine's syllogism as his own, and it summarizes a lifelong commitment that has made him a productive, if nettlesome, citizen of four societies. It also explains his continuing attachment to the GDR, despite long periods of official opprobrium there.

Implicit in Heym's declaration is the belief that certain ends justify the means, and Heym has often argued that in revolutionary societies freedom must be curtailed to prepare a peoples' democracy. Although from *Uncertain Friend* to *Collin* he has grown increasingly sensitive to the dangers of dictatorship, in his 1989 autobiography he also shows himself defending censorship (providing it is intelligent) and the use of coercion (*Nachruf* 780, 771). Heym recounts the fashion in which he presented these ideas to Australian students who invariably responded with the question "Why are you afraid of freedom?" (*Nachruf* 771; my trans.).

Heym's latest novel, the as yet untranslated *Schwarzenberg* (FRG 1984, GDR 1990), tells the story of an incipient socialist experiment in a small area of Germany that, at the conclusion of World War II, the United States and the Soviet Union briefly leave unoccupied. One of the heroes attempts to write a constitution for the tiny republic. The constitution guarantees a socialist economy, but it also insists on civil liberties:

> Freedom was a wager, the greatest one imaginable, but the risk that it brought was less than the danger of decay that every dictatorship, even the most well-intentioned, brought with it, and the danger of corruption that resulted from the concentration of power in only a few hands. "Freedom of thought," he wrote . . . "the right to free expression in whatever form, are guaranteed in the Schwarzenberg Republic. No one may be persecuted on account of his or her convictions, be they political, religious, philosophical, or artistic. Mail may not be opened. There will be no censorship of the press." (148; my trans.)

Heym has been persecuted for much of his life, either on account of his parents' religion or his own political persuasion, and an ambivalent attitude toward democracy has informed his work. He maintains great faith—theoretically—in the people, yet in practice he has remained distrustful of their gullibility and malleability, especially when the people are German. After over two decades experience with a "well-intentioned" dictatorship in the GDR, however, Heym presents in *Schwarzenberg* his most unequivocal support for the "bourgeois" freedoms that he dismissed in *The Eyes of Reason* as shams.

Heym's growing emphasis on freedom of expression relates intimately to his second great theme—the role of the writer. His novels have always contained authors, though in the beginning they generally constituted peripheral figures. Later, especially in such works as *The Lenz Papers, The Queen against Defoe, The King David Report,* and *Collin,* writers function as protagonists, as oppositional figures and repositories of truth. Implicitly Heym thematizes his own struggles as a politically committed writer in the United States and the GDR, a process that becomes explicit in his autobiography, where author Heym functions unabashedly as hero.

Heym's relationship with the United States, like that with Germany, was and remains an ambivalent one. In his *Crusaders* one finds the gratitude of the immigrant, the fervor of the antifascist, and the suspicion of the socialist. With time, the suspicion gained central place. Even in his later work, however, one finds the *idea* of America: in *The Lenz Papers,* he speaks of the Civil War as a great revolution; in *Uncertain Friend* the goal for many German leftists is an American-style republic; and Heym models his utopian constitution for twentieth-century Schwarzenberg in part, as we have seen, on the eighteenth-century American Bill of Rights.

Heym did not originally match his growing suspicion of, and distance from, the United States with a comparable skepticism regarding the Soviet Union or other Stalinist governments, a problem he discusses in his autobiography (*Nachruf* 559–61). In his later writings—*Uncertain Friend, The King David Report,* and *Collin*—he sheds his illusions, and at the conclusion of *Schwarzenberg,* the Soviets arrive to block the German road to socialism.

The democratic socialism of *Schwarzenberg* epitomizes Heym's utopian hope for Germany and explains why the author stubbornly remained in his adopted country, despite public vilification in 1965 and again in 1979 (when he defied GDR copyright laws designed to prevent critical authors from publishing in the West) with subsequent periods as a nonperson. During the 1980s, under the influence of *glasnost* and at the public urging of Stephan Hermlin, East German authorities initiated a hesitant "rehabilitation" of Heym. *The Wandering Jew* could appear in 1988, and even before the collapse of the dictatorship, the GDR planned to publish *Five Days in June* and *Schwarzenberg.*

Heym has written of the writer as hero and played the role himself. His apotheosis came on 4 November 1989, when, at an imposing and crucial oppositional rally, he was introduced as the doyen of the movement. Heym's writing had helped initiate and focus the opposition, but ultimately the people wanted something different than he. In the heady days of late November 1989, after the opening of the Wall, he joined Christa Wolf, Volker Braun, and others in calling for a separate, socialist German Democratic Republic, one worthy of the name. For a brief, shining moment, Stefan Heym lived in "Schwarzenberg," but as in his novel, the experiment could not last.

NOTES

1. See his discussion of his unpublished *No Turnpike Gates* in *Nachruf* 227–30, 237–38.
2. Zachau incorrectly lists the GDR publication date as 1977.
3. For an exception to the general praise, see Fritz Raddatz in the *Süddeutsche Zeitung* 27 Jan. 1974.
4. See, for example, *Der Sonntag* 28 April 1974 or Neubert, "Reports."
5. *Collin* exhibits clear parallels in this respect to Rolf Schneider's *November*, also published only in West Germany in 1979. For a discussion of *November*, see chapter 4.
6. See, for example, the *Frankfurter Rundschau* 10 March 1979 or Konrad Franke in the *Süddeutsche Zeitung* 28 April 1979.

7

Erasing Borders: The Literature of Convergence

"Based on my experience and my observation of readers' reactions, I'm no longer able to confirm this territorial division of literature as one of social orders, defined by different social backgrounds, states, and economic systems."
—Christa Wolf, Interview with Meyer-Gosau (1982)

In the turbulent fall of 1989, thousands of rebellious GDR citizens marched in the streets and demanded revolutionary change. Defiantly mocking a government that had long presumed to speak in their name, they proclaimed, "*We* are the people." Before long, however, the demonstrators unfurled West German flags and began chanting, "We are *one* people." When a desperate East German government opened the Wall, it unwillingly opened the way to German unity, to a single people.[1] The subsequent unification stunned many observers, but GDR literature had for some time suggested the convergence of the two Germanys.

In the GDR the decay of Marxism (at least in its Soviet form) as a viable ideology represented the dominant development of the 1980s. The dramatic events of the later 1980s demonstrated that SED programs had never taken hold of the masses, but for some time the artists and intellectuals, those who had clung most tenaciously to a vision of socialism, had also begun to question the inherited truths. Many younger artists no longer defined themselves by Marxist maxims. They did not seek to reform existing GDR socialism or even to

279

dissent from it. Rather they attempted to withdraw from their society into bohemian niches, where they wrote, painted, and performed for each other, scorning integration into the organized cultural activity of the state.[2] Others simply left. Even older, more established and committed writers, such as Christa Wolf, began to express doubts; as we have seen, in *Accident* (1987) Wolf asks whether utopias necessarily breed monsters (30).

As the utopian dream dimmed, GDR literature began to lose one of its distinctive, even defining, qualities. East German writers attempted to fill the ensuing void with other commitments, which in turn brought their literature closer to books written in the West. In 1963 Christa Wolf could entitle a novel *Divided Heaven*, but *Accident* demonstrated that the heavens were no longer divided, that radiation from nuclear reactors knows no borders. Wolf's *Cassandra* (1983) replaces Marxist ideas of class struggle with those of gender conflict, a process one also finds to a degree in Irmtraud Morgner's *Amanda: A Novel of Witches* (1983). Both novels condemn the arms race supported by East and West, and they implicitly side with the GDR independent peace movement, as does Stefan Heym's *The Wandering Jew* (FRG 1981; GDR 1988). Germans on both sides of the Wall knew that any superpower conflict would devastate Germany, and that brought their literatures together.

Cassandra, Amanda, The Wandering Jew, and *Accident* demonstrate a growing distrust of both superpowers, and Heym's *Schwarzenberg* (1984) depicts the collapse of a tiny German experiment in socialism wedged between the U.S. and Soviet spheres of influence. In the 1980s important GDR texts began to display signs of what Timothy Garton Ash, writing a review of *Schwarzenberg* for the *New York Review of Books* (31 Jan. 1985), termed "equivalency theories," theories long held by numerous West European leftists who perceived no moral difference between the United States and the Soviet Union.

I have discussed Wolf and Heym elsewhere; in this chapter I examine Monika Maron's *Flight of Ashes* (FRG 1981), which deals with environmental pollution; *The Distant Lover* (1982), Christoph Hein's novella of alienation; and Jurek Becker's *Bronstein's Children* (1986), a novel that describes the unabated effects of the German national-socialist past. Becker wrote his book while living in West Berlin with West German and East German passports. He set the story in East

Berlin, but it concerns all Germans. Is it East German literature or West German? In the 1980s a German literature emerges that is not limited in theme or quality—or geography of origin—to East or West. These three works from the 1980s, as well as those from Heym and Wolf, prefigure the most important German event of the 1990s— German unification.

Monika Maron, *Flight of Ashes* FRG 1981, GB 1986

Flight of Ashes describes the story of thirty-year-old Josepha Nadler, journalist and divorced custodial parent of a five-year-old son. Nadler visits the GDR industrial city of B., and she rejects the formulaic language of the newspapers in order to describe as accurately as possible the hazardous conditions in the local industry and the toxic environmental situation in the city onto which a nineteenth-century power plant daily spreads mountains of fly ash.

Nadler writes an uncompromising report for the *Illustrated Weekly*, where her friend and supervisor Luise supports her. The Party watchdog Strutzer blocks the article. Maron's novel recalls other GDR books about journalists and their difficulties—Hermann Kant's *The Masthead* (1972) or Erich Neutsch's *The Quest for Gatt* (1973)—though *Flight of Ashes* is more uncompromising and continues the tendency of critical authors during the 1970s to emphasize themes of writing and censorship.[3] As the Party subjects Nadler to increasing coercion, she escapes with pills and alcohol, with increasingly dark and violent dreams, with suicidal fantasies, or with surrealistic hallucinations of flying over Berlin. Her visions often occur at moments of intense societal pressure—while presenting Luise her manuscript (50–52), or during interviews with the Comrade in Charge (132) or with "King" Strutzer (158–59). Near the conclusion, Josepha's lover Christian suggests psychiatric help, but Josepha, who compares herself to an automobile being driven with the handbrake on (56), refuses. She fears she will end like her colleague Jauer, who, the novel implies, has been lobotomized (144, 172, 178).

Born in 1941, Monika Maron grew up as the stepdaughter of GDR Interior Minister Karl Maron. She worked in film and, like her protagonist Josepha Nadler, as a journalist. *Flight of Ashes* is her first novel—one begun, Maron noted, in the spirit of reform; only after the expatriation of Wolf Biermann did her efforts grow more radical. According to Maron, she also wished to tell the story of a woman's attempts at emancipation (Emmerich, 2d ed. 320). Her treatment of environmental issues, however, provided the novel with its most innovative aspect within GDR literary history.

The GDR raised itself to a leading industrial nation through a callous disregard for the environment, the devastation of which has become clear in the new openness following the demise of the SED. Many rivers in the former GDR are dead, the soil is contaminated, forests are dying, and air pollution levels rank among the world's highest. In exchange for hard currency, the GDR had also become a dumping site for West German nuclear waste. Yet in a 1986 interview with *Die Zeit*, Erich Honecker would not allow that his country suffered serious environmental problems. Thus he underscored the taboo surrounding the theme (Menge 244–45).

As usual, writers broke the silence. In the early 1960s, novels by Christa Wolf (*Divided Heaven*) and Erwin Strittmatter (*Ole Bienkopp*) had already called attention to pollution, though in Wolf's novel the narrator's pathos-laden evocation of Sputnik and the wonders of technological progress more than offset the concern expressed regarding urban industrial waste. A similar celebration of "progress" at the expense of nature can be found in Karl-Heinz Jakob's *Description of a Summer* (1961), Joachim Wohlgemuth's *Egon* (1962), and in the early poetry of Volker Braun (Reid 205). It was not until the mid-1970s that GDR writers began to examine consistently and relentlessly the environmental effects of the technological developments they had earlier welcomed.

In *Flight of Ashes* Nadler journeys to the industrial city of B. (for Bitterfeld) and is staggered by its reality, one carefully excluded from GDR newspapers:

> And these fumes could serve as road signs. Please go straight ahead to the ammonia, then turn left at the nitric acid. When you feel a stabbing pain in your throat and bronchial tubes, turn around and call the doctor, that was sulphur dioxide. . . . I'm staring my eyeballs out of my head: everywhere this filth. When you meet the dwarfs from the kindergarten you have to think how many of them must have bronchitis. You wonder about every tree that hasn't died. (8)

Similar descriptions recur throughout the text, as Nadler struggles to describe this city that, in the first sentence of her suppressed journalistic essay, she characterizes as the "filthiest town in Europe" (24).

Writing about B., Maron invites comparisons with the Bitterfeld Program from the late 1950s and early 1960s. Echoes, variations, and ironizations of that program occur when Nadler urges an employee to write a complaint about working conditions to the Party secretary, or when she, the intellectual, contemplates life as an industrial worker:

> I've been travelling through steelworks, textile mills, chemical plants, engineering collective combines for six years without being able to get used to the violence of industrial labor, without losing the horror that gets hold of me when I see the maiming that labor still does to people. Flayed wind pipes, crushed legs, deaf ears, growths jutting out of bones. Not to mention the invisible deformation through constant unvarying signals to the brain. . . . Eight hours a day. I can't, Luise, I can't do that. It would be slow, very slow suicide for me. (59)

One goal of the Bitterfeld Program was to narrow, if not overcome the gap in experience and understanding between white- and blue-collar workers. In Maron's novel Josepha recognizes her own "socially-veiled class arrogance" and the "class barrier" that continued to exist in her society (106).

The failure of the Bitterfeld Program epitomizes the failure of the GDR to make manual labor in any way more attractive, and Josepha begins to question the ideology underpinning SED socialism. Discussing the power plant, she writes:

> Built 1890 or '95, what difference do five years make anyway? It was new then, now it's worn out; twenty years ago a fireman stoked two furnaces, now he stokes four and in the meantime most firemen are women. In return they're now in a socialist collective. (11)

This passage implies what the novel will depict: socialism has worsened some dilemmas inherited from capitalism.

Although *Flight of Ashes* demonstrates that GDR environmental problems were exacerbated by outdated technologies, cynicism, and a lack of public scrutiny (which resulted from a closed society), it also shows that many forms and causes of East German industrial pollution were indistinguishable from those in the West. Josepha demands: "Why shouldn't the housewives, who are so obsessed with their wash that they do a whole load for as little as two shirts, know who pays for their laudable sense of cleanliness? Why shouldn't the active home gardeners think about whose health is ruined by their well-fertilized rose beds?" (12). She returns to her complaints later in the story: "Insecticides, fabric softeners, fertilizers. Couldn't they at least do without the fabric softeners?" (102). In a direct reference to Christa Wolf's *Divided Heaven*, Josepha muses: "The indivisible sky, no, it was divisible, sovereign territory, the word existed but the clouds flew against air traffic regulations obeying only the wind" (154). Clouds transcend ideological divisions. Within the novel, the clouds serve as metaphors for the poetic imagination, but they can also represent polluted air, acid rain, or as in Wolf's *Accident*, nuclear fallout.

Other themes in the novel demonstrate convergence with the West. Alone, Josepha struggles to raise her five-year-old son. She attempts to sort out her own ambivalent feelings about "equal rights" within a man's society (122–24), and she deals as best she can with the uneasy relationship between her desired self-image and her emotions: "But emancipated women don't shiver, much less scream, and they cross the word 'longing' from their vocabulary. I shiver, I scream, I feel longing" (13). Josepha's sense of emptiness and alienation, a condition Christoph Hein will analyze in *The Distant Lover*, also overlaps with such preoccupations in Western literature: "The uneasy feeling remains that somewhere, something is going on—there's life, that life is passing me by" (19).

Finally, Maron's novel converges with Western literature in its use of surrealistic techniques. In company with several other GDR authors from the late 1970s and early 1980s, Maron employs fantasy and dream sequences to break free from the stifling quotidian. As *Flight of Ashes* progresses, the narrative perspective changes abruptly, and realistic writing increasingly defers to the surrealistic. Maron continues to develop these techniques in her second novel, *The Defec-*

tor (FRG 1986), whose dust jacket features a picture by the Belgian surrealist René Magritte.[4] Maron's employment of such narrative devices represents another attempt by GDR authors to liberate themselves from the provincialism of the socialist-realist legacy.

Finished in 1978, Maron's novel could not appear in the GDR. At the 1981 Leipzig Book Fair, Vice Minister for Culture Klaus Höpcke noted that Maron had refused to make "aesthetic" corrections. Reception of the novel in West Germany accordingly underscored its documentary qualities, its societal criticism, and its suppression by the GDR government. Nonetheless, West German reviewers also glimpsed those aspects of the novel that signaled convergence. A headline in the *Deutsches Allgemeines Sonntagsblatt* characterized the novel as a "German-German Story: Sand in the Machinery of Two Cultures." In the review, Tilman Jens compares Bitterfeld as a symbol of industrial progress with the West German Hoechst Dye Works, and he also associates Maron's B. with West German Brokdorf, where protesters attempted to hinder the opening of a nuclear power plant. Jens concludes that one "must grasp [the novel] in its private and political radicalism to realize how much about us there is to read in this book from East Berlin" (22 March 1981; my trans.). Jörg Bernhard Bilke of *Die Welt* called *Flight of Ashes* the first "Ecology-Novel from East Berlin (24 March 1981; my trans.), and later in *Die Welt der Bücher* he asserted that there was no doubt that "the ecology debate, which here has already assumed terrorist forms, is now showing hesitant stirrings in the GDR" (No. 6, Christmas 1981; my trans.). *Die Tageszeitung* reviewed Maron's novel together with new works by Margaret Atwood, Saul Bellow, Jurek Becker, Nicolas Born, Doris Lessing, and others, arguing that all these writers criticize the fashion in which the media uphold the status quo (21 May 1984). A review by Norbert Schachtsiek-Freitag in *Deutschland Archiv* concludes with the reminder that despite the political scandal ignited by the novel, its description of the difficulties in a male-female relationship makes the reader forget East-West differences (1339).

In the United States the *Voice Literary Supplement* praised Maron's style and noted the environmental issues: "short-term economic gain always wins out over longer-term planning. Meanwhile, the citizens of B. suffer quietly, resigned to washing their windows every day and looking out at leafless trees" (May 1987). *Publishers Weekly* saw the book's value for U.S. readers in its feminist statement and in its treatment of environmental themes: "In light of recent events at Chernobyl, this is an especially timely novel" (5 Sept. 1986).

At least since the mid-1970s, GDR writers of science fiction had warned of ecological or nuclear disasters. The taboo however lay in a specific description of East German problems (Reid 218). Although Maron's novel was suppressed, GDR writers continued to press similar issues. In 1982 Hans Cibulka published his diarylike novel *Swantow*, which contains environmental protest. J. H. Reid notes that Cibulka, like Maron, attacks "our search for ever more material comforts in the cause of so-called progress. Here, too, the socialist countries are merely imitating the capitalist ones" (206). An extract from *Swantow* appeared in the GDR journal *Neue Deutsche Literatur* in 1981, but when the book was published a year later, two passages from the previous text had been censored. Even so, Klaus Höpcke complained publicly that the book had not been sufficiently "edited" (qtd. in Bohm 75–76). In 1979 Höpcke had also attacked the GDR writer Günter Kunert for his equation of capitalist and socialist industrialization (Reid 207).

Gabriele Eckart was able to publish excerpts from her book of candid interviews with farmers, and an East German publisher planned to print it, but the book finally appeared only in the West as *That's How I See It* (1984). In 1985 Lia Pirskawetz *could* publish her novel *The Still Earth* in the GDR. Discussing the economic and hence human hardships involved in choosing the environment over standard notions of progress, the book received generally favorable reviews. In 1987 Christa Wolf's *Accident* attempted to locate the causes for the environmental disaster of Chernobyl in patriarchal structures common to both East and West blocs.

At the Tenth GDR Writers' Congress, also in 1987, Jurij Koch passionately attacked the practice of rapacious strip-mining in his region. A few months later at the Leipzig Book Fair, Klaus Höpcke asserted that there should no longer be taboos against the discussion of environmental issues. Such victories grew increasingly common in the 1980s. Writers and artists would tacitly or explicitly join forces with unofficial, grass-roots peace or environmental movements to expand the limits of expression and to move the literature of their country into congruence with that of West Germany.

Christoph Hein, *The Distant Lover* GDR 1982, FRG 1983, USA 1989

As the son of a Protestant minister, Christoph Hein (born in 1944) could not attend a college preparatory school in the GDR. Starting in 1958 he went to school in West Berlin. After his graduation he worked in the GDR at a variety of odd jobs—assembly line worker, bookseller, waiter, journalist, actor, and assistant theater director. Between 1967 and 1971 he studied philosophy and logic in Leipzig and East Berlin. After his studies he worked for the East Berlin *Volksbühne* as a dramaturge and later as a resident author, becoming a free-lance writer in 1979.

In the following decade Hein built a reputation as a leading GDR writer of drama and prose. In 1980 he published his first collection of stories, followed in 1981 by a volume of plays. But it was his novella *The Distant Lover* (1982) that proved a literary sensation, one that established his renown in both Germanys.

Hein's protagonist Claudia is a forty-year-old doctor who lives alone in an East Berlin high-rise apartment building. Divorced, she has no children but has undergone two abortions. She maintains little contact with the other residents of her building and remains unsure whether she has any friends at all. She considers her parents "people I have no real ties with." Before visiting them she regrets that the "accidental bond continues to be asserted, some unidentified obligation, requiring senseless activity like these superfluous visits" (33).

Narrated by Claudia, the novella reconstructs her relationship with her lover Henry, now deceased. With Henry, as with everyone, Claudia had resisted intimacy: "The distance between us gave our relationship a cool familiarity that I found pleasant. I had no desire to reveal myself completely to another person again" (32). Her almost fetishistic need to shower, or to wash her hands and feet, symbolizes her attempts to keep distance, as does her phobia of being touched.

Claudia's efforts to avoid emotional involvements cannot entirely succeed, and the novella documents the moments when her defense mechanisms lapse. Henry's casual revelation that he is married shatters her, as does his sudden death. Claudia's reaction to these and other crises (when she discovers, for example, that her ex-husband is involved with her sister) disclose much to us, but they reveal less to Claudia, who possesses little desire for self-knowledge: "Repression is self-defense, defense against danger. . . . A healthy natural mechanism" (98). At the conclusion of the story, six months after Henry's death, Claudia asserts that she, like Siegfried, had bathed in dragon's blood, but that unlike Siegfried, no leaf had left her vulnerable. Her narrative concludes with a litany of repression: "I can't think of anything I lack. I've made it. I'm fine" (179).

Hein's novella is doubly coded, functioning both as political and as cultural critique. As the former, it is clearly a story from and about the GDR. Claudia mentions, for example, a poetry reading in a church, one of the few partially tolerated public spheres in the former GDR. She alludes to people who flee the country (82) and implies that her former husband has joined the Party to further his career (156).

More importantly, GDR history has crippled Claudia's personality. After the workers' uprising on 17 June 1953, Claudia, still a child, finds herself frustrated in her attempts to understand the event. The revolt becomes a taboo, one to be breached neither at school nor at home: "I sensed that even a conversation could be dangerous. . . . I learned to keep quiet" (123). Only with her best friend Katharina can she speak of the uprising. Claudia and Katharina maintain their friendship despite pressure from Claudia's family and from GDR society as a whole—during the 1950s the government organized antireligious campaigns designed to break the power of the churches, and Katharina's family (like Hein's) was devout. Nonetheless, Claudia ultimately denounces Katharina, who later leaves with her family for the West.

Stalinism has deformed Claudia's life, but the story explicitly refers to the German fascist past as well. Claudia is not the only denunciant in her family, for in the 1950s GDR authorities arrest a favorite uncle of hers for having provided the Nazis with information on leftists.[5] Through her uncle, Claudia feels herself implicated in fascist crimes. But her attempts to articulate that only embarrass or anger her friends, parents, and teachers:

> In the twelfth grade one of my classmates told me she considered my behavior affected. She said I shouldn't be so self-important; it made me seem ridiculous and high-flown. I contradicted her violently. But from then on, I kept quiet about it. At home no one mentioned Uncle Gerhard, not even me. If the topic of

fascism came up, I said little or nothing. I realized that I was a problem, insoluble, impossible to get rid of, inexplicable. And I began to keep quiet so as not to annoy others. (131)

Claudia's silence and her self-alienation have their roots not only in a history peculiar to the GDR, but in a German history common to both postwar German states.

Hein's novel presents more than a political critique of the GDR. As David Roberts writes:

> Claudia is the product of social emancipation, the (privileged) recipient of a scientific training in medicine. Theoretically, she is . . . in control of her own life, the autonomous personality of the Enlightenment. Practically, her social emancipation has been bought at the price of total emotional impoverishment. As a member of the singles' society, she is the product of a process of modernization that has distanced her from her family and from the little town of her childhood. The isolation, privatization, and anonymity of her existence in a Berlin block of flats is typical of contemporary industrial society and applies to both its state socialist and Western capitalist forms. The "costs of civilization" (Hein) are shared by both systems. ("Surface" 482)

In this second function, as cultural critique, Hein's novella most strongly represents the literature of convergence.

The characters in *The Distant Lover* suffer in quiet despair, and they long to shatter the ennui of their routines. Henry only feels alive when driving recklessly. Like Maron's Josepha, restless teenagers impatiently wait for "life" (107), as does Claudia on her fortieth birthday (166). Claudia's acquaintance Fred directs verbal aggression at his wife and others: "And his horrible whims and the tears or outbursts he provoked, all the little humiliations, were merely devices to keep his boredom at bay" (69). Everyone in this novella struggles with solitude: Claudia's supervisor; the elderly in the anonymity of high-rise buildings; or a caricatured West German who is, we are twice told, very alone (76). Hein's diagnosis extends beyond East German society.

David Roberts correctly notes that Christopher Lasch's *The Minimal Self: Psychic Survival in Troubled Times*, written about American society, describes salient features of Hein's society as well. Lasch's study defines the "survival mentality" as "characterized by emotional anesthesia, the refusal of long-term emotional commitments, a sense of impotence, and a defensive contraction of the self," all distinguishing features of Claudia's personality (qtd. in Roberts, "Surface" 483–84). Hein's protagonist embodies a rationalized, secular society. One result of the antireligious campaigns of the 1950s is demonstrated in the 1970s, when Claudia and Henry visit a church service sparsely attended by elderly people. "We didn't belong there, so we left," Claudia remarks (161). Following Max Weber, David Roberts asserts that Hein portrays a thorough "disenchantment of the world," one in which funerals, weddings, or a holiday such as Christmas have become empty rituals ("Surface" 486).

The language used to describe those rituals has also become hollowed out, meaningless. At Henry's funeral Claudia encounters "prescribed songs, prescribed gestures" (15); her wedding ceremony had consisted of "prepackaged sentences poured out of little foil pouches" (85). Claudia recognizes the entropy of language, especially in the newspaper announcements she reads: "the conventional flourishes of the ads, life support for the inarticulate misery of the linguistically impaired" (26). Her own communication nonetheless takes on this quality. Though the empty forms lame her, she has nothing to substitute:

> I sent Henry two postcards, meaningless comments about commonplace feelings. Stupid remarks which made even me uncomfortable. I didn't feel capable of really telling him anything. The postcards themselves paralyze me. The carefully allotted space for a personal message compressed into illiterate three-word sentences. Then the retouched photographs imposing themselves on both sender and message. Sometimes even a prefabricated greeting, a bold expression of cordiality. Of course I could have written him letters, but I had nothing to say. (65)

Similarly, she attempts to write her father but finds herself imprisoned in the same banalities, the same inability to communicate:

> I wanted to make it a long letter, but after half a page of fancy phrases I couldn't think of anything else to say. So I apologized

for that. On the way to the post office, I tore it up. It seemed so phony. I would have liked to write him an affectionate letter, but once the empty page was in front of me I didn't know what to say. (96–97)

We can trace Claudia's speechlessness to her experiences with Stalinism and fascism, but it also results from the disenchantment of the world, where everything, including language, has lost its magic.

Without language, Claudia cannot begin to know herself. She tells her mother she lives alone so she can better reflect on her life (38), but in fact she rarely does, practicing instead a rigorous repression of thought and feeling. When on rare occasion she does attempt to analyze those experiences that move her, she fails. After Henry's funeral Claudia makes an effort to commemorate him silently:

Later I drank some brandy in a café near my apartment, trying to remember Henry. An act of piety I thought I owed him. . . . I wanted to think of Henry, of Henry who was dead, of the funeral, of the soft, sexy voice of the minister. Then I gave up. (18)

After a troubling visit with her parents, she tries briefly to make sense of it: "In bed I thought about my parents, but with no real clarity. Just a vague kind of remembering. Soon I went to sleep" (40). Claudia cannot analyze her experience with any lucidity, in part because she does not possess the language to do so.

In the GDR any hint that the two Germanys shared increasingly similar problems was ideologically suspect, and there is a certain skittishness in East German reviews of Hein's novella. Six pieces in the "Pro and Contra" section of the *Weimarer Beiträge* praised the literary qualities of *The Distant Lover* but parted ways about its ideological message. Those who supported Hein, Gabriele Linder for example ("Für und Wider"), utilized a strategy already employed successfully in defense of another GDR antihero, Plenzdorf's Edgar Wibeau. The reviewers acknowledged that such problems existed and suggested that the author, in urging his society to consider how it might better integrate its Claudias (or Edgars), had in fact made a positive contribution. Indeed, the reviewers added, precisely a socialist society should be capable of helping such people.

Other reviewers were less supportive. Rüdiger Bernhardt noted that not only Claudia but all the novella's characters evince stunted personalities, an approach he dismisses decisively as ahistorical ("Für und Wider"). Ursula Wilke rejected the novella as untruthful. She regretted that Hein failed to show the developmental possibilities available to individuals in socialism, or the role of the GDR in the "world-wide conflict between humanity and organized inhumanity" ("Für und Wider" 1655; my trans.). To do that, she concluded, Hein would have needed a more mature weltanschauung.

GDR reviewers noted elements of Camus and Kerouac in the story, but writing for *Sinn und Form,* Ursula Heukenkamp provided the most explicit discussion of the similarities between Hein's book and Western literature. Hein's writing reminded her of the West German Martin Walser or the Austrian Peter Handke; in form and content, Hein imitated "a process of decline which is that of the bourgeois individual" (632; my trans.). She criticized his lack of distance, his lack of irony with regard to his material, for he implied that such problems were not limited to the bourgeoisie. Playing on the title *Der fremde Freund—The Foreign* (Strange, Distant) *Friend* (Lover)—Heukenkamp asserted that Hein had been trapped by the "foreign form."

Western reception confirmed the novella's importance for a literature of convergence. Jörg Bernhard Bilke asserted in the *Rheinischer Merkur/Christ und Welt* that the circumstances of Claudia's life were hardly GDR-specific, and he added that if Hein did not describe several trips to the provinces one would not know at first in which part of Germany his story occurred (14 Oct. 1983). Similar statements can be found in reviews by Uwe Wittstock in the *Frankfurter Allgemeine Zeitung* (17 Sept. 1983), Rolf Michaelis in *Die Zeit* (11 Nov. 1983), Karl Corino in the *Stuttgarter Zeitung* (10 Dec. 1983), Gabriele Kreis in the *Deutsches Allgemeines Sonntagsblatt* (18 Dec. 1983), and Heinz Mudrich in the *Saarbrücker Zeitung* (8 March 1984).

In the United States a review in the *Washington Post* praised the "universality" of Hein's insights (25 June 1989), while *Publishers Weekly* spoke of the "paralyzing ennui of modern existence" and the "meaninglessness of much of the busyness that we call civilization, East or West" (17 Feb. 1989). In the *New York Times Book Review* Katharina Washburn asserted that Claudia's "well-being, like that of certain of her Western counterparts, depends on a self-congratulatory emotional and physical 'fitness,' together with acquiring . . . as many material gratifications as possible." Washburn concludes that Hein "will afford some readers a small sharp stab of familiarity and connection, like that felt by a transatlantic traveler picking up the newspaper and finding in the international weather reports that all the instruments agree: in both East Berlin and New York the temperatures were identical and the barometric reading constant on a given day" (7 May 1989).

Hein followed *The Distant Lover* with several plays, numerous essays, and two novels: *Horn's End* (1985) and *The Tango Player* (1989). Published simultaneously in the Federal Republic and the GDR but ignored for several years in the latter country, *Horn's End* advances a scathing indictment of GDR Stalinism during the 1950s. *The Tango Player* was one of the first literary works that could both criticize East German participation in the suppression of the Prague Spring and be published in the GDR (a film version appeared in 1990 and an English translation in 1991). Hein set *The Knights of the Round Table* (1989), his final play published in what was still the GDR, in King Arthur's court. The piece parodies a geriatric and doddering politburo.

The Distant Lover hovers between cultural and political critique, but Hein's subsequent writing from the 1980s moved clearly in a political direction. Not only as a literary author but as a journalist and as a public figure (the dividing lines were in any case fluid in the GDR), Hein launched increasingly open criticism at his government. He attacked censorship at the Tenth GDR Writers' Congress in 1987 and wrote stinging critiques of GDR political practices for West German papers and for the *New York Times Magazine* (17 Dec. 1989). He delivered speeches and made television appearances during the eventful days of the nonviolent uprising in late 1989. After the fall of the Honecker regime, he served on an independent commission investigating the police brutality that had been directed at protesters. Hein's work was necessary and important. But after the collapse of the GDR and the eradication of the political abuses against which Hein struggled in the 1980s, the problems implied by Claudia and her "survival mentality" will remain in a united Germany, and not merely in that country.

Jurek Becker, *Bronstein's Children* FRG 1986, GDR 1987, USA 1988

With his first novel, *Jakob the Liar* (1969), Jurek Becker made a lasting contribution to the project of remembering the past. In his sixth novel, *Bronstein's Children*, he continues his preoccupation with the traumas resulting from Nazi extermination policies by demonstrating, as had Christa Wolf and others in the 1970s, that the past is neither dead nor past. Although set in East Berlin, the novel was written by Becker while living in West Berlin. His double perspective helped him craft a story with relevance for both Germanys.

Bronstein's Children refers overtly to Becker's earlier novel *The Boxer* (1976), which deals with the difficulties of a Jewish survivor in postwar Germany. Freed from a concentration camp, *The Boxer's* protagonist Arno Blank (he changes his name from Aron to make it sound less Jewish) attempts to begin a new life in the Soviet Zone of Occupation. With the assistance of a U.S. Jewish organization, he locates Mark, a boy who may or may not be his son. Unlike the protagonists in the East German "Literature of Arrival," protagonists who overcome initial difficulties to become productive citizens in socialism, Arno Blank cannot adjust to postcamp existence. Like Primo Levi, he believes that you can take a Jew out of the camps, but that you cannot take the camp out of the Jew. His relationship with his son is characterized by misunderstandings, and Mark, who has not received a religious education, surprises his father by emigrating to Israel. His letters to his father abruptly cease during the 1967 war.

Bronstein's Children takes place in the GDR in the early 1970s, at about the time *The Boxer* concluded. It is narrated by Hans Bronstein, the teenage son of a Jewish survivor named Arno. Hans's mother is dead, and his older sister Elle, who survived the war in hiding, lives in an asylum. While attempting to use the family summer cottage for a tryst with his girlfriend Martha, Hans discovers that his father and two other survivors have kidnapped Heppner, a former concentration camp guard. They have handcuffed the man to a bed in the cottage, where they interrogate him, not gently. Ultimately, Arno dies of a heart attack in the cottage, and Hans frees Heppner. Hans then narrates the story, in which he attempts to discover a meaning.

The identical names of the fathers in *The Boxer* and *Bronstein's Children* indicate the most obvious of numerous similarities between the two novels. Both fathers are concentration camp survivors. Both work after the war in the black market. Both are widowers, and both raise sons with whom they cannot or will not communicate. Like Mark Blank, Hans Bronstein has no religious instruction, but, like Mark, he feels himself to be Jewish, though against his will. Both fathers encounter difficulties relating their experiences to outsiders. Arno Blank communicates most comfortably with Kenik and Ostwald, other victims; and in a key passage, Arno Bronstein converses with two survivors in Yiddish, a language Hans did not know his father could speak. Both novels are told by people who can only guess at the thoughts, feelings, and motivations of the two fathers. Containing numerous gaps, both narratives are "open."

Arno, Hans, and Elle suffer from the unresolved history they carry within themselves. Elle is the victim of a mysterious disease that causes her to assault strangers. Doctors surmise that her aggression stems from her war experiences—a German family hid her, for money, from the fascists. Arno believes Elle attacks people she considers Nazis (109–10), and his explanation appears plausible, especially since she never directs her aggression against children, that is, those born after the war.

Although Hans thinks his father "normal" (27) and "wonderfully intact" (219), he admits that Arno, like Elle, distrusts older Germans: "I must add that, in dealing with people over fifty, Father tended to be unjust and rude" (47). Arno's accomplice, Gordon Kwart, insists that East German Jews continue to reside in "hostile territory" (161), and Hans remembers one conversation with his father, during which the younger Bronstein realizes he had been living with a stranger:

> [Father], Kwart, and Rotstein agreed that they were living in an inferior country, surrounded by second-rate people who didn't deserve any better. He could imagine, he said, how such a view would surprise me, yet why should he have discussed it with me before? Unfortunately, I had to learn to deal with these creatures; there would have been no point in representing my surroundings to me as unbearable. It was true that the concentration-camp guard would be severely punished if they handed him over to a court of law. But on what basis? Solely because one occupation power rather than the other happened to have conquered the country. If the border had been drawn

slightly differently, the same people on either side would have
opposite convictions. Anyone strong enough could impose his
convictions on this German rabble. (66)

This is German history viewed by the victims. For Arno Bronstein,
the governments of the Federal Republic and the Democratic Republic are accidents, formalities, facades: there are no good Germans.

Hans has not thought about Jewish issues (66), and he generally
engages in a massive act of repression, a project Martha exposes
(219). Hans admits only once, tentatively, that the past may have
damaged his present: "Perhaps I *am* a victim of Fascism after all and
refuse to admit it" (194). He will not utilize the official designation
"victim of Fascism" to secure himself a scarce apartment (176), but
he does include himself in that category to facilitate his acceptance
at the university (5).

That ambivalence governs many of Hans's thoughts and actions.
After hitting a boy who bullies him in a shower, he imagines a teacher
telling the boy: "Hans is a Jew. There may well be sensitive areas
there of which people like us have no idea" (37). Hans also wonders
whether his philo-Semitic teacher cheats on his behalf during a swim-
ming competition. Significantly, the novel leaves it open whether
these two incidents occurred or whether Hans simply imagines them.
Similarly, when he meets a man involved in making a film about the
Nazi persecution of the Jews, Hans thinks that "his eyes, which first
glanced at me fleetingly but then turned back to me, *seemed* to regret
that a face like mine wasn't appearing in the movie" (171; my emphasis).

Hans's ambivalence reflects Becker's own experience with Judaism, an experience he discusses in an essay published in 1978. In the
essay, Becker remembers his father's remark, "If anti-Semitism did
not exist—do you think I would have felt like a Jew for a single
second?" ("My Way" 418).[6] Similarly, in *Bronstein's Children* Hans
recalls his father's theory: "There were no Jews at all. Jews were an
invention" (37). In his autobiographical essay Becker argues that the
decision whether or not to be Jewish should be an intellectual choice
("My Way" 419–20). He admits, however, that choice constitutes
only a part, and perhaps the less powerful one, of a larger construct:
"I know that we are not merely the person we imagine ourselves to
be; for better or worse, we must also be the person others believe us

to be. That is the sad part. Seen in this way, I am cursed many times over, because I am the person that many people have obligingly decided I should be: a Jew" ("My Way" 420).

The dilemma in Becker's essay, one which finds literary expression in *The Boxer* and in *Bronstein's Children*, resembles the examination by Jean-Paul Sartre in *Anti-Semite and Jew*. For Sartre, the "Jew is one whom other men consider a Jew" (69). He writes that if Jews "have a common band, if all of them deserve the name of Jew, it is because they live in a community which takes them for Jews" (67). Jews are a successful invention. In Sartre's terms, "authentic" Jews understand, accept, and live to the full their condition as Jews; "inauthentic" Jews attempt to deny or escape their Jewishness. Max Frisch dramatized Sartre's thesis in his play *Andorra* (1961), and later Jean Améry, a Belgian author of Austrian birth, grappled with these issues in his essay "On the Necessity and Impossibility of Being Jewish."

Whether or not Hans Bronstein wishes to be a Jew, his environment regards him as one. Arno, Kwart, and Rotstein urge Hans to take sides; the Jews in the story constantly speak of "us" or of "our people." Martha's father attributes the fact that Hans has no friends to his Jewishness (98). After hitting his schoolmate, Hans is excused (or imagines he is) because of his Jewishness, and he remembers his father's theory that Jews were an invention (37). Similarly, when he visits Martha on a film set, he sees actors portraying SS men sitting in one group, while those playing Jews sit in another: "The fact that they were all actors apparently united them less than their *roles* divided them" (174; my emphasis). Bronstein family members must also play roles.

But the actors playing Jews on the film set are Jews, thus obscuring the line, as Sander Gilman notes, between societal determinism and "innate" characteristics (285). Becker suggests the latter with metaphors of genetic transmission. After Hans has discovered that his father is keeping the guard captive, he hits a boy who has a "camp-guard look" (33). He then wonders if that act constitutes a symptom of the same illness affecting his sister (34). Similarly, Hans notes of his father, "I only hope I have not inherited his compulsion to complicate every discussion and burden it with an extreme touchiness" (108). Numerous examples demonstrate Hans's hope to be illusory, the most telling one a conversation between Gordon Kwart and Hans, of which the latter recalls, "Then he says that my father had such an infinite number of good qualities that I should not pick out his only strange one, his prickliness, as an example to follow" (176). As Arno continues his self-destructive activities, Hans wonders whether his father suffers from mental illness, and whether that constituted a "family defect" that also affected him (236–37). Not surprisingly, he writes his final examination for high school biology on "The Cell as Transmitter of Hereditary Factors" (77). In this modern family tragedy, genes have assumed the role of fate.

In a letter to the East German translator of his works, Primo Levi speaks of a German sin that cannot be expiated with human justice, a sin that fills the lives of Jewish survivors with a venomous hatred, hatred that can express itself as a thirst for revenge, as moral collapse, and as exhaustion and resignation (Wander, "Brief" 22). In *The Boxer* Arno Blank demonstrates the qualities of exhaustion and resignation. In *Bronstein's Children* Arno Bronstein expresses the urge for revenge. When Hans suggests the inevitability of the novel's tragedy (326), he underscores an antagonistic contradiction, one inherited from history, one which must be played out inexorably to a grim conclusion. For Arno, there can be no reconciliation.

Of a different generation, Hans confronts a different problematic. Betwixt and between, he is at once insider and outsider, victim and bewildered observer. Becker illustrates Hans's interstitial position at the conclusion, as Hans packs his belongings and prepares to move to a new room. Hans cannot decide whether to destroy the guard's wallet confiscated by his father. It appears he would do so if the action could obliterate memory: "If I had destroyed Heppner's wallet, would he then have vanished even more completely?" (88) Hans also cannot decide whether the wallet belongs in a container reserved for his father's things, one reserved for his own, or one marked "miscellaneous." It seems to fit everywhere and nowhere; Heppner belongs to Hans *and* to his father. Hans is gratified that a Wall stands between him and Heppner, who now lives in the West—he feels fully "separated" from him (88). But like the guard's wallet, the problem will not disappear, and one wonders whether Hans has learned very much about history, or even about his story.

Originally entitling his novel *How I became a German*, Becker ultimately called it *Bronstein's Children*, thus emphasizing generations. The novel continues a revisionist project pursued by GDR writers at least since the 1970s, that concerned with exposing the East German myth of an abrupt, revolutionary rupture with the negative traditions of German history. Becker asserts that a mortgage remains, at least with the victims. Hans generally considers himself to be neither Jewish nor a victim of fascism, but the text demonstrates that in crucial regards he is both.

The narrative makes several gestures toward topoi that were standard in GDR literature. Hans repeatedly compares West Germany unfavorably with his country, and at the conclusion the former camp guard flees West. The film being made in the story recalls the traditional GDR emphasis on communist antifascist resistance. While reading the script Hans muses:

> The story was about a Resistance group, of which one member was a Jewish girl—Rahel. All the members lived with false documents and were in the same danger. Consequently it made no difference to Rahel that she was Jewish—at least that's how I took it. (92)

Becker ironizes here the GDR equation of Jews and communists as equivalent victims of fascism. Implicit is also a rejection of the illusion common to many Jews on the left that their communism "offset" their Jewishness. As Hans Mayer wrote: "Trotsky always dismissed his Judaism—and not without elements of self-hatred—as an accident of birth. His life history disproved this thesis" (257; my trans.). Mayer then speaks of Stalin's anti-Semitic purges and trials. Trotsky's original surname was Bronstein (that name is mentioned in Becker's title but not in the text). By raising the specificity of the "Jewish question," Becker interrogates official and literary versions of "a time together" (to speak with Stephan Hermlin), either during World War II or in the GDR.

We can read *Bronstein's Children* as an East German novel, for it was written by an East German citizen, and it makes reference to an East German literary and historical context. At the same time, Becker was living in West Berlin with a West German passport. While Becker was writing *Bronstein's Children*, West Germans heatedly debated the attempts of well-known theater and film director Rainer Werner Fassbinder to perform his play *Trash, the City, and Death*. The play deals with real estate speculation in Frankfurt/Main and features as villain an unnamed character called the "Rich Jew." Much heated debate ensued, and an attempt to perform the play in Frankfurt during October 1985 was stopped by West German Jews who occupied the stage.

During 1985–86 West German intellectuals furthermore debated, in leading journals and newspapers, the assertion by some West German historians that the history of World War II has been written by the victors and is in need of revision. The respected historian Ernst Nolte suggested that Hitler may have had legal justification for interning (not murdering) Jews. He also argued that the Nazi policy of genocide represented little that was new or unique in a century that has produced mass murders of Armenians, Soviets, or Cambodians.

Bronstein's Children was thus of moment in both East and West Germany. Becker provided his novel with a more universal dimension as well, for he entered into dialogue with Sartre, Frisch, and Améry, exploring what it means to be Jewish. The novel is, finally, pan-German, if only due to Arno Bronstein's implacable hatred of all Germans, East and West. Bronstein is fictional, but his attitude is not. In 1988, when Polish-American Holocaust survivor Isaac Nauman assumed the duties of rabbi in East Berlin, he demanded of reporters, "Can you really see any difference between a German on this side [of the Wall] and on the other side?" (qtd. in Mertens 52).

As if to emphasize the all-German nature of *Bronstein's Children,* it appeared almost simultaneously in East and West Germany, where it generally received positive reviews. The *Süddeutsche Zeitung* (20–21 Sept. 1986), *Die Welt* (30 Sept. 1986), *Die Zeit* (10 Oct. 1986), the *Frankfurter Rundschau* (18 Oct. 1986), and the East German *Sonntag* (20 May 1988) cited Arno Bronstein's fierce condemnation of the "German rabble," a passage that the former GDR writer Bernd Jentzsch, writing in *Die Welt,* characterized as a "pan-German rebuke." In one of the few negative reviews of the novel, Jentzsch disapproved of the fact that "the state itself is disavowed; one is a Jew and not a Jewish citizen of the 'GDR'" (30 Sept. 1986; my trans.). Writing in the *Frankfurter Allgemeine Zeitung,* Uwe Wittstock saw the novel as a condemnation of the "misplaced, superficial, self-serving use of history equally evident in Germany East and West," and he speaks of the "historical entanglements with which one must live in *Germany*" (30 Sept. 1986; my trans.; my emphasis).

Becker's novel also possesses international appeal, and the translation was well received in the United States. The *New York Times Book Review* did not emphasize the East German context, asserting instead that the novel explores "various responses to being a Jewish survivor in Germany" (27 Nov. 1988). Similarly, the *Los Angeles Times* remarked that the novel takes place in "East Germany, but Becker's point goes wider" (11 Dec. 1988). *Publishers Weekly* wrote that the book offered "a disquieting parable on the relationship between victim and persecutor, the thirst for justice and on the abyss separating Germany's affluent postwar generation from the not-so-distant past" (16 Sept. 1988).

Literature of Convergence; Or, What Remains of GDR Literature?

In its forty-one years of existence, the best GDR literature provoked and prefigured reform. It functioned as a seismograph, registering paradigm shifts sometimes long before other elements of society could, or would, acknowledge them. In the 1980s GDR literature presaged the united German literature of the 1990s. It did so in part by extending its concerns beyond parochial problems to those of a pan-German and/or international scale.

After Erich Honecker's approval of a more liberal GDR cultural policy in 1971, GDR literature began to converge, in matters of form, with that of the West. In the 1980s the themes grew ever more indistinguishable as well. In part, that resulted from the fading hopes for Marxist utopia, a process GDR literature registered well before the governments of the Warsaw Pact fell. Many of the younger GDR artists and writers turned their backs ostentatiously on a socialism they found crippling and repressive.

For the older writers, however, the dream did not die easily. Like her protagonist Josepha, Monika Maron long considered herself a reformer. Josepha insists to a French journalist that she does not want "to break off the dialogue with [the Party] or emigrate later on. I'm the black sheep now, but I belong to the flock." To which the Frenchman replies, "Perhaps you don't even belong to it now, and you just don't want to admit it" (83). Despite her inability to publish, Maron remained in the GDR until 1988, at which point she accepted, with the blessings of her government, a long-term visa for West Germany. Christoph Hein remained in the GDR to the end, but in *The Distant Lover* nothing remains of the socialist utopia. Instead we encounter a bleak landscape of boredom, alienation, and despair. As David Bathrick correctly asserts, Hein's book "signals the end of the wall before the end of the wall" (6). In *Bronstein's Children* Jurek Becker, who left the GDR with a long-term visa in 1978, problematizes the East German self-definition as an antifascist state. His GDR Jews (not necessarily mouthpieces for Becker himself) characterize their country as "hostile territory" (161).

Flight of Ashes, The Distant Lover, and *Bronstein's Children* are all doubly coded, responding to a GDR context but transcending it as well. *Flight of Ashes* deals with GDR censorship, with the difficulties of a reformer within a severely limited public sphere. But the novel furthermore investigates the price of technological progress, and it queries the very definition of progress. From a somewhat different perspective, Christoph Hein also interrogates an ideal of rational progress, a dialectic of enlightenment that has impoverished the present. Additionally, Hein examines the effects of the German past on German citizens, the project of Becker's *Bronstein's Children.*

Prior to 1989, scholars often disputed whether discrete East and West German literatures existed. Addressing the vexed problem in 1990, Jurek Becker argued that the defining qualities of East German literature were the conditions under which it was produced and the audience expectation—one internalized by authors—that literature would prove somehow oppositional, that it would in some fashion undermine the status quo while creating an ersatz public sphere ("Wiedervereinigung" 360). With the erasure of the German-German border, with the demise of the GDR and its system of censorship, there will be no more East German literature according to Becker's first definition, and *Bronstein's Children,* written in the West, would not qualify by that standard as a GDR book. But *Bronstein's Children* also demonstrates that the dialogic aspect of literature written by (former) GDR writers, that insistent desire to intervene in public debate, will constitute one quality that many eastern Germans will bring to a unified German literature, a literature that will surely continue to address such issues as the environment, women's rights, German history, and the discontents of civilization.

NOTES

1. Developments after 1989 have demonstrated that mental "Walls" have outlasted physical ones. Many Eastern and Western Germans regard each other today with incomprehension, mistrust, resentment, and/or outright hostility. Pastor Friedrich Schorlemmer, who played an active role in the GDR civil rights movement that culminated in the collapse of the SED dictatorship, accused some Western Germans in the early 1990s of waging a kind of civil war against Eastern Germans.

Additionally, revelations about the activities of the former East German secret security police (Stasi), which maintained about six million files in a country of about seventeen million people, have occasioned bitter divisions among former GDR citizens. When in December 1991 the Bundestag passed a law allowing Stasi victims access to their files, many Eastern Germans could read how colleagues, religious leaders, friends, and even family members had reported on them to the secret police.

2. See Introduction, note 5.

3. For a detailed discussion of GDR literature dealing with authors, see Müller.

4. For a more detailed discussion of surrealism, see Vallance.

5. It is not clear in the text whether the uncle was in fact an informant or whether he, a social democrat, fell victim to Stalinist purges.

6. In the essay Becker also notes that his father gave him no religious education and did not speak to him of the past.

Chronology of Cultural/Political Events

The date of first publication is given for literary works. Unless otherwise indicated, the place of publication is the GDR.

1942 S. Heym, *Hostages* (USA)
      A. Seghers, *The Seventh Cross*
      (Mexico, USA)

1944 S. Heym, *Of Smiling Peace* (USA)
      A. Seghers, *Transit* (USA)

1946 A. Seghers, "The Excursion of the   Founding of Socialist Unity party
      Dead Girls" (USA)   (SED).

1947   Return of A. Seghers.

1948 S. Heym, *The Crusaders* (USA)   Return of B. Brecht.

1949 A. Seghers, *The Dead Stay Young*   Founding of German Democratic
      S. Hermlin, "The Time Together"   Republic (7 Oct.).

1951 S. Heym, *The Eyes of Reason* (USA)   Beginning of campaign against
                                             formalism.

1952		Return of S. Heym.
1953	S. Heym, *Goldsborough*	Stalin dies (3 March); S. Heym revokes U.S. citizenship; workers' uprising on 17 June.
1956		Khrushchev's secret denunciation of Stalin; Anglo-Franco invasion of Egypt; E. Bloch forcibly retired; Brecht dies.
1957		W. Harich, W. Janka, E. Loest, and others tried and given severe prison sentences.
1958	B. Apitz, *Naked Among Wolves*	
1959	U. Johnson, *Speculations about Jakob* (FRG) A. Seghers, *The Decision*	First Bitterfeld Conference; U. Johnson leaves GDR; A. Seghers awarded GDR National Prize.
1961		Construction of Berlin Wall (13 August).
1962	F. Fühmann, *The Car with the Yellow Star*	
1963	S. Heym, *The Lenz Papers* E. Strittmatter, *Ole Bienkopp* C. Wolf, *Divided Heaven*	Introduction of New Economic System; P. Huchel loses post as editor of *Sinn und Form*; S. Hermlin loses post at Academy of Arts.
1964	J. Bobrowski, *Levin's Mill*	
1965		Eleventh Plenum of the Central Committee of the SED: criticism of W. Biermann and S. Heym, among others; J. Bobrowski dies
1966	F. R. Fries, *The Road to Oobliadooh* (FRG)	
1967		New Economic System replaced by Economic System of Socialism.

1968	G. de Bruyn, *Buridan's Ass* A. Seghers, *Trust* C. Wolf, *The Quest for Christa T.*	GDR troops join other Warsaw Pact nations in suppressing Prague Spring.
1969	J. Becker, *Jacob the Liar* S. Heym, *Uncertain Friend* (FRG)	
1970	S. Heym, *The Queen against Defoe* (Switz.)	
1971	F. Wander, *The Seventh Well*	W. Ulbright resigns (May) and is replaced by E. Honecker; Eighth Party Conference (June): thaw begins; Fourth Plenum of the Central Committee of the SED: Honecker speaks of art "without taboos" (Dec.); G. Lukács dies.
1972	S. Heym, *The King David Report* (FRG, USA) U. Plenzdorf, *The New Sorrows of Young W.* (*Sinn und Form* version)	
1973	F. Fühmann, *Twenty-Two Days or Half of a Lifetime* C. Wolf, "Self-Experiment" (*Sinn und Form*)	
1974	S. Heym, *Five Days in June* (FRG)	
1975	V. Braun, Unfinished Story (*Sinn und Form*)	
1976	R. Kunze, *The Wonderful Years* (FRG) C. Wolf, *Patterns of Childhood*	R. Kunze ejected from Writers' Association (Oct.); W. Biermann forcibly expatriated (Nov.); artists protest expatriation of Biermann.
1977	H. J. Schädlich, *Approximation* (FRG)	R. Kunze and H. J. Schädlich leave GDR.
1978	J. Becker, *Sleepless Days* (FRG)	J. Becker leaves GDR with long-term visa.

1979 S. Hermlin, *Evening Light*
      S. Heym, *Collin* (FRG)
      R. Schneider, *November* (FRG)
      C. Wolf, *No Place on Earth*

Sanctions against S. Heym; nine critical authors ejected from Berlin section of the Writers' Association; R. Schneider leaves GDR with long-term visa.

1981 S. Heym, *The Wandering Jew* (FRG)
      M. Maron, *Flight of Ashes* (FRG)

1982 C. Hein, *The Distant Lover*

1983 C. Wolf, *Cassandra*

A. Seghers dies.

1984

F. Fühmann dies; U. Johnson dies.

1986 J. Becker, *Bronstein's Children* (FRG)

C. Wolf awarded GDR National Prize.

1987 C. Wolf, *Accident*

Tenth GDR Writers' Congress: C. Hein and G. de Bruyn protest censorship.

1988

Mass arrests after demonstrations disrupt official Luxemburg/ Liebknecht parade; M. Maron leaves GDR with long-term visa.

1989

Hungary begins to open border to Austria (May); flight of GDR citizens through Hungary or through FRG embassies in Prague and Warsaw; Honecker resigns (18 Oct.); replaced by E. Krenz; border to FRG is opened (9 Nov.); Krenz resigns (6 Dec.) and is replaced by G. Gysi and H. Modrow.

1990

Free elections (March) won by Christian Democrats; GDR incorporated by FRG (4 Oct.).

Works Cited

Albrecht, Friedrich. "Interview mit Fritz Rudolf Fries." *Weimarer Beiträge* 25.3 (1979): 38–63.

———. "Zur Schaffensentwicklung von Fritz Rudolf Fries." *Weimarer Beiträge* 25.3 (1979): 64–92.

Allenstein, Bernd, and Manfred Behn. "Volker Braun." Arnold, 7th printing, 1–7, A–F.

Altbach, Edith Hoshino, et al., eds. *German Feminism. Readings in Politics and Literature*. Albany: State U of New York P, 1984.

Améry, Jean. *At the Mind's Limits. Contemplations by a Survivor on Auschwitz and Its Realities*. Trans. Sidney Rosenfeld and Stella P. Rosenfeld. Bloomington: Indiana UP, 1980.

———. "On the Necessity and Impossibility of Being Jewish." Améry, *Mind's Limits* 82–103.

Amnesty International. "Laws in the German Democratic Republic Restricting Freedom of Expression: How Writers are Affected." New York: Amnesty International, 1983.

Anderson, Edith, ed. [*Bolt out of the Blue*] *Blitz aus heiterm Himmel*. Rostock: Hinstorff, 1975.

———. "Genesis and Adventures of the Anthology *Blitz aus heiterm Himmel*." Gerber, *Studies* 4 1–14.

Anderson, Sascha, and Elke Erb, eds. [*Contact Is Only a Peripheral Phenomenon*] *Berührung ist nur eine Randerscheinung*. Cologne: Kiepenheuer and Witsch, 1985.

Angress, Ruth. "A 'Jewish Problem' in German Postwar Fiction." *Modern Judaism* 5 (1988): 215–33.

Apitz, Bruno. *Naked Among Wolves.* Trans. Edith Anderson. Berlin: Seven Seas, 1960. Trans. of *Nackt unter Wölfen.* Halle: Mitteldeutscher Verlag, 1958.

Arnold, Karl-Heinz. *Kritisches Lexikon der deutschsprachigen Gegenwartsliteratur.* Munich: Text und Kritik, 1978.

Auer, Annemarie. "Gegenerinnerung." *Sinn und Form* 29.4 (1977): 847–78.

Bahr, Gisela E. "*Blitz aus heiterm Himmel:* Ein Versuch zur Emanzipation in der DDR." Paulsen 223–36.

Bammer, Angelika. "The American Feminist Reception of GDR Literature (With a Glance at West Germany)." *GDR Bulletin* 16.2 (1990): 18–24.

Bathrick, David. "Productive Mis-Reading: GDR Literature in the USA." *GDR Bulletin* 16.2 (1990): 1–6.

Becker, Jurek. [*The Boxer*] *Der Boxer.* Rostock: Hinstorff, 1976.

———. *Bronstein's Children.* Trans. Leila Vennewitz. New York: Harcourt Brace Jovanovich, 1988. Trans. of *Bronsteins Kinder.* Frankfurt/Main: Suhrkamp, 1986; Rostock: Hinstorff, 1987.

———. *Jacob the Liar.* Trans. Melvin Kornfeld. New York: Harcourt Brace Jovanovich, 1975. Trans. of *Jakob der Lügner.* Berlin: Aufbau, 1969.

———. [*Leading the Authorities Astray*] *Irreführung der Behörden.* Rostock: Hinstorff, 1973.

———. "My Way of Being a Jew." Trans. Claudia Johnson and Richard A. Zipser. *Dimension* 11.3 (1978): 417–23.

———. *Sleepless Days.* Trans. Leila Vennewitz. New York: Harcourt Brace Jovanovich, 1979. Trans. of *Schlaflose Tage.* Frankfurt/Main: Suhrkamp, 1978.

———. "Die Wiedervereinigung der deutschen Literatur." *German Quarterly* 63.3–4 (1990): 359–66.

Behn, Manfred, ed. *Wirkungsgeschichte von Christa Wolfs "Nachdenken über Christa T."* Königstein: Athenäum, 1978.

Bernhardt, Rüdiger. "Für und Wider: *Der fremde Freund.*" *Weimarer Beiträge* 29.9 (1983): 1635–38.

Bettelheim, Bruno. *The Uses of Enchantment: The Meaning and Importance of Fairy Tales.* New York: Alfred Knopf, 1977.

Biele, Peter. "Nochmals—'Die neuen Leiden' . . . " Brenner, ed. 205–12.

Biermann, Wolf. *Nachlaß 1.* Cologne: Kiepenheuer and Witsch, 1977.

———. *The Wire Harp.* Trans. Eric Bentley. New York: Harcourt Brace Jovanovich, 1968. Trans. of *Die Drahtharfe: Balladen, Gedichte, Lieder.* Berlin: Wagenbach, 1965.

Bobrowski, Johannes. "Boehlendorff." Bobrowski, *Bitterness* 25–47.

———. *I Taste Bitterness: Short Stories.* Trans. Marc Linder. Berlin: Seven Seas, 1970.

———. *Levin's Mill.* Trans. Janet Cropper. London: Calder and Boyars, 1970. Trans. of *Levins Mühle: 34 Sätze über meinen Großvater.* Berlin: Union, 1964.

———. [*Lithuanian Pianos*] *Litauische Claviere.* Berlin: Union, 1966.

Bohm, Gunhild. "Bewegungen in Literatur und Literaturpolitik der DDR." *Neue Deutsche Hefte* 33.1 (1986): 75–92.

Bohnert, Christiane. "Stefan Heym: *Der König David Bericht*. Die Ohnmacht der Macht vor der Geschichte." *Jahrbuch für die Literatur der DDR*. Vol. 5. Ed. Paul Gerhard Klussmann and Heinrich Mohr. Bonn: Bouvier, 1985. 143–95.

Brand, Matthias. "Stacheldrahtleben: Literatur und Konzentrationslager." *Sammlung 4: Jahrbuch für antifaschistische Literatur und Kunst*. Ed. Uwe Naumann. Frankfurt/Main: Röderberg, 1981. 133–42.

Brandes, Ute. "Probing the Blind Spot: Utopia and Dystopia in Christa Wolf's *Störfall*." Gerber, *Studies 9* 101–14.

———. "Real Existing Stalinism as Fact and Literary Mirror: Anna Seghers and Walter Janka." *Gegenwartsbewältigung*/Coming to Terms with the Present: A Symposium. U of Michigan, Ann Arbor, 25–27 Oct. 1990.

Brandt, Sabine. "Politische Polemik um einen deutschen Film." *Reiner Kunze: Materialien zu Leben und Werk*. Ed. Heiner Feldkamp. Frankfurt/Main: Fischer, 1987. 241–49.

Brasch, Thomas. [*The Sons Die before the Fathers*] *Vor den Vätern sterben die Söhne*. Berlin: Rotbuch, 1977.

Braun, Volker. ["Büchner's Letters"] "Büchners Briefe." *Connaissance de la RDA* 7 (Nov. 1978): 8–17.

———. [*Hinze-Kunze-Novel*] *Hinze-Kunze-Roman*. Frankfurt/Main: Suhrkamp, 1985.

———. [*Lenin's Death*] *Lenins Tod. Sinn und Form* 40.1 (1988): 37–85.

———. *T. Gesammelte Stücke*. Vol. 1. Frankfurt/Main: Suhrkamp, 1989.

———. [*The Uncoerced Life of Kast*] *Das ungezwungene Leben Kasts. Drei Berichte*. Berlin: Aufbau, 1972. Expanded ed. Berlin: Aufbau, 1979.

———. ["Unfinished Story"] "The English Translation of Volker Braun's 'Unvollendete Geschichte.'" Trans. Yvonne Veronika Fiala. MA Thesis. U of Illinois, 1983. Trans. of "Unvollendete Geschichte." *Sinn und Form* 27.5 (1975): 941–79.

Brecht, Bertolt. *Poems, 1913-1956*. Ed. John Willett and Ralph Manheim. New York: Methuen, 1979.

Brenner, Peter J., "Einleitung." Brenner, ed. 11–68.

———, ed. *Plenzdorfs "Neue Leiden des jungen W."* Frankfurt/Main: Suhrkamp, 1982.

Brüning, Elfriede. "Heaven on Earth." Trans. Marjorie Tussing and Jeanette Clausen. Altbach et al. 68–76. Trans. of "Himmel auf Erden." *Neue Deutsche Literatur* 22.4 (1974): 126–37.

Bruyn, Günter de. *Buridan's Ass*. Trans. John Peet. Berlin: Seven Seas, 1973. Trans. of *Buridans Esel*. Halle: Mitteldeutscher Verlag, 1968.

———. *Das Leben des Jean Paul Friedrich Richter*. Halle: Mitteldeutscher Verlag, 1975.

———. [*New Splendor*] *Neue Herrlichkeit*. Frankfurt/Main: Fischer, 1984.

———. [*Presentation of a Prize*] *Preisverleihung*. Halle: Mitteldeutscher Verlag, 1972.

Büchner, Georg. Lenz. *Complete Works and Letters*. By Büchner. Trans. Henry

J. Schmidt. Ed. Walter Hinderer and Henry J. Schmidt. New York: Continuum, 1986. 139–59.

Büscher, Wolfgang. "Geschichte als Denk- und Spielraum: Die DDR-Historiker im Lutherjahr." Gerber, *Studies 4* 243–53.

Celan, Paul. *Paul Celan: Poems, a Bilingual Edition.* Ed. and trans. Michael Hamburger. New York: Persea, 1980.

Childs, David. *The GDR: Moscow's German Ally.* London: Allen and Unwin, 1983.

"Chronik." *Deutschland Archiv* 23.1 (1990): 161–76.

Cibulka, Hanns. *Swantow: Die Aufzeichnungen des Andreas Flemming.* Halle: Mitteldeutscher Verlag, 1982.

Conquest, Robert. *Stalin and the Kirov Murder.* Oxford: Oxford UP, 1989.

Conrad, Joseph. *Heart of Darkness.* Heart of Darkness: *A Case Study in Contemporary Criticism.* Ed. Ross C. Murfin. New York: St. Martin's, 1989. 17–94.

Corino, Karl. " 'Die neuen Leiden des jungen W.' " Brenner, ed. 251–54.

Czollek, Walter. "Begegnung mit der Vergangenheit." *Neue Deutsche Literatur* 19.2 (1971): 156–58.

Damm, Sigrid, and Jürgen Engler. "Notate des Zwiespalts und Allegorien der Vollendung." *Weimarer Beiträge* 21.7 (1975): 37–69.

Demetz, Peter. *After the Fires: Recent Writing in the Germanies, Austria, and Switzerland.* New York: Harcourt Brace Jovanovich, 1986.

———. *Postwar German Literature: A Critical Introduction.* New York: Pegasus, 1970.

Dölling, Irene. "Les femmes de RDA après le 'tournant.' " *Connaissance de la RDA* 30/31 (Jan. 1991): 119–29.

Droste-Hülshoff, Annette von. "The Jews' Beech Tree" *Three Eerie Tales from 19th Century German.* Ed. Edward Mornin. New York: Ungar, 1975. 99–151.

———. "On the Tower" Trans. Ruth Angress. *The Defiant Muse: German Feminist Poems from the Middle Ages to the Present.* Ed. Susan Cocalis. New York: Feminist, 1988. 29.

Dvorak, Paul F. Rev. of *The New Sufferings of Young W.,* by Ulrich Plenzdorf. *Modern Language Journal* 64 (1980): 519–20.

Eagleton, Terry. *Criticism and Ideology: A Study in Marxist Literary Theory.* London: Humanities, 1976.

Eckart, Gabriele. [*That's How I See It*] *So sehe ick die Sache.* Cologne: Kiepenheuer and Witsch, 1984.

Ehlert, Beate. "Dichterische Ich-Konstanten im Geschichtsprozeß. Über Stephan Hermlins autobiographische Utopie der Stille: 'Abendlicht.' " *Jahrbuch zur Literatur der DDR.* Ed. Gerhard Klussmann and Heinrich Mohr. Vol. 3. Bonn: Bouvier, 1983. 73–87.

Einhorn, Barbara. *Der Roman in der DDR 1949–1969.* Kronberg: Scriptor, 1978.

Elling, Barbara, and Andreas Mielke, eds. "Voices from the German Democratic Republic. An Anthology of Contemporary East German Prose." *Slavic and East European Arts* 3.2 (1985) 1st ed.

Emmerich, Wolfgang. *Kleine Literaturgeschichte der DDR*. Darmstadt: Luchterhand, 1984.

———. *Kleine Literaturgeschichte der DDR: 1945–1988*. 2nd ed., expanded. Darmstadt: Luchterhand, 1989.

Fassbinder, Rainer Werner. [*"The Bitter Tears of Petra von Kant"; "Trash, the City, and Death."* Two Plays] *Die bitteren Tränen der Petra von Kant; Der Müll, die Stadt und der Tod: Zwei Stücke*. Frankfurt/Main: Verlag der Autoren, 1984.

Feher, Ferenc. "'The Jewish Question' Reconsidered: Notes on Istvan Bibo's Classic Essay." Rabinbach and Zipes 315–55.

Fehervary, Helen, and Sara Lennox. Introduction. C. Wolf, "Self-Experiment" 109–12.

Firchow, Peter E., and Evelyn S. Firchow, eds. and trans. *East German Short Stories: An Introductory Anthology*. Boston: Twayne, 1979.

Flores, John. *Poetry in East Germany: Adjustments, Visions, and Provocations 1954–1970*. New Haven: Yale UP, 1971.

Fries, Fritz Rudolf. [*The Air Ship*] *Das Luft-Schiff: Biografische Nachlässe zu den Fantasien meines Großvaters*. Rostock: Hinstorff, 1975.

———. [*Alexander's New Worlds*] *Alexanders neue Welten: Ein akademischer Kolportageroman aus Berlin*. Berlin: Aufbau, 1982.

———. "Frauentags Anfang oder das Ende von Arlecq und Paasch." *Sinn und Form* 34.2 (1982): 359–72.

———. "Das Kloster im Walde." F. R. Fries, *Leipzig am Herzen* 122–130.

———. *Leipzig am Herzen und die Welt dazu: Geschichten von Reisen*. Berlin: Aufbau, 1983.

———. *The Road to Oobliadooh*. Trans. Leila Vennewitz. New York: McGraw-Hill, 1968. Trans. of *Der Weg nach Oobliadooh*. Frankfurt/Main: Suhrkamp, 1966; Berlin: Aufbau, 1989.

———. [*Sea Pieces*] *Seestücke*. Rostock: Hinstorff, 1973.

———. [*The Television War*] *Der Fernsehkrieg*. Halle: Mitteldeutscher Verlag, 1969.

Fries, Marilyn Sibley, ed. *Responses to Christa Wolf: Critical Essays*. Detroit: Wayne State UP, 1989.

Frisch, Max. *Andorra: Stück in zwölf Bildern*. Frankfurt/Main: Suhrkamp, 1961.

Fühmann, Franz. *The Car with the Yellow Star: Fourteen Days out of Two Decades*. Trans. Joan Becker. Berlin: Seven Seas, 1968. Trans. of *Das Judenauto: 14 Tage aus 2 Jahrzehnten*. Berlin: Aufbau, 1962.

———. *Twenty-Two Days or Half of a Lifetime*. Trans. Leila Vennewitz. Berlin: Seven Seas, 1980. Trans. of *Zweiundzwanzig Tage oder Die Hälfte des Lebens*. Rostock: Hinstorff, 1973.

Gerber, Margy, ed. *Studies in GDR Culture and Society: Proceedings from the Seventh International Symposium on the German Democratic Republic*. Lanham: UP of America, 1982.

———, ed. *Studies in GDR Culture and Society 4: Selected Papers from the Ninth New Hampshire Symposium on the German Democratic Republic*. Lanham: UP of America, 1984.

———, ed. *Studies in GDR Culture and Society 9: Selected Papers from the Fourteenth New Hampshire Symposium on the German Democratic Republic*. Lanham: UP of America, 1989.

Gerber, Margy, and Judith Pouget. *Literature of the German Democratic Republic in English Translation: A Bibliography*. Lanham: UP of America, 1984.

Gerlach, Rainer, and Matthias Richter, eds. *Uwe Johnson*. Frankfurt/Main: Suhrkamp, 1984.

Gilbert, Sandra M., and Susan Gubar. *The Madwoman in the Attic: The Woman Writer and the Nineteenth-Century Literary Imagination*. New Haven: Yale UP, 1979.

Gilman, Sander. "Jüdische Literaten und deutsche Literatur." *Zeitschrift für deutsche Philologie* 107.2 (1985): 270–94.

Girnus, Wilhelm. " . . . kein 'wenn und aber' und das poetische Licht Sapphos: Noch einmal zu Christa Wolf." *Sinn und Form* 35.4 (1983): 1096–1105.

———. "Wer baute das siebentorige Theben? Kritische Bemerkungen zu Christa Wolfs Beitrag in *Sinn und Form* 1/83." *Sinn und Form* 35.2 (1983): 439–47.

Goethe, Johann Wolfgang von. *The Sorrows of Young Werther; Elective Affinities; Novella*. Trans. Victor Lange and Judith Ryan. Ed. David E. Wellbery. New York: Suhrkamp, 1988.

Grambow, Jürgen. "Heimat im Vergangenen." *Sinn und Form* 38.1 (1986): 134–57.

———. "Zur Prosa von Fritz Rudolf Fries: Sein erster und sein jüngster Roman." *Weimarer Beiträge* 36.8 (1990): 1311–28.

Greiner, Bernhard. "Autobiographie im Horizont der Psychoanalyse: Stephan Hermlins 'Abendlicht.'" *Poetica* 14.3–4 (1982): 213–49.

———. "Sentimentalischer Stoff und fantastische Form: Zur Erneuerung frühromantischer Tradition im Roman der DDR." *DDR-Roman und Literaturgesellschaft*. Ed. Jos Hoogeveen and Gerd Labroisse. Amsterdam: Rodopi, 1981. 249–328.

Gruner, Petra, ed. *Angepaßt oder mündig? Briefe an Christa Wolf im Herbst 1989*. Berlin: Volk und Wissen, 1990.

Hage, Volker. "Zur deutschen Literatur 1987." *Deutsche Literatur 1987: Jahresüberblick*. Ed. Franz Josef Görtz, Volker Hage, and Uwe Wittstock. Stuttgart: Reclam, 1988. 7–49.

Hahn, Manfred. "Franz Fühmann: 'Zweiundzwanzig Tage oder die Hälfte des Lebens.'" *Weimarer Beiträge* 20.10 (1974): 143–55.

Hamburger, Michael, ed. *East German Poetry. An Anthology*. New York: E. P. Dutton, 1973.

Handke, Peter. *A Moment of True Feeling*. Trans. Ralph Mannheim. New York: Avon, 1979. Trans. of *Die Stunde der wahren Empfindung*. Suhrkamp: Frankfurt/Main, 1975.

Heiduczek, Werner. [*Death at the Seaside*] *Tod am Meer*. Halle: Mitteldeutscher Verlag, 1977.

Hein, Christoph. *The Distant Lover*. Trans. Krishna Winston. New York: Pantheon, 1989. Trans. of *Der fremde Freund.* Berlin: Aufbau, 1982; *Drachenblut.* Darmstadt: Luchterhand, 1983.

———. [*Horn's End*] *Horns Ende.* Berlin: Aufbau, 1985.

———. [*The Knights of the Round Table: A Comedy*] *Die Ritter der Tafelrunde: Eine Komödie.* Frankfurt/Main: Luchterhand, 1989.

———. *The Tango Player.* Trans. Philip Boehm. New York: Farrar, Straus, and Giroux, 1991. Trans. of *Der Tangospieler.* Berlin: Aufbau, 1989.

Herminghouse, Patricia. "The Rediscovery of Romanticism: Revisions and Reevaluations." Gerber, *Studies* (1982), 1–17.

———. "Wunschbild, Vorbild oder Porträt? Zur Darstellung der Frau im Roman der DDR." Hohendahl and Herminghouse 281–334.

Hermlin, Stephan. *City on a Hill.* Trans. Joan Becker. Berlin: Seven Seas, 1962. Trans. of *Die Zeit der Gemeinsamkeit.* Berlin: Volk und Welt, 1949

———. *Evening Light.* Trans. Paul F. Dvorak. San Francisco: Fjord Press, 1983. Trans. of *Abendlicht.* Leipzig: Reclam, 1983.

———. "Das Hier ist es." *Sinn und Form* 39.2 (1987): 274–84.

———. "The Time Together." ["Die Zeit der Gemeinsamkeit"] Hermlin, *City* 85–158.

———. "Wo sind wir zu Hause? Gespräch mit Klaus Wagenbach." *Äußerungen 1944–1982.* By Hermlin. Ed. Ulrich Dietzel. Berlin: Aufbau, 1983. 396–408.

Heukenkamp, Ursula. "Die fremde Form." *Sinn und Form* 35.3 (1983): 625–32.

Heym, Stefan. *The Cannibals and Other Stories.* Leipzig: List, 1957. German: *Die Kannibalen und andere Erzählungen.* Trans. Ellen Zunk and Heym. Leipzig: List, 1953.

———. *Collin.* Secaucus: Lyle Stuart, 1980. Trans. of *Collin.* Munich: Bertelsmann, 1979; Berlin: Der Morgen, 1990.

———. *The Crusaders: A Novel of Only Yesterday.* Boston: Little, Brown, and Co., 1948; German: *Kreuzfahrer von heute.* Trans. Werner von Grünau. Leipzig: List, 1950.

———. *The Eyes of Reason.* Boston: Little, Brown, and Co., 1951. German: *Die Augen der Vernunft.* Trans. Ellen Zunk. Leipzig: List, 1955.

———. *Five Days in June.* London: Hodder and Stoughton, 1977; Buffalo: Prometheus, 1978. Trans. of *Fünf Tage im Juni.* Munich: Bertelsmann, 1974; Berlin: Der Morgen, 1989.

———. *Goldsborough.* New York: Blue Heron, 1954. Trans. of *Goldsborough.* Leipzig: List, 1953.

———. *Hostages.* New York: G. P. Putnam's Sons, 1942. German: *Der Fall Glasenapp.* Leipzig: List, 1958.

———. *The King David Report.* New York: G. P. Putnam's Sons, 1973. German: *Der König-David-Bericht.* Munich: Kindler, 1972; Berlin: Der Morgen, 1973.

———. *The Lenz Papers.* Berlin: Seven Seas, 1968. First Eng. edition. London: Cassell, 1964. German: *Die Papiere des Andreas Lenz.* Trans. Helga Zimnik. Leipzig: List, 1963.

———. *Nachruf*. Munich: Bertelsmann, 1988.

———. *Of Smiling Peace*. Boston: Little, Brown, and Co., 1944.

———. *The Queen Against Defoe and Other Stories*. New York: Lawrence Hill and Co., 1974. German: *Die Schmähschrift oder Königin gegen Defoe: Erzählt nach den Aufzeichnungen eines gewissen Josiah Creech*. Zurich: Diogenes, 1970; Leipzig: Reclam, 1974.

———. *Schwarzenberg*. Munich: Bertelsmann, 1984; Berlin: Der Morgen, 1990.

———. *Shadows and Lights: Eight Short Stories*. London: Cassell, 1963. German: *Schatten und Licht: Geschichten aus einem geteilten Land*. Trans. Helga Zimnik and Heym. Leipzig: List, 1960.

———. "*Über Collin*: Interview mit ARD-Korrespondent Fritz Pleitgen." Mallwitz 374–77.

———. *Uncertain Friend: A Biographical Novel*. London: Cassell, 1969. German: *Lassalle: Ein biographischer Roman*. Munich: Bechtle, 1969; Berlin: Neues Leben, 1974.

———. *The Wandering Jew*. New York: Holt, Rinehart, and Winston, 1984; New York: Grove, 1985. Trans. of *Ahasver*. Munich: Bertelsmann, 1981; Berlin: Der Morgen, 1988.

Hieblinger, Inge. "The Advancement of Women in the GDR." *East Germany: A New German Nation under Socialism?* Ed. Arthur W. McCardle and A. Bruce Boenau. Lanham: UP of America, 1984. 248–63.

Hillich, Reinhard. "*Ole Bienkopp*—eine wichtige Zäsur im Schaffen Strittmatters." *Erwin Strittmatter: Analysen, Erörterungen, Gespräche*. Ed. Kollektiv für Literaturgeschichte. Berlin: Volk und Wissen, 1984. 70–104.

Hirdina, Karin. *Günter de Bruyn: Leben und Werk*. Berlin: Volk und Wissen, 1983.

Hohendahl, Uwe, and Patricia Herminghouse, eds. *Literatur und Literaturtheorie in der DDR*. Frankfurt/Main: Suhrkamp, 1981.

Hollis, Andy. Introduction. "Unvollendete Geschichte." By Volker Braun. Ed. Andy Hollis. Manchester: Manchester UP, 1988. 1–29.

Hörnigk, Therese. *Christa Wolf*. Göttingen: Steidl, 1989.

Jäger, Manfred. "Die Grenzen des Sagbaren: Sprachzweifel im Werk von Christa Wolf." *Christa Wolf: Materialienbuch*. Ed. Klaus Sauer. Darmstadt: Luchterhand, 1983. 43–162.

Jakobs, Karl-Heinz. [*Description of a Summer*] *Beschreibung eines Sommers*. Berlin: Verlag Neues Leben, 1961.

Janka, Walter. [*Difficulties with the Truth*] *Schwierigkeiten mit der Wahrheit*. Reinbeck: Rowohlt, 1989.

Jarausch, Konrad H. "The Failure of East German Antifascism: Some Ironies of History as Politics." *German Studies Review* 14.1 (1991): 85–102.

Jay, Martin. "Anti-Semitism and the Frankfurt School: Critical Theory's Analysis of Anti-Semitism." Rabinbach and Zipes 287–301.

Johnson, Uwe. *Speculations about Jakob: A Novel*. Trans. Ursule Molinaro. New York: Harcourt Brace Jovanovich, 1963. Trans. of *Mutmaßungen über Jakob*. Frankfurt/Main: Suhrkamp, 1959.

————. *The Third Book about Achim.* No trans. New York: Harcourt, Brace, and World, 1967. Trans. of *Das dritte Buch über Achim.* Suhrkamp: Frankfurt/ Main, 1961.

Joho, Wolfgang. "Tragikomische Ouvertüre." *Neue Deutsche Literatur* 12.5 (1964): 129–34.

Kant, Hermann. "Abendlicht." Kant, *Zu den Unterlagen* 149–53.

————. "Kindheitsmuster." Kant, *Zu den Unterlagen* 137–44.

————. [*The Masthead*] *Das Impressum.* Berlin: Rütten and Loening, 1972.

————. "Die Verantwortung des Schriftstellers in den Kämpfen unserer Zeit." Kant, *Zu den Unterlagen* 205–34.

————. *Zu den Unterlagen: Publizistik 1957–1980.* Ed. Leonore Krenzlin. Berlin: Aufbau, 1981.

————. "Zu wissen, wo man steht in den politischen Kämpfen unserer Zeit." Kant, *Zu den Unterlagen* 235–44.

Kaufmann, Hans. "Dringliches Forschen." *Neue Deutsche Literatur* 35.8 (1987): 134–38.

————. "Wider die troianischen Kriege." *Sinn und Form* 36.3 (1984): 653–63.

Kirsch, Sarah. *The Panther Woman: Five Tales from the Cassette Recorder.* Trans. Marion Faber. Lincoln: U of Nebraska P, 1989. Trans. of *Die Pantherfrau: Fünf unfrisierte Erzählungen aus dem Kassetten-Recorder.* Berlin: Aufbau, 1973.

Klausenitzer, Hans-Peter. "Der Erfolg hat viele Väter: Hans Joachim Schädlichs 'Versuchte Nähe' im Spiegel der Kritik." *Deutschland Archiv* 11.7 (1978): 745–48.

Knobloch, Heinz. *Herr Moses in Berlin: Auf den Spuren eines Menschenfreundes.* Berlin: Der Morgen, 1979.

Koerner, Charlotte W. "*Divided Heaven*—by Christa Wolf? A Sacrifice of Message and Meaning in Translation." *German Quarterly* 57.2 (1984): 213–30.

————. "Volker Brauns 'Unvollendete Geschichte': Erinnerung an Büchners 'Lenz.'" *Basis 9.* Ed. Reinhold Grimm and Jost Hermand. Frankfurt/Main: Suhrkamp, 1979. 149–68.

Korey, William. *The Soviet Cage.* New York: Viking, 1973.

Krisch, Henry. *The German Democratic Republic: The Search for Identity.* Boulder: Westview, 1985.

Kuhn, Anna. *Christa Wolf's Utopian Vision: From Marxism to Feminism.* Cambridge: Cambridge UP, 1988.

————, ed. *Deckname "Lyrik."* Frankfurt/Main: Fischer, 1990.

Kunze, Reiner. [*Dedications*] *Widmungen.* Bad Godesberg: Hohwacht, 1963.

————. [*Letter with a Blue Seal*] *Brief mit blauem Siegel.* Leipzig: Reclam, 1973.

————. [*Sensitive Ways*] *Sensible Wege.* Reinbeck: Rowohlt, 1969.

————. *The Wonderful Years.* Trans. Joachim Neugroschel. New York: G. Braziller, 1977. Trans. of *Die wunderbaren Jahre.* Frankfurt/Main: Fischer, 1976.

Kwiet, Konrad. "Historians of the German Democratic Republic on Anti-Semitism and Persecution." *Leo Baeck Institute Yearbook* 21 (1976): 173–98.

Leistner, Bernd. "Der Einsatz des Geschichtenerzählers: Zur Erzählweise des

318 / Works Cited

Romans 'Levins Mühle.'" *Johannes Bobrowski: Studien und Interpretationen.* By Leistner. Berlin: Rütten and Loening, 1981. 109–22.

Lennox, Sara. "'Der Versuch, man selbst zu sein': Christa Wolf und der Feminismus." Paulsen 217–22.

Linder, Gabriele. "Für und Wider: *Der fremde Freund.*" *Weimarer Beiträge* 29.9 (1983): 1645–48.

Loest, Erich. [*It Takes Its Course: Or, The Difficulties of the Plains*] Es geht seinen Gang: oder, Mühen in unserer Ebene. Halle: Mitteldeutscher Verlag, 1978.

Lüdke-Haertel, Sigrid, and W. Martin Lüdke. "Jurek Becker." Arnold, 29th printing, 1–12, A–J.

Ludz, Peter Christian. *The German Democratic Republic from the Sixties to the Seventies: A Socio-Political Analysis.* Cambridge: Harvard Center for International Affairs, 1970.

Lukács, Georg. *Essays on Realism.* Cambridge: MIT, 1980.

Macherey, Pierre. *A Theory of Literary Production.* Trans. Geoffrey Wall. Boston: Routledge and Kegan Paul, 1978.

Mallwitz, Peter, ed. *Stefan Heym: Wege und Umwege.* Munich: Bertelsmann, 1980.

Marcuse, Herbert. "Marxism and Feminism." *Women's Studies* 2.3 (1974): 279–88.

Maron, Monika. *The Defector.* Trans. David Newton Marinelli. London: Readers International, 1988. Trans. of *Die Überläuferin.* Frankfurt/Main: Fischer, 1986.

———. *Flight of Ashes.* Trans. David Newton Marinelli. London: Readers International, 1986. Trans. of *Flugasche.* Frankfurt/Main: Fischer, 1981.

Marx, Karl. *Economic and Philosophical Manuscripts.* Trans. T. B. Bottomore. *Marx's Concept of Man.* Ed. Erich Fromm. 15th Printing. New York: Fredrick Ungar, 1970. 87–196.

Mayer, Hans. "Hans Mayer." *Mein Judentum.* Ed. Hans Jürgen Schultz. 2d ed. Stuttgart: Kreuz, 1979. 248–60.

McCauley, Martin. *The German Democratic Republic since 1945.* New York: St. Martin's, 1983.

Menge, Marlies. "'Miteinander leben, gut miteinander auskommen': Ein ZEIT-Gespräch mit Erich Honecker." *Reise ins andere Deutschland.* Ed. Theo Sommer. Reinbeck: Rowohlt, 1986. 239–71.

Mertens, Lothar. "Jews in the GDR Today." *GDR Monitor* 20 (Winter 1988/89): 43–56.

Meyer-Gosau, Frauke. "Culture is What You Experience—An Interview with Christa Wolf." Trans. Jeanette Clausen. *New German Critique* 27 (Fall 1982): 89–100.

Mews, Siegfried. *Ulrich Plenzdorf.* Munich: C. H. Beck, 1984.

Milosz, Czeslow. *The Captive Mind.* Trans. Jane Zielonko. New York: Vintage, 1961.

Mohr, Heinrich. "Productive Longing: Structure, Theme, and Political Relevance in Christa Wolf's *The Quest for Christa T.*" M. Fries 196–232.

Morgner, Irmtraud. [*Amanda: A Novel of Witches*] *Amanda: Ein Hexenroman.* Berlin: Aufbau, 1983.

———. "The Glad Tidings of Valeska." Trans. Friedrich and Karen R. Achberger. *New German Critique* 15 (1978): 121–46. Trans. of "Die gute Botschaft der Valeska in 73 Strophen." Morgner, *Leben und Abenteuer,* 646–83.

———. [*Life and Times of Troubadour Beatriz as Chronicled by Her Minstrel Laura: Novel in Thirteen Parts and Seven Intermezzi*] *Leben und Abenteuer der Troubadora Beatriz nach Zeugnissen ihrer Spielfrau Laura: Roman in dreizehn Büchern und sieben Intermezzos.* Berlin: Aufbau, 1974.

———. "The Rope." Trans. Karen R. Achberger. Altbach et al. 215–19. Trans. of "Dritte Bitterfelder Frucht: Das Seil." Morgner, *Leben und Abenteuer.* 594–603.

———. "Shoes." Trans. Karen R. Achberger. Altbach et al. 213–14. Trans. of "Schuhe." Morgner, *Leben und Abenteuer.* 411–13.

Mörike, Eduard. "The Lovely Beech." *German Poetry from 1750–1900.* Ed. Robert M. Browning. The German Library. Vol 39. New York: Continuum, 1984. 228–31.

Moskin, J. Robert. "The Creator and the Commissars: An Encounter with Stefan Heym." Heym, *The Queen Against Defoe* 3–13.

Müller, Wolfgang. *Dichter-Helden in der DDR-Literatur der siebziger Jahre.* New York: Lang, 1989.

Nägele, Rainer. "Trauer, Tropfen und Phantasmen: Ver-rückte Geschichten aus der DDR." Hohendahl and Herminghouse 193–223.

Neubauer, John. Rev. of *The New Sufferings of Young W.,* by Ulrich Plenzdorf. *German Quarterly* 54.1 (1981): 125–26.

Neubert, Werner. "Niete in Hosen—oder . . . ?" Brenner, ed. 213–20.

———. "Reports über Geschichte." *Neue Deutsche Literatur* 22.4 (1974): 153–55.

———. "Der Sinn für das Wesentliche." *Neue Deutsche Literatur.* 22.8 (1974): 140–42.

Neumann, Bernd. *Utopie und Mimesis: Zum Verhältnis von Ästhetik, Gesellschaftsphilosophie und Politik in den Romanen Uwe Johnsons.* Kronberg: Athenäum, 1978.

Neusüß, Arnhelm. "Über die Schwierigkeiten beim Schreiben der Wahrheit: Gespräch mit Uwe Johnson." Gerlach and Richter 39–48.

Neutsch, Erich. [*The Quest for Gatt*] *Auf der Suche nach Gatt.* Halle: Mitteldeutscher Verlag, 1973.

Nickel, Hildegard M. "Women in the GDR: Will Renewal Pass Them By?" *Women in German Yearbook 6: Feminist Studies and German Culture.* Ed. Jeanette Clausen and Helen Cafferty. Lanham: UP of America, 1991. 99–107.

Norton, Roger C., ed. and trans. *Voices East and West: German Short Stories since 1945.* New York: Frederick Ungar, 1984.

Novalis. *Henry von Ofterdingen: A Novel.* Trans. Palmer Hilty. New York: Frederick Ungar, 1964.

Paulsen, Wolfgang, ed. *Die Frau als Heldin und Autorin: Neue kritische Ansätze zur deutschen Literatur*. Bern: Francke, 1979.

Pirskawetz, Lia. [*The Still Earth*] *Der stille Grund*. Berlin: Verlag Neues Leben, 1985.

Plate, Friedrich. "'Neue Leiden' ohne Standpunkt." Brenner, ed. 224–29.

Plavius, Heinz. "Gegenwart im Roman: Gespräch mit Günter de Bruyn." *Neue Deutsche Literatur* 16.6 (1968): 9–13.

Plenzdorf, Ulrich. *The New Sufferings of Young W. A Novel*. Trans. Kenneth P. Wilcox. New York: Frederick Ungar, 1979. Trans. of *Die neuen Leiden des jungen W*. Rostock: Hinstorff, 1973. Published as a play in *Sinn und Form* 24.2 (1972): 254–310.

Poche, Klaus. [*Choking*] *Atemnot*. Olten: Walter, 1978.

Popp, Hansjürgen. "Einführung in Mutmaßungen über Jakob." Gerlach and Richter 49–69.

Prutz, Robert. *Die deutsche Literatur der Gegenwart: 1848–1858*. Vol. 2. Leipzig: n.p., 1859.

Rabinbach, Anton, and Jack Zipes, eds. *Germans and Jews since the Holocaust*. New York: Holmes and Meier, 1986.

Raddatz, Fritz. "Mein Name sei Tonio K." Behn 73–76.

———. *Traditionen und Tendenzen: Materialien zur Literatur der DDR*. Frankfurt/Main: Suhrkamp, 1972.

———. "Ulrich Plenzdorfs Flucht nach innen." Brenner, ed. 303–9.

Rectanus, Mark W. "GDR Literature in the International Book Market: From Confrontation to Assimilation." *GDR Bulletin* 16.2 (1990): 11–18.

Reich-Ranicki, Marcel. "Bruno Apitz." Reich-Ranicki, *Deutsche Literatur* 456–60.

———. "Christa Wolfs unruhige Elegie." Behn 59–64.

———. *Deutsche Literatur in West und Ost: Prosa seit 1945*. Munich: Piper, 1966.

———. *Entgegnung: Zur deutschen Literatur der siebziger Jahre*. Stuttgart: Deutsche Verlags-Anstalt, 1979.

———. "Der Fänger im DDR-Rogen: Ulrich Plenzdorfs jedenfalls wichtiger Werther-Roman." Brenner 262–69.

———. "Die kommunistische Erzählerin Anna Seghers." Reich-Ranicki, *Deutsche Literatur* 354–85.

———. "Roman vom Ghetto." Reich-Ranicki, *Entgegnung* 289–93.

———. "Ein trauiger Zettelkasten." Reich-Ranicki, *Entgegnung* 212–17.

Reid, J. H. *Writing Without Taboos: The New East German Literature*. New York: Berg, 1990.

Reimann, Brigitte. [*Arrival in the Quotidian*] *Ankunft im Alltag*. Berlin: Verlag Neues Leben, 1961.

———. *Franziska Linkerhand*. Berlin: Verlag Neues Leben, 1974.

Reinhold, Ursula. "Stefan Heym: *Ahasver*." *Weimarer Beiträge* 35.3 (1989): 495–502.

Reso, Martin. "Karl Erp und die Heuhaufen: Zu Günter de Bruyns Roman 'Buridans Esel.'" *Sinn und Form* 21.3 (1969): 757–64.

Rey, William H. "Blitze im Herzen der Finsternis: Die neue Anthropologie in Christa Wolfs *Störfall.*" *German Quarterly* 62.3 (1989): 373–83.

Riedel, Nicolai. *Uwe Johnsons Frühwerk: Im Spiegel der deutschsprachigen Literaturkritik.* Bonn: Bouvier, 1983.

Roberts, David. "Stefan Heym: *Der König David Bericht.*" *AUMLA* 48 (November 1977): 201–11.

———. "Surface and Depth: Christoph Hein's *Drachenblut.*" *German Quarterly* 63.3–4 (1990): 478–89.

Romero, Christiane Zehl. " 'Remembrance of Things Future': On Establishing a Female Tradition." M. Fries 108–27.

———. "*Seghersmaterial* in Heiner Müller and Volker Braun." Gerber, *Studies* 9 57–83.

———. " 'Weibliches' Schreiben—Christa Wolf's *Kassandra.*" Gerber, *Studies* 4 15–29.

Roos, Peter, ed. *Exil: Die Ausbürgerung Wolf Biermanns aus der DDR.* Cologne: Kiepenheuer and Witsch, 1977.

Ryan, Judith. *The Uncompleted Past: Postwar German Novels and the Third Reich.* Detroit: Wayne State UP, 1983.

Sachs, Nelly. *O the Chimneys.* Trans. Michael Hamburger. New York: Farrar, Straus, and Giroux, 1967.

Sartre, Jean Paul. *Anti-Semite and Jew.* Trans. George J. Becker. New York: Schocken, 1965.

Sauer, Klaus. *Anna Seghers.* Munich: Beck, 1978.

Schachtsiek-Freitag, Norbert. "Eine so nicht erwünschte Reportage." *Deutschland Archiv* 14.12 (1981): 1337–39.

Schädlich, Hans Joachim. *Approximation.* Trans. Richard and Clara Winston. New York: Harcourt Brace Jovanovich, 1980. Trans. of *Versuchte Nähe.* Reinbeck: Rowohlt, 1977.

———. [*Eastwestberlin*] *Ostwestberlin.* Reinbeck: Rowohlt, 1987.

———. *Tallhover.* Reinbeck: Rowohlt, 1986.

Schlenstedt, Silvia. *Hermlin: Sein Leben und Werk.* Berlin: das europäische buch, 1985.

Schmelzkopf, Christiane. *Zur Gestaltung jüdischer Figuren in der deutschsprachigen Literatur nach 1945.* Hildesheim: Georg Olms, 1983.

Schmitt, Hans-Jürgen. "Von den *Mutmaßungen* zu den *Neuen Leiden:* Zur Wirkungsgeschichte der DDR-Literatur." *Die Literatur der DDR: Hansers sozialgeschichte der deutschen Literatur vom 16. Jahrhundert bis zur Gegenwart.* Ed. Hans-Jürgen Schmitt. Vol. 11. Munich: Carl Hanser, 1983. 15–41.

Schneider, Rolf. *Bridges and Bars: Short Stories.* Trans. Michael Bullock. New York: Viking, 1967.

———. *November.* Trans. Michael Bullock. New York: Alfred Knopf, 1981. Trans. of *November.* Hamburg: Knaus, 1979; Rostock: Hinstorff, 1990.

Schulz, Max Walter. "Das Neue und das Bleibende in unserer Literatur." Behn 70–72.

Schütte, Wolfram. "Zu spät fällt die Figur dem Autor ins Wort: Ulrich

Plenzdorfs Erzählung 'Die neuen Leiden des jungen W.'" Brenner, ed. 274–79.

Seghers, Anna. *Benito's Blue and Nine Other Stories.* Berlin: Seven Seas, 1973. Trans. of "Das wirkliche Blau. Eine Geschichte aus Mexiko." Berlin: Aufbau, 1967; *Die Kraft der Schwachen: Neun Erzählungen.* Berlin: Aufbau, 1965.

——. [*The Companions.*] *Die Gefährten.* Berlin: Kiepenheuer, 1932.

——. *The Dead Stay Young.* No trans. Boston: Little, Brown, 1950. Trans. of *Die Toten bleiben jung.* Berlin: Aufbau, 1949.

——. [*The Decision*] *Die Entscheidung.* 11th ed. Berlin: Aufbau, 1973.

——. ["Encounter on a Journey."] "Die Reisebegegnung." *Sonderbare Begegnungen.* By Anna Seghers. Berlin: Aufbau, 1973. 109–48.

——. "The Excursion of the Dead Girls." Firchow and Firchow 57–81. Trans. of "Der Ausflug der toten Mädchen." New York: Aurora, 1946.

——. [*On the Way to the American Embassy*] *Auf dem Weg zur amerikanischen Botschaft und andere Erzählungen.* Berlin: Kiepenheuer, 1930.

——. *A Price on his Head.* Trans. Eva Wulff. *Two Novelettes.* Berlin: Seven Seas, 1962. 111–293. Trans. of *Der Kopflohn: Roman aus einem deutschen Dorf im Spätsommer 1932.* Amsterdam: Querido, 1933.

——. "The Reed." Seghers, *Benito's Blue* 144–57. Trans. of "Das Schilfrohr." *Die Kraft der Schwachen: Neun Erzählungen.* Berlin: Aufbau, 1965. 63–75.

——. *The Revolt of the Fishermen.* Trans. Margaret Goldsmith. London: Elkin, Mathews, and Marrot, 1929. Trans. of *Aufstand der Fischer von St. Barbara.* Berlin: Kiepenheuer, 1932.

——. ["The Righteous Judge"] "Der gerechte Richter." Berlin: Aufbau, 1990.

——. *The Seventh Cross.* Trans. James A. Galston. Boston: Little, Brown, 1942. German: *Das siebte Kreuz.* Berlin: Aufbau, 1946.

——. [*The Strength of the Weak*] *Die Kraft der Schwachen.* See Seghers, *Benito's Blue.*

——. *Transit.* Trans. James A. Galston. Boston: Little, Brown, 1944. German: *Transit.* Konstanz: Weller, 1948.

——. [*Trust*] *Das Vertrauen.* Berlin: Aufbau, 1968.

——. [*The Way Through February*] *Der Weg durch den Februar.* Paris: Edition du Carrefour, 1935.

Sevin, Dieter. *Christa Wolf: "Der geteilte Himmel"; "Nachdenken über Christa T.": Interpretationen.* Munich: R. Oldenbourg, 1982.

Silbermann, Marc. *Literature of the Working World: A Study of the Industrial Novel in East Germany.* New York University Ottendorfer Series. Vol. 9. New York: Lang, 1976.

——. "Writing What—for Whom? 'Vergangenheitsbewältigung' in GDR Literature." *German Studies Review* 10.3 (1987): 527–38.

Spittmann, Ilse. "Der 17. Januar und die Folgen." *Deutschland Archiv* 21.3 (1988): 227–32.

Spriano, Paolo. *Stalin and the European Communists.* London: Verso, 1985.

Stephan, Alexander. *Christa Wolf*. Amsterdam: Rodopi, 1986.

Stinglwagner, Wolfgang. "Kein Anlaß zur Euphorie: Die wirtschaftliche Lage der DDR." *Deutschland Archiv* 22.2 (1989): 129–33.

Strittmatter, Erwin. *Ole Bienkopp*. Trans. Jack and Renate Mitchell. Berlin: Seven Seas, 1966. Trans. of *Ole Bienkopp*. Berlin: Aufbau, 1963.

———. [*Oxcart Drivers*] *Ochsenkutscher*. Potsdam: Märkische Druck- u. Verlags GmbH, 1950.

Stroop, Jürgen. *The Stroop Report: The Jewish Quarter of Warsaw is no more!* Intro. Andrzej Wirth. New York: Pantheon, 1979.

Sudau, Christel. "Women in the GDR." Trans. Biddy Martin. *New German Critique* 13 (1978): 69–81.

Tate, Dennis. *The East German Novel: Identity, Community, Continuity*. New York: St. Martin's, 1984.

Tetzner, Gerti. *Karen W.* Halle: Mitteldeutscher Verlag, 1974.

Vallance, Margaret. "Monika Maron: Harbinger of Surrealism in the GDR." *GDR Monitor* 20 (Winter 1988/89): 57–64.

Wallmann, Jürgen. "In der Fantasie liegt die Wahrheit." *Deutschland Archiv* 8.8 (1975): 870–71.

———, ed. *Reiner Kunze: Materialien und Dokumente*. Frankfurt/Main: Fischer, 1977.

Wander, Fred. "Brief an Primo Levi." *Sammlung 5: Jahrbuch für antifaschistische Literatur und Kunst*. Ed. Uwe Naumann. Frankfurt/Main: Röderberg, 1982. 21–27.

———. *The Seventh Well*. Trans. Marc Linder. Berlin: Seven Seas, 1976. Trans. of *Der siebente Brunnen*. Berlin: Aufbau, 1971.

Wander, Maxie. [*Good Morning, My Lovely*] *Guten Morgen, du Schöne: Frauen in der DDR. Protokolle nach Tonband*. Berlin: Buchverlag Der Morgen, 1977.

Weimann, Robert. "Diskussion." Brenner, ed. 173–88.

Werner, Klaus. "Toleranz und Entschiedenheit." *Sinn und Form* 32.2 (1980): 484–92.

Werth, Wolfgang. "Rebell mit positiver Haltung: Plenzdorfs neuer Werther." Brenner, ed. 284–88.

Wieghaus, Georg. "Fred Wander." Arnold, 19th printing, 1–6, A–D.

Wilke, Ursula. "Für und Wider: *Der fremde Freund*." *Weimarer Beiträge* 29.9 (1983): 1652–55.

Will, Wilfried van der. "The Nature of Dissidence in the GDR." *The GDR in the 1980s. GDR Monitor*. Special Series 4. Ed. Ian Wallace. Dundee: n.p., 1984. 31–43.

Wohlgemuth, Joachim. [*Egon and the Eighth Wonder of the World*] *Egon und das achte Weltwunder*. Berlin: Verlag Neues Leben, 1962.

Wolf, Christa, *Accident/A Day's News*. Trans. Heike Schwarzbauer and Rick Takvorian. New York: Farrar, Strauss, and Giroux, 1989. Trans. of *Störfall: Nachrichten eines Tages*. Berlin: Aufbau, 1987.

———, ed. *Anna Seghers: Glauben an Irdisches. Essays*. Leipzig: Reclam, 1974.

———. "Anna Seghers über ihre Schaffensmethode: Ein Gespräch." C. Wolf, *Anna Seghers* 340–47.

———. *Cassandra: A Novel and Four Essays*. Trans. Jan van Heurck. New York: Farrar, Straus, and Giroux, 1984. Trans. of *Kassandra*. Darmstadt: Luchterhand, 1983; *Voraussetzungen einer Erzählung: Kassandra*. *Frankfurter Poetik-Vorlesungen*. Darmstadt: Luchterhand, 1983; *Kassandra: Vier Vorlesungen. Eine Erzählung*. Berlin: Aufbau, 1983.

———. *Divided Heaven*. Trans. Joan Becker. 4th Printing. New York: Adler's Foreign Books, 1983. Trans. of *Der geteilte Himmel*. Halle: Mitteldeutscher Verlag, 1963.

———. "Faith in the Terrestrial." C. Wolf, *Reader* 111–37.

———. *Der geteilte Himmel*. Halle: Mitteldeutscher Verlag, 1963.

———. *Lesen und Schreiben: Neue Sammlung. Essays, Aufsätze, Reden*. 4th ed. Darmstadt: Luchterhand, 1983.

———. *No Place on Earth*. Trans. Jan van Heurck. New York: Farrar, Straus, and Giroux, 1982. Trans. of *Kein Ort. Nirgends*. Berlin: Aufbau, 1979.

———. "Nun ja! Das nächste Leben geht aber heute an. Ein Brief über die Bettine." C. Wolf, *Lesen* 284–318.

———. *Patterns of Childhood*. Trans. Ursule Molinaro and Hedwig Rappolt. New York: Farrar, Straus, and Giroux, 1984. Trans. of *Kindheitsmuster*. Berlin: Aufbau, 1976. First translated as *A Model Childhood*. Trans. Ursule Molinaro and Hedwig Rappolt. New York: Farrar, Straus, and Giroux, 1980.

———. *The Quest for Christa T.* Trans. Christopher Middleton. New York: Farrar, Straus, and Giroux, 1970. Trans. of *Nachdenken über Christa T.* Halle: Mitteldeutscher Verlag, 1968.

———. *The Reader and the Writer: Essays, Sketches, Memories*. Trans. Joan Becker. New York: International Publishers, 1977. Trans. of *Lesen und Schreiben: Aufsätze und Betrachtungen*. Berlin: Aufbau, 1972.

———. "Remembrance and Memorial—Fred Wander: *The Seventh Well*." C. Wolf, *Reader* 97–107.

———. "Der Schatten eines Traumes: Karoline von Günderrode—Ein Entwurf." C. Wolf, *Lesen* 225–83.

———. "Self-Experiment: Appendix to a Report." Trans. Jeanette Clausen. *New German Critique* 13 (1978): 109–31. Trans. of "Selbstversuch: Traktat zu einem Protokoll." *Sinn und Form* 25.2 (1973): 301–23.

———. " 'Shall I Garnish a Metaphor with an Almond Blossom?': Büchner Prize Acceptance Speech." Trans. Henry J. Schmidt. *New German Critique* 23 (1981): 3–11. Trans. of "Büchner-Preis-Rede." C. Wolf, *Lesen* 319–32.

———. "Subjective Authenticity: A Conversation with Hans Kaufmann." M. Fries 55–75.

———. *Unter den Linden: Drei unwahrscheinliche Geschichten*. Berlin: Aufbau, 1974.

———. [*What Remains*] *Was bleibt*. Frankfurt/Main: Luchterhand, 1990.

———. "Worte des Gedenkens." *Sinn und Form* 36.5 (1984): 1017–22.

———. "Zur Information." *Sinn und Form* 35.4 (1983): 863–66.

Wolf, Gerhard. " 'Der Mensch braucht Zeit, um klüger zu werden.' " *Neue Deutsche Literatur* 2.12 (1954): 154–63.

————. [*Poor Hölderlin*] *Der arme Hölderlin*. Berlin: Union, 1972.

Wolter, Christine. "I Have Remarried." Trans. Friedrich Achberger. Altbach et al. 220–25. Trans. of "Ich habe wieder geheiratet." C. Wolter. *Wie ich meine Unschuld verlor*. Berlin: Aufbau, 1976. 26–35.

Woods, Roger. *Opposition in the GDR under Honecker, 1971–85: An Introduction and Documentation*. New York: St. Martin's, 1986.

Worgitzky, Charlotte. "Karriere abgesagt." C. Worgitzky. *Vieräugig oder blind: Erzählungen*. Berlin: Der Morgen, 1978. 77–91.

Zachau, Reinhard K. *Stefan Heym*. Munich: C. H. Beck, 1982.

Zeindler, Peter. "Glück des einzelnen vor dem Plansoll? Eine Begegnung mit dem DDR-Dramatiker Ulrich Plenzdorf." Brenner, ed. 313–18.

Zipes, Jack. "Christa Wolf: Moralist as Marxist." C. Wolf, *Divided Heaven* v–xxxvii.

Zipser, Richard A. "Interview with Jurek Becker." *Dimension* 11.3 (1978): 407–16.

Zipser, Richard A. and Karl-Heinz Schoeps. *DDR-Literatur im Tauwetter*. 3 vols. New York: Lang, 1985.

"Zuschriften an Wilhelm Girnus." *Sinn und Form* 35.5 (1983): 1087–96.

Index